English in the World

History, Diversity, Change

This book is part of the series *Worlds of English* published by Routledge in association with The Open University. The three books in the series are:

English in the World: History, Diversity, Change
(edited by Philip Seargeant and Joan Swann)

ISBN 978-0-415-67421-8 (paperback)

ISBN 978-0-415-67420-1 (hardback)

ISBN 978-0-203-12456-7 (ebook)

Communicating in English: Talk, Text, Technology
(edited by Daniel Allington and
Barbara Mayor)

ISBN 978-0-415-67423-2 (paperback)

ISBN 978-0-415-67422-5 (hardback)

ISBN 978-0-203-12454-3 (ebook)

The Politics of English: Conflict, Competition, Co-existence
(edited by Ann Hewings and Caroline Tagg)

ISBN 978-0-415-67424-9 (paperback)

ISBN 978-0-415-67425-6 (hardback)

ISBN 978-0-203-12455-0 (ebook)

This publication forms part of the Open University module U214 *Worlds of English*. Details of this and other Open University modules can be obtained from the Student Registration and Enquiry Service, The Open University, PO Box 197, Milton Keynes, MK7 6BJ, United Kingdom (Tel. +44 (0)845 300 60 90, email general-enquiries@open.ac.uk).

www.open.ac.uk

English in the World

History, Diversity, Change

Edited by Philip Seargeant and Joan Swann

Routledge
Taylor & Francis Group

Published by

Routledge
2 Park Square
Milton Park
Abingdon OX14 4RN

in association with

The Open University
Walton Hall
Milton Keynes MK7 6AA

Simultaneously published in the USA and Canada by

Routledge
711 Third Avenue
New York, NY 10017

Routledge is an imprint of the Taylor & Francis Group,
an informa business

First published 2012

Edited and designed by The Open University.

Typeset by The Open University.

Printed and bound in the United
Kingdom by Latimer Trend &
Company Ltd., Plymouth.

British Library Cataloguing in Publication Data:
A catalogue record for this book is available from the
British Library.

Library of Congress Cataloging-in-Publication Data

English in the world : history, diversity, change / edited
by Philip Seargeant and Joan Swann.
    p. cm.
  ISBN 978-0-415-67420-1 (hardback) -- ISBN 978-0-
415-67421-8 (pbk.) -- ISBN 978-0-203-12456-7 (ebook)
1. English language--Globalization. 2. English
language--Variation. 3. English language--History.
4. English language--Foreign countries. I. Seargeant,
Philip. II. Swann, Joan.
  PE1073.E5485 2012

420.9--dc23

                                    2011037811

ISBN 978-0-415-67421-8 (paperback)

ISBN 978-0-415-67420-1 (hardback)

ISBN 978-0-203-12456-7 (ebook)

1.1

Contents

Series preface

The books in this series provide an introduction to the study of English, both for students of the English language and the general reader. They are core texts for the Open University module U214 *Worlds of English*. The series aims to provide students with:

- an understanding of the history and development of English, and a critical approach to its current global status and influence
- skills and knowledge to use in analysing English-language texts
- an appreciation of variation in the English language between different speakers and writers, and across different regional and social contexts
- examples of the diversity of English language practices in different parts of the world
- an understanding of how English is learned as a first language or as an additional language, and of its role as a language of formal education around the world
- an appreciation of how media, from print to the internet, have affected the English language and contributed to its position in the world today
- an understanding of how English is promoted around the world and the controversies surrounding the politics and economics of such decisions and its impact on other languages and the people who speak them
- informed reflections on the likely future role of English.

The readings which accompany each chapter have been chosen to exemplify key points made in the chapters, often by exploring related data, or experiences and practices involving the English language in different parts of the world. The readings also represent an additional 'voice' or viewpoint on key themes or issues raised in the chapter.

Each chapter includes:

- **activities** to stimulate further understanding or analysis of the material
- **boxes** containing illustrative or supplementary material

- **key terms** which are set in coloured type at the point where they are explained; the terms also appear in colour in the index so that they are easy to find in the chapters.

The other books in this series are:

Allington, D. and Mayor, B. (eds) (2012) *Communicating in English: Talk, Text, Technology*, Abingdon, Routledge/Milton Keynes, The Open University.

Hewings, A. and Tagg, C. (eds) (2012) *The Politics of English: Conflict, Competition*, Coexistence, Abingdon, Routledge/Milton Keynes, The Open University.

Ann Hewings
Series Editor

Biographical information

Joan Beal

Joan Beal is Professor of English Language at the University of Sheffield where she teaches modules on the history of English and on varieties of English. She is the author of several textbooks, including *English in Modern Times 1700-1945* (2004), *Language and Region* (2006) and *An Introduction to Regional Englishes* (2010).

David Crystal

David Crystal is Honorary Professor of Linguistics at the University of Bangor. Formerly Professor of Linguistics at Reading, since the 1980s he has worked as an independent scholar from his home in Holyhead, North Wales. His publications include *The Cambridge Encyclopaedia of the English Language* (1995/2003), *Evolving English* (2010) and *The Story of English in 100 Words* (2011).

Dick Leith

Dick Leith worked as a freelance writer and, prior to this, was Senior Lecturer in Linguistics at Birmingham Polytechnic (now University of Central England). His books include *A Social History of English* (2nd edn, 1997) and, with George Myerson, *The Power of Address: Explorations in Rhetoric* (1989).

Kay McCormick

Kay McCormick is Emeritus Professor in the Department of English at the University of Cape Town (South Africa). Her research fields are sociolinguistics – in particular language contact and narrative studies – especially the analysis of oral life histories. Her current sociolinguistic work is on changing forms and uses of bilingual and multilingual vernaculars.

Miriam Meyerhoff

Miriam Meyerhoff is Professor of Linguistics at the University of Auckland (New Zealand). She conducts research on a wide range of sociolinguistic topics; principally, issues of language variation and change, but also language and gender, creoles and language contact, ideologies of language, social networks and communities of practice.

She is the author of *Introducing Sociolinguistics* (2010) and co-editor of *The Handbook of Language and Gender* (2003).

Philip Seargeant

Philip Seargeant is Lecturer in Applied Linguistics in the Centre for Language and Communication at The Open University. He is author of *The Idea of English in Japan: Ideology and the Evolution of a Global Language* (2009), and *Exploring World Englishes* (2012), and editor of *English in Japan in the Era of Globalization* (2011). He has also published several articles in journals such as *World Englishes, the International Journal of Applied Linguistics, Language Policy, Language Sciences*, and *Language & Communication*.

Jennifer Smith

Jennifer Smith is Senior Lecturer in English Language and Linguistics at the University of Glasgow. After a career teaching English in Athens, Greece, she returned to university, graduating with an MA from Durham and PhD from York. Her research is in sociolinguistics, and language variation and change. She has published in a number of areas, including dialect acquisition in pre-school children, Scottish dialects and their relationships to colonial Englishes in North America and bidialectalism in situations of dialect levelling.

Anna Strycharz

Anna Strycharz is a PhD candidate at the University of Edinburgh. Her research interests focus around language variation and change in Japanese, especially in the area of honorifics in the dialect of Osaka. She has taught introductory sociolinguistic courses at the University of Edinburgh and the University of Auckland.

Joan Swann

Joan Swann is Director of the Centre for Language and Communication in the Faculty of Education and Language Studies at the Open University. Recent books include *Creativity in Language and Literature* (2011, co-edited with Ronald Carter and Rob Pope) and the *Companion to English Language Studies* (2010, co-edited with Janet Maybin).

General introduction

Philip Seargeant

The English language had been around for about four hundred years before it began to be called English. It first emerged sometime during the fifth century AD, when a number of Germanic tribes from the north of Europe – whom we now refer to collectively as the Anglo-Saxons – arrived in Britain, bringing with them their several indigenous dialects. Over the next few hundred years, as these tribes established roots and began spreading out across the country, the language slowly developed. Yet it was not until the ninth century that the term 'English' began to be regularly used to refer to the language (Crystal, 2005, p. 27). English did not become 'English' until at least four centuries into its existence.

During this early period of its history, English was just one of many languages spoken on the British mainland. The *Anglo-Saxon Chronicles* – the earliest history of Britain written in English – begin their account of the country by explaining that:

> The island of Britain is eight hundred miles long and two hundred broad. There are five languages, English, Brito-Welsh, Scottish, Pictish and Latin. The first inhabitants of this land were the Britons.

> (The *Peterborough Chronicle*, *c.*1150, translated in Freeborn, 2006, p. 13)

So in the beginning, English was just one language among several; it was a language without a particularly strong identity and with no special status. For the first few centuries of its life, it was very much a *local* language, spoken by one section of the population of an island off the western coast of continental Europe.

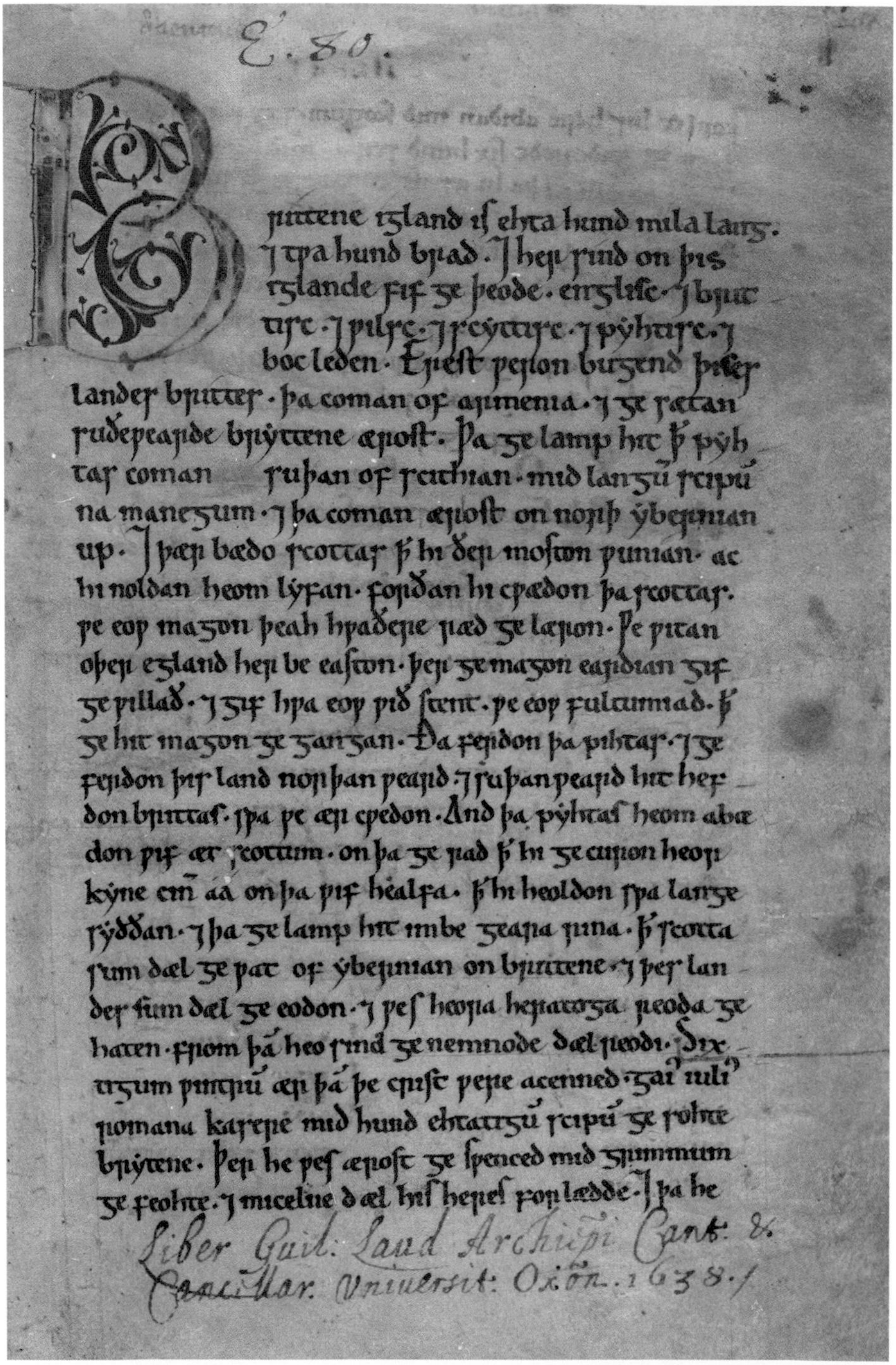

E. 80.

Brittene igland is ehta hund mila lang.
⁊ twa hund brad. ⁊ her sind on þis
iglande fif geþeode. englisc. ⁊ brit
tisc. ⁊ wilsc. ⁊ scyttisc. ⁊ pyhtisc. ⁊
boc leden. Erest weron buend þises
landes brittes. þa coman of armenia. ⁊ gesætan
suðewearde bryttene ærost. Þa gelamp hit þ pyh
tas coman suþan of scithian. mid langū scipū
na manegum. ⁊ þa coman ærost on norþ ybernian
up. ⁊ þær bædo scottas þ hi ðer moston wunian. ac
hi noldan heom lyfan. forðan hi cwædon þa scottas.
we eow magon þeah hwaðere ræd gelæron. We witan
oþer egland her be easton. þer ge magon eardian gif
ge willað. ⁊ gif hwa eow wið stent. we eow fultumiað. þ
ge hit magon gegangan. Ða ferdon þa pihtas. ⁊ ge
ferdon þis land norþan weard. ⁊ suþan weard hit hef
don brittas. swa we ær cwedon. And þa pyhtas heom abæ
don wif æt scottum. on þa gerad þ hi gecuron heora
kyne cin̄ aa on þa wif healfa. þ hi heoldon swa lange
syððan. ⁊ þa gelamp hit imbe geara rina. þ scotta
sum dæl gewat of ybernian on bryttene. ⁊ þes lan
des sum dæl geeodon. ⁊ wes heora heratoga reoda ge
haten. from þā heo synd genemnode dælreodi. Six
tigum wintrū ær þā þe crist wære acenned. gaius iulius
romana kasere mid hund eahtatigū scipū gesohte
bryttene. Þer he wes ærost geswenced mid grimmum
gefeohte. ⁊ micelne dæl his heres forlædde. ⁊ þa he

Liber Guil: Laud Archiepi Cant: & Cancellar: Universit: Oxon. 1638.

Figure 1 The opening lines of the *Peterborough Chronicle* in the original Old English

Fast-forward one a half millennia and English is now spread extensively across the globe. Today, it is used, in one form or another, by more people, in more areas, and for a wider set of purposes, than any other language. That unnamed language which began life as a parochial dialect spoken by one faction of a group of invading tribes from northern Europe now has a status unmatched by any other language on earth. The question this raises – and one of the questions we'll be addressing in this book – is how and why this dramatic shift took place. What happened to transform English from that small parochial language into the pre-eminent medium of international communication in the modern world? Why has this particular language, from all the other countless systems of speech that the human race has developed throughout its history, risen to such a position of prominence?

The emergence of English as a global language is not the end of the story, though. The fact that English is now established as an important linguistic force in countless communities around the world does not mean that there is little more to say about it. Nor does it mean that those same processes of change and development that brought the language to this position are not still happening. In fact, in the opinion of some scholars the present moment is a critical juncture in the history of the language. In their opinion, English is now going through a transformation almost on a par with what happened when those Germanic tribes first arrived in Britain 1500 years ago. Now, as then, both the form and status of English are in a state of dynamic change – and this is producing a great deal of debate about the nature of English itself.

The focus and structure of the book

This book takes as its starting point the global existence of the English language and looks at both how and why it came to occupy this position, and what the consequences of its global spread are for the way it is used and perceived around the world. In the first half of the book, we will examine the history of the language, beginning with its arrival in Britain in the fifth century and moving up to the present day and its status as a language with a truly global reach. The first four chapters cover the historical story, with Chapter 1 opening up the questions that the book as a whole will address, and Chapters 2, 3 and 4 then tracking the history of the language, first within England and the British Isles, then to various territories overseas in the wake of colonial expansion, and finally to its current existence as a language which has a presence in diverse contexts all across the globe.

The second half of the book then considers the forms that the language takes around the world, how it is used as a means of expression, and how it relates to issues of both personal and cultural identity. Building on the historical context established in the first half, Chapters 5, 6 and 7 examine, in turn, contemporary varieties of English, how English is used alongside other languages, and how English itself continues to vary and change. An important point that recurs across these chapters is the role that English plays in people's lives. For although the subject of the book is nominally the English language, language would not exist without the people who speak it, and for this reason our examination situates English firmly within the social, cultural and political contexts in which it is used.

Finally, throughout our exploration, we will reflect on the way that English is and has been studied, and on *how* we know what we know about the language. In other words, we shall look at the methods and approaches linguists use to explore its history and to investigate the processes of variation and change. For not only does an understanding of these methods offer us an insight into the working practices of language studies as an academic area, it can also contribute to our overall understanding of the language itself, and of the ever-evolving role that English plays in the lives of millions of people around the globe.

Note to readers

In addition to features such as readings, activities, boxes and key terms that are described in the series preface, the book also includes two appendices. These comprise a timeline indicating key dates in the history of the English language (Appendix 1) and a note on conventions for describing the language (Appendix 2). We point you to these at various stages during the course of the book, but you may also like to use them for general reference purposes as you are reading through the chapters.

1 English in the world today

Philip Seargeant

1.1 Introduction

In an essay written towards the end of the twentieth century, the linguist Michael Toolan suggested that the English that is now used as an international language around the world – that's spoken, for instance, by a Turkish businesswoman communicating with a Korean sales representative at a convention in Sao Paulo, or by a Finnish diplomat discussing climate change with a Romanian scientist at a conference in Johannesburg – is so culturally removed from the traditional national language of England that it should not be called 'English'. The name 'English', he argues, is no longer appropriate; it no longer reflects the identity the language has in the modern world. He suggests that the language should be renamed. As an alternative, he proposes 'we call it Global'. English, he contends, at least as it's used in the context of international communication, 'is becoming increasingly released from a sense of rootedness in one or more ethnic homelands (whether that is thought of as England, or the Anglo-Saxon world, or the Anglo-American world)' (Toolan, 1997, p. 8), and so the time is ripe for a strategy of radical renaming.

So far, of course, this alternative name hasn't really taken off. However persuasive Toolan's arguments may be, people's actual naming practices have not followed his suggestion. But other scholars have voiced similar qualms, some of which have been highly influential. The linguist Braj Kachru, for example, has suggested that because 'English now has multicultural identities … [t]he term "English" does not capture [the] sociolinguistic reality' of the language (Kachru, 1992, p. 357). Instead, he suggests that the plural form 'English*es*' should be used. It is no longer possible to speak of a *single* English language, he contends; around the world there are now several different varieties of English being spoken, each of which is distinct enough to be accorded the status of a separate language. So while Kachru doesn't go quite as far as Toolan in suggesting that a completely new name is required, he still feels that a fundamental reconceptualisation of the language is necessary.

I shall return to Kachru's arguments about the 'multicultural identities' of English towards the end of this chapter. For now, the point to note is that at the beginning of the twenty-first century, and despite its emergence as *the* international language of the present time, the status of English is, in certain respects, no more settled than it was at any previous stage in its history. In addition to the question that was posed in the general introduction about how English has emerged to occupy its current prominent position in global society, we can therefore ask what it is about the nature of the language in the world today that leads scholars like Toolan and Kachru to make such radical suggestions about the need to change the very name of the language. After all, if people were to adopt Toolan's suggestion, the entire subject of this book would be changed. Our present discussion would be about the pre-history of Global rather than the second millennium of English. So are suggestions such as these from Toolan and Kachru entirely fanciful? Are they ultimately simply misguided approaches to the subject? Or do they actually identify some underlying truth about the state and status of English in the world today?

This first chapter will take an initial look at this complex of questions. In doing so, it will introduce you to examples of the variety and diversity of the English language, both as it exists around the world today and as it has developed through history. We shall look at what counts as English today and how the diversity of the language reflects its social history. In addition, we will examine the roles that English plays in people's lives, and consider why it is that debates about the language, and about how people use the language, can sometimes be highly controversial. We'll begin, though, by asking a simple, but fundamental, question: *what exactly is the English language?*

1.2   What is English?

It seems sensible to begin an exploration of the English language by determining what we mean by 'English'. If we want to study its development, its use and its status, it's worth clarifying exactly what *it* is. From one perspective, of course, this may seem a rather empty task. Given that you are reading this book – and are therefore presumably a fluent English reader – English is very likely to be almost as integral a part of your life as the air you breathe. You probably get on perfectly well on a day-to-day basis without ever having to reflect on what exactly comprises the language. It's what you're reading now. If you live in an English-speaking country, it's probably what you use on a daily basis to converse with your friends, colleagues and family. In other words, speaking and reading English is something you just *do*. You may have the odd argument with people about certain aspects of English usage

('Is it okay to say *My sister and me had an argument about correct grammar?*'), or may occasionally consult a dictionary to check the meaning or spelling of an unusual word ('What does deontic mean?'; 'When is it *complement* and when is it *compliment?*'). But as an expert speaker of the language, you can use English without ever needing to be able to give a scientific definition of what it is – just as you can breathe without needing any knowledge of the chemical constituents of air.

Activity 1.1

Allow about
10 minutes

For the purposes of this introduction, spend a few minutes writing down a short definition of what you understand by the 'English language'. Imagine you're defining the language to someone who has no conception of what it is: how would you sum it up in a few sentences?

Comment

You may well have started your definition by saying that English is the language spoken in England. This is how Dr Johnson defined it in his dictionary of the English language, composed back in the mid-eighteenth century:

> ENGLISH. *adj.* Belonging to England; thence English is the language of England.

Of course, as I've noted above, in today's world, English is much more than this. English has spread extensively in the two and a half centuries since Johnson's time. Modern dictionaries mostly augment Johnson's definition by adding something about the global scope of the language. The *Chambers Dictionary* (11th edition), for example, defines it as:

> A Germanic language spoken in the British Isles, USA, most parts of the Commonwealth, etc.

while the *Oxford English Dictionary* extends this slightly further:

> Of or relating to the West Germanic language spoken in England and also used in many varieties throughout the world.

As we can see, these definitions all concentrate on a number of key elements – and your own definition may well have focused on some or all of these as well. These elements are: the communities with which the language is most associated (it's the national language of the UK, the USA, etc.); its history (i.e. being of Germanic origin); and the way it's now used in various places around the world. In other words, all these definitions link the language with the people who speak it now or who spoke it in the past. As such, they're all *social* definitions of the language – describing it not in terms of the structure it has (they don't mention, for example, that it predominantly uses a subject-verb-object word order), but in terms of the communities who use it and – importantly – who identify with it. That's to say, the language doesn't exist as an abstract entity out there in the ether. It's something people actually use; something they both speak *and* write/read (although these definitions mostly privilege the notion of speaking). And it's something which plays a significant role in their lives. For this reason any investigation into the language will involve an investigation into the social and historical context in which the language flourishes. In other words, when studying the language we also need to study the people who use the language – we need to study *how* they use it, *why* they use it and what they *think* about it.

More detail on the statistics of English speakers can be found in Chapter 4.

Before moving on to a discussion of these issues, let us first pursue the definition of the language in a little more detail. In textbooks on the subject, it is common practice nowadays to add statistical information about how many people in the world speak the language. Latest estimates suggest that English is currently spoken by between 1500 and 2000 million people, in hundreds of countries, and operates as the main form of communication in important domains such as global business and science. It is precisely because of statistics such as these that some people feel the language has developed in such a way that, conceptually, it is now a quite different entity from its pre-globalised incarnation.

We need to be a bit careful, however, when we make assertions about English using figures like these. While statements of this sort may seem fairly straightforward in one respect, there are a number of hidden issues in the way they are phrased which can complicate the picture. For example, what do we actually mean when we say that 'English is spoken by almost two billion people in the world today'? What counts as 'English' in this context? And who qualifies as having the competence to be a 'speaker' of it? Is the English that is spoken in a town on the south coast of England the same as that spoken on the north island of New Zealand or in the centre of Singapore? And if there are significant differences between the way it is spoken in these places, at what point do we say that they are different varieties of the language, or that perhaps they are actually different *languages*? And does a 'speaker' of the language need to have perfect fluency in it? Does someone learning the language count as a 'speaker'? And finally, is there any significance in the fact that these statements privilege *speaking* over *writing*? Should we consider spoken English and written English in the same way, or are there important differences between them which mean we should view them as distinct entities?

Once we start scrutinising some of these issues and concepts we can see that a statement such as 'English is spoken by almost two billion people in the world' is an abstraction, and one which raises almost as many questions as it answers. So rather than talk only in abstractions, let us consider some concrete examples of the use of the language around the world in an attempt to determine more closely what counts as English, and who qualifies as an English speaker.

Activity 1.2

Allow about 20 minutes

Have a look at the three passages below. They are all excerpts from poems or songs. Which of them look recognisably like 'English' to you? How much can you understand of each of them? (In each case, the original is given first, followed where necessary by a translation into standard British English.)

1   As they was a-ridin' back to camp
A-packin' a pretty good load,
Who should they meet but the Devil himself,
A-prancin' down the road.

Sez he, "You ornery cowboy skunks,
You'd better hunt yer holes,
Fer I've come up from Hell's Rim Rock,
To gather in yer souls."

Sez Sandy Bob, "Old Devil be damned,
We boys is kinda tight,
But you ain't a-goin' to gather no cowboy souls,
'Thout you has some kind of a fight."

So Sandy Bob punched a hole in his rope,
And he swang her straight and true,
He lapped it on to the Devil's horns,
An' he taken his dallies too.

(Gardner, 'The Sierry Petes, or Tying Knots in the Devil's Tail')

2   Wark's dattin a ill-trikkit dug,
Unbiddibil ay, fir aa du roars.
Hit winna byd, hit nivir faetchis.
an du winds up kaain aa.
An luv, wiel hit's a haaf-wyld kat
Du mebbie maets, bakk an foar.
Hit'll tak dy kloo an ryv dy sokk,
Till du shæsts da bæst awa.

Naen firby a tøtak'r sænt
Wid aks da pær ta ly tagiddir.

[Work is such a mischievous dog
which never does as it's told no matter how loud you shout at it
It won't stay, it won't fetch, and you end up herding the flock yourself.
And love, well it's a half wild cat
you feed occasionally.
It makes off with your ball of wool and tears your knitting in pieces
so you chase the creature away.

Nobody except an idiot or a saint
would expect the two of them to lie down together.]

(Jamieson, 'Varg', with a translation 'The difficult and messy business of
living' by the author)

3   So I called and called *sampai* you answer
You *kata* "Sorry *sayang. Tadi tak dengar.*
My phone was on silent, I was at the gym"
Tapi latar belakang suara perempuan lain

Sudahlah, sayang, I don't believe you
I've always known that your words were never true
Why am I with you? I *pun tak tahu*
No wonder *lah* my friends *pun tak suka you*

[So I called and called until you answered
You said, "Sorry darling, I didn't hear you
My phone was on silent, I was at the gym"
But in the background was another woman's voice

Enough darling, I don't believe you
I've always known that your words were never true
Why am I with you? I really don't know
No wonder even my friends don't like you]

(Avi, 'Kantoi')

Comment

1   The first excerpt is from a 'cowboy poem' from the Arizona region
    dating from the early part of the twentieth century by Gail I. Gardner.
    It tells the story of two cowboys who run into the devil on their way
    home from a bar. You probably found it almost all intelligible, although
    there are one or two dialect words (some of them related specifically
    to their profession) which might be a little obscure. 'Dally', for
    example, refers to a method of winding a rope around the saddle;
    while 'ornery' is originally a colloquial pronunciation of 'ordinary', and
    means 'cantankerous' or 'mean'. There are also a few distinctive
    grammatical constructions, such as 'you ain't a-goin' to gather no',
    which aren't common in standard English, although similar
    constructions do still occur in some contemporary colloquial forms of
    the language.

2   The second example is in Scots, the traditional Germanic language
    spoken in Lowland Scotland, the Northern Isles and parts of Ulster.
    Along with Gaelic and Scottish English, this is one of the three main
    languages spoken in Scotland. It has its roots in the Anglo-Saxon
    dialects which arrived on the British mainland in the fifth century, so
    it's related to English but has developed mostly independently. Some
    people consider it to be a dialect of English, while others regard it as
    an entirely separate language. These stanzas are from a poem called
    'Varg' by the contemporary poet Robert Alan Jamieson. As you can
    see, although some words are obviously close cousins of modern
    standard British English (e.g. 'wark' = work; 'luv' = love), for the most

part it's quite different. And even these words which sound similar when spoken, are spelt in non-standard ways. It also includes some characters such as ø and æ which aren't used in modern standard British English. So unless you're a Scots speaker, you'd probably have difficulty understanding it without the translation.

3   The third example is from a song titled 'Kantoi' by the Malaysian singer Zee Avi. This is in what is colloquially known as 'Manglish', a blend of English and Malay. In Malay, this type of language use is known as *bahasa rojak*, which means 'mixed language'. Such mixed or 'hybrid' languages are quite frequent around the world – in later chapters we'll look at other examples. But they're also often quite controversial, and are viewed by some as being sloppy or incorrect uses of 'proper English'. In 2006, for example, the Malaysian government banned the use of *bahasa rojak* on television and radio, saying that it was adversely affecting people's proficiency in both standard English and Malay (*The Star,* 2006). On the other hand, many people consider it to be a distinctive aspect of Malaysian culture and, when used in songs such as this, see it as a way of expressing a unique cultural identity.

Chapter 4 looks at 'Singlish', a mixed variety of English spoken in Singapore. Chapter 6 gives examples of a mixed variety found in Cape Town known as 'Kitchen English'.

So what do these different examples tell us about the nature of English around the world? One of the points I hope they illustrate is that the language is very diverse – that in different communities it has developed in such a way that its form is noticeably different.

You may feel, however, that some of the examples above are not necessarily 'real' English at all. Manglish, for instance, can be thought of as a mixture of English and a quite separate language. And while modern Scots and English developed from a common ancestor, Scots is now often viewed as a distinct language (although this decision is as much a political issue as it is a linguistic one, as we'll discuss later in the book). As I mentioned above, in these two cases there is a great deal of controversy about the status of these as independent or legitimate languages. So were you to make the argument that neither of them are really English at all, you wouldn't be alone in doing so. The question that follows from this, though, is at what point do we decide to call these varieties a different language? At what point are they no longer 'English'? Is the Arizonan example also a different language? Or is it similar enough to standard English that it should still be called English? In other words, where does the tipping point come? Given the fact that English is being used on an everyday basis in these diverse forms around the globe, how does one decide what counts as the core of the language? Is there a central version of the language which we should think of as *authentic* English? Or are each of these varieties equally valid systems of linguistic expression which just happen to be different?

For the moment I will simply pose these as questions and won't attempt to answer them. As you can probably imagine, the answers are complex and extensive, and much of the rest of the book will be focused on addressing them.

Languages, varieties and dialects

So far I have been discussing what counts as the English **language** – but in doing so I have introduced a number of related concepts such as **variety**, **dialect** and **accent**, which have been used to distinguish between certain different aspects of the general phenomenon we are calling English. Before we go any further, it is worth clarifying the differences between these various concepts, and how exactly they are used in language studies. It is easiest to define them in relation to one another, as they are used to highlight different systematic patterns in the way language manifests itself in society. Of the three, **variety** is the more general term and is used to refer to any distinct form of a language. It is also more neutral than the others which – as I shall discuss below – can be used to suggest that one form of a language is more prestigious or legitimate than another. **Dialect** then refers specifically to a language variety in which aspects of the vocabulary and grammar indicate a person's regional or social background. For example, the Geordie dialect is the distinctive and systematic use of certain grammatical and vocabulary features that are associated with the population of Newcastle and the Tyneside region. Standard British English is itself considered a dialect by linguists, indicating a speaker's social origin. This is contrasted with the concept of **accent**, which refers specifically to differences in pronunciation. So a New York accent refers to the distinctive and systematic pronunciation which is associated with the population of the city of New York.

Both the Geordie dialect and the New York accent could be described as varieties of English, as could Australian English or Hong Kong English. These latter two examples would usually be referred to using the more general term variety rather than dialect because they are associated with large-scale or autonomous communities, whereas the communities of Newcastle or New York are part of the wider populations of the UK and the USA respectively. However, the dividing lines between the concepts of a language, a variety and a dialect are not absolutely clear-cut. As noted earlier, one of the issues at the heart of English language studies at the moment is how different varieties are perceived, and how they should be referred to. To refer to something as a language rather than a dialect is to afford it more status. That is to say, if something is viewed as a language in its own right, it is accorded a greater respect than a dialect is. For this reason, in cases where the communities using the variety have clear political and geographical boundaries and distinct institutions, and perhaps also have established literary or cultural histories, the variety is more likely to be accorded the status of a language in its own right. The example that is often given to illustrate this is the relationship between Swedish and Danish. These are linguistically very similar to each other in their spoken form (so much so that they are mutually comprehensible), but are nonetheless thought of as different languages because they are associated with different nation states. So a question which often arises when considering the nature of English around the world is whether certain varieties are distinct enough from both a linguistic *and* a political point of view to qualify as different languages. To put it another way, is English a language which, because of its global spread, has several different varieties around the world – or is there now a *family of English languages* (McArthur, 1998)? And what are the consequences of viewing the current situation from one perspective rather than the other?

English through history

I'll return to these questions at the end of the chapter. For now, however, let's consider a related question. To what extent is modern-day English – the English you are reading now – the same language as that introduced to the British Isles one and a half millennia ago?

Allow about 40 minutes

Activity 1.3

Have a look at the following passage, which is written in **Old English** and dates back to the late tenth century AD. If you came across this passage with no introduction, do you think you'd recognise it as English? Can you understand any of it? While reading it through, make a note of any words that you recognise:

> eac swylce seo næddre wæs geapre þonne ealle þa oðre nytenu þe God geworhte ofer eorþan. and seo næddre cwæþ to þam wife.

> hwi forbead God eow þæt ge ne æton of ælcon treowe binnan
> paradisum.

Comment

At first glance this might seem entirely incomprehensible to you. There
are only five words in the passage which have a form which is the same
as modern standard British English. These are: *God, and, to, wife* and *of*.
There's at least one other word which resembles a modern English word:
paradisum looks a little similar to *paradise*. But other than that the words
mostly look distinctly alien, and some of them even include letters which
are no longer part of the alphabet we use for modern-day English.

Now let's look at another passage from approximately four hundred years
later. This is in what's known as **Middle English**, and was written around
the late fourteenth century. How much of this passage can you read?

> But the serpent was feller than alle lyuynge beestis of erthe which
> the Lord God hadde maad. Which serpent seide to the womman
> Why comaundide God to ʒou that ʒe schulden not ete of ech tre
> of paradis.

As you might have noticed, both these passages are translations of the
same section of the Bible, namely Genesis chapter 3, verse 1. The
Middle English version is much closer to modern-day English, and you
were probably able to read a great deal more of it than of the Old English
version. However, there are still a few features which differ from the
language we now use. For example, the character ʒ (known as *yogh*) is
used in place of a *y*. Also, the spelling of many words is rather different
from how it is today. For instance, in the first line the word 'living' is spelt
lyuynge (*y* is used instead of *i*, and *u* instead of *v*), and the word 'beasts'
is spelt *beestis*. Some of the vocabulary is also no longer regularly used
in contemporary English. The word 'feller' in the first line, for example,
means 'crueller' or 'more ruthless'. It was still to be found in
Shakespeare's time – for example, in the phrase 'this fell sergeant,
Death, is swift in his arrest' in *Hamlet* (5.2.341) – but is not in common
usage today (except in rather specialised contexts). All in all, though,
you'd probably identify this as being English.

Finally, let's look at two more translations of the same passage. The first
is in **Early Modern English** and dates from the seventeenth century.
This is, in fact, a passage from one of the most renowned translations of
the Bible: the King James or Authorised Version of 1611. The second is
in **Modern English**, and was translated in 1961.

Now the serpent was more subtill then any beast of the field, which the Lord God had made, and he said vnto the woman, Yea, hath God said, Ye shall not eat of euery tree of the garden?

The serpent was more crafty than any wild creature that the LORD God had made. He said to the woman, 'Is it true that God has forbidden you to eat from any tree in the garden?'

(texts adapted from Freeborn, 1992, p. 407)

The Early Modern English version is closer still to present-day English, although there are still a few features which mark it out as archaic. For example, nowadays *ye* meaning 'you' is only found in certain dialects, and is no longer used in standard British or American English.

Before going on to discuss what conclusions we can draw from the way the language has changed over the years, let's have another look at the first translation again and see if we're able to recognise more similarities between it and the others than might have been apparent at first glance. It will help if you know that the character þ, known as 'thorn', is used for the sound *th* in words such as *thin*; that ð, known as 'eth', is used for the sound *th* in words such as *that*; and that æ, known as 'ash', is used for the vowel sound in words such as *nap*. If you compare the words in this translation with the equivalent words in the other translations – and if you try speaking them out loud – you may well find that you're able to read much more than you originally thought.

eac swylce seo **næddre** wæs geapre þonne ealle þa **oðre** nytenu þe God geworhte ofer eorþan. and seo næddre **cwæþ** to þam wife. **hwi** forbead God eow þæt ge ne æton of ælcon treowe binnan paradisum.

It's not possible to work through the passage word by word here, but I've highlighted a few words which we can scrutinise in a little more detail:

- From looking at the later translations, you can probably see that *næddre* is in the equivalent position to 'serpent'. If you separate the first letter from the rest of the word, you'll perhaps be able to identify a connection. The meaning has changed somewhat – the Old English word was used to refer to snakes generally, whereas the modern word is used for a particular type of snake – but the Old English word is the original form of the modern word 'adder'.

- Moving on to *oðre*, if we replace the *ð* with a *th*, we can recognise this as the word 'other'.

- A similar shift in spelling conventions can be seen in the word *cwæþ*, where we now use *qu* instead of *cw*. If we then substitute *th* for *þ* in this word, we end up with something which would be pronounced 'quoth' – which we still have in the modern form of 'quote'.

- In the case of the word *hwi*, if we simply reverse the first two letters of the word we get modern-day 'why'.

So we can see that there is indeed a fair amount of continuity between Old English and Modern English, albeit that surface features such as spelling conventions have changed quite considerably.

It's also worth noting that one of the words we were able to identify from the very beginning – 'wife' – actually has a slightly different meaning in this first translation from its modern sense. In all the later translations of the passage it's given as 'woman'. This is because the word's meaning has narrowed since the tenth century. Nowadays we use 'wife' specifically to refer to a married woman, whereas back in the centuries of the first millennium it simply meant 'woman'.

So in conclusion, we can see that the language has changed considerably over the last thousand or so years. It has changed in terms of its **lexis** (vocabulary), its **orthography** (spelling) and its **semantics** (meaning). And, although we haven't commented on it here, it's also changed in terms of its **syntax** (word order). At the same time, however, we can still discern a very definite line of continuity back through all the passages, which justifies us in referring to them as being instances of a single developing language.

One of the reasons for the change that has happened to English over the centuries is that, since its very beginnings, English has always been in contact with other languages. The influence from this contact can be seen most clearly in the way that English is full of what are known as **loanwords**. The term loanword, or **borrowing**, is used to refer to an item of vocabulary from one language which has been adopted into the vocabulary of another. The process is often the result of **language contact**, where two or more languages exist in close geographical or social proximity. The dominant language often absorbs new items of vocabulary, either to cover concepts for which it has no specific word of its own, or to generate a slightly different function or nuance for concepts for which it does have existing words.

Some loanwords retain their 'foreign' appearance when they are adopted, and people will often then use them specifically for the sense of exoticism that they impart. One can talk of a certain *je ne sais quoi*, for example, or of a *joie de vivre* when speaking English – in both cases invoking images of French culture to enhance the meaning of what is being communicated. Other loanwords, however, become completely naturalised, until speakers of the language no longer notice their 'foreignness' at all. Below is a short selection of words of foreign origin which are in use in modern-day English. As you can see, they come from languages from all parts of the globe.

freckle	from the Old Norse *freknur*, first recorded in English in 1386
steak	from the Scandinavian, *steik*, 1420
bamboo	from the Malay, *bambu*, 1563
barbecue	from the Spanish, *barbacoa*, 'a framework of sticks set upon posts', 1697
ketchup	from the Chinese (Amoy dialect), *ketchiap,* a sauce, 1711
ghoul	from the Arabic, *ghul,* an evil spirit, 1786
dinghy	from the Hindi, *dengi*, 1794
pyjamas	from the Urdu, *paejamah*, 1801
cafeteria	from the Spanish, 1839
tycoon	from the Japanese, *taikun,* meaning 'great lord', 1857
rucksack	from the German, 1866

The extent to which English is made up of words of foreign origin was satirised during the diplomatic row between the United States and France over support for the Iraq war in 2003. The newspaper article below plays on the idea that some factions within the United States were so displeased with the French for not offering support for the war that they tried to remove all influence of French culture from their everyday lives.

English Sans French

The Franco-American ~~dispute~~ *falling out* over the best ~~approach~~ *way* to ~~disarming Iraq~~ *take away Iraq's weapons* has resulted in perhaps the highest level of anti-French feeling in the United ~~States~~ *Lands* since 1763.

A French-owned ~~hotel~~ *innkeeping* firm, Accor, has taken down the ~~tricolor~~ *three-hued flag*. In the House of ~~Representatives~~ *Burghers*, the ~~chairman~~ *leader* of the ~~Committee~~ *Body* on ~~Administration~~ *Running Things* has ~~renamed~~ *named anew* French fries 'freedom fries' and French toast 'freedom toast' in House ~~restaurants~~ *eating rooms*.

To which the ~~question~~ *asking* arises: Why stop with Evian, Total gasoline, and the Concorde (~~just~~ *only* the Air France flights)? Let's get to the heart of the ~~matter~~ *thing*: A ~~huge~~ *big* percentage of the words in ~~modern~~ *today's* English are of – gasp! –French ~~origin~~ *beginnings*. What if, as a result of the ~~current diplomatic dispute~~ *today's falling out between lands*, the French ~~demand~~ *ask for* their words back? We could all be linguistic ~~hostages~~ *captives*.

It is time for English-speaking ~~peoples~~ *folk* to throw off this cultural ~~imperialism~~ *lording-it-over-others* and ~~declare~~ *say* our linguistic freedom. It is time to ~~purify~~ *clean* the English ~~language~~ *tongue*. It will take some ~~sacrifices~~ *hardship* on everyone's part to get used to the new ~~parlance~~ *speech*. But think of the ~~satisfaction~~ *warm feeling inside* on the day we ~~are all able to~~ *can all* stare the *Académie Française* in the eye and say without fear of ~~reprisal~~ *injury*: '*Sumer is icumen in ...*'

(*Christian Science Monitor*, 14 March 2003)

If the journalist had been even more rigorous with the linguistic analysis, he or she might also have put a line through *level, percentage, cultural* and *captives*, all of which have their etymology based partly in French. The point is well made though, that if we wish to remove all French influence from English we have to step well back into the history of the language. In the article, this earlier form of English is symbolised by the popular twelfth-century song, *Sumer is icumen in*, which appears a great deal more 'foreign' to us now than many of the loanwords that have become part of our vocabulary.

In Chapters 2, 3 and 4 we'll look in more detail at the history that resulted in these words entering the English language. For the time being, the point to make is simply that English has, over its lifetime, absorbed influences from countless sources – and so just as English is now a presence in diverse contexts all across the globe, so diverse contexts from across the globe also have a presence in the language itself.

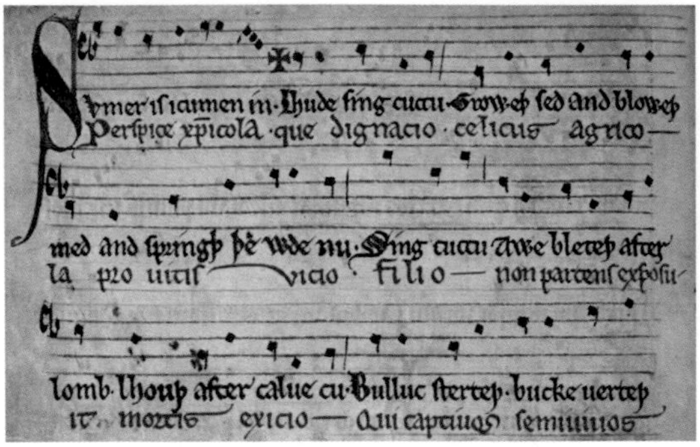

Figure 1.1 Manuscript of *Sumer is icumen in*

1.3 Who speaks English?

History is not simply about the passage of time, of course. It is what people do, and the changes that occur in society as a result of people's actions over time. The history of English can therefore be seen as a record of the changes that have occurred in the populations of those who speak the language. When two languages come into contact, what actually happens is that two communities who speak different languages engage with each other, and the nature of that engagement will determine how the languages influence one another. In other words, as was noted in the general introduction, it is important when we study English not to forget that what we are actually studying is the language as it is and was used by real people.

I remarked earlier that there is a problem in talking about statistics such as those which say that English is spoken by almost two billion people the world over because they make large generalisations about the nature of the English involved, and the relationship that people have to the language. Such statistics can never fully represent the diversity of experiences that speakers of the language have, either about whether they feel they are 'authentic' English speakers or about what they themselves understand English to be. In this section, therefore, I shall consider the role English plays in the lives of people in various parts of the world, and look at how the opinions people hold about the language are related to their personal histories, to the histories of their communities and to their interpretations of the history of the language.

Activity 1.4

Language plays a very important part in people's identities, and in this activity I'd like you to reflect on the role that your own experiences with English have played in your life. What is your own 'personal language history'? Spend a few minutes thinking about the questions below. In the discussion that follows we'll look at extracts from a selection of other people's reflections, and at how their experiences of English relate to their own identity.

- What languages or dialects were you exposed to when you were growing up?

- Who had the most influence on the language you learnt as a child?

- How did your education affect your attitudes to language? Were there any experiences related to language from your school days which have left a strong impression on you?

- How have the activities you've engaged in since school (e.g. work, family life, pastimes) affected your language use?

Comment

Here is a short selection of extracts from English speakers from around the world who were asked the same questions. The first extract is from a woman who was born and brought up in Birmingham in the UK. She reflects here on her time since university and the influences on her use and perception of language during this period of her life:

> I went to University in Swansea and for the first time was first made aware of my 'English' (and apparently 'posh') accent. My first job after leaving was in the North East of England, and here I was perceived (again, for the first time) as a 'Southerner'. In neither place was anyone able to place my place of birth from my accent. I think what I noticed most was that people made assumptions about my socio-economic background purely on the basis of my accent (or perceived lack of local accent) and saw me as 'middle-class' which was not how I saw myself. Since then, I have taught in various primary schools, mainly in Birmingham, where, as my parents did, I am aware of my responsibilities of being a language role model, particularly where pupils are new (or relatively new) to English. Though I am back on home ground (in fact, teaching at the school I first attended), people still can't tell where I come from!

The second excerpt is from a man who was born and brought up in Iran but now lives in Ontario, Canada. His native language is Farsi. In between his childhood in Tehran and his current life in Canada, he also spent some time living in the UK:

> I was educated in a mixed Farsi and English language school until grade eight. My father was keen to send me to England for my education. In those days a lack of university places and the annual university entrance competition were a major concern for parents. In 1978, just before the Iranian Revolution, I started my education at a college in Bedford, England. My minimal English and studying this subject further helped me to get through my course work every year. After finishing my O-Levels and A-Levels, I went to Liverpool University. I decided to study Structural Engineering with a view to going back to Iran one day.
>
> I had to learn a lot of engineering professional jargon like 'stress', 'strain', 'fatigue', 'moment', 'shear', 'curvature', etc. With my solid English background, I could put together the basic vocabulary and, without this, my understanding and learning of the Structural Engineering concepts and syllabus would have been impossible.
>
> After receiving my Masters degree in 1992, I found a good position at the International Institute of Earthquake Engineering in Tehran, Iran. After 14 years I was returning with not much Farsi ability to write at advanced levels. It took me almost one year to read and learn the engineering terms in Farsi. But I found out in some cases that the technical words were taken from the engineering literature in English.

The final extract is from a woman currently living in London. She writes here of the periods of her life spent in both her birthplace, Taiwan, and the UK:

> I was born in Taipei, Taiwan and brought up with Mandarin Chinese. I first moved to London with my family when I was ten years old, knowing my alphabet up to K. The only two English words I knew were 'apple' and 'hat', which I pronounced more like 'epple' and 'het' due to the more dominant American influence in Taiwan.

After I graduated from my Fine Art degree, I went to Taiwan to get reacquainted with Chinese culture. While I was there I worked at an art gallery, an English language school and a bilingual newspaper. Most of my western friends were American. I was shocked to be labelled British. In order to work at the language school in Taiwan, I had to adapt my accent moderately so that kids didn't fail their KK (the phonetic system used there). My accent was all mixed up. I remember being mistaken for being an Australian when I spoke to a British guy! I hated listening to the local American station and clung to BBC World Service for my sanity.

I married an American and then moved back to the UK. I found work in East London at a university library. For the first time in my life, I became fascinated by the different accents I was coming across. Some of my colleagues are of proud, East End, working class origin, some are from Essex, some are from the Midlands, the North, from Scotland, from Italy, Bulgaria, Kenya … Here we are in multicultural Britain! Not to mention the new slangs used by colleagues who are a decade or so younger than me, or the foreign students we encounter from all over the world!

From these brief examples we get a picture of the way that different people can have very different experiences of the 'same' language, and that these experiences often have a formative influence on how they perceive their own identity.

Figure 1.2 The multilingual landscape of London: Chinatown and the Brick Lane area

So as we can see, the attitudes people have towards the language are a part of their own personal history. But this personal history is always a part of the wider history of the community in which they live. It is often the case that not only is the language of importance to the individual's sense of identity, but that it also plays a part in the cultural identity of a group or nation. It is within this context that the history of English – and especially the reasons behind its global spread – can be of great significance for the attitudes people have towards the language.

Activity 1.5

Turn now to Reading A: *Gĩkũyũ: recovering the original*. This is part of an essay by the Kenyan author Ngũgĩ wa Thiong'o about his experiences growing up, and how the political attitudes towards English affected his life and his sense of identity. While reading the passage, think about the relationship between language choice and the wider political climate. Why do you think that the act of speaking one language rather than another should have such political significance?

Comment

What this piece illustrates very starkly is the way that the politics of language impact on an individual's language biography, and how the history of English – especially its colonial history – has meant that the language can become a very politicised issue in certain contexts. Ngũgĩ wa Thiong'o's career as a writer has been profoundly influenced by this history and by the symbolism that he feels is attached to English because of it. After the publication of his third novel, Ngũgĩ chose to stop writing in English, despite the literary success he'd achieved with it. Instead, he now writes all his fiction in his native Gĩkũyũ. Doing so is an overt political action – and one which conflicts with commercial or utilitarian interests. The readership for a book in Gĩkũyũ is far smaller than for one in English; yet this is the readership Ngũgĩ wishes to address first and foremost, and this is the language community with whom he wishes to associate himself. The reasons for this decision are clearly shown in the opening section of this essay, in which he describes events in his life which remain in his consciousness as vivid instances of the way that English is inextricably tied up with a history of colonisation, and was symbolically implicated in the domination of his native culture by an alien culture.

Figure 1.3 Ngũgĩ wa Thiong'o

Activity 1.6

Now turn to Reading B: *English in China after the revolution
(1949–present)* by Kingsley Bolton. This provides a different Illustration of
the way in which historical change has an influence on English. Not only
is English important in the lives of individuals, but it's also important in
the lives of communities as a whole. While reading, think about how the
changing history of China has influenced attitudes to English. What
reasons are given for English being an important language for
China today?

Comment

What Kingsley Bolton charts in this reading is the way that attitudes to
English have changed according to political trends in China. Today, a
major motivation for learning the language is that it's seen as a way to
access the global economy. For both individuals and the state, English is
seen as an essential tool for economic success. In earlier decades, on
the other hand, the rationale for English language education was quite
different. It was promoted as a means of teaching communist values, or
for spreading Maoist ideals to an international audience. At each juncture
in the history of modern China then, specific values have been

associated with the language, and these have reflected the wider social and political concerns of the population at the time.

One further important point that's illustrated in this reading is the crucial role that the education system plays in the way that English is viewed in society. In a world in which more people now speak English as a second language rather than as their mother tongue (an issue I'll explore in more detail below), a majority of English speakers have been introduced to the language through formal education. And this means that *how the language is taught* has a great influence on people's attitudes towards it.

Figure 1.4 A multilingual street sign in present-day China

What we can see from examples such as these is that the development of the language is influenced by social forces. Decisions about the language made by institutions such as national governments and education systems have an impact on the form of the language and on the way it is perceived and used. In contexts such as these, English cannot simply be considered a neutral medium of communication; instead it is a politically charged social practice embedded in the histories of the people who use it.

1.4   How do we model the spread of English?

What we have seen so far, then, is that the English language is and always has been a diverse entity. It has changed dramatically over the centuries since it first arrived on the shores of Britain from the north of Europe, and these changes mean that the language that was spoken at that time is almost incomprehensible to us now. As the language has spread beyond Britain it has continued to change, and to change in different ways in different contexts. It has diversified to such an extent that some scholars suggest that it is no longer accurate to talk of a single 'English'; that instead there are many different English languages around the world today. Given this great diversity, then, how can we best approach the study of the language?

People who study language like to do so in a systematic way. They like to develop models to explain how it is that a language such as English has ended up the way it is, and to explain why one form of the language is different from another, what the nature of the similarities and differences between varieties is, and what processes occur to produce this change. In this final section I shall consider how people have modelled the existence of English around the world, and in doing so I will introduce some key concepts and terminology which will then be used in the rest of the book.

A first distinction that is often made is between the English that is spoken by **native speakers (NS)** and by **non-native speakers (NNS)**. The word 'native' is derived from the Latin *natus* meaning 'to be born', so one's native language is the language one acquires from birth. An alternative term for this is **mother tongue**, which again refers to the language of one's early childhood environment. (It's worth adding here that people growing up in bilingual or multilingual environments might learn more than one language from birth, so have more than one mother tongue.) A native speaker is therefore someone who has learnt a particular language – in this case English – since early childhood, in contrast to a non-native speaker, who will have learnt it later in life. The significance of the distinction is that people acquire language in a different manner depending on the age at which they learn it. Learning a second or additional language later in life may, for example, result in speaking it with an accent influenced by one's native language.

There is a widespread perception in society that non-native speakers are not able to attain the same level of competence as native speakers, but this is by no means necessarily the case. Often, an expert non-native speaker can have an equal or even superior proficiency to a native speaker – it all depends on their environment, their educational background, and the purpose for which they learn and use the language. For example, a non-native English-speaking diplomat working at the United Nations might possibly have a wider vocabulary and a greater rhetorical prowess than a native-speaking farmer working in the south of England, simply because his or her job requires an expert use of language in the way that the farmer's does not. In this case, the life-stage at which the language was learnt is likely to be less important than a host of other environmental factors such as occupation, educational background and identity. As we can see, then, the concept of the mother tongue or the native speaker (and the related notion of **English as a Native Language (ENL)** countries) is as much to do with the biography of the speaker as with the nature of the language itself.

Another long-standing distinction used in the discipline is that between **English as a Second Language** and **English as a Foreign Language**. These are often abbreviated by use of the acronyms **ESL** and **EFL**. ESL refers to the use of English in countries where it has some **official** or legal status, most often as the result of a colonial history. For example, English is an official language in India – and is thus used in administrative and educational contexts – although it is not the mother tongue for the majority of the population.

English as a Foreign Language is a term used in contrast to ESL, and refers to contexts where English has no special official status. Instead, the language is taught in schools as something specifically associated with the UK, the USA or other countries that are traditionally perceived as English-speaking. For example, in Japan, children will learn English at school for the same purposes as children in the UK learn French or German – they are not expecting to use it as part of their everyday life in Japanese society, but as a useful tool should they travel abroad or want to learn about the cultures of English-speaking nations.

This, at least, was traditionally how the language was taught up until quite recently. Since English has emerged as the pre-eminent language of international communication it is beginning to be seen less as a *foreign* language and more as an **international language**. In other words, English is not useful simply because it allows one to communicate with people from the UK or the USA, but because it allows communication with people from an increasingly wide range of places. Indeed, statistically the language is now more often used for encounters between non-native speakers than it is with native speakers. So countries such as

Japan now view English as an essential skill for the modern citizen, despite the fact that the language has no official status in the country concerned. In a policy document on the nation's 'Goals in the twenty-first century', for example, the Japanese government suggests that:

> The advance of globalization and the information-technology revolution call for a world-class level of excellence. Achieving world-class excellence demands that, in addition to mastering information technology, all Japanese acquire a working knowledge of English – not as simply a foreign language but as the international lingua franca. English in this sense is a prerequisite for obtaining global information, expressing intentions, and sharing values.
>
> (CJGTC, 2000, p. 10)

So whereas for a long time there was a straight distinction between ENL, ESL and EFL, we now have to add **EIL** or **English as an International Language** as a further conceptualisation of how the language is used in today's world. There is a growing perception that English is now the world's **lingua franca** – that it operates as a means of communication for people across the globe who do not share a mother tongue and yet, given the globalised society in which we now live, have the need to interact.

The Three Circles of English

The above is, then, a brief overview of the ways in which scholars traditionally categorise the different ways in which English is used around the world. While these terms may identify how people use the language, however, they do not explain anything about the dynamics of the spread or the nature of the distribution of English. To do this, we need to introduce a model which expands on these categories and maps them on to different social and historical processes.

A number of models for describing the spread of English around the globe have been put forward over the last few decades, but by far the most influential has been the one devised by Braj Kachru and known as the *Three Circles of English*.

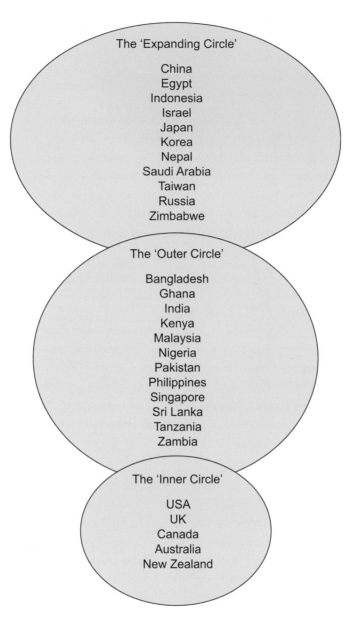

The 'Expanding Circle'

China
Egypt
Indonesia
Israel
Japan
Korea
Nepal
Saudi Arabia
Taiwan
Russia
Zimbabwe

The 'Outer Circle'

Bangladesh
Ghana
India
Kenya
Malaysia
Nigeria
Pakistan
Philippines
Singapore
Sri Lanka
Tanzania
Zambia

The 'Inner Circle'

USA
UK
Canada
Australia
New Zealand

Figure 1.5 The Three Circles of English (adapted from Kachru, 1992)

As Kachru explains it:

> The current sociolinguistic profile of English [around the world] may be viewed in terms of three concentric circles. These circles represent the types of spread, the patterns of acquisition, and the functional allocation of English in diverse cultural contexts. The

Inner Circle refers to the traditional cultural and linguistic bases of English. The Outer Circle represents the institutionalized non-native varieties (ESL) in the regions that have passed through extended periods of colonization … The Expanding Circle includes the regions where the *performance* varieties of the language are used essentially in EFL contexts (i.e. varieties that lack official status and are typically restricted in their uses).

(Kachru, 1992, pp. 356–7)

Let us take the three circles in turn and see how Kachru expands on the categories discussed above. For each circle, Kachru's model reflects the following three issues:

- the historical process that has resulted in English occupying its current position in particular countries
- how members of particular countries usually come to acquire the language
- the purposes or functions to which the language is put in particular countries.

The **Inner Circle** of English-speaking countries is composed of those places where the language is the mother tongue for the vast majority of the population and where it operates as the default language for almost all domains of society. This circle comprises not only the UK, but also those countries colonised by the British where English displaced indigenous languages and is now firmly embedded as the majority language. It includes therefore the USA, Canada, Australia, New Zealand, etc. Kachru explains that these countries are what he calls 'norm-providing' in that the English here operates as the model for the type of English that is taught around the world. In other words, when people learn English as a foreign language in a country such as China, they are likely to look to standard British or standard American English as an appropriate model to which to aspire.

The **Outer Circle** also comprises countries in which the current status of English is the result of colonisation, but with the difference that in these countries the language did not displace the indigenous languages, but instead was used alongside them for certain specific roles. These then are the ESL countries, where English is not the first language for the majority of people, but is rather an additional language used in institutional contexts such as bureaucracy and education. Kachru calls these countries 'norm-developing' in that the varieties of English spoken here are now securely rooted in the culture – they are **indigenised varieties** – and yet they do not yet have the same status as ENL varieties. As he explains, 'In the Outer Circle the varieties of English have their own local histories, literary traditions, pragmatic contexts, and communicative norms' (Kachru, 1992, p. 359).

Finally, there is the **Expanding Circle**, which refers to the rest of the world. In these countries English is predominantly viewed and taught as a foreign language, as this has been defined in the section above. These countries have no significant number of first or second language speakers, and as such they are 'norm-dependent' – that is to say, they do not have the base of first-language speakers which would allow them to develop their own norms, and so they follow a UK or US standard English as their model. They are traditionally EFL countries, in that the education system assumes that English is taught for purposes such as tourism or to read foreign literature.

Table 1.1 The Three Circles of English and their attributes

	Cause of spread	Pattern of acquisition	Functional allocation	Countries
The Inner Circle	Settlement by first language English speakers	As a native language	All functions	e.g. UK, USA, Canada, Australia, New Zealand
The Outer Circle	Colonisation (by the British)	As a second language	Administration, education, literature	e.g. India, Kenya, Singapore
The Expanding Circle	Globalisation	As a foreign language	Tourism, diplomacy, business	e.g. China, Japan, most countries in Europe

The strengths and limitations of the model

The Three Circles model has several advantages, but it also has its limitations. One of its strengths has been the way it has advocated the need to see the presence of the language around the globe as consisting of several **world Englishes** rather than as a single, monolithic entity. As Kachru says:

> We must ... cease to view English within the framework appropriate for monolingual societies. We must recognize the linguistic, cultural, and pragmatic implications of various types of pluralism; that pluralism has now become an integral part of the

English language and the literatures written in English in various parts of the non-Western world.

(Kachru, 1992, p. 362)

The model has indeed helped focus scholarly interest on non-native varieties, and has done a great deal to legitimise them as valid linguistic systems. Whereas previously, non-native varieties – especially those of the Outer Circle – had been viewed as deficient versions of Inner Circle varieties (Quirk, 1990), Kachru's model makes a case for seeing them as legitimate varieties in their own right, which are both linguistically stable and firmly embedded in the culture of the communities that use them. This is in part achieved by referring to them as separate Englishes, rather than simply non-native dialects. In addition, the model draws attention to the importance of historical and political processes – of the sort we have looked at with respect to Kenya and China – in the state of Englishes around the world.

As I mentioned, though, people have also pointed to its limitations (e.g. Bruthiaux, 2003; Pennycook, 2007). Like any theoretical model, it is a generalisation, and so it necessarily simplifies the phenomena it's dealing with. It identifies what it sees as broad trends within the pattern of English spread across the globe, but in doing so invariably overlooks – for reasons of pure practicality – many important details. Some of the limitations that people have pointed to are discussed below.

First, the model deals with language only at the level of the nation state. All the varieties it refers to are associated with whole countries. But of course, there is also a great amount of variety *within* countries, in the shape of regional and social dialects and the specific registers people use at work. To group everything that happens within a country together ignores this variety, and so the criticism is that the model does not adequately capture the heterogeneity of English. Furthermore, some scholars say that the focus on *varieties* is itself limiting, and that people often mix the language with other languages in an ad hoc manner, throwing in words and phrases in English while nominally speaking other languages (Pennycook, 2007). With English now having a global status this happens with greater frequency, and it disrupts the neat categories, such as Indian or Malaysian English, with which Kachru's model works.

The model also fails to take account of countries which do not fit neatly into its scheme. Kachru himself points to the case of South

Africa, where there are now eleven official languages, and where English will be learnt as a mother tongue by large sections of the population, but not by others. Yet even core 'Inner Circle countries' such as Canada and New Zealand are officially bilingual, and thus do not fit unproblematically into the model.

The model is also unable to accommodate countries whose status is shifting. For example, in several European countries – especially those in Scandinavia – English may have traditionally been a foreign language, but today it is such an integral part of everyday life that it is moving towards a situation where it almost has the status (in practice if not in name) of a second language. Furthermore, as was noted above, in many countries the notion of English as a foreign language is being challenged or replaced by English as an international language – and again, the model does not fully recognise this.

What we need to bear in mind is that the terms we use for discussing English in the world are the result of a simplification of what are often very complex sociolinguistic circumstances. In other words, they are convenient generalisations, and although useful as tools for description and analysis, they should not be seen as a direct representation of the full complexity of how language operates in real-life situations. Nevertheless, this model – along with the caveats that accompany it – provides a good starting point for an investigation of modern-day English. Over the next few chapters we shall continue our examination of the language by focusing in more detail on its history, and we will do this in stages which roughly parallel the Three Circles. Chapter 2 will begin with the first emergence of English, and give the background to the Inner Circle variety that developed on the British mainland. In Chapter 3 we will track the spread of English beyond the British Isles, and give the background for Outer Circle or 'postcolonial' varieties. And in Chapter 4 we shall look at how the language finally went global, how it spread through the Expanding Circle, and how it came to occupy its present position in the world. In the second half of the book we will then go on to look at how people use the language today, and at how history and current practice combine together in everyday acts of communication.

1.5   Conclusion

What is of particular interest about English in the world today is that as it spreads around the globe, and as it is adopted by or imposed on different social groups, it diversifies and develops into various and distinct incarnations. Yet at the same time, English exists in the world today as a means of international communication – as a way for people from *different* social groups to communicate with each other – and to fulfil this function it would seem that variation in the language needs to be curtailed to a certain extent. That is to say, if the language becomes *too* diverse it will not remain mutually comprehensible across different social groups. So we have two impulses at work that are seemingly incompatible, or perhaps even in conflict, and the question we are faced with is how to render them as consistent, as both being part of the existence of a single entity we call 'English'. This is one of the central problems in English language studies today – and it's a very modern problem because it has come about as a direct result of the position that English now occupies in the world. As we have already remarked, however, to understand the position that English does now occupy in the world, we first need to understand how it has been shaped by the history it has inhabited, and it is this that we shall turn to in the next chapter.

READING A: Gĩkũyũ: recovering the original

Ngũgĩ wa Thiong'o

Source: wa Thiong'o, N. (2004) 'Recovering the original' in Lesser, W. (ed.) *The Genius of Language*, New York, Pantheon Books, pp. 102–5.

He lay on his tummy on a high table in the assembly hall with all the students and staff present. Two teachers held his head and legs and pinned him to the table and called him monkey, as the third whip lashed his buttocks. No matter how horribly he screamed and wriggled with pain, they would not let him go. Scream Monkey. Eventually the shorts split and blood spluttered out, some of it on the shirts of those who held him down, and only then did they let him go. He stood up barely able to walk, barely able to cry, and he left, never to be seen in the precincts of that government school or any other again; I have never known what happened to him. His fault? He had been caught in the act of speaking Gĩkũyũ in the environs of the school, not once, not twice, but several times. How did the teachers come to discover his sins?

Speaking African languages in the school compound was a crime. If a student caught another speaking an African language, he would pass a token called a monitor to the culprit, who would carry it around his neck till he caught another speaking the forbidden tongues; he would pass the dreaded thing to the new culprit, and so on – children spying on one another, all day, or even tricking each other into speaking the leprous language. The one with the monitor at the end of the day was the sinner and would be punished. The above recipient of whiplashes had been a sinner for so many weeks that it looked as if he was deliberately defying the ban on Gĩkũyũ. The teachers were determined to use him as an example to teach others a lesson.

This was the Kenya of the fifties in the last century. The country was then a British settler colony, with a sizeable white settlement in the arable heartland, which they then called White Highlands. But from its colonization in 1895, Kenya was always contested, the forces of colonial occupation being met by those of national resistance, with the clash between the two sides climaxing in the armed conflict of the fifties, when Kenyans grouped around Mau Mau (or, more appropriately, Kenya Land and the Freedom Army) took to the forests and mountains to wage a guerrilla struggle against the colonial state. The outbreak of the war was preceded by a heightened nationalist cultural awareness, with songs, poetry, and newspapers in African languages abounding. The outbreak of the war was followed by a ban on performances and publications in African languages. A similar ban applied to African-run schools – they were abolished.

I first went to Kamandūra primary, a missionary set-up, in 1947. But we must have been caught up by the new nationalist awareness, because there were rumors that missionary schools were deliberately denying us children real education (*Gūthimira ciana ūgī*). Such schools were alleged not to be teaching Africans enough English, and some of us were pulled out of the missionary school and relocated to Manguū, a nationalist school where the emphasis was on the history and culture of Africans. In religion, some of the nationalist schools, which called themselves independent, aligned themselves with the orthodox church, thus linking themselves to the unbroken Christian tradition of Egypt and Ethiopia, way back in the first and fourth centuries of the Christian era.

I was too young to know about this linkage; all I knew was that I was going to a school where we would be taught 'deep' English alongside other subjects and languages, in our case Gĩkũyũ. I can't remember if the English in the nationalist school was 'deeper' than that taught in the previous school – I doubt if there was any difference in approach to the teaching of English – but I do recall that a composition in Gĩkũyũ was good enough to have me paraded in front of the class, in praise. That is how to write good Gĩkũyũ, the teacher said after reading it aloud to the class. So in the nationalist school of my early primary schooling, mastering Gĩkũyũ and knowing English were not in conflict. One got recognition for mastering one or both.

This peaceful co-existence of Gĩkũyũ and English in the classroom changed suddenly a few years later, when the African independent schools were shut down, with some of them resurrected as colonial state-run institutions. Manguū was one of these and the emphasis on humiliating the Gĩkũyũ language-users, as the pre-condition for acquiring English, was the most immediate outcome of the changes. It was under the new dispensation that terror was unleashed on Gĩkũyũ. The screaming student was being thrashed to take him out of the darkness of his language to the light of English knowledge.

I enjoyed English under all dispensations, but the image of the screaming student haunted me and even puzzled me for a long time. The student was hounded out of the school for speaking Gĩkũyũ, the language I had once been praised for writing well. Maybe there was something wrong with the teachers who had so praised me; the evidence of this was that they had all lost their jobs under the new colonial position on the importance of English. The new teachers, all African, all black, all Gĩkũyũ, devised all sorts of methods for associating African languages with negative images, including making linguistic sinners carry placards that asserted that they were asses. It was a war of attrition that gradually eroded pride and confidence in my language. There was nothing this language could teach me, at least nothing that could make me become educated and modern. Gore to the students who spoke Gĩkũyũ; glory to those who showed a mastery of English. I grew up distancing myself from the gore in my own language to attain the glory in English mastery.

READING B: English in China after the revolution (1949–present)

Kingsley Bolton

Source: Bolton, K. (2006) *Chinese Englishes: A Sociolinguistic History*, Cambridge, Cambridge University Press, pp. 246–58.

A number of trends emerged in foreign-language teaching after the establishment of the People's Republic in 1949. Up until the 1990s, Chinese education would experience a roller-coaster ride of changing policy directives, most dictated by the prevailing political winds. Immediately after the revolution, Russian began to replace English as the major foreign language in schools. By the beginning of the 1960s, however, with the weakening of the Soviet influence, English was reintroduced as a school language, but, shortly after, its resurgence was abruptly halted by the Cultural Revolution (1966–76), which devastated not only the national education system, but the whole of the Chinese nation. Many English teachers were attacked, physically and otherwise, during this period, for various crimes including spying, and 'worshipping everything foreign' (Adamson and Morris, 1997, p. 15).

Politically, the years between the end of the Cultural Revolution and the 1997 handover were dominated by the need to implement the 'four modernisations' in agriculture, industry, defence, and science and technology. By the early 1980s, English had begun to receive increased attention in the national curriculum, particularly in major urban schools, as it was seen as increasingly necessary for university studies and employment and was widely referred to as 'the language of international communication and commerce' (Ross, 1993, p. 40). At the same time, anxiety about the 'spiritual pollution' associated with foreign cultures and languages persisted, and the 1978 English syllabus was justified politically in the following terms:

> English is a very widely used language throughout the world. In certain aspects, English is a very important tool: for international class struggle; for economic and trade relationships; for cultural, scientific and technological exchange; and for the development of international friendship … To uphold the principle of classless internationalism and to carry out Chairman Mao's revolutionary diplomacy effectively, we need to nurture a large number of 'red and expert' people proficient in a foreign language and foreign disciplines.
>
> (1978 English syllabus, cited in Adamson and Morris, 1997, p. 17)

When the syllabus was revised in 1982, the emphasis was changed from politics to economics, sentiments that were reiterated in the 1993 English syllabus for junior secondary schools which stipulated that:

> A foreign language is an important tool for interacting with other countries and plays an important role in promoting the development of the national and world economy, science and culture. In order to meet the needs of our Open Door Policy and to accelerate socialist modernization, efforts should be made to enable as many people as possible to acquire command of one or more foreign languages.
>
> (1993 English syllabus, Adamson and Morris, 1997, p. 21)

The aims of the 1993 syllabus also include the fostering of communication, and the acquisition of knowledge of foreign cultures (Adamson and Morris, 1997, p. 22), aims which were repeated in the revised 2000 English syllabus for junior secondary schools.

The changing styles of official English teaching over the last thirty years may be illustrated by the changes in English-language textbooks in this period. Figures [1] and [2] below are taken from a People's Educational Press (PEP) primary English textbook of 1960, and graphically illustrate the political content of the textbooks of that period. The copperplate handwriting beneath the printed text provides an interesting contrast to the stark slogans of communism […] One can compare these two illustrations with a page from a more recent PEP secondary textbook, shown in [F]igure [3] below, which discusses the subject of Christmas. This is taken from a course book called *Junior English for China*, and is representative of more culturally open approaches to textbook design.

Figure [1] Driving a train
(PEP, 1960, p. 3)

Figure [2] Paper tiger
(PEP, 1960, p. 15)

The inclusion of such a passage in a recent textbook seems genuinely indicative of the liberalisation of aspects of education in the contemporary PRC. It would have been unthinkable to have printed such a culturally loaded text in earlier books in the post-1949 era. In the supplementary text that follows Lesson 54, even Jesus Christ receives a mention:

What does Christmas mean? Christmas Day is the birthday of Jesus Christ. When Christ was born nearly two thousand years ago, many people, rich and poor, gave him presents. So today, people still do the same thing to each other. Of course, everyone likes presents. But Mr Green says: 'It is better to give than to receive.' What do you think?

(People's Educational Press, 1992, p. 55)

Lesson 54

Read

Christmas is an important festival in Britain and many other parts of the world. Read the passage below very quickly and find out "Who is Father Christmas?" Then read it again and answer the questions on page 54 of your workbook.

CHRISTMAS DAY

On Christmas Eve — the night before Christmas Day — children all over Britain put a stocking at the end of their beds before they go to sleep. Their parents usually tell them that Father Christmas will come during the night.

Father Christmas is very kind-hearted. He lands on top of each house and climbs down the chimney into the fireplace. He fills each of the stockings with Christmas presents.

Of course, Father Christmas isn't real. In Jim and Kate's house, "Father Christmas" is really Mr Green. Mr Green doesn't climb down the chimney. He waits until the children are asleep. Then he quietly goes into their bedrooms, and fills their stockings with small presents. When they were very young, Mr Green sometimes dressed up in a red coat. But he doesn't do that now. The children are no longer young, and they know who "Father Christmas" really is. But they still put their stockings at the end of their beds.

Use your dictionary

1 Try to guess what these words mean:
   Britain   stocking   chimney   kind-hearted   top
2 Now look up the words in a dictionary.

Read the end of the text in the next lesson for homework.

Figure [3]   'Christmas Day' in a recent English textbook (PEP, 1992, p. 54)

Other lessons in the same textbook discuss such topics as the life of a British family resident in China, the biography of Thomas Edison, life in Australia, soccer and the spread of English as an international language.

Today, despite the fact that English continues to grow in importance as a school subject throughout China, attitudes to the language vary. Zhao and Campbell (1995) report that many students resent having to learn the language, and only do so because of the importance of the language for educational advancement, learning English 'purely because they have to'. They claim that 'most Chinese learners of English are not learning English for international communication but for social and economic mobility' (1995, p. 383, 385). Despite this, the importance of English in education is increasing and, in the last ten years, a number of colleges and universities on the Chinese mainland have experimented with the use of English as a teaching medium. For example, the Guangdong Education Commission recently announced its intention to establish English-medium courses in selected schools 'to equip Guangdong students in urban and Pearl Delta areas with the same command of English as their counterparts in Hong Kong and other Southeast Asian countries by 2005' (Yow, 2001, p. 2). The same article reported that there were also plans to employ 'native-speaker' teachers in many of the best schools in the province.

Outside the national education system, the study of English has continued to spread. Over the past twenty years, successive 'English crazes' have found expression in a range of ways: in the English-speaking corners that were set up in many cities; in the growing popularity of certification of various kinds, including the TOEFL examination and Business English diplomas; and in various other activities associated with learning the language. English is a strong second language within the Chinese media, and several English-language newspapers and magazines are published for domestic as well as international consumption, including the *China Daily* 中國日報, the *Beijing Review* 北京周報 and a range of smaller publications in cities such as Beijing, Guangzhou and Shanghai. English-language books are widely available from bookshops, and include reprints of western 'canonical' texts as well as Chinese literature in English translation. English-language radio programmes for language learning have had a large following for many years, as do such news channels as the Voice of America. In addition, China Central Television Station (CCTV) now has regular broadcasts in English. The increasing availability of the internet in China has also opened further channels for communication in

English, as has the growing popularity of e-mail communication
(Li, 2000).

For those remaining in China to study [rather than studying abroad],
there are now a number of alternatives to English teaching in state
schools, including a small but growing number of private schools and
tutorial centres (Lai, 2001). But the most radical approach to English
teaching in the late 1990s has been a nationwide campaign by a
charismatic English teacher named Li Yang 李楊, who claims to have
lectured to over 13 million people nationwide. His approach is known
everywhere throughout China by the striking name of *Feng kuang ying yu*
瘋狂英語 or 'Crazy English'.

Li Yang's 'Crazy English'

The 1999 documentary film *Crazy English* produced and directed by
Zhang Yuan provides a fascinating insight into Li Yang's popularity, as
it follows the celebrity English teacher on a nationwide tour from sports
stadium to university to school to government enterprise.[1] Li Yang is a
youthful thirty-something with a popstar image and entourage to match,
who has turned his teaching method into a multi-million business. No
mean feat for a self-confessed educational failure.

His method relies on a small number of basic principles, which are
constantly drilled into audiences of various sizes, but which can number
up to several thousand. Three core principles are 'speak as loudly as
possible', 'speak as quickly as possible' and 'speak as clearly as possible'.
The training sessions he provides on tour are actually fairly simple
sessions of elementary English practice, where he instructs his audiences
in pronunciation techniques using a modified 'total physical response'
technique in combination with mnemonic hand signals. Interestingly
enough, his own pronunciation is characterised by a marked American
accent.

In addition to his public appearances, Li also earns money from the sale
of books and tapes, but the key to his success is the accompanying
psychological pitch, which is geared to the aspirations of his audience.
In many of his public appearances, Li relates his own earlier difficulties
in mastering the language, urging his devotees to follow his own
example of determination and will-power in overcoming adversity, and
teaching his audiences such slogans as 'I enjoy losing face!', 'Welcome

---

[1] The film *Crazy English* is produced by Chen Ziqiu and Zhang Yuan, and is directed by
   Zhang Yuan. The video version in VCD format is distributed by Asia Video Publishing
   Co., Ltd.

setbacks!', 'Relish suffering!' and 'Seek success!' In a radio broadcast that occurs early in the film, Li Yang puts across a message of self-help and self-improvement:

> Hello everybody! My name is Li Yang. This probably sounds strange. People have asked if I've fabricated my hardships. My parents, classmates and teachers will testify that I lacked confidence. I didn't know where to end up. I had an inferiority complex, felt ignorant. I didn't feel capable of anything. I was always telling myself to be determined: I'll start tomorrow! I'll start tomorrow! Everyone wants to succeed, I want to serve as an example. My Crazy English consists of many philosophies of life and success … Money is no longer a problem. In one day, I could make 20 to 30 grand, 30 to 40 grand. That time is past. I've moved onto another stage. Once I've accomplished something, it becomes dull. I think I've found a bigger goal. To tell thousands of people about my process of struggle. Everyone needs to do his work well. Because Chinese people lack confidence. Chinese people need to put their noses to the grindstone.

Li Yang's message of hope also combines with a message of monetary gain that seems to capture the spirit of the state-sanctioned materialism ('to get rich is glorious') of the late 1990s. Occasionally, however, this crosses all boundaries of the possible, as on the occasion when he tells Tsinghua University students of the money to be made teaching English abroad:

> For teaching English in Japan, the highest salary is US$30,000 per hour. Native speakers from America who go to Japan to teach for Sony, Toshiba, Sharp and National, earn up to US$30,000 per hour … My advertising slogan is already thought out. To learn English, look for a Chinese person. Where I'd advertise? *Yomiuri Shimbun* and *Asahi Shimbun* [two leading Japanese newspapers]. The market for English teachers in Japan is large. This is good news … So with this idea in mind, for the sake of making money, start to learn English tonight. Money is the biggest motivation for studying. How do you come to repay your parents in the future? Buy them an airplane ticket around the world. 'Go travel around

the world!' This is the best way to repay your parents. This is one of the biggest motivations for studying.

Another important element of the Crazy English philosophy is a sharp and focused nationalism which Li expresses in a number of ways, including the repetition of patriotic slogans such as 'Never let your country down!', and the employment of a chubby, balding and buffoonish American as an onstage butt. In some performances, Li Yang's self-help philosophy is extended from the individual to the nation:

> What's the US industry and agriculture output for 1995? Almost 7,400 billion US dollars. How about for China? 550 billion US dollars. This is just small change for America. There's a Japanese bank called Mitsubishi Bank. One bank's deposit is 700 billion US dollars. More than that of all the banks in China combined. There's another American company, Microsoft. Bill Gates' Microsoft Company. Its value has exceeded 200 billion US dollars. There's another American company, General Electric, whose value will reach 400–600 billion US dollars by the year 2000. The value of one company is almost equal to the GNP of China. I'm telling you all of this, hoping you will remember it. Don't be blinded by the claim 'China's the biggest market'. We should teach our children that China is by no means the biggest market. Where is the biggest market? America, Japan, Europe! What is China's aim? To occupy these three markets, right? Here is a question for everybody. What's the purpose of studying English? Repeat after me. Occupy … America … Japan … Europe … these three big markets. Make money internationally! Say it loudly! Make money … internationally! Make money internationally!

In the two stills from the film reproduced as [F]igures [4] and [5], Li Yang is standing on the Great Wall of China, giving instruction to a few hundred soldiers from the People's Liberation Army (PLA). In the film, the PLA soldiers are being trained to chant in unison such useful phrases as 'How're you doing?', 'Never let your country down!', 'I have been looking forward to meeting you!', 'Brilliant!', 'No pain, no gain!', 'Nineteen ninety-seven!' and 'The PLA is great!'

Figure [4] 'How're you doing?' (Still from the 1999 documentary film *Crazy English*, produced and directed by Zhang Yuan.)

Figure [5] 'The PLA is great' (Still from the 1999 documentary film *Crazy English*, produced and directed by Zhang Yuan.)

As McArthur has pointed out, in terms of numbers of speakers and a range of other factors, English and Chinese represent two of the most important language traditions and cultures in the world today (McArthur, 2000). A recent study by Dalby (2001) places Chinese as the most widely spoken language in the world, with 1,155 million speakers worldwide, of whom 800 million speak Mandarin as a first language, and 200 million speak the variety as a second language. In addition, it is estimated that there are 85 million speakers of Wu dialects

(Shanghainese, etc.) and 70 million speakers of Yue dialects (Cantonese, etc.). English is in second place with a total of 1 billion speakers. Of these, 400 million are first-language speakers, and 600 million are second-language speakers. Much more could be said, and doubtless will be said and written, about the linguistic and cultural contacts between these two traditions, and the growing 'interface' between them (McArthur, 2000) [...] In the case of Li Yang's 'Crazy English', we see [a particular type of] modernity at work, that of a rapidly industrialising China in which capital and capitalism serve the needs of Maoist Marxist-Leninism reinvented as 'socialism with Chinese characteristics'. Creolists explain Canton 'jargon' as an early variety of 'business English' and, as China enters the World Trade Organisation, Li Yang's approach appears to give voice to the material hopes of millions of Chinese in a variety of brash English that twangs American but rings global with its exhortation 'Make the voice of China be widely heard all over the world!'

Acknowledgements

People's Educational Press of Beijing (for permission to reproduce the textbook illustrations).

References for this reading

Adamson, B. and Morris, P. (1997) 'The English curriculum in the People's Republic of China', *Comparative Education Review*, vol. 41, no. 1, pp. 3–26.

Dalby, D. (2001) 'The linguasphere: kaleidoscope of the world's languages', *English Today*, vol. 17, no. 1, pp. 22–6.

Lai, E. (2001) 'Teaching English as a private enterprise in China', *English Today*, vol. 17, no. 2, pp. 32–6.

Li, Y. (2000) 'Surfing e-mails', *English Today*, vol. 16, no. 4, pp. 30–4.

McArthur, T. (2000) 'The English-Chinese interface', talk given at the University of Hong Kong, March 2000.

People's Educational Press (1992) *Junior English for China*, Beijing, People's Educational Press.

Ross, H. A. (1993) *China Learns English: Language teaching and social change in the People's Republic*, London, Yale University Press.

Yow, S. (2001) 'Guangdong to trial English as medium', *South China Morning Post*, 20 October, p. 2.

Zhao, Y. and Campbell, K. P. (1995) 'English in China', *World Englishes*, vol. 14, no. 3, pp. 377–90.

2 A national language

Joan Beal

2.1 Introduction

We begin our look at the history of English by addressing the question of how it was that English initially rose to become a **national language**. English was not, after all, the original, indigenous language of England. Prior to the arrival of the Anglo-Saxons in Britain in the 400s, the inhabitants of the island spoke Celtic languages. Yet English shows few traces of Celtic, emerging instead from the mix of dialects brought by the Germanic invaders. Nor was the subsequent growth of English within England a smooth or inevitable trajectory. After the Norman Conquest of 1066, for example, English was not even the first language of the ruling classes. For several centuries, French and Latin were spoken in England as well as English which, in its many regional forms, was the language of everyday life and of the lower classes. Yet somehow by the fourteenth century, when official government documents were first written in English, a sense of a national, standard variety of English had begun to emerge.

From the 1300s, much of the story of English is an account of **standardisation**: the social and political processes by which norms of language usage are agreed and enforced. Today we can talk of a **standard English** in Britain, one that is codified in dictionaries and grammars, prescribed in schools and promoted by the media. However, it is important not to see the history of English as simply a move from diversity to homogeneity: variation still exerts its pull on English even within England, not only in the dialects spoken across the country, but also in the changing make-up of the languages with which it co-exists. Nor should the history of English be seen in any sense as 'finished'; as well as its spread throughout the British Isles and beyond (which will be the topic of Chapters 3 and 4), English continues to shift and develop within England itself.

In this chapter, I trace the history of English in England and explore many of the issues touched on above: the hybrid nature of English and the continuing impact of language contact, the social and political nature of standardisation, the diversity that continues to characterise English in England, and the extent to which, in different historical periods, including our own, English can be considered a *national* language. The

'Seven Ages of English' below, which you can use for reference throughout this chapter and the next two, will help you start thinking about this last question. The historical timeline (Appendix 1), gives more detailed information about many of the key dates that relate to the history of the language.

Seven Ages of English

1 Pre-English period (– *c*.AD 450)

Local languages in Britain are Celtic, and the inhabitants known as Celts or Britons. After the Roman invasion *c*.55 BC, Latin becomes the dominant language of culture and government. Many communities in Britain are bilingual Celtic-Latin. The island (excluding Scotland) is widely known by its Latin name, Britannia (Britain).

2 Early Old English (450 – *c*.850)

Anglo-Saxon invasion *c*.AD 449 after the Romans have withdrawn (410). Settlers bring a variety of Germanic dialects from mainland Europe. First English literature appears *c*.AD 700. English borrows many words from Latin via the Church.

3 Later Old English (*c*.850 – 1100)

Extensive invasion and settlement from Scandinavia. In the north of England dialects of English become strongly influenced by Scandinavian languages. In the South King Alfred arranges for many Latin texts to be translated.

4 Middle English (*c*.1100 – 1450)

Norman conquest and Norman rule. English vocabulary and spelling now affected by French, which becomes the official language in England. Educated English people trilingual (French, Latin, English). Chaucer. England begins to become recognised as a political entity within Britain.

5 Early Modern English (*c*.1450 – 1750)

Includes the Renaissance, the Elizabethan era and Shakespeare. The role of the Church, of Latin and of French declines and English becomes a language of science and government. Britain grows commercially and acquires overseas colonies. English taken to the Americas, Australia, India. Slave trade carries African people speaking different African languages to Caribbean and America, giving rise to English creoles. English acquires a typographic identity with the rise of printing. Many attempts to 'standardise and fix' the language with dictionaries and grammars. Union of England and Scotland, 1707.

6 Modern English (*c.*1750 – 1950)

Britain experiences Industrial Revolution and consolidates imperial power, introducing English medium education in many parts of the world. English becomes the international language of advertising and consumerism.

7 Late Modern English (*c.*1950 –)

Britain retreats from empire. New standardised varieties of English emerge in newly independent countries. English becomes the international language of communications technology.

Activity 2.1

Allow about 15 minutes

Before going on to explore the history of English, it is worth thinking about the evidence on which this history is based, as the availability and use of different sources will shape the story told. What different kinds of evidence do you think language historians can use?

Comment

Today, we have many sources of evidence for the ways in which English is spoken and written for different purposes, by different types of people and in different places, but the further back in time we go, the sparser the evidence is. In this chapter, I use two main types.

- **Internal evidence** is linguistic evidence that comes from examples of language use, such as texts written in the language; it can also be described as **direct evidence**.

- **External** or **indirect evidence** comes from sources such as commentaries on the language, or archaeological finds.

So, when discussing Middle English dialects, we can use the direct evidence of words, spellings and grammatical structures found in texts from different parts of the country and the indirect evidence of writers who comment on what they see going on around them. One important early source is Bede's account of the Anglo-Saxon invasions of Britain in the 400s (*Historia Ecclesiastica Gentis Anglorum* or *Ecclesiastical History of the English People*), although this was a historical text written 300 years after the events Bede describes (around 730). It is important when evaluating such commentaries to bear in mind the position of the writer: Bede, who lived in the land settled by the Anglo-Saxons, would not necessarily share the viewpoint of Celtic-speaking Britons displaced by the invasion.

Another problem for historians of English is that for earlier periods, direct evidence is particularly sparse and patchy. We have no written records of English before the conversion of the Anglo-Saxons to Christianity in the seventh century (when ecclesiastical texts began to be produced by the Church). Even after the conversion, surviving manuscripts are scarce and do not reflect the whole spectrum of usage because they were written by clerics. As we get nearer to the present day, more texts are available, but they still reflect only the usage of the literate. Direct evidence of spoken usage is not available until the invention of sound recording in the late nineteenth century, so we have to piece together our knowledge of pronunciation from clues in spelling, rhymes and commentaries on usage.

2.2   The beginnings of English

England before English

The Pre-English and Early Old English periods

What was the linguistic situation in Britain before English, and how did it shape what was to become English? One enduring puzzle is why Old English (or Anglo-Saxon) was not more heavily influenced by the languages spoken in Britain before the Anglo-Saxon invaders arrived in the fifth century. The Britons living in England at the time spoke Celtic languages similar to present-day Welsh, Cornish and Breton. Because these latter day Celtic languages are now spoken in the west of Britain (Wales and Cornwall), it had previously been thought that the Anglo-Saxons drove the Britons away from the more fertile lands in the East, but archaeological and genetic evidence has since suggested that many Britons may have lived alongside Anglo-Saxons, albeit as a subject people. This is reinforced by the fact that the word 'Welsh' comes from the Old English *wealh* meaning 'foreigner' or, in some contexts, 'servant' or 'slave'. If the Anglo-Saxons viewed the Britons as alien and inferior, they would be unlikely to learn their language.

Such evidence as we have of the Celtic language at that time comes largely from names: *Avon* and *Ouse* come from Celtic words for 'water' or 'stream', and the county name *Cumbria* comes from the same Celtic root as the Welsh *Cymru* (meaning 'Wales'). Other words borrowed from the Celtic-speaking Britons by the Anglo-Saxons are few, but include *broc* ('badger') and *dunn* ('dun' as in 'dun cow'). The full extent of Celtic influence on Old English is a matter of dispute, but the general consensus is that the vast majority of the vocabulary of Old English for which we have written records is of Germanic origin. Latin would also have been spoken in Britain at least until the Roman withdrawal in 410 (although little archaeological or textual evidence of it remains), not only by the occupying Roman forces but presumably also by bilingual Celtic-speaking Britons. However, most Latin words now used in English come not from the Roman occupation of Britain which ended before the arrival of the Anglo-Saxons, but were brought over by the Germanic invaders whose languages had acquired them during the Roman occupation of their own lands.

'English' before England

What do we know about the dialects of the Germanic tribes that were to come to Britain, and from which English emerged? Figure 2.1 shows the continental homelands of the Angles, Jutes and Saxons, and their settlements in England and Southern Scotland.

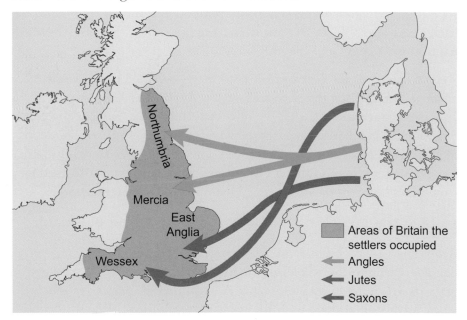

Figure 2.1 Areas of Britain where the Angles, Jutes and Saxons settled

Our knowledge of the Germanic tribes on the continent comes largely from the Roman historian Tacitus, who wrote the *Germani* in AD 98. The Germani, to use Tacitus's term, were not literate, so we have no direct evidence of their languages. By comparing related languages for which there is written evidence, however, historical linguists have reconstructed a Germanic family of languages and its hypothetical ancestor, Proto-Germanic. This family is divided into three groups:

- the West Germanic, including the ancestors of present-day German, Dutch and English
- the North Germanic or 'Norse', including Norwegian, Danish, Swedish and Icelandic
- the East Germanic, of which the only surviving records come from Gothic.

All the languages of the Anglo-Saxon invaders belonged to the West Germanic group, hence the continuing similarities between English, German and Dutch demonstrated in words like English 'foot', modern German *Fuß* and Dutch *voet*. Along with this Germanic word-stock, the Anglo-Saxons brought over words that had been borrowed from Latin, either as a result of trade or of the Roman occupation of Germania. These include *stræt* ('paved road'), *candel* ('candle'), *cypian* ('to buy', from which the modern English word 'cheap' derives), the Anglo-Saxon ancestors of culinary terms including 'butter', 'cheese', 'pepper' and 'wine', and terms of measurement and finance including 'mint' from Latin *moneta* ('coin') and 'pound'.

Tacitus described the Germani as comprising separate tribes, some of which will have been the ancestors of the Anglo-Saxon invaders. The continental ancestors of what we now call 'English' were related – but diverse. The immediate linguistic heritage of the Anglo-Saxon invasions of the fifth century was not therefore a unified language called 'English', but a variety of West Germanic languages or dialects spoken by settlers from across present-day Germany, Denmark and the Netherlands.

English in England

According to the *Oxford English Dictionary* (*OED*), the first instance of a name referring to the whole of the Anglo-Saxon peoples was by Pope Gregory I, writing in 595 and using the Latin word *Anglus*. Although when the historian Bede used the term *gentis Anglorum* ('English people') he was referring to all the Anglo-Saxons, it is often unclear whether other writers used this just with reference to the Angles who, according to Bede, settled in the north and east of the country. Throughout the Old English period, several kingdoms existed; these are usually described as the Heptarchy, consisting of Northumbria, Mercia, East

Anglia, Essex, Kent, Sussex and Wessex (see Figure 2.2). Much of the period was turbulent, and borders shifted as one kingdom conquered another's territory. There was no notion of a politically unified 'England' until the time of King Alfred (849–899), and even he did not rule over all of what we now call England.

Of the seven kingdoms (names in capitals), three dominated the Anglo-Saxon period: Northumbria in the 7th century, Mercia (with its dyke marking the Welsh border) in the 8th century and Wessex from the 9th century.

Figure 2.2 Map of Britain showing the political geography of the Old English period

Even though Alfred was never king of all England, his reign as king of Wessex saw a revival of learning in which texts were composed in West Saxon English (the dialect of Old English used in Wessex) or translated into it from Latin. Although it could be argued that these texts exemplify an evolving and incipient form of standard, written English, West Saxon was never a *national* standard. However, the mistaken impression that it was *the* standard dialect of Old English is conveyed by the predominance of surviving texts in this variety – an illustration of how our access to evidence shapes the story we tell. Records of other dialects are patchy: we have important texts such as the English glosses of the *Lindisfarne Gospels* from Northumbria (as illustrated in Figure 2.3 below), some from Kent and from the Lichfield area of Mercia, but none from East Anglia, which, as we shall see, was to be an influential area in later centuries. Most extant texts from the Old English period were written in and around important ecclesiastical centres: Durham in Northumbria, Lichfield in Mercia, Winchester in Wessex and Canterbury in Kent. This is not surprising, since Christianity brought literacy and the Roman alphabet, and the skill of writing and illustrating manuscripts was largely confined to clerics. As with West Saxon, this focusing of literacy and literary resources led to a certain amount of local standardisation, at least in the texts that survive.

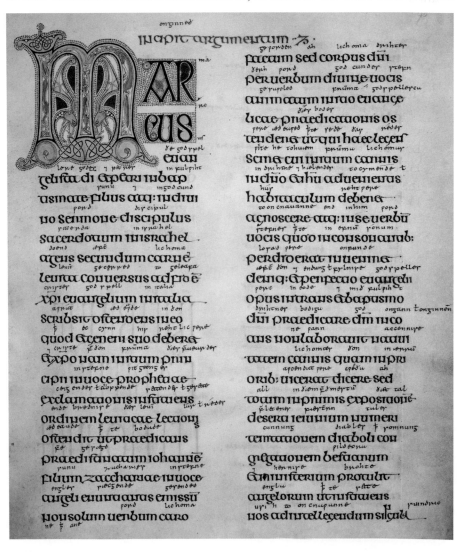

Figure 2.3 The *Lindisfarne Gospels c.*700 (The British Library)

Activity 2.2

**Allow about
20 minutes**

To illustrate differences between these Old English dialects, we can examine two versions of the same text. The text is *Caedmon's Hymn*; Caedmon is often described as the first English poet and Bede tells the story of how, as an illiterate peasant, Caedmon was divinely inspired to compose this poem. The first version was written in Northumbrian in 737, and the second at a later date in West Saxon. The two Old English versions are followed by a translation into Modern English.

Compare the two versions and make a note of any differences. Can you identify any regularities? What do you think the significance of these might be?

1 Northumbrian version

Nu scylun hergan hefaenricaes uard
metudæs maecti end his modgidanc
uerc uuldurfadur sue he uundra gihuaes
eci dryctin or astelidæ
he aerist scop aelda barnum
heben til hrofe haleg scepen.
tha middungeard moncynnæs uard
eci dryctin æfter tiadæ
firum foldu frea allmectig

2 West Saxon version

Nu sculon herigean heofonrices weard,
meotodes meahte and his modgeþanc,
weorc wuldorfæder, swa he wundra gehwæs,
ece drihten, or onstealde.
He ærest sceop eorðan bearnum
heofon to hrofe, halig scyppend;
þa middangeard moncynnes weard,
ece drihten, æfter teode
firum foldan, frea ælmihtig.

3 Modern English version

> Now let me praise the keeper of Heaven's kingdom,
> the might of the Creator, and his thought,
> the work of the Father of glory, how each of wonders
> the Eternal Lord established in the beginning.
> He first created for the sons of men
> Heaven as a roof, the holy Creator,
> then Middle-earth the keeper of mankind,
> the Eternal Lord, afterwards made,
> the earth for men, the Almighty Lord.

Comment

We can see certain consistent differences between the two Old English texts; you may have found others as well as the ones I detail here. Where the West Saxon text has <ea> in *herigean*, *bearnum* and *weard*, the Northumbrian version has <a> in *hergan*, *barnum* and *uard* meaning 'praise', 'children' and 'guardian' respectively. Although we can never be sure of the exact relationship between spelling and pronunciation in this period, we might infer that in West Saxon the vowel had the gliding sound heard in present day 'pier' (a diphthong); while Northumbrian had a shorter vowel sound, perhaps like that in 'pan' (a monophthong). Another difference can be seen in certain vowels on the ends of words. The Northumbrian text has a variety of spellings: <æ> in *astelidæ*, *tiadæ*, <i> in *mæcti*, and <e> in *hrofe*, where the West Saxon text has only <e>. One suggestion is that these were unstressed vowels which in West Saxon were pronounced like many unstressed vowels in English today as /ə/ (such as at the end of 'teacher'). You may be able to speculate about other possible connections between spellings in the above texts and the pronunciations they suggest. Although these two texts are separated by time as well as place, they provide a glimpse of the dialectal diversity of Old English, both spoken and written.

As we have seen, a kind of standardisation occurred in major religious centres, and the dominance of Wessex towards the end of the period of Old English could have resulted in West Saxon being selected as the standard language of England. However, this process was interrupted by the Norman conquest of 1066, after which English would not fulfil the functions of a standard language for several centuries. Even in the Old

English period, English was not the only language spoken and written in what is now England: Latin was the language of the Church, Cornish survived in the South-West, and, as we shall see below, the North Germanic (or Norse) languages of the Vikings were to have a major influence on the North and East.

2.3   Foreign influence

Danes and the Danelaw

According to the *Anglo-Saxon Chronicle*, the Vikings first came to England from Scandinavia in 783, although the date most often cited as that of the first Viking raid is 793, when a group landed on Lindisfarne off the coast of Northumbria. They stayed only long enough to slaughter the monks and steal the monastery's treasure, but many other raids followed and by the middle of the ninth century groups of Scandinavians were beginning to winter in England. In the second half of the century, Danish invaders brought armies over with a view to conquest and permanent settlement. Northumbria, Mercia and East Anglia were conquered, with only Alfred in Wessex holding out. In 878, a treaty was signed acknowledging the rule of the Danish king Guthrum in an area north and east of a line drawn from London to Chester. This area, shown on the map in Figure 2.4, was known as the Danelaw.

The Later Old English period

Within this area, we find place names with Norse elements such as:

- *-by* meaning 'village' as in Grimsby and Whitby
- *-thorpe*, meaning 'farmstead' as in Grimethorpe and Scunthorpe
- *-toft* meaning 'plot of land' as in Lowestoft.

Place names provide a great deal of evidence for the kinds of settlement that developed in these periods, as well as clues about the nature of interaction between people speaking different languages.

Within the Danelaw, it appears that Danes and Angles lived together and intermarried. They probably understood each other's languages to a certain extent, and the English that developed in this area was strongly influenced by the Norse language, perhaps to the extent that a hybrid variety developed. We do not have written records of this Anglo-Norse variety but, when written records from this area emerge in the Middle English period, the density of Norse loanwords is striking. Many of these words were to find their way into standard English where they remain widely used: 'egg', 'husband', 'skin', 'sky'. They are mostly words relating to everyday life, bearing witness to the intimate relationship between those of Danish and Anglian descent in the Danelaw. Other words of Norse origin survive in the present-day dialects of regions once within the Danelaw. Orton and Wright (1974, p. 17) state that 'several thousands of Scandinavian loans are found in the present-day dialects of the North and East Midlands'. These include words such as *gimmer* ('ewe lamb'), *lake* ('to play'), *lop* ('flea') and *slape* ('slippery').

The southern limit of the Danelaw (shown with the line) coincided in part with the route of the Roman road known as Watling Street, running from London to Wroxeter in Shropshire. North of that line the Danes ruled until the West Saxon kings reconquered the Danelaw in the 10th century. The purple portion represents the area where place names derive from the languages spoken by the Vikings – Danes in the East, Norwegians in the West. Vikings from Norway also settled in Ireland, the north-east and west of Scotland and along the coast of Wales.

Figure 2.4 Map showing the extent of the Danelaw (adapted from Barber et al., 2009, p. 139)

Between 1950 and 1961, the Survey of English Dialects (SED) collected examples of British dialects before, as the researchers believed, these died out through increased social mobility and media influence (in fact, as we shall see in Chapters 5 and 7, the effect of these changes was more complex). These researchers devised a questionnaire to elicit dialect vocabulary items from rural dialect speakers where contact with other dialects was felt to be minimal. Figure 2.5 shows the results from the item in the SED questionnaire which asked people to name the word they used for 'any stretch of running water smaller than a river'.

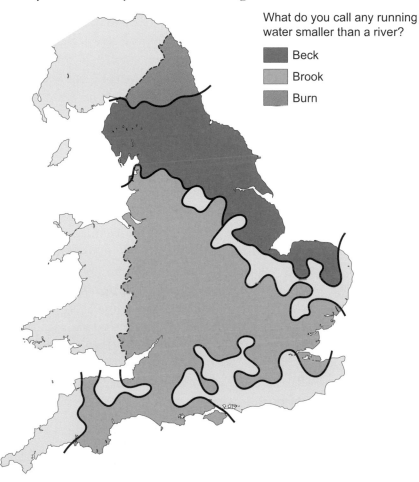

Figure 2.5 Words for 'rivulet' (adapted from Survey of English Dialects)

Apart from the standard English word 'stream', three main responses were elicited: 'burn' in the far North-East, 'brook' in the West and much of the South and, in an area roughly corresponding with the Danelaw, 'beck'. Only 'beck' has a Norse etymology: 'burn' and 'brook' are derived from Old English.

We can still see the influence of Viking settlers in street names. York at the heart of the Danelaw and Chesterfield on its border both have a number of 'gate' streets where the Norse word *gata* is used instead of the Old English *stræt*: *Coppergate* and *Micklegate* in York, for example, and *Glumangate* and *Knifesmithgate* in Chesterfield. Figure 2.6 shows the signage for the shopping centre at Coppergate in York, the barrel revealing that 'copper' comes not from the metal but from *cooper*, 'barrel-maker'.

Figure 2.6
Sign for
Coppergate,
York

The influence of Norse in the Danelaw affected grammar as well as vocabulary. For example, the northern dialects of Middle English adopted the Scandinavian pronouns *they*, *them* and *their* for third person plural pronouns. These were much more functional than the Old English forms *hī*, *hira* and *him*, which were likely to be confused with the singular forms corresponding to modern English *he*, *her* and *him*. These 'th-' forms would find their way into standard English in the fifteenth century. The legacy of the Scandinavian settlers in England can thus be found today both in the regional dialects of the area and in the standard language.

The Middle English
period

The Norman Conquest and French in England

We have seen that, by the middle of the eleventh century, the written English of Wessex (West Saxon) was beginning to be used as a literary language, but Latin was still used in the Church and an Anglo-Norse dialect was used in the Danelaw. These were accompanied by a myriad of other dialects across the country, which I will discuss in the next section. The Norman Conquest of 1066 was to introduce another elite language which would take over from English in higher-status functions: Norman French. The Norman French of the conquerors and the more prestigious Central (Parisian) French of their descendants were to have a deep and lasting effect on English.

There is a plaque in Durham cathedral, showing the names of bishops from the tenth century onwards. It is noticeable that all the bishops from Aldhun (995–1018) to Aethelwine (1056–1071) have Anglo-Saxon names but, just five years after the conquest, a bishop with the typically Norman name William Walcher is installed, and throughout the rest of the eleventh and twelfth centuries, all the bishops likewise have French names. This is a striking example of how William of Normandy gave the important posts of Church and state to his followers; at a stroke, the English governing classes were deposed. From this time until the thirteenth century, the ruling and governing classes of England would have French (or Anglo-Norman, the variety of French which developed in England) as their first language. The nobility retained lands in Normandy, so England was a colony rather than their homeland. Although there must have been a certain amount of French-English bilingualism for the sake of communication, English in this period was a vernacular rather than a language of status. The language of the Church, and of learning, was Latin and courtly literature was composed in French, because this was the preferred language of the kings of England. Other languages were spoken in specific parts of England during this period: immigrants from the Low Countries (present-day Belgium and the Netherlands) brought Low German to East Anglia, and Cornish was still spoken in Cornwall. Without even taking into consideration the dialectal diversity of English, it is evident that England at this time was a multilingual nation.

The difference in status between French and English was commented on by Robert of Gloucester, who wrote a *Chronicle of English History* in the late thirteenth century:

> þus com, lo, Engelond in-to Normandies hond:
> And þe Normans ne couþe speke þo bote hor owe speche,
> And speke French as hii dude atom, and hor children dude also teche,
> So þat heiemen of þis lond, þat of hor blod come,
> Holdeþ alle þulke speche þat hii of hom nom;
> Vor bote a man conne Frenss me telþ of him lute.
> Ac lowe men holdeþ to Engliss ...

(cited in Barber et al., 2009, pp. 145–6)

This can be translated into modern-day English as follows:

> Thus England came into Normandy's hands and the Normans could only speak their own language and spoke French as they did at home and also taught their children [French]. So that noblemen of this country, of their blood, keep to the language they received from them: for unless a man knows French, people don't think much of him. But men of low status stick to English.

The words borrowed from French into English at this time bear witness to this difference in status. Although Old English 'earl', 'king' and 'queen' were retained, words for other ranks of nobility came from French: 'baron', 'count', 'duke', 'duchess', 'prince'. Words relating to government, such as 'chancellor', 'council', 'government' itself, 'nation' and 'parliament', and legal terms such as 'accuse', 'court', 'crime', 'judge', 'justice', 'prison' and 'sentence', were all borrowed from French (although 'law' itself had been taken from Norse). Words describing refinements of cuisine and fashion were also taken from French, suggesting that it was the French-speaking elite who ate well and set the fashions. Anglo-Saxon 'shirt' or the related Norse 'skirt' were retained as words for the simple tunics of the lower classes, but the more refined clothing of the nobility was referred to with French words such as 'apparel', 'costume', 'dress', 'fashion' and 'robe'. When animals were in the fields, they retained their English names 'calf', 'ox', 'sheep', 'swine', but when served up at table they were given the French names 'veal', 'beef', 'mutton', 'pork'. The Normans were dominant in warfare and castle building; the words 'war' and 'castle' come from the Norman dialect of French, which had <w> where modern French has <gu> (hence the Conqueror's name was William, not Guillaume) and <c> where modern French has <ch>, hence England has 'castles' while France has *châteaux*. The word 'war' was first recorded in the *Anglo-Saxon Chronicle* of 1154, and 'castle' as early as 1075, but the majority of French loans into English are first cited in the *OED* in the thirteenth century. This does not mean that they were first used then, but they are not recorded in extant texts in English before that time because, as we have seen, writing was mainly in French or Latin in the intervening period. It was not until 1204, when King John lost his lands in Normandy and the nobility consequently had to decide whether to keep their lands in England or France, that there was any real incentive for the ruling classes to learn English.

English and ideas about diversity in the fourteenth century

The beginnings of the Early Modern period

During the fourteenth century, the use of French in England began to decline, although it was not until Henry IV came to the throne in 1399 that England had its first king since the conquest who spoke English as his first language. The gradual shift in balance between the two languages is illustrated in the following passage written by John of Trevisa in 1385. Trevisa was translating an earlier text by Ranulf Higden, in which Higden complains that children are forced to learn

French in grammar schools, to the detriment of their own language. Trevisa added the following:

> þys manere was moche y-used tofore þe furste moreyn, and ys seþthe somdel ychaunged. For Iohan Cornwal, a mayster of gramere, chayngede þe lore in gramerscole and construction of Freynsh into Englysch; and Richard Pencrych lurnede þat manere techyng of hym, and oþer men of Pencrych, so þat now, þe 3er of oure Lord a þousond þre hondred foure score and fyue, of the secunde kyng Richard after þe Conquest nyne, in al þe gramerscoles of Engelond childern leueþ Frensch, and construeþ and lurneþ an Englysch.
>
> (cited in Barber et al., 2009, p. 153)

This can be translated into modern-day English as follows:

> This custom was much in use before the first plague, and since then has changed somewhat. For John Cornwall, a grammar teacher, changed the teaching in grammar schools and construing from French to English and Richard Pencrich learned this method of teaching from him, and others from Pencrich, so that now, in 1385, in the ninth year of the reign of King Richard II, in all grammar schools in England, children are abandoning French and construing and learning in English.

Trevisa bears witness here to an important turning point in the history of the standardisation of English: although the grammar school curriculum was to be dominated by Latin for several centuries after this, once English became a medium of education there was a need for some kind of standard for instruction.

At this time (the fourteenth century), however, there was little concept of a standard version of English (i.e. a prestige form of English recognised across England as standard), and diversity was the norm.

Dialects of Middle English can be divided into five main groups, with much variation within each group (Crystal, 2003, p. 50):

- Southern, a continuation of Old English West Saxon
- Kentish (or South-Eastern), a continuation of Old English Kentish
- East Midland, the east part of the Old English Mercian area
- West Midland, the west part of the Old English Mercian area
- Northern, north of the Humber, a continuation of Old English Northumbrian.

See Appendix 2 for the conventions used to describe phonological features.

With respect to the dialects of Middle English, it is worth making three observations. First, some of the distinctive features of Middle English dialects have left traces in the corresponding regional varieties today. The West Midland dialect used for the poem *Sir Gawain and the Green Knight* had a rounded vowel /ɒ/ where other dialects had /a/ before /n/ and the traditional dialects of this region (e.g. Cheshire) still have pronunciations like /mɒn/ for 'man'. Northern dialects did not participate in a sound change whereby Old English /a:/ was rounded to /ɔ:/ in words like *bān* corresponding to present-day English 'bone'. We can still see this in the distinction between Scots *hame* and English 'home' and in northern place-names such as Stanley ('stone meadow') in County Durham. Southern dialects of Middle English had voicing of the fricatives /f/ and /s/ so that they were pronounced like present-day /v/ and /z/ at the beginnings of words, so that 'cider', for example, would be pronounced 'zyder' in the county of Somerset (or 'Zumerzet') where it is produced. These traces testify to the longevity of what are now considered to be 'non-standard' dialects which diverge from the 'norm'. Although often evaluated negatively in comparison with standard English in Britain today, regional dialects can be traced back to a time when dialect diversity itself was the norm, and no one variety had yet been raised above the others as a 'standard'.

This leads us to the second point which is that dialectal diversity was still the norm in the 1300s even in written or formal domains (such as literature or official documents) where today we would expect adherence to a **national standard**. Chaucer, for example, who had great prestige as Richard II's (1367–1400) court poet, wrote in his native London dialect while poets from other parts of the country used their own dialects. The author of *Sir Gawain and the Green Knight* used a

North-West Midland variety and *Piers Plowman* was written in a South-West Midland variety. There was no sense that these poets were deviating from a literary norm in writing in their own regional varieties. However, and this is the third point, there are hints in fourteenth-century literature that the dialect of London and the South was gaining prestige, no doubt because of its association with the capital and the Court. Accompanying the prestige awarded to the London dialect was a derogatory attitude towards other varieties.

Activity 2.3

Allow about
15 minutes

Trevisa's 1385 translation of Higden, which I have already cited as evidence for the decline of French, also embellishes the original author's remarks about northern dialects of English, as evident in this extract from the modernised version of his translation. Can you identify the different criteria that he uses in evaluating 'the language of the Northumbrians' here?

> All the language of the Northumbrians, and especially at York, is so sharp, slitting and frotting and unshaped, that we southern men can barely understand that language. I believe that is because they are near to strange men and aliens … that speak strangely.

(By 'aliens', Trevisa presumably means Scots: Scotland at that time was a separate nation with its own monarchy, government and language.)

Comment

It is interesting that Trevisa's observations are statements not only about *language*, but also about the *social* and *political* status of Northumbrians. The linguistic criterion relates to the sound of the dialect and the basis seems to be aesthetic. Trevisa employed descriptive, sound-symbolic terms which represent what he perceived as the harshness of the northern dialect. The social and political criteria relate to the wider relations between 'we southern men' and the Northumbrians: not only are the two communities so distant that they can barely be understood (presumably the Northumbrians also had problems understanding the southerners), but the Northumbrians also inhabited that dangerous area close to the 'aliens', the Scots. As we shall see in the next section, the proximity of the far north of England to the Scottish border was for some time after this cited as a reason for the outlandishness of its dialect. As Katie Wales (2006, pp. 61–2) points out, the mention of York could well be evocative of that city's history as one of the most important centres in the Danelaw. So, Trevisa's remarks suggest, not only were fourteenth-century authors beginning to notice differences between dialects of English, but they were starting to evaluate some negatively in favour of others. In doing so, they were linking linguistic features with particular social characteristics – Chaucer even has the first comic northerners in his *Reeve's Tale*. We have already seen that at one time all dialects were considered equal, and any one could have emerged as a standard; indeed, we saw earlier that West Saxon may have taken on the attributes of a standard, due to its political dominance from the 800s, if not for the Norman Conquest. It is worth bearing in mind that, as dialectal diversity became a matter of concern and the need for a standard variety arose, decisions were often based on social and political, rather than linguistic, grounds.

Chapter 8 of the third book in this series – Hewings and Tagg (eds) (2012) – discusses how people make judgements about others based on their dialect.

2.4 Standardisation

The Early Modern period and beyond

The beginnings of standardisation: selecting a standard variety

In discussing the development of standard English, I use a model of standardisation first proposed by Einar Haugen (1966) and later modified by James and Lesley Milroy (1985). The stages of standardisation as outlined by Haugen are:

- **selection** of a variety to be the standard
- **codification**, by which norms are elucidated and captured in dictionaries or grammars
- **elaboration**, which involves the extension of the standard to a wider variety of functions
- **implementation**, whereby norms are imposed and variability suppressed.

Milroy and Milroy expand the model to include **prescriptivism**, by which judgements about the correctness and desirability of certain linguistic features serve to maintain the standard. They also stress that the stages of standardisation need not be successive and may overlap, and that the processes involved in the implementation of a standard are ongoing, as successive generations attempt to suppress the variability which is the inevitable result of linguistic change. For example, we have seen that the first stage of selection comes very late in the history of English (the initial emergence of West Saxon as a candidate was halted by the Norman Conquest, and a London-based variety only began to take on prestige after the decline of French in England). It will also become evident that, in the case of English, elaboration precedes, or at least overlaps with, codification; and, although prescriptivism intensifies after the codification of standard English norms in the eighteenth century (it is easier to prescribe norms if you have access to authoritative written sources), it is still with us in the twenty-first.

In 1490, William Caxton produced an English translation of Virgil's *Aeneid*, titled *Eneydos*. Caxton had introduced the new technology of printing into England about fourteen years earlier, and, as a businessman, wanted to ensure that his books had as wide a market as possible. Dialectal diversity was problematic for him, as he needed his texts to be read and understood throughout the country. He complains about this in the preface to his *Eneydos*, with the example of a misunderstanding over a request for eggs:

> [T]hat comyn englysshe that is spoken in one shyre varyeth from a nother. In so moche that in my dayes happened that certayn marchauntes were in a ship in tamyse for to haue sayled ouer the see into zelande and for lacke of wynde thei taryed atte forlond. and wente to lande for to refreshe them And one of theym named sheffelde a mercer cam in to an hows and axed for mete. and specyally he axyd after eggys And the goode wyf answerde. that she coude speke no frenshe. And the marchaunt was angry. for he also coude speke no frenshe. but wolde haue hadde egges and she vnderstode hym not. And thenne at laste a nother sayd that he wolde haue eyren. then the good wyf sayd that she vnderstod hym wel. Loo what sholde a man in thyse dayes now wryte. egges or eyren. certaynly it is harde to playse euery man bycause of dyuersite & chaunge of langage.

Although Caxton here portrays himself as caught in a dilemma about which dialect to use in order to 'please every man', he was in fact writing this in a variety that was already taking on the functions of a standard. His use of this in printing played a part in its dissemination. As we saw in the previous section, the close of the fourteenth century brought the first post-conquest king of England whose first language was English. This meant that English would now be the language of government. From about 1430, government documents began to be written in English and, since it was considered vital that these be understood throughout the country, it was felt that the language used in these documents needed to be consistent and uniform. Since government documents were produced by clerks in the Chancery in Westminster, it was these bureaucrats who decided which variants were chosen. These clerks came from various parts of the country, but were all resident in London. The variety of English used in their documents appears to have been based on London English, with some features originating further north, probably from the East or Central Midlands. We know from population records that prosperous immigrants came from these areas to London at this time, and East Anglia in particular was a very wealthy area due to the wool trade. Some of the more northerly features in what has become known as Chancery Standard English could also have been a matter of pragmatic choice: the 'northern' form *they*, for instance, was a more distinctive marker of the third-person plural subject form than the contemporary southern form *he*. Although some variability is still evident in Chancery documents (both *hem* and *them* are used for third-person plural object, for instance), in most respects spellings in these documents are much more consistent than those of other documents. For instance, Chancery documents have *such* or *suche*, where others have *sich*, *sych*, *seche*, *swich* or *sweche* for present-day English 'such'. As in many cases, the Chancery variant is most similar to that used in present-day standard English. Since the process of standardisation involves the reduction of variants, it is evident that the Chancery documents mark the first stage in the process of standardisation: the selection of a variety.

Allow about 15 minutes

Activity 2.4

On what basis was the London variety (with some northern features) selected as the Chancery Standard? What sort of problem do you foresee in assuming that the adoption of this as the standard would provide an English that would 'be understood throughout the country'?

Comment

As with Trevisa's judgements above, decisions made by the Chancery in fifteenth-century London were not solely linguistic or pragmatic ones. The variety was selected not only because it was familiar to the bureaucrats involved, but because it was spoken by elite individuals (hence the adoption of East Anglian terms). This variety was not inherently (or linguistically) superior to any of the others still being used by writers across the country. However, the fact that it was used by the government bureaucracy and that people therefore encountered it in official documents meant that it was endowed with prestige, which paved the way for its acceptance. Although a standard was seen as a necessary step in the effective governance and union of the country, it should be borne in mind that that it was a written standard only and dialects continued to be used in speech and informal writing. The prestige given to this one regional variety would give those who used it within their home communities (who were often among the elite) greater access to public documents and presumably to participation in public life, but could exclude those who came from other regions and spoke different dialects. At this time, of course, the effect of the selection of this variety of English may have been minimal; Latin, for example, was still the language of religion and scholarship, although Caxton's translations were beginning to make classical texts available in English for the unlatined literate.

Elaboration of function

By the sixteenth century, there is evidence of a consensus of opinion as to what constituted the 'best' English, at least for writing. The most frequently quoted text from this period is an extract from George Puttenham's *Arte of English Poesie* (1589):

> This part in our maker or Poet must be heedyly looked unto, that it be naturall, pure, and the most usuall of all his countrey: and for the same purpose rather that which is spoken in the kings Court, or in the good townes and Cities within the land, then in the marches and frontiers, or in port townes, where straungers haunt for traffike sake ... But he shall follow generally the better brought up sort ... men civill and graciously behavoured and bred ... neither shall he take the termes of Northern-men, such as they use in dayly talke, whether they be noble men or gentlemen, or of their best clarkes all is a matter: nor in effect any speach used beyond the river of Trent, though no man can deny but that theirs is the purer English Saxon at this day, yet it is not so Courtly nor so currant as our Southerne English is, no more is the far Westerne mans speach: ye shall therefore take the usuall speach of the Court, and that of London and the shires lying about London within lx myles, and not much above.

Puttenham is very specific here about the geographical boundaries of the variety he recommends: within a sixty mile radius of London; but he also makes statements about social class: 'the better brought up sort'. The further from London, the more outlandish the dialect: like Trevisa in 1385, he warns against using northern dialects, but also mentions the far West, as well as border areas and ports, where English speakers came into contact with other languages. (Scots is now often described as a dialect of English, but would have been considered a separate language in the 1500s.) This text tells us that a London-based standard had been selected and accepted by influential people, though not yet diffused throughout the country, since, in the North, not even 'noble men or gentlemen' used it. These distant varieties, however, along with Scots and the English spoken in Wales and Ireland, were treated as 'other' in texts of this period. The 'four nations' scene in Shakespeare's *Henry V* has an English character, Gower, whose speech is represented as standard English, while his interlocutors Fluellen, Macmorris and Jamie are represented as using stereotypical features of Welsh English, Irish English and Scots respectively. Other sixteenth-century texts represent the North and the South-West as 'other': we have already seen how Puttenham singles out these areas for comment, and a Northumbrian character in William Bullein's *Dialogue against the Fever Pestilence* (1564) is represented as the 'barbarian at the gates'. Even if standard English was not yet used in these areas, an emerging belief in the need for, and the superiority of, a standard variety led to it being treated as the norm, at least for writing.

Puttenham's text was one of several guides for aspiring writers produced at this time, which testify to the beginnings of elaboration of function as the standard variety begins to take over functions previously carried out in Latin. Until this time, ideas of good style in writing were based on classical rhetoric, which was taught in grammar schools through the medium of Latin. At the beginning of the sixteenth century, there was a feeling that English was not a suitable medium for serious writing, because it lacked 'eloquence'. The publication of style guides such as Puttenham's *Arte of English Poesie* (1589) and Thomas Wilson's *Arte of Rhetorique* (1560) provided examples in English of the figures of rhetoric that had previously been learnt in Latin, and so enabled writers to gain confidence in English as a literary medium. The earlier part of the sixteenth century is marked by a proliferation of complaints and apologies, all of which tell the same story: the author is ashamed of writing in such a crude medium, but feels obliged in order to reach readers who don't know Latin. For example, in 1545 Ascham writes:

> And as for ye Latin or greke tonge, every thyng is so excellently done in them, that none can do better: In the Englysh tonge contrary, every thinge in a maner so meanly, bothe for the matter and handelynge that no man can do worse.

The unfavourable comparison with Latin and Greek is understandable, given that these were still the languages of learning, but English was also described as failing to measure up to the Romance vernaculars, because the Renaissance had reached these countries earlier and their languages were further ahead in the process of standardisation. Thus, Andrew Borde wrote in 1548 that 'the speche of Englande is a base speche to other noble speches, as Italion, Castylion [i.e. Spanish], and Frenche.' The key words here are 'base' and 'mean', but other authors complain that English is 'barren' and 'barbarous'. These terms signify that English was perceived as wanting, which may be a precursor to the process of elaboration of function: it was considered 'barbarous', 'base' and 'mean' because it lacked the eloquence of these other languages and 'barren' because it lacked the vocabulary. The problem of eloquence was overcome by a combination of the provision of rhetoric manuals with examples in English and the work of literary figures who, even in their lifetimes, were celebrated as models of good style. Among these, Shakespeare was just one among many and the poet viewed as the flower of the age was Sir Philip Sidney.

Activity 2.5

Now turn to Reading A: *Shakespeare and the English language* by Jonathan Hope. In the reading, Hope challenges the common portrayal of Shakespeare as a timeless and outstanding master of words, and instead describes the playwright and his language use as firmly embedded in, and to an extent typical of, his times. As you read, take notes on the evidence and arguments that Hope presents in relation to word coinages allegedly found in Shakespeare's work, the size of his vocabulary, the way in which his puns would have been received, and his unusual syntax. What are the implications of Hope's discussion for understanding language use at the time of the Renaissance (i.e. around the sixteenth and early seventeenth centuries)?

Comment

Hope's reading makes it clear that our present-day understanding of Shakespeare as a lone and highly innovative genius stems from Romanticism (a cultural movement of the late 1700s which emphasised aesthetic and emotional values) and distorts the wider picture of what was actually going on in the sixteenth and seventeenth centuries. We can see this in the way that puns were interpreted, as well as Shakespeare's role in the development of English vocabulary. In comparison with contemporaries such as Ben Jonson or Sir Philip Sidney, Shakespeare was not exceptional but one of many writers who made a contribution at a time when English vocabulary was greatly expanding. The onus on 'newness' is also of our making: at the time Shakespeare was writing, authority rather than originality was valued. It must therefore be borne in mind that Renaissance writers were also borrowing from other, earlier works, from each other and from the local speech they heard around them, often in the process using pre-existing words in new ways and in unexpected syntactic constructions.

As Reading A suggests, literary figures were instrumental in overcoming the problem of barrenness: the sixteenth century, and especially the last decade, saw a huge influx of new words into English, most of which were adapted from Latin. This filled a gap in the language left by centuries in which only Latin had been used for learned writing, meaning that English simply did not have a vocabulary for registers used in domains such as philosophy, science and religion. In the course of the sixteenth century, the Renaissance and the Reformation gave impetus to translating classical texts and writing learned and religious works in English, in order to make learning available to a wider spectrum of society. As the authors producing these works would have had a classical education, it would be easy for them to adapt words from Latin and, to a lesser extent, Greek into English. The efforts of these authors certainly bore fruit, for, by the end of the 1500s, the prevailing view had changed from English being a cause for apology, to being a source of national pride. Richard Carew, writing in 1602, boasts of the superiority of English to other European vernaculars, drawing on national stereotypes to personify the languages:

> I come now to the last and sweetest point of the sweetness of our tongue, which shall appear the more plainly, if ... we match it with our neighbours. The Italian is pleasant, but without sinews, as a

still fleeting water. The French, delicate, but even nice as a woman, scarce daring to open her lips for fear of marring her countenance. The Spanish, majestical, but fulsome, running too much on the O, and terrible like the devil in a play. The Dutch, manlike, but withal very harsh, as one ready at every word to pick a quarrel. Now we, in borrowing from them, give the strength of consonants to the Italian, the full sound of words to the French, the variety of terminations to the Spanish, and the mollifying of more vowels to the Dutch, and so (like Bees) gather the honey of their good properties and leave the dregs to themselves.

(Carew, in Camden, *Remains concerning Britain*, 1674, p. 50)

Of course, there was also a political dimension to this upsurge of pride: we need to view Carew's jingoistic remarks in the context of the Tudor dynasty's foreign policy and the growth of nationalism and imperial expansion. The Reformation, when the newly established Protestantism broke with the Catholic Church in the early fifteenth century, also provided a political and religious impetus to favouring English over the language of the Roman church: some texts praise the 'plainness' and 'honesty' of English compared to the obfuscation of Latin. The publication of the King James Bible in 1611 was an important milestone in elaboration of function, providing as it did a sacred text in the vernacular standard. By the beginning of the seventeenth century, then, standard English had gone a long way down the path of elaboration of function, but this process was to continue for some time: Latin was still to a large extent the language of science and higher scholarship. Right to the end of the seventeenth century, major scientific texts were being written in Latin: Isaac Newton's *Philosophiæ Naturalis Principia Mathematica* (1687) was, as the title indicates, written in Latin. However, his later work *Opticks* (1704) was written in English, which demonstrates that, by the eighteenth century, elaboration of function was almost complete.

Activity 2.6

The influx into English of Latin (and, to a lesser extent, Greek) words was to have a lasting effect on the English lexicon. We now have a 'two-tier' vocabulary in which more common, everyday words from Old English or Norse often have more 'intellectual' synonyms with Latin or Greek origins. This is especially noticeable in fields such as science, but can also be seen in less specialised genres. The text below is taken from a report in the British newspaper *The Guardian* on 1 September 2010, in

**Allow about
30 minutes**

which the introduction of a smoking ban in public places in Greece is discussed.

Using a dictionary which provides etymologies, find five words which have Latin or Greek etymologies. What do you notice about these words?

> A ban on lighting up in enclosed public areas comes into force in Greece today as part of an effort to curb the country's high smoking rates.
>
> Offenders will be fined up to €10,000 (£8,260), and tobacco advertising will also be prohibited under the measures.
>
> Some 42% of Greeks over the age of 15 smoke, well above the European average of 29%. The campaign will include an advertising blitz and the distribution of anti-smoking board games to children.
>
> The prime minister, George Papandreou, said: 'It will contribute to the work we're doing today that's aimed at changing attitudes, norms and behaviour to improve our quality of life and to make our country viable – not just its economy but in everyday life.'
>
> ('Greece bans smoking in enclosed public spaces', guardian.co.uk, 1 September 2010)

Comment

This passage contains words with Old English, French, Latin and Greek etymologies, as well as a few from other modern languages, such as *blitz* from German. Some of the words with Latin origins are not the specialised or technical words we might expect, but have expanded their range of meanings to become everyday words: 'area' comes from the Latin *ārea* meaning a vacant piece of level ground in a town, and 'part' from Latin *part-*, *pars*.

Other words from Latin are more specialised: 'prohibit' comes from Latin *prohibere* (to forbid). 'Forbid' means roughly the same as 'prohibit' but, coming from Old English, it seems less 'official': we are more likely to see 'prohibit' on public notices and it is unlikely that parents would tell children that they were 'prohibited' from doing something.

'Distribute' and 'contribute' both come from Latin verbs, and show how the adoption of Latin words into English follows regular patterns. 'Distribute' is from Latin *distribut-*, the past participle stem of *distribuere*, and 'contribute' from *contribut-*, the past participle stem of *contribuere*. In both cases, the English verb has been taken directly from the Latin past participle, adding an <e> to the end in spelling. 'Norm' is from Latin *norma* and was first introduced into English with the Latin spelling in 1676. The anglicised form we use today was first recorded in 1821.

'European' is derived from *Europe*, which was taken into English from Latin but came to Latin from Greek. The prefix *anti-* comes directly from Greek, but can now be attached to words of any origin to mean 'opposite' or 'against'.

You may have noticed that some of the words you looked up came into English from French rather than Latin. French is a Romance language, and so these words ultimately have Latin roots. Sometimes it is difficult to tell whether a word has come into English from French or Latin, but this exercise shows that both languages have contributed a great deal to present-day English vocabulary.

Codification

Although most sixteenth- and seventeenth-century texts printed in English used the standard variety, this standard incorporated a good deal of variability. As we saw in the reading by Jonathan Hope, with regard to a number of morphological and syntactic features which were changing in this period, authors such as Shakespeare made use of conservative and innovative variants. It is now accepted that this variability was not unstructured or random, but reflected the sociolinguistic structure of the speech community: for example, as we saw earlier, spelling variation could reflect regional differences in pronunciation. The process of standardisation is defined by Einar Haugen (1966, p. 935) as involving both the 'maximal variation of function' (i.e. the range of different purposes the language can be used for), and 'minimal variation in form' brought about by the reduction of variability. The implementation of reduction in variability involves codification, which had barely begun in the early seventeenth century. The first extant monolingual English dictionary, Robert Cawdrey's *A Table Alphabeticall* (1604), was not intended as a guide to correct spelling or appropriate use of vocabulary, but as a guide to the 'hard words' which had been brought in from Latin and other languages in the process of elaboration of function. Likewise, the few grammars of English that appeared at this time, such as Wallis's *Grammatica Linguae Anglicanae* (1653), were intended as pedagogical aids to teaching English rather than prescriptive guides to correct usage. The implementation of the standard, involving the processes of codification and prescriptivism, begins in the eighteenth century.

Activity 2.7

Now turn to Reading B: *Johnson among the Early Modern grammarians* by Linda Mitchell. This shows how linguistic authority was distributed between two emerging groups of language codifiers: grammarians (writers of grammar books) and lexicographers (producers of dictionaries). Pivotal in the development of the dictionary as we know it today is Samuel Johnson's *Dictionary of the English Language*, published in 1755. As you read, think about the following questions:

- What were the differences in the developing roles of grammarians and lexicographers?
- In what ways can Johnson's dictionary be seen as a milestone in the history of the codification of English?
- To what extent do you think dictionaries, then and now, serve to 'stabilise' or to document changes in a language?

Comment

By the late 1700s, the role of grammarians had shrunk: much of the impetus towards grammar writing came from the increasing importance of English in the school curriculum, and most of the authors of these grammars were teachers, perceived as preoccupied by the finer details of English grammar. Lexicographers, meanwhile, began to provide what was seen as a comprehensive, authoritative and accessible inventory of the language. The publication of Johnson's *Dictionary of the English Language* was an important milestone both for lexicography and for standard English. Johnson made choices between variant spellings which, with a few exceptions, are still with us today and his overt proscription of words that he considered 'barbarous' also point to a prescriptive agenda. Johnson's *Dictionary* was certainly received as a codifying text. In his *Lectures on Elocution* (1762), Thomas Sheridan stated that 'if our language should ever be fixed' Johnson 'must be considered by all posterity as the founder, and his dictionary as the cornerstone'. Johnson realised that he could never 'fix' the language, but he saw it as the duty of a lexicographer to at least hold back the tide of linguistic change. The dictionary today remains this curious mixture of description and prescription: it is usually accepted as the ultimate authority, yet at the same time it follows usage, incorporating new words and meanings as they arise.

An area of language that I have so far not discussed with regard to standardisation is pronunciation. Although sixteenth-century authors such as John Hart chose to describe the pronunciation of educated speakers in and around London, their primary objective was spelling reform, and there was at this stage no attempt to impose a standard pronunciation. Some seventeenth-century phoneticians, such as Christopher Cooper (1687), singled out certain pronunciations as 'barbarous', but this was primarily because they deviated from the way they were spelt: Cooper warns that he who 'would write exactly' should avoid pronunciations like *chimbley* and *sarvice*.

The codification of pronunciation began in the late eighteenth century, when elocutionists such as Thomas Sheridan and John Walker produced explicit guides to correct pronunciation in the form of pronouncing dictionaries. Walker especially pulled no punches in pointing out the 'faults' of the Irish, Scots, Welsh and his 'countrymen', the Cockneys. The latter were singled out for condemnation because, living as they did in the capital, they had access to correct speakers and so had no excuse for faults such as 'h'-dropping. Walker was to be highly influential in setting standards for 'correct' pronunciation: his *Critical Pronouncing Dictionary* (1791) was reprinted over 100 times between 1791 and as late as 1904. Of course, it would be impossible to 'fix' pronunciation, and not all of Walker's prescriptions survived beyond the nineteenth century: he considered the pronunciation of 'basket', for example, with /a:/ to be 'bordering very closely on vulgarity', yet today this pronunciation is generally considered to be the standard one and the short vowel recommended by Walker is often denounced as 'flat'. Likewise, Walker provides some of the earliest evidence for loss of /r/ after consonants as in 'bar', 'card', 'regard' (now considered the norm in England), but implies that this is a London innovation and not recommended. What is important to note is that Walker and his fellow elocutionists selected the speech of educated Londoners as a model, but that linguistically the features granted prestige were no better or worse than those used by other speakers. However, by disseminating this pronunciation via their dictionaries and lectures and beginning to codify it, the elocutionists brought ideas about the necessity of standardisation of pronunciation in line with that of grammar, spelling and vocabulary.

Known as non-prevocalic /r/, this feature varies considerably across different dialects of English. It is discussed in relation to contemporary variations and changes in English in Chapters 5 and 7.

There was a political impetus towards promoting a stable and uniform variety at this time. In 1707, the Act of Union was passed, incorporating Scotland into what would now be called Great Britain. (Throughout the eighteenth century, the word *British* in the title of a book on grammar and pronunciation was politically loaded, referring as it did to the relatively recent Union.) Several authors expressed the view that unity of language would promote the unity of the nation. Educated Scots in particular sought to eradicate 'Scotticisms' from their language and brought in elocution teachers from England to help them. James Buchanan wrote what is acknowledged to be the first pronouncing dictionary of English *Linguae Britannicae Vera Pronunciatio* (The True Pronunciation of the Language of Britain) in order to help his fellow Scots to 'speak as properly and intelligibly as if they had been born and bred in London' (Buchanan, 1757, p. xv). The expansion of English to become the national language not simply of England but of Great Britain was integrally bound up with political attempts to consolidate the new boundaries of the nation.

As the British Empire expanded in the nineteenth century, there was even more incentive to learn and propagate 'correct' English in order to set an example to the rest of the Empire. Although we can see the beginnings of prescriptivism in the pronouncements of eighteenth-century codifiers like Johnson, Walker and the grammarian Robert Lowth (1710–1787), their statements are permissive in comparison with those found in nineteenth-century texts. Richard Bailey writes:

> If there is one heritage of the nineteenth-century language culture that survives most vigorously, it is the institutionalization of hierarchy among linguistic variants. The nineteenth century is, in short, a century of steadily increasing linguistic intolerance.
>
> (Bailey, 1996, p. 82)

The nineteenth century saw the dawn of descriptive linguistics, but it also brought a proliferation of cheap prescriptive handbooks and 'penny manuals' providing quick answers for those who wanted to avoid the social embarrassment of making linguistic mistakes. Titles like *Don't: a Manual of Mistakes* and *Poor Letter H, its Use and Abuse* are typical.

What Bailey also suggests is that prescriptivism is still thriving: in fact, it is flourishing in the twenty-first century. In 2003, the best-selling non-fiction title in the UK was Lynn Truss's *Eats, Shoots and Leaves*, a humorous guide to correct punctuation, and 'old-fashioned' grammar books such as *My Grammar and I (or Should that Be 'Me')?* subtitled *Old-school Ways to Sharpen Your English* are proliferating. The continuing perception of a need for such texts highlights their futility in the face of inevitable linguistic change. Eighteenth-century codifiers did not succeed in 'fixing' the language, so much as endorse a belief in the need to reduce variability and inhibit change. Even in its secured position as a national language, there will always be those who consider innovations in English to be 'incorrect' and who make prescriptive pronouncements to this effect.

2.5   Conclusion

English has, in a sense, 'come a long way' since its emergence as a clutch of dialects on a small island at the periphery of the recently fallen Roman Empire. It is tempting to trace its rise as a smooth progression from relative obscurity to the national language of England (and on to its current global status). As we have seen in this chapter, its 'rise' was anything but a story of inevitable and uninterrupted progress, but rather one of chance, shaped by encounters (often violent) between social groups who brought various languages into contact with one another, as well as by political and social decisions such as the selection of a Chancery Standard or the commercial impetus provided by the advent of printing. Furthermore, the development of modern-day English in England is as much the result of people's changing *ideas* about the language as it is about any actual linguistic situation. For example, we saw that prior to the 1800s diversity was the norm – not only was there no standard form in the modern sense, but there was no expectation that there should be one. With the growing, often politically motivated beliefs in a standard English came the parallel feeling that other dialects could be considered inferior – a prescriptive attitude that prevails today but which appears not to have always been the dominant way of thinking.

Despite the prescriptive beliefs that have in some ways shaped the English spoken in England today, its history shows us that the language has always been underpinned by hybridity, diversity and change. English is a result of a mix of different influences on the varied Germanic dialects from which it emerged – Scandinavian, Latin, Norman, French – and it continues to be shaped by its speakers' encounters with other languages, even within the British Isles. To say that English is the national language of England is not to say that twenty-first century England is monolingual, far from it: at the turn of the millennium, for example, a study reported that London schoolchildren spoke over 300 languages between them (Baker and Eversley, 2000). England also remains a place of great dialectal diversity, as will be explored further in Chapter 5; the story of English is as much about changing attitudes towards diversity as it is about actual homogenisation as far as regional spoken dialects are concerned. Finally, the history of English illustrates the inevitability of linguistic change. Although a standard form of written English has been established in England, that standard is always evolving, and as English has spread around the world, several different standard varieties of English now exist.

READING A: Shakespeare and the English language

Jonathan Hope

Specially commissioned for this book.

Introduction

When Shakespeare's plays were first printed together, Ben Jonson provided a poem describing Shakespeare as 'not of an age, but for all time'. Subsequent criticism built on this, constructing what has been called the 'myth' of Shakespeare as a cultural phenomenon: a 'universal' genius whose qualities transcend history, and who can 'speak' to us across time (e.g. Dobson, 1995).

The myth of Shakespeare's universality is powerful but it is also very dangerous, especially in relation to his language. Shakespeare used English at a particular moment in its history: its vocabulary was expanding rapidly while its grammar standardised. He had choices to make about grammatical constructions, pronouns and nouns that are no longer open to us. But Shakespeare's culture also thought about language differently, and applied different aesthetic values to it. If we see Shakespeare as 'universal', we run the risk of blinding ourselves to the strangeness of Shakespeare's linguistic practice and culture.

In this reading, I will outline briefly some of these issues, which I discuss at length in Hope (2010). First, how imposing our own aesthetic values leads us to misjudge Shakespeare's vocabulary. Second, how a failure to understand what the Renaissance thought about meaning stops us appreciating Shakespeare's wordplay. In a final section, I move away from words, to suggest that Shakespeare's real linguistic genius might instead be found in grammar.

Words

One of the commonest claims about Shakespeare's language is that he invented hundreds of words. For example, the writer and broadcaster Melvyn Bragg states that Shakespeare declared himself to be 'A man on fire for new words' (Bragg, 2003, p. 144). A fine rhetorical flourish, but unfortunately not only a careless misquotation of *Love's Labour's Lost* ('a man of fire-new words' 1.1.175), but also a gross misrepresentation of what the line actually means. It is about the character Armado, not

Shakespeare, and it implies that the new words he invents are a foolish, linguistic pretention.

This should give us pause, but did Shakespeare nonetheless invent a lot of words? It is true that his name crops up regularly as the first citation for new words, and new meanings for old words, in the *Oxford English Dictionary* (*OED*). However, since Jürgen Schäfer's work in the 1980s (Schäfer, 1980), we have known that such apparent creativity has to be treated with caution. The army of readers who read English books for examples for the *OED* searched Shakespeare more carefully than they did other contemporary writers, and in many cases they missed earlier uses by writers other than Shakespeare. Furthermore, wider studies of English in Shakespeare's time have shown that almost *all* writers coined new words in the period: the English vocabulary expanded more quickly at this time than at any other (though many words were used once or twice and never again) (Nevalainen, 1999). Once the bias in the *OED* collecting is allowed for, Shakespeare does not look unusual when compared to his contemporaries. In fact, Marvin Spevack has suggested that Shakespeare avoids one of the main sources of new words – Latin – using up to 50 per cent fewer Latin-derived terms than the average of his contemporaries (and this would match the implied criticism of Armado's Latinate vocabulary in *Love's Labour's Lost*) (Spevack, 1985). Shakespeare's preference seems to have been to extend, often by dazzling metaphorical leap, the meaning of familiar words, rather than conjure entirely new ones from the semantic deep.

So we must be cautious about statistics claiming to show that Shakespeare was the first user of many words. What, though, of another common claim: that Shakespeare, as befits his genius, had a much bigger vocabulary than any of his contemporaries? This is expounded by David Crystal (Crystal, 2008, p. 6), for example, who makes this 'largeness' claim even while debunking other language myths about Shakespeare. Again, at first sight the evidence seems clear: Shakespeare uses more words (*c.*20,500) than contemporaries like Ben Jonson (*c.*19,000) and Thomas Middleton (*c.*14,000). But it is not quite as simple as this: more writing by Shakespeare survives – so he had more opportunity to use different words. When we compare the *rate* at which he uses words he has not employed before, he turns out to be strictly average (see Craig, 2011; and Elliott and Valenza, 2011). It is as if we were comparing the careers of three goalscorers: Jackie Milburn, Malcolm Macdonald and Alan Shearer, say. Below are their career totals.

(All three strikers played for Newcastle United: Milburn 1943–57; Macdonald 1971–76; Shearer 1996–2006.)

Name	Total goals scored
Jackie Milburn	200
Malcolm Macdonald	121
Alan Shearer	206

(Figures taken from www.nufc.com/2010–11html/players.html, accessed 31 August 2010)

On these figures, it looks as though Milburn and Shearer were clearly more prolific strikers than Macdonald – if they were writers, we might be talking about them having larger vocabularies. But we are overlooking a crucial extra piece of evidence: how many games they played. When we add this in, the picture changes:

Name	Total goals scored	Total games played
Jackie Milburn	200	397
Malcolm Macdonald	121	228
Alan Shearer	206	395

A player who plays more games, like a writer who writes more texts, gives him- or herself more opportunities to score – we need to look at the rate at which a striker scores:

Name	Total goals scored	Total games played	Goals per game
Jackie Milburn	200	397	0.504
Malcolm Macdonald	121	228	0.531
Alan Shearer	206	395	0.522

Now we see that their rates of scoring are rather similar: about 0.5 goals per game, with Macdonald and Shearer slightly ahead of Milburn. Similarly with Shakespeare: he uses more words (scores more goals) than his contemporaries, but he writes more plays (plays more games). Once we look at the rate at which he uses words he has not used before, he looks very similar to those around him.

Why is our culture so keen on the false notion of an 'exceptional' Shakespeare, inventing words and wielding a gargantuan vocabulary? Our notions of poetic genius come from the Romantics, and for them, originality and newness were key elements in aesthetic theory. Even today, essentially Romantic notions of what art should be underlie most of our aesthetic judgements. Newness is all: adaptation, remaking (in film and elsewhere) occupy lowly rungs on the scale of artistic achievement.

But the Renaissance had no such fetish for newness: indeed, it was more likely to be viewed suspiciously. Throughout Shakespeare's plays, characters who speak with authority, disparage the new, and the fashionable, as ephemeral (Mercutio dismisses linguistic fashion when he derides 'new tuners of accent' *Romeo and Juliet* 2.4.29). 'Original' did not have the positive connotations for Shakespeare it has for us – and nor was 'artificial' pejorative. Where the Romantics celebrated the poet's ability to create out of nothing, Renaissance thinkers were wary of the dangers of inventing things that had never existed, and could never exist: not because they were inherently bad, but because their relationship to truth was unstable. Defenders of poetry and the imagination celebrated the access it offered to the ideal: to how things should be. But many distrusted 'new' or fictional ideas as likely to be false. Shakespeare, we should remember, was an adapter, not an originator, of stories.

We can see, then, that our own, historically conditioned, aesthetic values lead us to assume that Shakespeare must have exceeded his contemporaries in linguistic invention and potential. In terms of his vocabulary, however, as the statistics show, Shakespeare is resolutely average.

Meanings and puns

If our aesthetic theories have led us to overestimate Shakespeare's vocabulary, they have also caused us to reject his use of the pun (another aspect of his language which is typical of its time). Dr Johnson dismissed Shakespeare's puns as trivial, and most subsequent criticism has agreed. Is it not strange, though, that the greatest writer in English (and his culture) should have spent so much energy on pointless linguistic games? If we put Shakespeare back into history, it becomes possible to explain, and perhaps even appreciate, his wordplay.

The Renaissance had two competing theories about how language worked, and specifically how words came to have meanings. The dominant one was Aristotle's, and it held that language was an arbitrary human construction: words had meaning because people agreed what each designated. Any word could just as easily mean something else – as long as convention allowed. Juliet gives a textbook account of this when she bemoans the fact that Romeo, as a Montague, is from a family bitterly at war with her own:

> 'Tis but thy name, that is my enemy:
> Thou art thyself though, not a Montague.
> What's Montague? it is nor hand nor foot,
> Nor arm, nor face, nor any other part
> Belonging to a man. O! be some other name.
> What's in a name? that which we call a rose,
> By any other word would smell as sweet;
> So Romeo would, were he not Romeo call'd,
> Retain that dear perfection which he owes,
> Without that title. – Romeo, doff thy name;
> And for thy name, which is no part of thee,
> Take all myself!

(Romeo and Juliet, 2.2.38–49)

The alternative to this arbitrary view of meaning was associated with Plato, and its crucial difference was in the rejection of the notion of arbitrariness in language. The Platonic view posited a deep (divine or occult) connection between the *form* of words (their sounds or spelling) and their *meanings*. 'Rose', by this view, did not just designate a particular plant because everyone agreed that it would: it somehow had the essence of 'rose' in its structure – in the same way that 'H_2O' tells you something about the nature of water that 'water' does not.

Generally in the Renaissance, commentators on language shift between the two viewpoints, seemingly untroubled by the fact that they are mutually exclusive. Writers who begin arguing for one position, are likely to revert to the other, consciously or not, a page or two later. This is, to some extent, a consequence of the rhetorical method which dominated intellectual life in the period. Rhetorical teaching tended to put more emphasis on the arrangement and treatment of material than on reaching a conclusive answer. In this case, however, there was another reason for vacillation between the positions. The Platonic position on meaning, irrational as it was frequently shown to be, had an allure it retains today. The dream of being able to do things with language – really *do* things – runs through magic, religion, even much early science.

The allure of the Platonic position can perhaps be seen in the way Shakespeare, and other writers at the time, treat puns. For us, puns are often rather feeble, mechanical exercises in spotting arbitrary similarity between the forms of words otherwise unrelated: 'son' and 'sun' for example, when Richard has the 'winter' of 'discontent' banished by the 'son of York' (*Richard III*, 1.1.1–2). But on a Platonic view, the similarity is not necessarily arbitrary – and this is reinforced by the fact that neither 'son' nor 'sun' had a fixed spelling in Shakespeare's time – so they are arguably not different words in our sense at all. Viewed this way, puns become witty plays on multiple meanings, all of which are kept alive, rather than static, laboured jokes: a true Shakespearean pun is one word with two simultaneous interpretations – not two words, each with a distinct meaning. And perhaps the Platonic position is not as irrational as we might think: after all, in Juliet's case, if Romeo's *name* was different, then *things* would be too, and they would be free to marry.

Grammar

If Shakespeare's linguistic genius is not manifest in the size or fecundity of his words, what is it that he does as a writer that makes him stand out? At the start of *Henry V*, a prologue introduces the play, apologising for the fact that the small theatre, and limited acting troupe, cannot do justice to the wide fields of France, or the huge armies that fought there. The audience, the prologue declares, must make up for this with their imaginations:

> Think, when we talk of horses, that you see them
> Printing their proud hoofs i' the receiving earth;

> (*Henry V*, 1:26–7)

These two lines are typical of the way Shakespeare creates effects out of entirely familiar language, rather than by inventing new words, and also the way he combines semantic effects (to do with meaning) with syntactic ones (to do with grammar).

Let's begin with semantic effects. Semanticists (linguists who study meaning) commonly identify a quality they call *animacy* in nouns. Animacy refers to the degree to which something is alive, and the extent to which it is capable of growth, movement and thought. Plants are thus animate, in that they can grow, but they generally lack the capacity for intentional movement, so they are less animate than birds and animals – which in turn are less animate than humans, as they lack the full range of human thought.

Of the three nouns in the passage ('horses', 'hoofs', 'earth'), we can argue that 'horses' are the most animate, 'hoofs' the next (since, although they consist of hard, inert matter, they are at least attached to a living thing), and 'earth' the least. However, if we look at the language of the passage, we discover that all three are treated as if they had more animacy than we might expect.

For example, the horses do not simply place or stamp their hooves in the earth: they *print* them. Printing is a specifically human activity – so the metaphorical use of it here functions to imply conscious volition on the part of the horses, and thus increases their animacy. Similarly, when the horses' hoofs are described as 'proud', the metaphor implies a degree of animacy not normally associated with the noun – hard, dead tissue cannot have feelings of pride. Finally, the earth is described as 'receiving' – again, an adjective which increases animacy by implying active volition.

Running in parallel with these semantic effects are syntactic ones with a similar purpose, and which are also typical of Shakespeare. The most normal order of elements in English clauses is:

[subject] + [verb] + [object]

which we can refer to as 'SVO'. There is an example of a clause which matches this in the first line quoted above:

^{Subject}[you] ^{Verb}[see] ^{Object}[them]

Normally in English, the subject is a highly animate noun or pronoun, and the object is often less animate. Here, the human, highly animate pronoun 'you' does something ('see') to the non-human, less animate, horses ('them'). This is, crudely speaking, how the world works: more animate things typically do things to less animate things. Now let's look again at Shakespeare's lines, with subjects, objects and verbs marked:

> Think, when S(we) V(talk) of O(horses), that S(you) V(see) O (them)
>
> V(Printing) O(their proud hoofs) i' the receiving earth

'them', as we have already seen, is the object of 'see'. But notice what happens: as soon as the horses are introduced in the role of object ('them'), they are transformed into the subject of 'Printing'. It is the horses (them) who are seen by us, but it is also the horses (they) who do the printing. By a sleight of grammatical hand, the horses are *simultaneously* the inactive object of 'see' and the active subject of 'Printing':

$$^{Subject}[\text{you}] \quad ^{Verb}[\text{see}] \quad ^{<Object}[\text{them}]^{Subject>} \quad ^{Verb}[\text{Printing}]$$

The rapid shift we have just observed from grammatical object to subject role, with an implied increase in activity and animation, is very common in Shakespeare, who seems to have a need to animate, and activate, almost everything he mentions, however inactive or inanimate we might think it. It is also typical of Shakespeare that he uses both grammatical and semantic means to achieve this (making 'them' simultaneously an object and a subject, and using the semantic implications of 'Printing' to increase the animacy of 'horses').

A further feature of Shakespeare's syntax is unusual word order. John Porter Houston has identified a tendency for Shakespeare to invert the object and the verb, producing subject-object-verb clauses (SOV), rather than the normal subject-verb-object (SVO) (Houston, 1988). At its simplest, this adds emphasis, and perhaps strikes us as archaic, without causing serious problems in understanding:

Queen: Hamlet, thou hast thy father much offended.
Hamlet: Mother, you have my father much offended.

(Hamlet, 3.4.8–9)

In present-day English we would expect 'S(thou) V(hast much offended) O(thy father)' and 'S(you) V(have much offended) O(my father)', with the objects 'thy father' and 'my father' in their more normal position after the verb. When Shakespeare employs SOV order in longer sentences, we may find it harder to follow the sense:

> What feast is toward in thine eternal cell,
> That thou so many princes at a shot
> So bloodily hast struck?

(Hamlet, 5.2.370–2)

Here, a more usual order would be, 'that S(thou) V(hast struck) O (so many princes) at a shot'.

This tendency in Shakespeare is useful to know about if we are trying to understand why we – or perhaps students we are teaching – have problems following Shakespeare's meaning. It will become even more interesting, however, if future research confirms Houston's claim, that Shakespeare uses SOV word order far more frequently than his contemporaries – and that the rate at which he uses it increases over his career. Recent linguistic work on other syntactic features has confirmed the frequent literary-critical observation that Shakespeare's late style is more complex syntactically than his early one: perhaps Houston has identified a key characteristic of Shakespeare's language – one that really does set him out from his contemporaries.

Conclusion

Many have felt that Shakespeare's language must hold the key to his genius – but analysis of his linguistic practice has lagged behind almost every other part of Shakespeare scholarship. Perhaps this is because Shakespeare's language can only be seriously studied in relation to what others were doing at the time: if we want to make a claim about Shakespeare's vocabulary, we must also know about, say, Middleton's; and yet the effect of the Shakespeare 'myth' has been to take Shakespeare out of history, and divorce the study of his work from the study of 'lesser' contemporary writers. This is an exciting time in the study of Shakespeare's language, however: digital technology will soon make it possible for individual scholars to search and compare the complete corpus of Early Modern printed texts on their laptops. We will be able to put Shakespeare back into history.

References for this reading

Bragg, M. (2003) *The Adventure of English*, London, Hodder and Stoughton.

Craig, H. (2011) 'Shakespeare's vocabulary: myth and reality', *Shakespeare Quarterly*, vol. 62, no. 1, pp. 53–74.

Crystal, D. (2008) *Think on My Words: Exploring Shakespeare's Language*, Cambridge, Cambridge University Press.

Dobson, M. (1995) *The Making of the National Poet*, Oxford, Clarendon Press.

Elliott, W. E. Y. and Valenza, R. J. (2011) 'Shakespeare's vocabulary: did it dwarf all others?' in Ravassat, M. and Culpepper, J. (eds) *Stylistics and Shakespeare's Language: Transdisciplinary Approaches*, London, Continuum.

Hope, J. (2010) *Shakespeare and Language: Reason, Eloquence and Artifice in the Renaissance*, The Arden Shakespeare Library, London, A&C Black.

Houston, J. P. (1988) *Shakespeare's Sentences: A Study in Style and Syntax*, Baton Rouge, LA and London, Louisiana State University Press.

Nevalainen, T. (1999) 'Early Modern English lexis and semantics' in Lass, R. (ed.) *The Cambridge History of the English Language*, vol. III 1476–1776, Cambridge, Cambridge University Press.

Schäfer, J. (1980) *Documentation in the O.E.D.: Shakespeare and Nashe as Test Cases*, Oxford, Clarendon Press.

Spevack, M. (1985) 'Shakespeare's language' in Andrews, J. F. (ed.) *William Shakespeare: His World, His Work, His Influence*, vol. 2, New York, Charles Scribner's Sons.

READING B: Johnson among the Early Modern grammarians

Linda C. Mitchell

Source: Mitchell, L. C. (2005) 'Johnson among the Early Modern grammarians', *International Journal of Lexicography*, vol. 18, no. 2, pp. 203–16.

Introduction

Although lexicographers in seventeenth- and eighteenth-century England had published some developed dictionaries, it was Samuel Johnson's *Dictionary of the English Language* (1755) that set the standards for lexicons in both England and America. Johnson's dictionary also marked a shift in language authority from grammarians to lexicographers. In the seventeenth century, dictionaries had consisted of crude lists of synonyms that served as rudimentary definitions to translate foreign languages like Latin or French, while grammar texts included many of what we would consider lexicographical components: pronunciation, spelling, definitions, etymology, and usage notes. Grammarians were primarily responsible for decisions about the English language, decisions they usually made by consulting Latin grammars that held a centuries-long tradition of authority.

In the eighteenth century, decisions about language increasingly fell under the purview of lexicographers. While grammarians continued to focus on grammar-related material, lexicographers developed more comprehensive dictionaries. Johnson was able to write his monumental *Dictionary* of 1755 because he made use of several techniques grammarians had used in grammar texts, such as incorporating usage notes, making decisions on correctness, illustrating meanings with quotations, and even attempting witticisms. Johnson's ability to use the most successful techniques of grammarians, as well as lexicographers, helped to shift language authority to lexicographers.

In the seventeenth century [however], grammarians still possessed the same authority to make language decisions they had held since antiquity, and lexicographers had not yet emerged as a distinct group.

Early eighteenth-century grammar texts and new lexicographical demands

In the early eighteenth century, the publication of grammar books for English created a greater demand for vocabulary in the vernacular. This demand increased even more as the vernacular lexicon began to stabilize and the dictionary-type material outgrew the parameters of grammar books. Dictionaries, however, were still elementary, with only a short definition, synonym, or commentary for each word; grammar books included the more analytic information: pronunciation, meaning, parts-of-speech classification, etymology, spelling, and usage. During this phase, grammarians (e.g. Guy Miège, 1688; Richard Johnson, 1706; Charles Gildon and John Brightland, 1712; Michael Maittaire, 1712; James Greenwood, 1722) tried to retain their authority in making decisions about language. One way they were able to sustain their authority was to increase the kinds of material in grammar texts. For example, Gildon and Brightland added rhetoric, logic, poetry, and composition to the 1712 edition of *Grammar of the English Tongue* [...]

The move on the part of early eighteenth-century lexicographers to have more control over language is not obvious as they were still making their mark. In this stage lexicographers did much to shape dictionaries as we know them today, but they continued many of the practices they had started in the seventeenth century with improvements in their presentation of the material. They continued the practice of using pictures in dictionaries because it was an efficient method of defining words. The pedagogy of connecting words with pictures is still used today, especially with young children and in foreign language classes.

The first dictionary to have a compendium of grammar is Thomas Dyche and William Pardon's *New General English Dictionary* (1735). Dyche, also a grammarian, was able to see the necessity of such an inclusion. He claimed that his work was for those who wanted to write 'correctly and elegantly,' and he covered difficult words, technical terms, spelling, accents, and pronunciation. The publication of Dyche and Pardon's dictionary indicates that grammarians had begun to lose ground, especially since this dictionary stressed grammar and pronunciation. Lexicographers were working with historical and empirical data and keeping abreast of linguistic changes. Grammarians, on the other hand, had become pedagogues, teaching students how to use language, publishing and republishing little-changed textbooks. The decline in the status of the grammarian was evident by the middle of the eighteenth century. In the preface to *A New General English Dictionary* (1744), Dyche and Pardon denigrate the grammarian as a person who spends too much time on insignificant niceties, and perhaps they could claim to know, since they were themselves both grammarians-turned-lexicographers. With Dyche and Pardon, the responsibility for protecting the standards of English usage from corruption and deterioration moved from grammarians to lexicographers, a transfer that is still in force today though perhaps not fully recognized by all language scholars. Grammarians who had in ancient times been pre-eminent were now criticized and questioned for their pedagogy and theories, while lexicographers were increasingly looked upon as authorities.

Johnson and the early modern grammarians

Johnson shared an anxiousness with grammarians that the English language would change beyond recognition. [...] However, while early grammarians were focused on *fixing* the English language, eighteenth-century lexicographers like Johnson aimed to slow the changes in language so that future generations would be able to read English. The vernacular had been growing and changing in unpredictable ways to the extent that sixteenth-century language contrasted significantly with that of the eighteenth century. Johnson even states, 'no dictionary of a living tongue ever can be perfect, since while it is hastening to publication, some words are budding, and some falling away' (1755, sig. C2v). However, Johnson's dictionary helped stabilize the changes in language so that future generations would recognize the English language.

The eighteenth century was a time of an expanding empire, and Johnson, more than fellow grammarians, recognized how a growing nation would change language. Language was affected by commercial trading in both foreign countries and England. Moreover, many foreigners were entering England to establish businesses. Johnson sees a natural progress taking place.

> Total and sudden transformations of a language seldom happen; conquests and migrations are now very rare; but there are other causes of change … commerce, however necessary, however lucrative, as it depraves the manners, corrupts the language; they that have frequent intercourse with strangers, to whom they endeavour to accommodate themselves, must in time learn a mingled dialect, like the jargon which serves the traffickers on the Mediterranean and Indian coasts. This will not always be confined to the exchange, the warehouse, or the port, but will be communicated by degrees to other ranks of the people, and be at last incorporated with the current speech.
>
> (Johnson, 1755, Preface sig. C2r)

Johnson argued that as a country grows, so does the language. The alternative would be a stagnant, isolated nation.

> There are likewise internal causes equally forcible. The language most likely to continue long without alteration, would be that of a nation raised a little, and but a little above barbarity, secluded from strangers, and totally employed in procuring the conveniences of life; either without books, or … with very few: men thus busied and unlearned, having only such words as common use requires, would perhaps long continue to express the same notions by the same signs.
>
> (Johnson, 1755, Preface sig. C2r)

Grammarians in the eighteenth century resisted change and moved to more conservative, prescriptive beliefs about *fixing* language. Lexicographers like Johnson, however, adopted more flexible, descriptive ideas of how language changes naturally.

Despite his recognition of the mutability of living language, Johnson wanted to do what grammar texts had not yet accomplished: codify and standardize the English language. In the Preface to his *Dictionary* Johnson urges his peers to protect the mother tongue: 'Tongues, like governments, have a natural tendency to degeneration; we have long preserved our constitution, let us make some struggles for our language' (1755, sig. C2v). With the help of books written by scholars and men of letters, Johnson claimed the role of lexicographer and seized the authority from grammarians to legislate rules of language, an authority that dictionary editors retain to this day. According to Johnson, it was the responsibility of lexicographers to record anomalies so that undesirable language habits were not perpetuated and reinforced. He states, 'every language has likewise its improprieties and absurdities, which it is the duty of the lexicographer to correct or proscribe' (Plan 1747).

Johnson shared the fear of early eighteenth-century grammarians (e.g. Charles Gildon, 1712; Michael Maittaire, 1712; John Garretson, 1719; James Greenwood, 1722) that the English language might deteriorate. Johnson acknowledges that some supporters of his dictionary 'will require that it should fix our language, and put a stop to those alterations which time and change have hitherto been suffered to make in it without opposition' (Preface, sig. C2r). In the Preface he anticipates the objections and concedes that it is impossible to keep language in a fixed state:

> With this consequence I will confess that I flattered myself for a while; but now begin to fear that I have indulged expectation which neither reason nor experience can justify … and with equal justice may the lexicographer be derided, who being able to produce no example of a nation that has preserved their words and phrases from mutability, shall imagine that his dictionary can embalm his language, and secure it from corruption and decay,

that it is in his power to change sublunary nature, and clear the world at once from folly, vanity, and affection.

(Johnson, 1755, Preface sig. C2r)

Thus, Johnson admits that a lexicographer has limitations. [...]

Grammarians among the lexicographers

Building upon Johnson's authoritative work, other lexicographers continued to go beyond the limited scope of the dictionary to cover both grammar and lexicon in even more detail. Lexicographers were also more alert than grammarians to issues of conforming to rules and standards, especially to the way people used language in social situations. John Entick, for example, promises in *The New Spelling Dictionary* (1765) to help the reader 'write and pronounce the English tongue with ease and propriety' (1765: title page). In the introduction, he reinforces his aim for people 'to speak and to write correctly and properly, to be instructed in the rules for right pronunciation, and in the art of true spelling; and or how to write every word with proper letters' (1765, p. ix). He wishes 'to assist young People, Artificers, Tradesmen and Foreigners, desirous to understand what they speak, read and write' (1765: title page). Entick claims that his grammatical introduction will facilitate the user's proficiency in English and help him gain necessary social and linguistic competence.

In *A New Dictionary of the English Language* (1773) William Kenrick states on the title page that he will include, for each entry, information on orthography, etymology, and idiomatic use in writing, all of which had appeared in the grammar books of the seventeenth century. He will also show the correct pronunciation according to the 'present practice of polished speakers in the Metropolis,' further proof of the increased lexicographic focus on communication at that time. He also includes what he calls a rhetorical grammar to help people with contemporary speech and communication. Two other publications aimed at the lower and middle classes are James Barclay's *A Complete and Universal English Dictionary on a New Plan* (1774) and John Ash's *The New and Complete Dictionary of the English Language* (1775). Both lexicographers include discussions of grammar and communication skills. Barclay also adds an outline of ancient and modern history, and Ash includes some essays on linguistic matters.

When lexicographers included grammar, they were unaware they were gaining an authority over grammarians in standardizing the language. While grammarians served as pedagogues, concentrating on classroom exercises and fighting battles over teaching methodologies, lexicographers quietly inventoried and researched usage. In sum, lexicographers became the guardians of language. The transfer of authority from grammar books to dictionaries was complete by the latter part of the eighteenth century. Dictionaries now held linguistic authority, while grammar texts served a purely pedagogical function.

As one might expect, the transfer of linguistic authority brought with it the propensity for controversy. The battles were not just about a word change, but about who controls language, what social classes are included, and what groups are excluded. Previously, such grammar books as Lily's [*A Short Introduction of Grammar* (1567)] had the power to decide those issues. As dictionaries became more influential and were able to reach more people, they began to dominate the linguistic sphere. They could encode values and reflect current language usage. Language is power, and dictionaries could wield that power by standardizing language.

Conclusion

Johnson saw himself as protector of the English language, despite its protean instability. No grammarian or lexicographer had ever approached language in such a complete and documented way. Johnson had a different aim from fellow grammarians and lexicographers; he wanted to entertain as well as inform his readers. Johnson's approach set a new standard for the authority of dictionaries: an educational tradition in which dictionaries would supply editorial comments and provide illustrative quotations that would increase knowledge. Although lexicographers such as Nathan Bailey had published a variety of dictionaries in the eighteenth century, it was Johnson who produced the authoritative dictionary that was used for at least one hundred years and that served as a basis for other dictionaries.

References for this reading

Ash, J. (1775) *The New and Complete Dictionary of the English Language*, London.

Barclay, J. (1774) *A Complete and Universal English Dictionary*, London.

Dyche, T. and Pardon, W. (1735) *A New General English Dictionary*, London.

Dyche, T. and Pardon, W. (1744) *A New General English Dictionary*, London.

Entick, J. (1765) *The New Spelling Dictionary*, London.

Garretson, J. (1719) *English Exercises for School-Boys to Translate into Latin*, London.

Gildon, C. and Brightland, J. (1712) *A Grammar of the English Tongue*, London.

Greenwood, J. (1722) *An Essay Towards a Practical English Grammar*, London.

Johnson, R. (1706) *Grammatical Commentaries*, London.

Johnson, S. (1755) *A Dictionary of the English Language* (First folio edition), London.

Kenrick, W. (1773) *A New Dictionary of the English Language*, London.

Lily, W. (1567) *A Short Introduction of Grammar*, London.

Maittaire, M. (1712) *The English Grammar*, London.

Miège, G. (1688) *English Grammar*, London.

3   A colonial language

Dick Leith and Philip Seargeant

3.1   Introduction

The idea that English had the potential to become a 'world language' began to emerge as early as the mid-eighteenth century. Prior to this, and in notable contrast to prevailing attitudes today, there was a belief that English people had a particular penchant for learning foreign languages. Such was this interest in other languages that there was concern that English itself was falling into a state of disrepair. In 1766, one anonymous commentator wrote of the condition of his national language that:

> The last objection that occurs to me at present, is, that our tongue wants [i.e. lacks] universality, which seems to be an argument against its merit. This is owing to the affectation of Englishmen, who prefer any language to their own, and is not to be imputed to a defect in their native tongue. But the objection, if such it be, is vanishing daily; for I have been assured, by several ingenious foreigners, that in many places abroad, Italy in particular, it is become the fashion to study the English Tongue.
>
> (cited in Bailey, 2006, p. 346)

The 'universality' that English did eventually achieve was not, however, the result of it simply being a fashionable thing to learn in continental Europe. The more fundamental reasons for its global spread are related to processes of geopolitical significance: to the history first of the British Isles, then of Europe, and ultimately of the world. For while the Italians in the mid-eighteenth century were apparently cultivating a fashion for the learning of English, at the same time England was spreading its power base well beyond its own shores, and English-speaking peoples were already dispersed across territories in several continents.

In the next chapter we will focus specifically on what it means to say that English is now a 'global' language – perhaps even *the* global language – and examine how it came to occupy this position. Before we turn to this issue, though, we need first to look at how the language spread beyond England, and at how the foundations were laid for its later emergence as a global force. Central to the expansion of the language is the history of **colonisation**. The concept of colonisation refers here to processes involving the establishment, often by force, of communities of English speakers in territories around the world. These communities positioned themselves in a relation of power to the indigenous or pre-existing populations of the territories in which they settled, while at the same time maintaining economic and cultural links with England. It was processes of this sort which played a significant and decisive role in the expansion of English usage around the world. In terms of Kachru's model of the spread of English that we looked at in Chapter 1, both the Inner and Outer Circle countries almost all trace their current usage of English back to some form of colonial relationship with England.

In this chapter, therefore, we will examine the relationship between colonisation and the spread of English, looking at the promotion of the language beyond England – first within the British Isles, and then to places such as the Americas, Africa and Australia. We will also consider the language contact that occurred as English rubbed up against other languages and cultures, and the influence this has had on the shape of the language as it has developed in diverse world contexts. Finally, we will consider the part that the history of colonisation has played in the political and cultural associations that English now has around the world, and look at the complex issues of cultural identity and divided language loyalties which accompany the language's global spread.

3.2   The colonial experience

David Crystal (1988, p. 1) has estimated that between the end of the reign of Elizabeth I (1603) and the beginning of the reign of Elizabeth II (1952) the number of mother-tongue English speakers in the world increased from between five to seven million to about 250 million, of whom four-fifths lived outside the British Isles. This growth was largely due to the colonial expansion of England to overseas territories which, he argues, began in the sixteenth century. In many ways, however, the process of colonisation began earlier than this within the British Isles themselves, when English first became established as the main language of the Celtic-speaking territories of Ireland, Scotland and Wales. We can say, therefore, that the spread of English has been closely associated with a colonial process from as far back as the twelfth century.

There was no single, universal colonial experience, however. Each colony provided a unique context politically, socially and linguistically. Nevertheless, it is possible to discern a common sequence of events in many of those colonies where English emerged as a main language:

- first, **colonisation**, whereby an original settlement was made by English speakers

- second, **political incorporation**, whereby the colonised territory was brought under the central control of the English/British government

- third, a **nationalist reaction** which sometimes, but not always, led to independence.

Each stage of this sequence had linguistic implications. In the sections below we shall first outline the nature of these different stages and their relationship to language-related issues, and then consider how they actually manifested themselves in different colonial contexts. In later chapters in the book – and specifically in Chapter 5 – we will look in detail at the linguistic consequences of this history in terms of the variety of different forms of English that are now spoken in postcolonial territories.

Stage 1: Colonisation

As was suggested above, the process of colonisation took different forms in different places. For a long period after the Germanic invasions of the fifth century which established English in England, Celtic languages continued to be widely spoken in three areas of the British Isles: Ireland, Scotland and Wales. After a time, though, the spread of English was extended into these areas as well. But although the spread of the language throughout the British Isles can be seen as part of a colonial process, it was not a simple matter of one nation state – 'England' – setting up a colony in another. Indeed, it was only during the Renaissance that nation states as we understand them today took form in Europe. How, then, can the spread of English from the twelfth century onwards be regarded as a colonial process?

According to the historian Robert Bartlett (1993), the peripheral areas in Europe were colonised during the Middle Ages from what he calls the 'centre', formed by Latin Christendom (Figure 3.1). In the north-western periphery, this process of colonisation affected all the Celtic territories of the British Isles. The motives were political and religious, involving both the subjugation of the population and the reinforcement

The development of the concept of the nation state is dealt with in another book in this series, *The Politics of English: Conflict, Competition, Co-existence* (Hewings and Tagg, eds, 2012, Chapter 5).

of Christianity as defined by the Pope. Following their conquest of England in 1066, the Norman monarchs encouraged the colonisation of first Wales and then Ireland by awarding land to knights in return for subduing the local population (the situation in Scotland was slightly different). The linguistic consequence was the introduction of varieties of English (along with other languages such as French and Flemish) into these territories.

Figure 3.1 The 'centre' in medieval Europe (adapted from Bartlett, 1993, p. xvi)

Moving next to the establishment of English colonies beyond the British Isles, this began at the end of the sixteenth century. The motives in these cases were threefold:

- **Economic**. Companies run by capitalist entrepreneurs were granted a monopoly over a certain commodity by the monarch, who gained by taxing the profit made in trading it.

- **Social**. In England, economic problems such as unemployment and inflation combined with population growth to create a large class of dispossessed 'vagrants' and political dissidents; these could help solve the problem of providing labour in colonies overseas.

- **Political**. Rivalries developed among European states, especially the Portuguese, Spanish and Dutch in the seventeenth century; the French in the eighteenth; and, by the end of the nineteenth, the Germans.

We shall see later in the chapter how the history of English in the colonies needs to be understood against this background.

Since the process of colonisation beyond the British Isles lasted more than 300 years and affected four continents, it is very difficult to make generalisations about its character. In this chapter, we will examine three distinct types of English colonisation, each with its own linguistic consequences.

- **Displacement**. A substantial settlement by first-language speakers of English displaced the precolonial population (examples are North America and Australia).

- **Subjection**. Sparser colonial settlements kept the precolonial population in subjection, allowing some of them access to learning English as a second, or additional, language (examples are Nigeria, Cameroon and India). This type of colonisation is often called 'indirect rule' – a principle developed by Lord Lugard, High Commissioner of the Protectorate of Northern Nigeria at the turn of the nineteenth century. It was widely employed throughout the British colonies.

- **Replacement**. A precolonial population was replaced by new labour from elsewhere, principally West Africa (examples are Barbados and Jamaica).

In the second half of the chapter we will look at these three types of colonisation in more detail and examine case studies exemplifying each of them, but first we look in more general terms at the other stages involved in processes of colonisation.

Stage 2: Political incorporation

As colonies developed and became of greater strategic importance to England, the English government took greater responsibility for their administration. The Celtic territories were the first to experience political incorporation in this way. In 1536, for instance, 'England' as the name of the state also included Wales. In dealing with Scotland, however, the English government revived the old term 'Britain'. Both territories were formally joined as 'Great Britain' in 1707. Ireland was formally incorporated in 1800 as part of what had come to be called 'the United Kingdom'. For the greater part of the nineteenth century all these territories were officially 'British', and many individuals from Ireland, Scotland and Wales played an active part in forming the British empire overseas. And in all of them, broadly speaking, English came to be identified as the language of the state.

Originally, colonists were subjects of the English monarchy, economically dependent on and controlled by 'the mother country'. Linguistically this meant that the language usage of England remained a powerful model. But political incorporation beyond the British Isles took a looser form than in the case of the Celtic territories. It was not until the nineteenth century that the British government, rather than the various trading companies, assumed the administration of the remaining colonies, creating the 'British Empire'. And by that time the issue of political incorporation had become complicated by nationalist reaction.

Stage 3: Nationalist reaction

The political incorporation of communities that feel they have a distinct cultural identity provides fertile ground for the emergence of nationalist reaction. From the late eighteenth century onwards, different forms of nationalist activity characterised political life in many of the areas colonised by the English. Language figured prominently in such nationalist reaction: in some cases, the precolonial language provided a focus for the assertion of a separatist identity, in others this role was played by English itself.

For example, by the end of the nineteenth century the newly emerging nationalisms in Ireland, Scotland and Wales were beginning to fear for the survival of the Celtic languages, and campaigns were mounted to promote them. One consequence of this was that they became taught languages, learnt by many people who otherwise knew only English. Another consequence was that they became increasingly sentimentalised, as much by the English as by the Celts themselves. The Victorian educationalist and literary scholar Matthew Arnold, for instance, spoke of the 'lively Celtic nature' expressed by Irish and Welsh writing.

Overseas, nationalist reaction began with North America in 1776. Originally motivated by concerns over taxation and parliamentary representation, political independence for the 'United States of America' was achieved by means of armed force, and the new state declared itself a republic. Fearing this might be a precedent, the British government offered a form of self-government to the United States' neighbour, Canada, in 1867. Dominion status, as this was called, was similarly granted to other, more recent colonies with substantial settler populations from the British Isles: Australia (in 1901), New Zealand (in 1907) and South Africa (in 1910; but this was complicated by the presence of a large Dutch settlement). In 1931, the Statute of Westminster confirmed the independence of the dominions, which continue to be linked to Britain in the 'Commonwealth of Nations'.

In the dominions, nationalist sentiment has tended to take a cultural rather than political form. Movements for *political* independence, on the other hand, emerged in India and many of the new African colonies during the twentieth century. The language of these movements was also English, even though this was a second (or at least additional) language for most of the inhabitants.

3.3   The linguistic consequences of colonisation

As we have noted, language-related concerns are often closely linked to the process of colonisation. One of the more striking linguistic consequences of colonisation has been the appearance of new varieties of English worldwide. Whenever the colonial process brought English into contact with other languages it did so within particular relations of power. Indeed, an important part of any definition of colonisation must relate to the pattern of social, economic and political inequalities which privileged the colonial language (in this case English) and those who spoke it. These colonial conditions of language contact played an important role in shaping the new varieties of English that emerged.

Allow about
10 minutes

Activity 3.1

Before we look in detail at the processes by which new varieties develop in colonial contexts, take a few moments to consider what factors occur when two languages come into contact, and what the linguistic consequences of these might be. In other words, what happens to language and language use when communities speaking different languages are thrown together by historical events?

Comment

Depending on the social and political conditions under which the different speech communities come together, contact between two or more languages can have a number of different linguistic consequences. It is usual, though, for the languages to influence each other in some form or another. This can be by means of the adoption of loanwords, changes in pronunciation, and also grammatical structure. The extent of the influence will depend on the length and depth of the contact between the two communities, as well as the political relationship between them.

Edgar Schneider (2007, pp. 32–55) has identified five broad stages of historical development for new varieties of English in the context of contact between different speech communities brought about by colonialism. These stages lead 'from the transplanting of English to a new land through a period of vibrant changes, both social and linguistic, to a renewed stabilization of a newly emerged variety' (p. 30). The process begins with the **foundation** stage, in which English is brought to a territory where it had not previously been spoken. At this initial stage the indigenous community and the newly arrived settlers see themselves very much as distinct groups (the former as owners of the territory, the latter as representatives of Britain), and although there is some language contact, communication between the two is usually confined to certain members of the communities, either interpreters or those with high status.

The second stage in the process is what Schneider calls **exonormative stabilisation**: English begins to be regularly spoken in the territory, though mainly in contexts such as administration, education and the legal system. The variety that is spoken is one modelled on norms from the settlers' 'home' country – that is, Britain – (it is an exonormative variety, or one that looks to external norms), and so has no distinct identity of its own.

The next stage in the process is the one Schneider considers to be the most important, from both a cultural and a linguistic point of view. This is the period of **nativisation**: by this point, the earlier cultural and political allegiances that had existed precolonisation are beginning to be seen as no longer relevant for the realities of the new situation in which people are living, and are being replaced by a new sense of cultural – and linguistic – identity for the territory. The territory is thus developing its own cultural practices and ways of doing things, and part of this is the development of a localised, or indigenised, variety of English.

Nativisation is followed by the fourth stage, **endonormative stabilisation**, during which the local variety of English begins not only to be accepted as legitimate in its own right, but also gets actively promoted as an important part of the territory's culture. By this point, therefore, the population no longer looks to the model of English that is used in Britain, but is instead relying on, and indeed promoting, local norms for the language. This often follows political independence for the territory, and issues related to language can play a key role in the establishment of a distinct political identity.

The final phase in the process is **differentiation**. By now the local variety is well established and what begins to happen is that a process of *internal* linguistic variation takes place within the territory, as different sectors of society (e.g. communities in different geographical regions) begin to establish their own particular usage patterns of English, which can be considered separate dialects of the variety now spoken in the territory. It is worth noting, however, that not all territories progress through all five of these stages, and depending on the particular historical circumstances involved, different aspects of the process will be more salient in different places.

Dialect levelling and internal variation

During this process of development for new varieties, there are two trends that are of particular interest and that it is worth looking at in a little more detail. In all the colonies – from that first established in Ireland in the twelfth century to much later ones, such as Australia, where settlement began in the late eighteenth century – the English-speaking settlers formed a diverse group of people. Many came from lowly social positions in England but found themselves in a position of power in relation to the original, precolonial populations. Some were economic migrants from rural communities (the most significant case of this is probably the migration from Ireland to North America during the Irish famines of the nineteenth century). Others were political or religious refugees (such as the Protestants who created some of the first North American colonies in the seventeenth century).

The restructuring of social identity is a typical colonial process and applies both to the incoming community (in this case British) and to members of the precolonial population who become incorporated into the colonial system. Ambivalent cultural and linguistic loyalties commonly arise. The mixed demographic background of early settlers (with people coming from different class backgrounds and different areas of Britain) suggests that the varieties of English taken to the colonies were diverse and often non-standard. When speakers of these different varieties were brought together in a new community, a process of **dialect levelling** often occurred. That is, differences between speakers tended over time to become eroded and a more uniform variety emerged. When political incorporation occurred, this model of a common standard across the community was reinforced by the high-status English speakers sent out as representatives of the British government (this is a factor in the stage Schneider calls exonormative stabilisation). Nationalist reaction, and the seeking of independent political and cultural identity, could then lead to the promotion of a different standard model, by encouraging the identification and codification (particularly in spelling books and dictionaries) of a local variety of English ('nativisation' in Schneider's model). The case of American English, which we shall look at below, is a notable example. The results of the nativisation process sometimes created a cultural and political tension over the legitimacy of any local variety of English (could this 'new' English be considered as valid as that spoken back in Britain?). And indeed, ambivalent attitudes to local forms of English are still sometimes evident in many of the former colonies; for example, while American English or Australian English may have secure independent status now, the same is not necessarily the case for Nigerian English or Singaporean English.

The processes described above are ones which tend to produce uniformity from a pattern of difference. But as the final stage of Schneider's model suggests, there were other tendencies that led to **internal variation** in usages of the language. As colonies expanded and became more established, different areas and groups usually developed a sense of local cultural and linguistic identity. This might be reinforced by contact with local languages, by new kinds of social hierarchies (often positioning precolonial people as low status), or by different forms of continuing relationship with Britain.

The most complex linguistic situation was found in those colonies where speakers became bilingual in English and a local language. This was the case in India and West Africa, where a relatively small number of Europeans imposed political and economic control over precolonial populations. Here, the English language came into the most intimate contact with other languages and new, sometimes radically divergent, forms of English arose. When a language is imposed on a community as part of a colonial process, local speakers tend to incorporate many linguistic features from their first language when speaking the new, imposed one. In situations such as these, the local language which influences the colonial language is described as a **substrate**.

At first, this might occur simply because local people learn English as a second or additional language, and knowledge of their first language interferes in a systematic way with their English, especially in terms of pronunciation and the adoption of certain grammatical patterns. However, as time goes on, a new variety of English establishes itself, acquires a stability and coherence, and becomes the target language learnt by young people (i.e. a process of endonormative stabilisation occurs). At that point, we can describe the emergent variety of English as possessing a distinct identity and, typically, as having a generally understood social status within the community.

A good example of a linguistic substrate is provided by Hiberno-English (also called Irish English), the variety that arose in Ireland as a consequence of contact between English and Irish. In this, several grammatical structures and features of accent seem to be the result of an Irish substrate, even though very few speakers of Hiberno-English learn Irish as their first language. An example is a sentence such as 'They are after doing the work', where the construction 'after' plus the '-ing' form of a verb indicates the immediate past (which, in standard British English, would be: 'They have just done the work'). The use of this construction in Hiberno-English is thought likely to be a result of the influence of the use of the prepositional phrase *tar éis* ('after') in Irish (Hickey, 2007, p. 136).

Perhaps the most extreme consequence of language contact, where only the vocabulary appears to be English and the grammar is derived from elsewhere, can be found in the English **pidgins** and **creoles** which have appeared in many parts of the world since the seventeenth century.

These are varieties which began as simplified forms of English that were originally developed as a means of communication between communities which did not share a common language. Many of them are a linguistic legacy of the slave trade which brought speakers of African languages to the American colonies. We will return to a fuller discussion of these later in the chapter, and then look in detail at their linguistic features in Chapter 5.

3.4 The spread of English within the British Isles

Having outlined the processes involved in colonisation, and looked also at its relationship with language issues, let us now turn our attention to some extended examples. A key argument in this chapter has been that the global spread of English began within the British Isles, towards the end of the twelfth century.

Figure 3.2 gives you a snapshot of the historical background to what we will cover in this section. It includes details of the situations in Scotland and Wales which we mentioned briefly earlier in the chapter. In this section though, we will use Ireland as our chief case study. Many aspects of the growth of English usage in the formerly Celtic-speaking territories of Ireland and, to a certain extent, Scotland can be seen as an early colonial process which in some ways provided a model for later English colonisation overseas. It is also the case that the new varieties of English which arose in these areas were influential in the development of English beyond the British Isles, since Irish and Scottish emigrants formed a substantial proportion of some English colonies.

The colonisation of Ireland

The first colonies were established in the south-east of Ireland towards the end of the twelfth century. English law was introduced to protect the colonists and disadvantage the Irish. New towns or boroughs – which were a distinctive form of Anglo-Saxon settlement that contrasted with local dispersed habitations – were built and became centres of Anglo-Norman influence (records from the late twelfth century show immigration to Dublin, Ireland's capital, from towns in the south-west of England and Wales). A century later, two-thirds of Ireland had been conquered after military campaigns against the Irish earls.

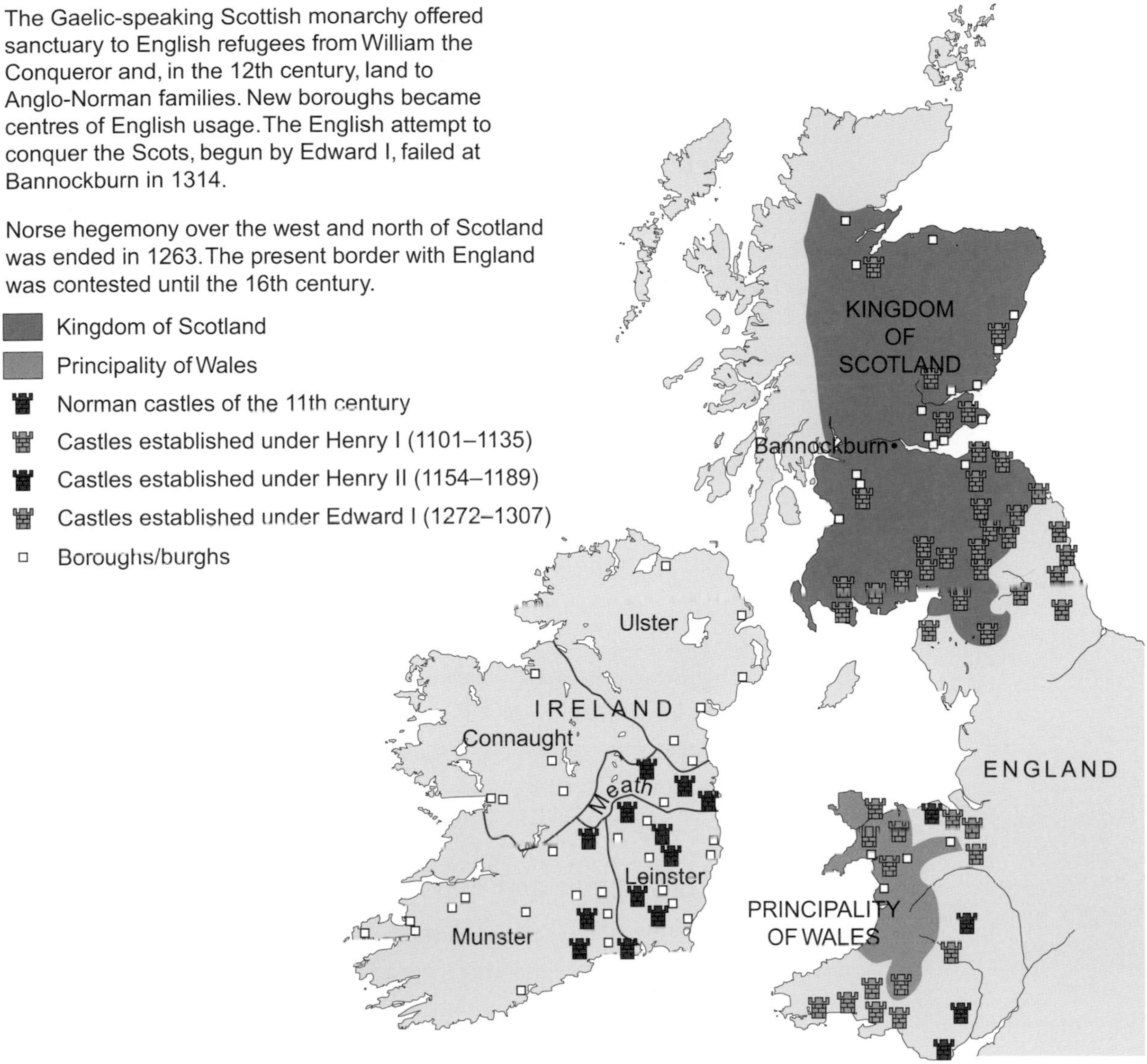
The Gaelic-speaking Scottish monarchy offered sanctuary to English refugees from William the Conqueror and, in the 12th century, land to Anglo-Norman families. New boroughs became centres of English usage. The English attempt to conquer the Scots, begun by Edward I, failed at Bannockburn in 1314.
Norse hegemony over the west and north of Scotland was ended in 1263. The present border with England was contested until the 16th century.
Kingdom of Scotland
Principality of Wales
Norman castles of the 11th century
Castles established under Henry I (1101–1135)
Castles established under Henry II (1154–1189)
Castles established under Edward I (1272–1307)
Boroughs/burghs
KINGDOM OF SCOTLAND
Bannockburn
Ulster
IRELAND
Connaught
Meath
Leinster
Munster
ENGLAND
PRINCIPALITY OF WALES

Anglo-Norman influence in Ireland began in 1167 under Henry II. Dublin was occupied and by 1250 only the North-West remained in Irish hands. English was established in the boroughs. But during the next 200 years the Irish reasserted control, leaving only the Pale – a small area around Dublin – in English hands.

Figure 3.2 Anglo-Norman expansion in the British Isles

It is a feature of colonial activity that personal identities and loyalties change. By the fourteenth century, it seems, many of the colonists had married among the Irish and adopted the 'manners, fashion' and, significantly, 'the language of the Irish enemies', in the words of a Statute of 1366. This process continued, so that by the late fifteenth century English control was limited to a small area around Dublin known as 'the Pale'.

English control, however, was reasserted during the sixteenth century, reflecting the monarchy's preoccupation with territorial boundaries. Henry VIII's Proclamation of 1541 urged that 'the king's true subjects' in Ireland 'shall use and speak commonly the English tongue'. The Protestant Reformation gave a new twist to Anglo-Irish relations, since the Irish continued to practise Roman Catholicism. Under Elizabeth I (1558–1603) England was at war with Catholic Spain and Irish Catholicism was seen as treachery. An English army was sent to overcome the resurgent Irish chieftains. In the course of long and bitter fighting, the invading English defined the enemy as the opposite of all those qualities claimed for the Protestant English. According to the attorney general for Ireland, Sir John Davies, in 1610 the 'wild' Irish did not 'build houses, make townships … or improve the land as it ought to be' (Stallybrass, 1988, p. 206). They were also described as filthy, long-haired and promiscuous. The Irish were eventually defeated, and their land confiscated and awarded to fresh colonisers. Many of these colonisers in the north-east of Ireland were Scots, who gave rise to the linguistic area known today as Ulster Scots. Among the other colonisers were the poorest sections of the English population in London, encouraged to go to Ireland because the government feared they would be 'seditious' if they stayed in England (Stallybrass, 1988).

Political incorporation and nationalist reaction in Ireland

The new colonists of the seventeenth century clung to their Protestant, non-Irish identities, while the Irish were resettled in the poorer west of the country. Anti-English sentiment among the Irish was strong enough to support any cause that threatened the British state, especially if a Catholic power were involved in that cause. But by the end of the eighteenth century new democratic and nationalist ideas had fuelled a movement for independence from English rule which also took root among sections of the Protestant population. It was after an uprising in 1798 that Ireland was incorporated into the United Kingdom by the Act of Union of 1800.

It has been estimated that by 1800, English was the first language of half the population of Ireland. In the course of the nineteenth century Irish was increasingly abandoned. Three reasons have been suggested for this (Harris, 1991, p. 38). One of these was depopulation. Famines in the 1840s greatly reduced the Irish-speaking population, either by death or by emigration (principally to America). Another reason was the introduction of universal English language education. The final one is significant in the context of ideas linking nationalism and language. English, not Irish, became the language of the two institutions which claimed to speak on behalf of the Irish population: the Catholic Church and the independence movement. The latter gathered pace in the course of the century, culminating in the establishment of the Irish Free State (Irish Republic) in 1922, whereby twenty-six counties in southern Ireland gained independence from the United Kingdom. Northern Ireland remained part of the UK.

Before the seventeenth century, Irish was the first language of the whole population. Today it is used as the main community and household language of about 3 per cent of the population of the Irish Republic (see Figure 3.3), although it remains the 'national' and 'first official language' (Government of Ireland, 2006, p. 10). As such, it is a compulsory subject in secondary schools and is cultivated as the language of literature, broadcasting and government publications. English is recognised in the Irish constitution as a 'second official language', but in practice is used alongside Irish. Despite the fact that an overwhelming proportion of Irish people speak English in their daily lives, they often explicitly express loyalty to the idea of Irish as part of their 'national' identity.

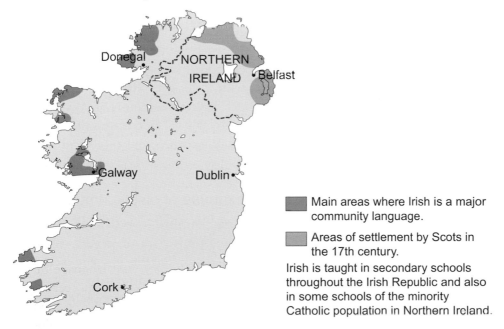

Main areas where Irish is a major community language.

Areas of settlement by Scots in the 17th century.

Irish is taught in secondary schools throughout the Irish Republic and also in some schools of the minority Catholic population in Northern Ireland.

Figure 3.3   The linguistic situation in Ireland

Both this language loyalty and the role of Irish in the Irish Republic today can be seen as the result of nineteenth-century language nationalism. By 1893, three organisations had been set up to revive the Irish language. They were largely led by literary figures and intellectuals, often from the upper class, for whom the Irish language was linked to the images of both an ancient literary culture and the non-literate usage of the peasantry in the west. For these movements, language was at the heart of Celtic culture: remove the language, and everything else dies.

In time, then, there emerged a distinctive form of English spoken in Ireland, now known as Hiberno-English or Irish English. As was mentioned above, this was influenced in various ways by the Irish language, which was the first language of many of its original speakers. Irish English gradually became the form of English learnt by monolingual English speakers in Ireland. We will look in detail at the nature of this variety – as well as others from the British Isles – in Chapter 5.

3.5   The spread of English beyond the British Isles

The establishment of English-speaking colonies in North America at the beginning of the seventeenth century was the first decisive stage in the colonial expansion of England that made English an international language. The first English settlers, however, were by no means the first Europeans to set up colonies. South America was the first to be 'discovered' by Europe – by the Portuguese and Spanish – in the late fifteenth century. This is a useful reminder that other European languages often came into contact with English in the colonies and influenced its development. The much later colonisation of Australia in many ways followed a pattern similar to that in North America. In both cases, large-scale immigration of English speakers and other Europeans displaced existing populations.

English in North America: an example of displacement

Although Newfoundland was discovered and had a small settlement earlier, in 1607 an expedition established the colony of Jamestown in Virginia. A group who became known as the 'Pilgrim Fathers' were among those who followed, landing from the 'Mayflower' to settle in Plymouth, Massachusetts, in 1620. Their colony was perhaps the most successful at attracting settlers: within twenty years a further 25,000 Europeans had migrated to the area.

The Pilgrims, like many of the early English settlers, sought religious freedom (one effect of the Reformation was the persecution of Puritans as well as Catholics). Pennsylvania, further south, was settled originally by a Quaker colony, but attracted English and Welsh settlers of various religious denominations too. In each direction, there were colonists from other European states: French to the north and north-west, and Dutch to the west.

The pattern of colonisation in the southern areas differed slightly from that of the North. Huge plantations and estates developed in the South – in contrast to the northern smallholdings – growing rice at first and later cotton. These colonies were settled by a high proportion of people from the south and west of England (many of them deportees and political refugees). Labour for the plantation was supplied by slaves who were transported from Africa. By 1724, slaves in South Carolina outnumbered free people by three to one. These estates formed the nucleus of what has come to be known as the American South.

The complex relationship between North American settlement and the slave trade is illustrated in Figure 3.4, which shows some of the main West African languages which were to influence the new forms of English that came to be spoken by slaves in North America and the Caribbean.

Any linguist examining the early period of settlement in North America is faced with two main questions. First, how and when did American English become differentiated from British English and recognised as an independent variety (i.e. at what point did exonormative stabilisation take place)? Second, how did internal dialect differences in American English arise?

The variety of English which was implanted in North America was that of the Early Modern period. It has sometimes been claimed that many of the differences between American and British English can be explained in terms of a 'colonial lag': the language of colonial settlers is more 'conservative' than that of the country they left. Thus, some features of American English, such as the widespread pronunciation of /r/ in words like 'cart' and 'far' (known technically as 'non-prevocalic /r/') might be attributed to the fact that /r/ in such words was generally pronounced in Elizabethan English. Although the speech of Londoners later became /r/-less, this was too late to influence the speech of those who had already left.

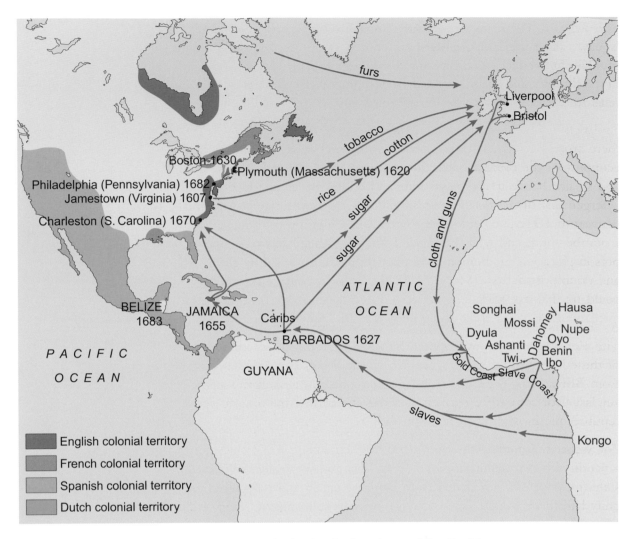

Figure 3.4   The Atlantic slave trade and colonisation in America and the Caribbean

The problem with this explanation is that in some areas on the east coast – the oldest settlements among them – there has long been an /r/-less tendency. This area seems to have maintained close cultural and trade links with England and the British model of speech remained a powerful model of social correctness. Other, more inland communities seem not to have maintained such close ties with England. Hence this feature, at least, of modern dialect variation is better explained by different patterns of contact with England after the first settlement.

It might be supposed that in North America some dialect variation arose from contact with different indigenous languages. The influence of precolonial languages on American English, however, has been relatively slight. What influence there was, was mostly in terms of lexical borrowings such as 'moose', 'racoon', 'persimmon', 'tomahawk' and 'squaw', all of which appeared in the early 1600s (Finegan, 2006, pp. 284–5). Several place names, such as Alabama, Manhattan, Massachusetts and Mississippi, are also derived from Native American ones (p. 390).

As English settlements in North America became more established, there arose a tendency towards internal differentiation. The different economy of the southern area, for example, gradually pulled its culture and speech habits in a different direction from that of the North. So emerged one of the major modern dialect boundaries of the USA: that between northern and southern speech. Southern American English has a number of distinctive features, such as the use of *y'all* for the second-person plural pronoun (where standard American English uses 'you'), and double modals such as *might could* as in the sentence 'he might could fix that car right up for you, if you asked him kindly'.

As these local economies developed, and conflicts of economic interest with England grew, the colonists themselves became increasingly aware of these linguistic differences. Once the colonies gained independence from Britain in 1783, the issue of a distinct linguistic identity became a key issue for some of those active in the process of founding the new republic, the most notable figure in this respect being Noah Webster.

For Webster, America in 1783 was no longer a colony but it was not yet a nation. A written constitution defined it politically as a republican state (more precisely, a federation of individual states), but national unity had to be worked for, and a crucial arena for this was language. Even if American speech was diverse, linguistic uniformity could follow from the achievement of a distinctive visual identity through spelling, which in turn could influence speech over the generations. And it was these beliefs about language which Webster attempted to embed within the local culture by means of the creation of his *American Dictionary*.

Activity 3.2

Why do you think that the production of a dictionary can be a useful tool in the promotion – and possibly even the construction – of an independent cultural identity?

Allow about 10 minutes

Comment

Producing a dictionary can be an influential way of validating the distinctive linguistic practices of a community, and promoting the bond between a language and a particular cultural or political identity. As we saw in Chapter 2 with the case of Dr Johnson's work, a dictionary of the national language is often used to symbolise the distinct cultural identity of a community, and thus has a political as well as a linguistic rationale. (See below for examples of such national dictionary projects.)

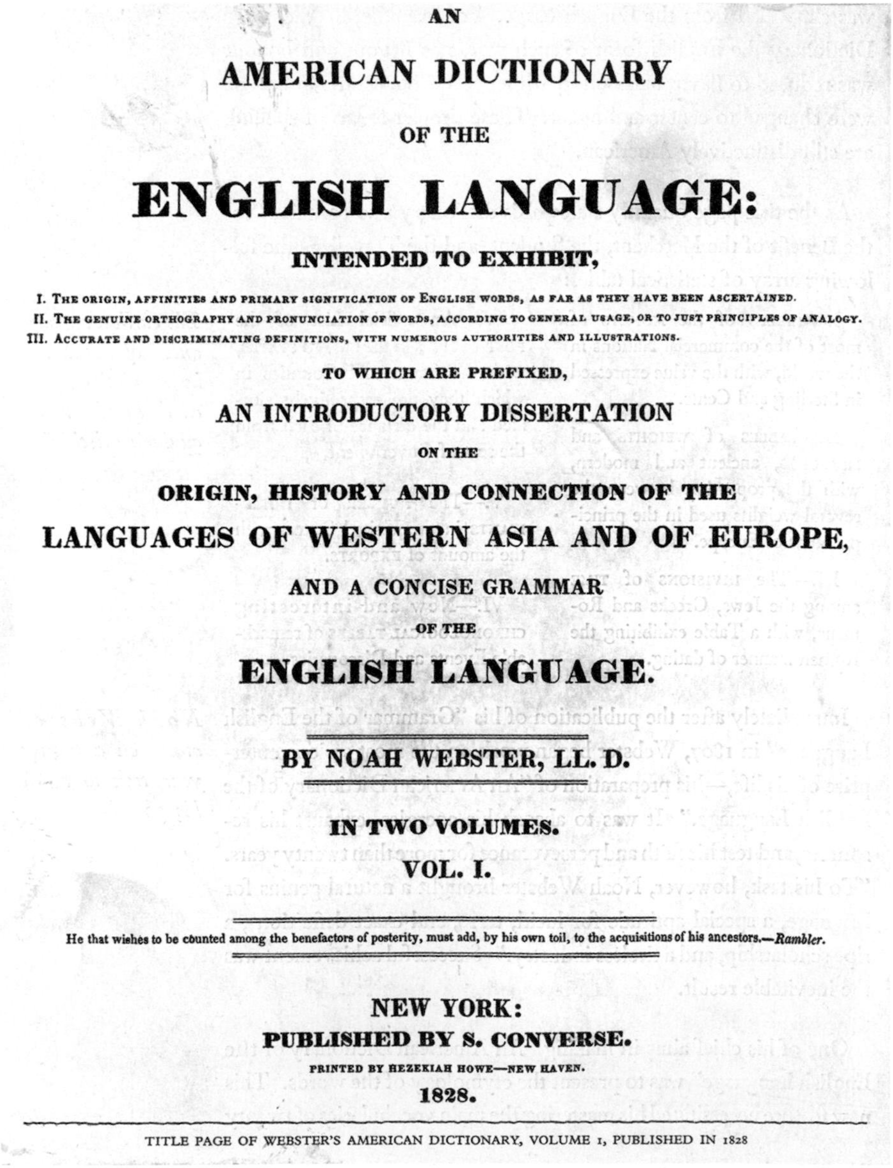

AN

AMERICAN DICTIONARY

OF THE

ENGLISH LANGUAGE:

INTENDED TO EXHIBIT,

I. THE ORIGIN, AFFINITIES AND PRIMARY SIGNIFICATION OF ENGLISH WORDS, AS FAR AS THEY HAVE BEEN ASCERTAINED.
II. THE GENUINE ORTHOGRAPHY AND PRONUNCIATION OF WORDS, ACCORDING TO GENERAL USAGE, OR TO JUST PRINCIPLES OF ANALOGY.
III. ACCURATE AND DISCRIMINATING DEFINITIONS, WITH NUMEROUS AUTHORITIES AND ILLUSTRATIONS.

TO WHICH ARE PREFIXED,

AN INTRODUCTORY DISSERTATION

ON THE

ORIGIN, HISTORY AND CONNECTION OF THE

LANGUAGES OF WESTERN ASIA AND OF EUROPE,

AND A CONCISE GRAMMAR

OF THE

ENGLISH LANGUAGE.

BY NOAH WEBSTER, LL. D.

IN TWO VOLUMES.

VOL. I.

He that wishes to be counted among the benefactors of posterity, must add, by his own toil, to the acquisitions of his ancestors.—*Rambler.*

NEW YORK:
PUBLISHED BY S. CONVERSE.
PRINTED BY HEZEKIAH HOWE—NEW HAVEN.
1828.

TITLE PAGE OF WEBSTER'S AMERICAN DICTIONARY, VOLUME 1, PUBLISHED IN 1828

Figure 3.5   Title page of Webster's *An American Dictionary of the English Language*

National dictionary projects

The dictionary produced by Noah Webster (1758–1843) in the years after American independence is a prime example of the promotion of a distinct cultural identity for political means. One of Webster's ambitions was to give his newly independent nation a language of its own. In the early stages of its development, Webster was planning to call his project a *Dictionary of the American Language*, and he wrote of American and English as being distinct languages (Finegan, 2006, p. 392). By the time he came to publish in 1828, however, he had settled on the less radical title of *An American Dictionary of the English Language*. Yet a key aim of his was still to use the dictionary as a means of distinguishing between the English that was used in Britain and that used in America. He did this primarily through attempts to reform the spelling system so that American English *looked* markedly different from British English.

Webster's motivations were expressly political, and based on his belief that 'a *national language* is a band of *national union*' (Webster, 1991 [1789], p. 87). He argued that the existence of a distinct language was an important attribute for a truly independent state:

> Let us then seize the present moment, and establish a *national language* as well as a national government. Let us remember that there is a certain respect due to the opinions of other nations. As an independent people, our reputation abroad demands that, in all things, we should be federal; be *national*.
>
> (Webster, 1991 [1789], p. 93)

One can find similar arguments in several subsequent 'national dictionary projects' including those of the recent past. In the second half of the twentieth century, as English began to cement its position as a truly global language, a number of dictionaries for the New Englishes were published, and all articulated cultural and political independence as part of their rationale. For example, the Australian *Macquarie Dictionary*, which first appeared in the early 1980s, sees itself as playing a key role in the process of nation building:

> the *Macquarie Dictionary*, the first comprehensive dictionary of Australian English, is one of the essential parts of Australian nationhood. When new nations were being formed in Europe in the nineteenth century, the preparation of dictionaries was one

of the basic parts of nation-building. We were a long time getting a dictionary like this. We should be proud of its service to the people of Australia.

(Horne, 1997, p. x)

The Canadian national dictionary project has a similar intention:

The *Canadian Oxford Dictionary* belongs to the age of the global village, but with a wholesome Canadian bias. This dictionary has dozens of mundane uses – clarifying meanings, settling spellings, suggesting pronunciations, providing synonyms, and all the rest – but the sum of all these uses is much greater than the parts. In the living language there is a reflection of where we have been and where we are likely to go next, and what we have considered important on the way. It is the codification of our common understanding.

(Chambers, 1999, p. x)

Whereas Webster's objective was to *establish* a national language, mainly by modifying the orthography of standard British English, these later national dictionary projects attempt instead to catalogue linguistic features that they feel are distinctive of their own national cultures. For example, the *Dictionary of Bahamian English* (Holm, 1982, p. iii) highlights the fact that 'This dictionary ... contains over 5,000 entries for words and expressions used in the Bahamas which are not generally found in the current standard English of Britain or North America'. And the *Australian National Dictionary* contends that 'In the simplest analysis Australian English, the English used by Australians, differs from that used elsewhere in the ways and the extent that the circumstances of life in this country and the history of its people have been distinctive' (Ramson, 1988, p. vii).

The nationalist ideal of linguistic uniformity in American English has not, however, been completely achieved. One reason is that the processes of internal differentiation mentioned above have not diminished. The economic and cultural division between North and South led to the Civil War of the 1860s, which ended with the North victorious. In part, the war was a confrontation between the forces of political centralisation, represented by the North, and those of regional autonomy. Ever since, the South has often been represented as a bastion of older, agricultural, hierarchical values outside those of mainstream America, and its dialect has also been vigorously defended as an intrinsic aspect of its distinct cultural identity.

Another source of differentiation is the sheer diversity in the American population since the late eighteenth century. By the mid-nineteenth century, settlers had advanced as far west as the Mississippi, their numbers swelled by thousands of land-hungry Scots Irish from Ulster. By the end of that century the West too had been settled, partly by millions of immigrants from various parts of Europe. A levelled form of pronunciation, which is sometimes referred to as 'general American', is associated with these states (although in practice there is a great deal of pronunciation diversity across this area). Theoretically, the newcomers were to form what is often called the 'melting pot' of American society, in which ethnic origin is subsumed by a common American citizenship; in practice, however, new composite identities such as 'Irish American' and 'Italian American' have been created, and European cultural practices maintained. Influences from other sources have produced further diversity in terms of other varieties, such as that spoken by Spanish-speaking immigrants from Mexico, which is known as 'Chicano English' (Fought, 2003), or African-American English (AAE), which shares many features with the American South, but also with many creoles (Finegan, 2006). The latter association has often been stressed by African-Americans themselves, as a means of claiming a separate, 'African' identity through language, an issue discussed in the next section.

English in West Africa: an example of subjection

At the beginning of the chapter we identified three types of English colony. America represented the first group: the wholesale immigration of native-speaking English settlers who displaced the local, precolonial population. We now move to an example of the second type, where sparser colonial settlements maintained the precolonial population in subjection.

Sierra Leone, where the first European slaving expedition occurred in the sixteenth century, was settled by escaped and (after 1807) freed slaves. A little later, Liberia was established by the USA for ex-slaves. The significance of these ventures was the association of slaves with an African 'homeland', an association based on the notion of 'descent' from African tribes. One eventual outcome of this development was the sense of common cause between black people in both America and

Africa. This commonality was aided in the British colonies by the existence of a shared language, English.

New British colonies were established in Africa after 1880. Between that date and the end of the century virtually the entire continent was seized and shared out among the European powers. In West Africa, however, there was no substantial settlement by people from the British Isles. Instead, the new colonies were administered by a small number of British officials. The population remained overwhelmingly African, with a select number receiving education in English from missionaries, and a larger number using English-based pidgins (see box) in addition to the languages they already spoke.

Pidgins and creoles

Pidgins are new languages which initially come into being through a particular type of language contact which occurs between speakers who need to develop a sustained means of communication (often for trading purposes) but do not share a common language. They are closely associated with creoles. The traditionally observed distinction is that pidgins are languages without native speakers – that is, they are learnt later in life by people who already have a first language. As a pidgin is then passed on to the children of a community, and used by them as a first language, it becomes a creole.

Pidgins typically have a small vocabulary and little grammatical complexity, and often depend heavily on context for understanding. Much of their vocabulary is taken from a specific language (e.g. English, French, etc.), and this is known as the **lexifier**. The process by which a pidgin becomes a creole is referred to as **creolisation**, and there is a certain amount of controversy about how exactly this takes place. Some pidgins change into creoles by means of a process whereby the language becomes a mainstay of everyday communication in the community, and children are thus brought up speaking it as their first language (Sebba, 2009). However, some scholars, such as Salikoko Mufwene, argue that the distinction is actually that 'creoles and pidgins developed in separate places, in which Europeans and non-Europeans interacted differently – sporadically in trade colonies [which gave rise to pidgins] but regularly in the initial stages of settlement colonies [which gave rise to creoles]' (Mufwene, 2006, p. 315).

Furthermore, although the two terms suggest two separate phenomena, the distinction between a pidgin and a creole is not always clear-cut. For example, Bislama is often referred to as a pidgin, although it is an official language of Vanuatu (an island in the South Pacific Ocean) and seems to be creolised in urban areas. The term **expanded pidgin** is therefore sometimes applied to a variety which is used in various different domains (e.g. for education and administration), has some native speakers, but is not considered to have quite the status of a creole. For example, West African Pidgin English is a generic name for a number of varieties which 'are spoken, sometimes as a pidgin and sometimes as a creole (i.e. as a first language), in Nigeria, Ghana, Gambia, Cameroon and some other costal countries of West Africa' (Sebba, 2009, p. 390).

Figure 3.6 shows some of the world's English-based pidgins and creoles.

During the nineteenth century, Britain came to see the role of colonies, such as those in Africa, as that of producing raw materials, while Britain remained the source of manufacturing. The precolonial populations were not given any rights as far as the vote and compulsory education were concerned, despite the fact that these had been granted to the working class in Britain. These economic and political arrangements were justified by appealing to contemporary theories of racial difference. The precolonial populations were considered to be at a lower stage of cultural and intellectual development than white Europeans. Colonial service could therefore be conceived as a duty and as a way of demonstrating 'manliness', a key aspect of nineteenth-century Englishness.

The system described above is often referred to by the word **colonialism**. First used in the nineteenth century, it reflects changes in the relationship between Britain and its colonies as they were incorporated into what was called the British Empire. The term is more loaded than 'colonisation', partly because it has been used most frequently by those who were opposed to it, on the grounds that it amounted to exploitation of the weak by the powerful. In one respect, it names the process from the point of view of the less powerful, and has often been used pejoratively.

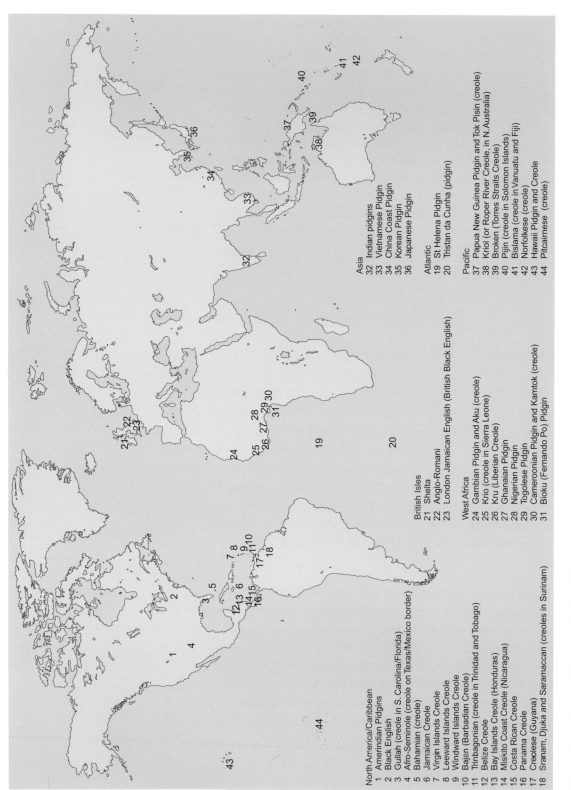

Figure 3.6 Some of the world's English-based pidgins and creoles

North America/Caribbean
1 Amerindian Pidgins
2 Black English
3 Gullah (creole in S. Carolina/Florida)
4 Afro-Seminole (creole on Texas/Mexico border)
5 Bahamian (creole)
6 Jamaican Creole
7 Virgin Islands Creole
8 Leeward Islands Creole
9 Windward Islands Creole
10 Bajan (Barbadian Creole)
11 Trinbagonian (creole in Trinidad and Tobago)
12 Belize Creole
13 Bay Islands Creole (Honduras)
14 Miskito Coast Creole (Nicaragua)
15 Costa Rican Creole
16 Panama Creole
17 Creolese (Guyana)
18 Sranam, Djuka and Saramaccan (creoles in Surinam)

British Isles
21 Shelta
22 Anglo-Romani
23 London Jamaican English (British Black English)

West Africa
24 Gambian Pidgin and Aku (creole)
25 Krio (creole in Sierra Leone)
26 Kru (Liberian Creole)
27 Ghanaian Pidgin
28 Nigerian Pidgin
29 Togolese Pidgin
30 Cameroonian Pidgin and Kamtok (creole)
31 Bioku (Fernando Po) Pidgin

Asia
32 Indian pidgins
33 Vietnamese Pidgin
34 China Coast Pidgin
35 Korean Pidgin
36 Japanese Pidgin

Atlantic
19 St Helena Pidgin
20 Tristan da Cunha (pidgin)

Pacific
37 Papua New Guinea Pidgin and Tok Pisin (creole)
38 Kriol (or Roper River Creole, in N. Australia)
39 Broken (Torres Straits Creole)
40 Pijin (creole in Solomon Islands)
41 Bislama (creole in Vanuatu and Fiji)
42 Norfolkese (creole)
43 Hawaii Pidgin and Creole
44 Pitcairnese (creole)

According to the African linguist Ali Mazrui, British colonialism, with its emphasis on the difference between the subject black population and its white rulers, set the tone for colonialism in Africa in general (Mazrui, 1973). And according to Mazrui, it was in the British colonies that Africans led the struggle for independence. This was partly because they felt a solidarity with the black ex-slaves in the USA, involved in their own struggles for full citizenship. A movement known as pan-Negroism emerged, based on what was seen as a shared ethnic identity. This gave way to pan-Africanism, an anti-colonial struggle for blacks in Africa alone. Mazrui argues that the language of both of these movements was English, and that this may have led Africans in French colonies to feel somewhat excluded from them.

Why was it that English was so bound up with the anti-colonial struggle? For Mazrui, the fact that the African elite could enjoy higher education in (English-speaking) North America as well as Britain meant that their attitudes were partly shaped by the issue of black emancipation there. But he also discusses the possibility that, in the French colonies, Africans – at least in theory – were considered citizens of France itself. Accordingly, many of them viewed the French language with affection. In the British colonies, on the other hand, attitudes to English seem to have been more pragmatic (as perhaps was also the case in nineteenth-century Ireland).

But there are other ways in which the movement for African independence and the English language have been linked. These have to do with supposed properties of the language itself. Edward Blyden, who was born in 1832 in the Caribbean and later became a professor of languages in Liberia, argued that English was best suited to unify Africans because it 'is a composite language, not the product of any one people. It is made up of contributions by Celts, Danes, Normans, Saxons, Greeks, and Romans, gathering to itself elements … from the Ganges to the Atlantic' (Blyden, 1888, quoted in Mazrui, 1973, p. 62). In other words, it is the perceived impurity and hybridity of English that makes it so useful. (It is worth noting however that, from a linguistic point of view, all languages are influenced by the contact their speakers have had throughout history with speakers of other languages, and so all languages are 'hybrid' to some extent or another.)

Another line of reasoning relates to the way that the diversity of African society, symbolised by the huge numbers of different languages spoken, is seen as a problem for the cause of independence. Observers have often explained this diversity as produced by 'tribalism'. For promoters of independence, this tribalism needs to be replaced by a different, European concept: that of nationalism, which involves a state with fixed territorial boundaries that represents the interests of, and has legitimate control over, its people. In this view, learning English helps Africans to recreate their identities as members of nations rather than tribes. It has sometimes been claimed that British colonialism has helped Africans to 'modernise' themselves by introducing them to the English language and, in so doing, to a new culture with concepts such as 'freedom' and 'national identity'.

This view raises a number of problems. For example, it claims that a particular language encodes particular ways of thinking. Many Africans have themselves expressed it, often in debates about the role of English in postcolonial society. Many writers of literature have argued that English is an inadequate medium for the expression of an authentically 'African' experience. Others, however, have argued that the postcolonial African identity is a hybrid one, and that an African exposed to the English language and to concepts derived from European experience is no less 'African' than any other. It is therefore the task of the writer to create a kind of English capable of expressing the 'authenticity' of Africa. So whereas an author such as Ngũgĩ wa Thiong'o rejects English outright because of its associations with a harsh colonial regime (as expressed in the reading in Chapter 1), others, such as Chinua Achebe and Amos Tutuola, cultivate and promote what could be described as a distinctive African English (Taiwo, 1976).

Activity 3.3

Now turn to Reading A, which is an extract from Edgar Schneider's book on 'postcolonial Englishes', and which examines the history of English in the West African country of Cameroon. Schneider outlines the various phases of development that English has gone through in Cameroon, in both colonial and postcolonial times, and considers how the country's colonial history has contributed to the current linguistic profile of the area. The linguistic situation in Cameroon is complicated by the fact that its history includes episodes of colonisation by a number of European countries, which has led to divided loyalties between different colonial languages. Another aspect of the language situation in the country is the use of West African Pidgin English, which we touched on briefly above.

While reading the extract, think about the following questions:

- How have the politics of the region shaped the language practices of the population?
- In what way does English have a 'symbolic' value for parts of the population?
- How is the English that is spoken in Cameroon itself diverse and varied?

Comment

The website *Ethnologue*, which logs statistics of languages around the world, records that there are currently 268 languages spoken throughout Cameroon, by far the overwhelming majority of which are indigenous African languages. Yet the official languages of the country are English and French, both of which are a legacy of the colonial history of the area. The **language ecology** of the country – that is to say, the way that different languages co-exist within society and the relationships they have with each other – is thus primarily structured around these two languages, with a sharp demarcation existing between the Anglophone and Francophone portions of the population. As Schneider notes, this results in a rather unusual situation for postcolonial countries, whereby many people's cultural identity is a product of their affiliations to one or other of the two colonial languages, rather than to 'traditional ethnic alignments'. And for this reason, English is a symbol of group identity for the Anglophone section of society, and attitudes towards the language in this sector are predominantly very positive.

Another aspect of the language ecology of the country is the relationship between (West African) Pidgin and standard English. While standard English is the variety taught in schools and used in administrative contexts, Pidgin is widely used in colloquial contexts. So different varieties of English exist within Cameroon (Wolf talks of a continuum of varieties existing between Pidgin and standard English), and these are used for different purposes and different contexts. Furthermore, for communities of urban youths, a mixed variety called 'Camfranglais' that includes elements from English, French, Pidgin and indigenous languages is developing. Thus, the language profile of Cameroon has been greatly influenced by a history of colonisation, but the result is not simply the imposition of the language of the colonisers on the colonised population, but of a more complex and disputed interplay of differing influences and affiliations.

English in Jamaica: an example of replacement

Let us now return to the role of the slave trade which brought Africans to America and elsewhere to supply cheap labour for the developing colonies. The long-term effect of the slave trade on the development of the English language is immense. It gave rise not only to Black English in the USA and the Caribbean, which has been an important influence on the speech of young English speakers worldwide, but also provided the extraordinary context of language contact which led to the formation of English pidgins and creoles. This language contact resulted from the third type of English colony identified above: where a precolonial population is replaced by new labour from elsewhere, principally West Africa.

The origins of the slave trade belong to the earliest stages of colonial activity. In 1562 an Elizabethan Englishman called Sir John Hawkins sailed with three ships and 100 men to the coast of West Africa and captured 300 Africans 'partly by the sworde, and partly by other meanes' (in the words of a contemporary account). He sold them in the Caribbean, filled his ships with local hides, ginger, sugar and pearls, and returned to England 'with prosperous successe and much gaine to himself and the aforesayed adventurers [London merchants]'. This venture marked the beginnings of the British slave trade (Walvin, 1993, p. 25). The Africans Hawkins took were from the area that is known today as Sierra Leone. It is possible that they had already had contact with the Portuguese, who had been trading in the area for about a century (Le Page and Tabouret-Keller, 1985, p. 23). We don't know what languages they spoke, or even whether they had any language in common (in Sierra Leone today twenty-five named languages are spoken, according to *Ethnologue*), but it is possible that they had some knowledge of a pidgin that was used between Africans and the Portuguese for the purposes of trade.

One trade controlled by the Portuguese was the shipment of slaves from Africa to the islands of the Caribbean colonised by the Spanish. They used their pidgin in dealing with African middle-men, who traded slaves (captured from other tribes) in return for other goods. In selling his slaves to the Spanish colonists of Hispaniola (later Haiti), Hawkins was taking trade from the Portuguese; but it seems that the Portuguese-based pidgin was used widely enough to survive the successful attempts by both the English and the Dutch to capture the slave trade (Le Page and Tabouret-Keller, 1985, pp. 29–30).

It is possible that on Hispaniola, Hawkins's slaves substituted Spanish words for the Portuguese ones in their pidgin, and thus created a Spanish-based pidgin. Or perhaps they were resold, as often happened, to another set of colonists in a different Caribbean territory. Lack of evidence makes it very difficult to keep track of every shipment of slaves. What we do have, from such contemporary accounts as Ligon's *A True and Exact History of the Island of Barbados* (1647), is a description of slaving practice and estimates of numbers in one of the earliest of the British colonies in the Caribbean, Barbados. According to Ligon, shipments of slaves were 'fetch'd from several parts of Africa, who speak severall languages, and by that means, one of them understands not another' (Ligon, 1647, p. 46).

Perhaps it is this statement that has encouraged linguists to take the view that the 'policy of the slave traders was to bring people of different language backgrounds together in the ships, to make it difficult to plot rebellion' (Crystal, 1988, p. 235). If this view is accepted then pidgin would have been the only form of communication available to slaves on the new plantations, and over the generations the African languages they spoke would have been abandoned. But since pidgin had only been used for very simple kinds of interaction, its vocabulary and grammar would have been limited. So it would have needed extending and adapting. As was explained in the box above, this process of extension and adaptation – whereby a pidgin develops into a fully functioning language – is called creolisation.

Creolisation happened in many parts of the English-speaking Caribbean, including Jamaica. This island was captured from the Spanish in 1655, rapidly turned over to sugar production, and settled by English speakers from Barbados and other Caribbean islands such as St Kitts and Nevis (settled in the 1620s), and by convicts from Britain. By 1673 these seem to have been matched in number by African slaves, but by 1746 the latter outnumbered the former by over ten to one, and the owners of the plantations (which were often very large) lived in perpetual fear of slave revolt. Even if the slaves were kept separate linguistically, this did not prevent them from rebelling, despite the severest punishments.

In what language did the slaves plot their revolts? Did they develop their creoles to create meanings unavailable to the slave owners? Or did they retain their African languages? It is noteworthy that if they did abandon the latter, they did so while still retaining their culture of religious, medical and artistic practices. They also often hung on to their names, despite the fact that they were renamed by the planters as a mark of ownership (Walvin, 1993, p. 63). On the other hand, Wolof, an African language spoken today in Senegal and Gambia, is said to have been quite widely spoken in the slave-owning southern states of America during the eighteenth century (McCrum et al., 1992, p. 226), where conditions seem to have been much less conducive to its retention than in Jamaica. This is because in America, plantations were generally smaller than in Jamaica, slaves were often resold or moved from one plantation to another and, above all, owners soon preferred to produce new slaves from within the existing slave community, rather than continue to import them from Africa (so contact with African languages from freshly imported slaves would have been lost).

Whether or not the African languages were abandoned, it seems that their influence can be traced in creoles. Words such as *adru* (a medicinal herb) from Twi, *himba* (an edible wild yam) from Ibo, and *dingki* (a funeral ceremony) from Kongo have all been found in Jamaican Creole.

Allow about 5–10 minutes

Activity 3.4

Reread the last sentence in the paragraph above. In the light of the discussion of slave culture and language, do you think there is anything especially significant about the meanings of these Africanisms and their use in Jamaica? Now look back at Figure 3.4 to find out where Kongo, Twi and Ibo are spoken. What does this suggest about the source of slaves?

Comment

The Africanisms refer to knowledge and practices the slaves brought with them to Jamaica. They also show the vast 'catchment area' for the slave trade. The English at first preferred slaves from the Gold Coast (now Ghana), but by the second half of the eighteenth century most of the slaves came from further east and as far south as Angola. When it is known that *Ethnologue* lists seventy-nine languages spoken in Ghana today, it is possible to infer that the slave traders hardly needed to ensure that slaves speaking the same language were kept separate.

Jamaican Creole also has words from Portuguese (*pikni*, 'a small child'), Spanish (*bobo*, 'a fool'), French (*leginz*, 'a bunch of vegetables for a stew'), Hindi (*roti*, 'a kind of bread'), Chinese (*ho senny ho*, 'how's business?') and even Arawak, the language of the precolonial population which had been mostly destroyed by the time English was first spoken in Jamaica (*hicatee*, 'a land turtle', adopted via Spanish).

Estimates suggest that around 94 per cent of the Jamaican population are Creole-dominant bilinguals, and that only around half the monolingual Creole speakers have a knowledge of English (Holm, 2000, p. 94). Since the nineteenth century, formal education, officially based on the teaching of standard English, has been available in Jamaica. But, as in the case of Ireland, access to the prescribed linguistic model, especially in relation to speech, has been limited. New varieties of Jamaican speech that can be described as more standardised, however, have evolved alongside Jamaican Creole. This is the process that some linguists call decreolisation. Individual Jamaicans are said to move along a continuum with creole at one end and more standardised English at the other. And as in many other parts of the Caribbean, use of creole is firmly linked to a sense of local identity.

3.6   Language education policies and colonialist agendas

In the final section of this chapter let us consider the role English – and specifically the teaching of English – played in the politics and policies of colonisation. As was noted above, in the context of the slave trade it has been suggested that the lack of a common language among the colonised population was exploited by the colonisers as a means of political control. Depending on the context, though, the introduction of English into the colony could serve a number of different functions, and English language education and the decision colonisers took with respect to how and when the language should be taught, has thus been a very important part of the history of colonisation.

Activity 3.5

Now turn to Reading B: *ELT and colonialism* by Alastair Pennycook, which examines the role played by English language teaching (ELT) in colonisation processes in various contexts, and also discusses the mutual influence that ELT and the colonial period had on each other. While reading, consider the following questions:

- What arguments have been given for and against the teaching of English to the local population in colonial contexts?
- How can the colonial period be said to have influenced current English language teaching practices?

Comment

Pennycook suggests that in many colonies the desire to mould a compliant and docile population was best served by education in local languages, with English being reserved for the instruction of a small elite who would mostly fulfil key administrative roles for the governing of the colony. English was not seen as something for the masses – and indeed, in many quarters it was considered dangerous for the population at large to have access to it. At the same time, however, English was promoted in colonial language policies as a 'superior language', and one which embodied the civilised values of the colonising power.

But the influence of the colonial period on English language practices did not flow in only one direction. Pennycook goes on to suggest that the discipline of ELT as it is practised today owes a great deal to the developments that occurred in colonial contexts. In other words, just as the English that is spoken in former colonies had and continues to have a profound influence on that spoken in the UK today (an issue we will return to in Chapter 5), so the language teaching practices that were developed in colonial times have also had an important influence on the practice and theories of the English language teaching industry.

3.7   Conclusion

In this chapter we have examined the spread of English from England, first to other parts of the British Isles and then to other areas of the world. The processes of colonisation, political incorporation and nationalist reaction suggest that these take different forms in different contexts and have different linguistic consequences. The varieties of English in all the case studies we have looked at have been shaped by contact: contact with other languages, other cultures and different political scenarios; as well as contact between different varieties of English used by settlers. And within the broad context of English as it exists in the world today, the ways it developed beyond England in the colonial period have had great import for its rise to its current global position, and for the diversity that it now exhibits. Ishtla Singh (2005) traces one motivating aspect for the diversity of English worldwide to an interesting paradox about language usage that dates from the beginning of the colonial period:

> What is particularly interesting in the context of [the change that English began to undergo in the Early Modern period] is the fact

that as norms and ideologies of 'correctness' in language use were explicitly beginning to take shape and to be perceived as important in the evolution of an intellectually progressive and increasingly powerful nation [i.e. Britain], the non-standard everyday use of socially ordinary English speakers was taking root in the colonies; and indeed, laying the foundations for the new directions of change the language would follow.

(Singh, 2005, pp. 172–3)

In other words, the diversity in the language around the world is in part a result of the various patterns of contact with other languages and cultures, but is also a product of the linguistic diversity that existed across the British Isles and was exported abroad by those embarking on colonial expansion. While the idea of the 'standard' was being enforced *in* England (as was outlined in Chapter 2), the native diversity of English was spreading around the globe.

As illustrated in Reading B, the worldwide spread of English has often been told as a progressive, even triumphalist story, reflecting the glory and international superiority of England and Englishness. But it is possible to regard the global success of English as the result of centuries of exploitation and oppression. For many users of English today, the story might feel more like one of imposition. Before the end of the twentieth century, however, it was also possible to see English as having become a genuinely 'world' language, transcending differences of culture, race and belief. And it is this stage in the story of English which we turn to in the next chapter, when we look at the emergence of English as a global language.

READING A: Cameroon

Edgar W. Schneider

Source: Schneider, E. W. (2007) *Postcolonial English: Varieties around the World*, Cambridge, Cambridge University Press, pp. 212–18.

Due to their geographical proximity and partially shared history […] the evolution of English in Cameroon is somewhat similar to the Nigerian process. While Nigeria was exclusively British in her colonial days, however, substantial differences in Cameroon can be explained by the country's earlier colonization by the Germans and the colonization of the southern and eastern (greater) parts of its territory by the French after World War I. It is especially marked by the heritage of the latter, resulting in the predominance of French on the national level and a much less prominent role of English and Pidgin in the country […]

Cameroon as a polity goes back no further than 1884. Before that date, the region shared coastal trade contacts and, beginning in 1844 in Bimbia near Douala, missionary activities with other West African coastal regions. At that time, the British practically controlled the coast of present-day Cameroon. However, they refrained from getting involved more deeply, and by the time they decided to accept formal authority in the region the Germans had forestalled them and signed a contract with the indigenous kings Bell and Akwa. Hence, from 1884 to 1919 Cameroon was a German protectorate. The Germans established plantations near the coast and gradually penetrated into the hinterlands. They were mainly interested in commercial exploitation, not in any kind of serious colonization; the number of administrators they sent remained small.

While there is no reason to assume that the original identities of the persons involved in early contacts were substantially modified, a basically positive attitude on the side of the indigenous populations toward the British may be deduced from the fact that in 1879 and 1881 the local kings explicitly sent petitions to the Queen requesting formal annexation, asking for 'English laws in our towns' and 'an English Government here' (quoted from Schmied 1991: 10–1; see Todd 1982: 6; Chumbow and Simo Bobda 1996: 403).

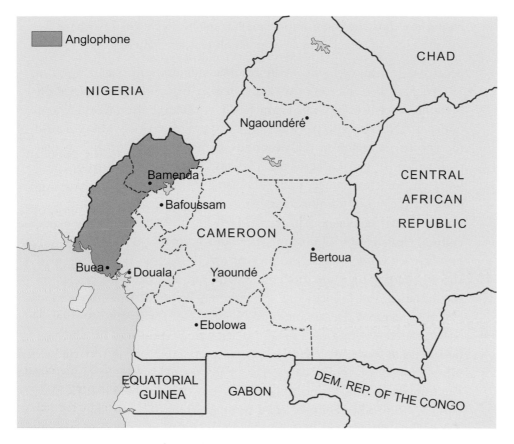

Figure 1   Map of Cameroon

As elsewhere in the region, by the late nineteenth century Pidgin English and English had been firmly established. Trading activities and missionary schools brought early bilingualism involving Pidgin and English, respectively. While some of the missionaries attempted to study and employ indigenous languages, in practice they mostly used Pidgin, which turned out to be most effective, and taught standard English. There was also a small number of English-medium schools, 'highly regarded by Cameroonians' (Todd 1982: 9). The Germans discouraged formal education in English but did nothing to impose their own language. In fact, they found Pidgin English useful themselves for evangelization and administration, so in reality the Pidgin and also English continued to thrive and spread during those years. In particular, the plantations which they established fermented further uses of Pidgin as a lingua franca among a multiethnic workforce, and these workers then took the language into the hinterlands when they returned home. As is typical of a trade colony, pidginization and the spread of the

pidgin are thus the most important linguistic effects of this phase
[of the cycle of development of postcolonial Englishes] [...]

[P]hase 2 [of the cycle, i.e. exonormative stabilisation] began when in
1919 a part of Cameroon was mandated to Britain by the League of
Nations, a relationship which practically continued after World War II
under a UN Trusteeship. However, this pertains to only about a fifth of
the country, a region in the west and northwest, adjacent to Nigeria,
then called 'British Cameroons.' The vast majority of the region,
however, went to France, under the same terms. Both colonial powers
installed their own administrative structures and institutions and
imposed their language, a process which institutionalized a linguistic and
cultural cleavage into 'Francophones' and 'Anglophones' which strongly
preoccupies Cameroon to the present day. While the French installed a
strictly centralized, Paris-oriented system and ultimately succeeded in
acculturating and Frenchifying the country, British Cameroons was
essentially treated like an annex to Nigeria, from where it was
administered – it had no capital, no separate administration, and no
budget of its own (Wolf 2001: 100). The principle of indirect rule relied
more strongly on traditional power structures in society. State-supported
English education was institutionalized, but only in the elitist form
familiar from other colonies. The prestige which English enjoyed,
indicating attitudes and identities in the [indigenous speech community]
strand, can be deduced from the fact that many pupils changed from
Basel missions, supportive of vernacular education, to other mission
stations where English was taught (Wolf 2001: 89) [...]

In theory, the British only wished to encourage vernacular primary
education and institutionalized English as a medium of instruction from
standard 5 onwards. In practice, however, this policy was frequently
undermined by the lack of qualified teachers and by the local demand
for the acquisition of English which led to the adoption of English as
the medium of education from the first grade of primary school starting
in the 1950s (Todd 1982: 10). Secondary education, first offered in
Nigeria only, was established gradually, and the quality of English was
regarded as high (1982: 11), with an exonormative orientation (Schmied
1991: 11). This has to be qualified, however, given that school
enrollment was generally low and secondary education was accessible to
only a tiny minority of the population. But basically during that phase
'English became the language of education and administration'
(Chumbow and Simo Bobda 1996: 405), and the number of English
schools rose (405–6).

The spread of the Pidgin continued vividly, promoted by the prestige accorded to English, with a clear division of labor between the two: English for scholastic and formal purposes, Pidgin for informal everyday interactions.

> Missionaries and administrators normally spoke English, ... but switched to Pidgin when their interlocutors (church-members, house-servants, or others) could not speak English. Teachers and pupils spoke English in class, but once outside they usually switched to Pidgin; even in the classroom Pidgin was not totally absent.
>
> (Chumbow and Simo Bobda 1996: 408)

Pidgin English was diffusing further as a lingua franca also in the French-administered part of Cameroon – not as vigorously as in the British one but persistently, primarily in cities, like in Douala (where it had always been important) [...]

As elsewhere in Africa, the dawning of independence after World War II caused a reversal of the policy and attitude, with the aim of modernizing the territory ruled by the British. This transition triggered phase 3 [of the cycle of development of postcolonial Englishes: nativisation]. Increased efforts were invested into the education and development of British Cameroons. The number of schools multiplied, and government activity was supported by the ongoing work of missionaries. In 1960 French Cameroons became independent. One year later, in a referendum in the British part the population could decide between being merged with Nigeria or joining Cameroon. While a northern region voted in favor of Nigeria, Southern British Cameroons, now the two south-western provinces, decided in favor of reunification with French Cameroon (perhaps surprisingly so) to form the new 'Federal Republic of Cameroon.'

In this new political entity, English remained the language of administration and education in the Anglophone zone, with French occupying the same role in the much larger part of the country. In 1972 the federation was considered strong enough to be transformed into a united, officially bilingual state, the 'United Republic of Cameroon,' in which both English and French were (theoretically) accepted as official languages everywhere, on equal terms. In practice, however, it turned out that the regional autonomy of the federation to some extent had been a protective shield, a period during which the predominance of French was not felt to be overwhelming. To the Anglophones, who have felt discriminated against, this situation has been a constant source of discontent and grievance to the present day. It is frequently stated that this conflict is not exclusively a linguistic but rather a cultural one, with institutions and organizational principles inherited from the British colonial days being threatened and in some cases replaced by French-derived conventions. The situation was epitomized in another highly symbolic step: in 1982 the word 'United' was dropped from the country's official name, thus attributing it the designation which the French part had had on its own before the reunification, viz. Republic of Cameroon/Republique du Cameroun. Anglophones have regarded this step as a 'breach to the 1972 Constitution' and as a forceful 'assimilation of the minority' (Chumbow and Simo Bobda 1996: 404). Furthermore, economic and political ties with France remain strong. The relationship is probably not quite that clear-cut – some of the British legacy has been successfully preserved, and, interestingly enough, in 'a remarkable foreign policy move in the direction of the English-speaking world' (Wolf 2001: 147), Cameroon recently joined the Commonwealth, but the basic tension remains and can be felt very strongly. Kouega (2002: 112) rightly observes a 'one-way expansion of bilingualism, with speakers of English operating increasingly or fully in French, but their French-speaking counterparts remaining largely monolingual.'

This situation has generated a rather unusual situation with respect to the identity construction of a substantial proportion of Cameroon's population: it is based upon a postcolonial, second-language construct rather than traditional ethnic alignments (Chumbow and Simo Bobda 1996: 425; Wolf 2001: 46). Therefore, for this group the English language assumes an important symbolic function as an identity carrier.

Thus, in the Anglophone provinces the functions of English and Pidgin are manifold, and generally comparable to their uses in Nigeria. English predominates in administration, education, the media, and generally in primarily urban and formal domains and interethnic communication; Pidgin complements it in informal settings and situations of social proximity [...] [M]ore than half of the urban population speak standard English. Pidgin is widely considered as a form of English, and it is encroaching upon traditional domains of standard English (Simo Bobda and Wolf 2003: 107).

Attitudes toward English are thoroughly positive, with English being 'a symbol of in-group solidarity' for Anglophones (Wolf 2001: 231). Pidgin profits from being widely considered English, and outside formal spheres it enjoys covert prestige (164). Pidgin and also English are far from homogeneous and come in several shades and variants, adjusted to the 'myriad of real-life encounters of persons with different mother tongues in all kinds of situations' (Wolf 2001: 154). In terms of both functional distribution and structural properties, the difference between the two is straightforward at the top and bottom ends of the sociostylistic continuum but gets blurred in the middle ranges, where one borrows from the other and speakers slip between relatively more casual and more distanced modes, depending upon the demands of the situation. Wolf sees them on a continuum, finding little sense in attempts at separating them and arguing that this position is in line with the local practice of using *English* as a cover term for both (2001: 187, 196). The structural gap between them is clearly shrinking (Simo Bobda and Wolf 2003: 101, 113). Most recently, this was documented by Ngefac and Sala (2006), who compared Gilbert Schneider's Cameroon Pidgin data from the 1960s with corresponding present-day forms and found that many basilectal Pidgin forms [i.e. those that diverged furthest from the English on which the pidgin first developed] have disappeared and that standard English has been exerting a strong influence on Pidgin English [...]

In the Francophone region Pidgin English has retained its strong position as a lingua franca from the early colonial days, though it competes with other lingua francas and carries no symbolic meaning (Todd 1982: 19–21; Wolf 2001: 155–63). Standard English is taught as a second language in secondary education, though the outcome is far from an effective bilingualism (or multilingualism, including African vernaculars; see Wolf 2001: 170–6).

Despite this perplexing growth of both Pidgin and English in Cameroon, however, it is noteworthy that the position of authorities and educators remains decidedly conservative: Pidgin English is officially not tolerated at all in the classroom, and the orientation of English teaching remains fully exonormative (Todd 1982: 12; Wolf 2001: 204–6; Ngefac 2001). There is even a mild form of a complaint tradition, lamenting falling standards of English and blaming Pidgin as a scapegoat (Schröder 2003: 55) [...]

The highly complex and multilingual situation in Cameroon has produced a phenomenon that has been observed in similar forms elsewhere in association with nativizing [postcolonial Englishes]: a highly mixed code used primarily by urban youths, associated with solidarity and an appreciation of cultural hybridity. In Cameroon it is called 'Camfranglais', consisting of French, English, Pidgin, and indigenous elements. Reportedly, it is in use 'mainly for relaxed and informal conversation among francophone youth' (Schröder 2003: 89; see also Menang 2004: 906), comparable to what Pidgin English means to young Anglophones.

Thus, Cameroonian English has moved on into phase 3 [of the cycle of development of postcolonial Englishes], especially in the Anglophone region, but it seems barred from making further progress by the overwhelming competition of French and by the fact that the region where it really thrives lacks statehood and thus the option of an independent identity symbolized by the language. English is under pressure, from Pidgin in the Anglophone part and from French elsewhere. Cameroonian Pidgin, on the other hand, is going strong in its grassroots development, certainly with a qualitative difference between the two parts of the country but basically almost everywhere. It has been suggested as a candidate for a national language, being indigenous, widely understood, and structurally close to the vernaculars (Todd 1982: 25; Chumbow and Simo Bobda 1996: 419; Schröder 2003: 196–243; Simo Bobda and Wolf 2003), but it lacks codification, and at present it is hard to see how it should overcome its strong overt stigmatization.

References for this reading

Chumbow, B. S. and Simo Bobda, A. (1996) 'The life cycle of post-imperial English in Cameroon' in Fishman et al. (eds) [no book title or publisher listed] 401–29.

Kouega, J-P. (2002) 'Uses of English in Southern British Cameroons', *English World-Wide*, vol. 23, pp. 93–113.

Menang, T. (2004) 'Cameroon Pidgin English (Kamtok): phonology' in Schneider et al. (eds) [no book title or publisher listed], pp. 902–917.

Ngefac, A. (2001) 'Extra-linguistic correlates of Cameroon English phonology'. PhD dissertation, University of Yaoundé 1.

Ngefac, A. and Sala, B. M. (2006) 'Cameroon Pidgin and Cameroon English at a confluence: a real-time investigation', *English World-Wide*, vol. 27, pp. 217–227.

Schmied, J. J. (1991) *English in Africa: An introduction*, London, New York, Longman.

Schröder, A. (2003) *Status, Functions, and Prospects of Pidgin English. An Empirical Approach to Language Dynamics in Cameroon*, Tübingen, Gunter Narr.

Simo Bobda, A. and Wolf, H-G. (2003) 'Pidgin English in Cameroon in the new milenium' in Lucko, P. and Wolf, H-G. (eds) [no book title or publisher listed], pp. 101–117.

Todd, L. (1982) *Cameroon*, (Varieties of English Around the World, T1), Heidelberg, Julius Groos Verlag.

Wolf, H-G. (2001) *English in Cameroon*, Berlin, New York, Mouton de Gruyter.

READING B: ELT and colonialism

Alastair Pennycook

Source: Pennycook, A. (2006) 'ELT and colonialism' in Cummins, J. and Davison, C. (eds) *International Handbook of English Language Teaching, Part 1*, New York, Springer, pp. 13–24.

Introduction

English expanded from a language spoken by about 6 million people in 1600, a little over 8 million in 1700, around 30 million in 1800, to about 120 million in 1900. Thus its growth can be seen first in the context of the growth of England as an imperial power, and second in the context of the spread of English as an imperial language. [I]n spite of the expansion in the number of English users by 1900, it is important to understand that British colonial language policy was not massively in favor of spreading English.

Colonial language policies can be seen as constructed between four poles (for much greater detailed analysis, see Pennycook, 1998; 2000): First, the position of colonies within a capitalist empire and the need to produce docile and compliant workers and consumers to fuel capitalist expansion; second, the discourses of Anglicism and liberalism with their insistence on the European need to bring civilization to the world through English; third, local contingencies of class, ethnicity, race, and economic conditions that dictated the distinctive development of each colony; and fourth, the discourses of Orientalism with their insistence on exotic histories, traditions, and nations in decline. By and large, these competing discourses on the requirements for colonial education produced language policies broadly favoring education in local languages (Brutt-Griffler, 2002): Vernacular education was seen as the best means of educating a compliant workforce and of inculcating moral and political values that would make the colonial governance of large populations more possible. English was seen as a dangerous weapon, an unsafe thing, too much of which would lead to a discontented class of people who were not prepared to abide by the colonial system.

There are, of course, ample examples of imperial rhetoric extolling the virtues of English, from Charles Grant's argument in 1797 [with reference to India] that:

> the first communication, and the instrument of introducing the rest, must be the English language; this is a key which will open to them a world of new ideas, and policy alone might have impelled us, long since, to put it into their hands ... (Bureau of Education, 1920, p. 83)

through Macaulay's infamous Minute of 1835[1] (1972), to Frederick Lugard's views on the use of English at Hong Kong University in the early part of the 20th century:

> I would emphasize the value of English as the medium of instruction. If we believe that British interests will be thus promoted, we believe equally firmly that graduates, by the mastery of English, will acquire the key to a great literature and the passport to a great trade. (1910, p. 4)

These arguments, however, had more to do with the construction of English as a language with particular benefits, an issue that will be discussed below, than with the expansion of English beyond a narrow elite.

The weight of argument by colonial administrators was much more in favor of education in local languages. In the 1884 report on education (Straits Settlements[2]), E. C. Hill, the Inspector of Schools for the colony, explained his reasons against increasing the provision of education in English that went beyond concerns about the costs and the difficulties in finding qualified teachers to teach English:

> As pupils who acquire a knowledge of English are invariably unwilling to earn their livelihood by manual labour, the immediate result of affording an English education to any large number of

Malays would be the creation of a discontented class who might become a source of anxiety to the community. (p. 171)

This position was extremely common and is echoed, for example, by Frank Swettenham's argument in the Perak Government Gazette:[3]

> I am not in favour of extending the number of 'English' schools except where there is some palpable desire that English should be taught. Whilst we teach children to read and write and count in their own languages, or in Malay ... we are *safe* (emphasis in original). (6 July 1894)

Thus, as Loh Fook Seng (1970) comments, 'modern English education for the Malay then is ruled out right from the beginning as an unsafe thing' (p. 114).

In an article on vernacular education in the State of Perak, the Inspector of Schools, H. B. Collinge (cited in Straits Settlements, 1894), explained the benefits of education in Malay as taking 'thousands of our boys ... away from idleness,' helping them at the same time to 'acquire habits of industry, obedience, punctuality, order, neatness, cleanliness and general good behaviour.' Thus, after a boy[4] had attended school for a year or so, he was 'found to be less lazy at home, less given to evil habits and mischievous adventure, more respectful and dutiful, much more willing to help his parents, and with sense enough not to entertain any ambition beyond following the humble home occupations he has been taught to respect' (p. 177). And not only does the school inculcate such habits of dutiful labor but it also helps colonial rule more generally since:

> if there is any lingering feeling of dislike of the 'white man', the school tends greatly to remove it, for the people see that the Government has really their welfare at heart in providing them with this education, free, without compulsion, and with the greatest consideration for their Mohammedan[5] sympathies. (p. 177)

Similarly, in Hong Kong, E. J. Eitel (Report, 1882), the Inspector of Schools, argued that by studying Chinese classics, students learn 'a system of morality, not merely a doctrine, but a living system of ethics.'

Thus, they learn 'filial piety, respect for the aged, respect for authority, respect for the moral law.' In the Government schools, by contrast, where English books are taught from which religious education is excluded, 'no morality is implanted in the boys' (p. 70). Thus, the teaching of Chinese is:

> of higher advantage to the Government … boys strongly imbued with European civilization whilst cut away from the restraining influence of Confucian ethics lose the benefits of education, and the practical experience of Hong Kong is that those who are thoroughly imbued with the foreign spirit, are bad in morals. (p. 70)

The implications of this understanding of colonial language policy are several. Education in vernacular languages was promoted both as a means of colonial governance and as an Orientalist project for the maintenance of cultural formations. While this has many implications for an understanding of mother tongue education and modes of governance (see Pennycook, 2002), it is also significant for the role of English both before and after the formal ending of colonialism. The effects of Anglicist rhetoric did not produce widespread teaching of English, but did produce widespread images of English as a superior language that could bestow immense benefits on its users […] Meanwhile the language had been coveted and acquired by social and economic elites with whom the British were now negotiating independence. This was to have significant implications for the neo-colonial development of English in the latter half of the 20th century. Finally, however, although English teaching was relatively limited as an imperial project, the very scale of the empire and the ELT that did occur within it has ironically often been overlooked.

Thus, in spite of the relatively limited role of ELT within the British Empire, this new global position of English nevertheless had significant implications for the development of ELT. Indeed, the origins of a great deal of thinking about English and English language teaching have their origins in the colonial context rather than in what is often assumed to be their provenance in Britain itself. In his history of English language teaching, Howatt (1984, p. 71) comments that ELT forked into two streams at the end of the 18th century; one being the development of ELT within the Empire, the other being the influence of continental Europe on ELT. Although Howatt is no doubt right in suggesting that to study the development of ELT throughout the British Empire would entail a vast and separate series of studies, it is a shame that he opts so completely for the European side of the fork, and even more so if one considers that it may indeed have been the imperial fork that was more significant. That is to say, it was not so much that theories and practices of ELT were developed in Britain (with a strong European influence) and then exported to the Empire, but rather that the Empire became the crucial context of development of ELT, from where theories and practices were then imported into Britain.

This argument is akin to Gauri Viswanathan's (1989) observation that although 'the amazingly young history of English literature as a subject of study (it is less than a hundred and fifty years old) is frequently noted,' far less appreciated is 'the irony that English literature appeared as a subject in the curriculum of the colonies long before it was institutionalized in the home country' (pp. 2–3). Viswanathan shows that because of the existence of an educated class of Indians who already exerted considerable control over their people, and because of the policy of religious neutrality in education, which prevented the British from promoting a firmer program of moral discipline through the educational system, English literature was called into service 'to perform the functions of those social institutions (such as the church) that, in England, served as the chief disseminators of value, tradition, and authority' (p. 7). The development of English literature as a subject, then, was a response to the particular needs of the colonial administration in India. It was only later that this newly developed cultural curriculum of English literature, designed to develop moral and traditional views in a secular state, was imported into Britain and used to fulfill similar functions […]

What I am […] suggesting here is that it is not merely the case that British colonial administrators tried out their teaching schemes in the empire rather than in Britain, nor merely that the empire was a more obvious site for developing English teaching than was Europe, but rather that the development of ELT was profoundly influenced by such contexts. Europeans have always attempted to write the colonized, and what they perceive as the periphery, out of the histories of what happened in the colonies (aside, of course, from treacheries, debaucheries, duplicities, and so forth), making all that has been deemed progressive to be only a product of European endeavor. Yet the development of English, the development of ELT, the development of

English literature could not have happened without the colonial encounter.

Notes

1. In 1835, Thomas Macaulay, a British politician who had a seat on the Supreme Council of India, wrote his famous 'Minute on Indian Education'. In this he sets out a language policy for the colony, based around the use of English in Indian administration. He explains the rationale for this as follows:

    > We must at present do our best to form a class who may be interpreters between us and the millions whom we govern; a class of persons, Indian in blood and colour, but English in taste, in opinions, in morals, and in intellect. To that class we may leave it to refine the vernacular dialects of the country, to enrich those dialects with terms of science borrowed from the Western nomenclature, and to render them by degrees fit vehicles for conveying knowledge to the great mass of the population. (1835/1972, p. 249)

2. The Straits Settlements were a British colony comprising Penang, Malacca (both of which are now part of Malaysia), and Singapore.

3. Perak is a state in modern Malaysia. It was a British colony during the end of the nineteenth and the first half of the twentieth centuries.

4. The reference simply to 'boys' here reflects the fact that education in this context was designed for boys only, not for girls.

5. 'Mohammedan' is an archaic word for a Muslim, or follower of the prophet Mohammed. As the *Oxford English Dictionary* notes, 'The term is not employed or favoured by Muslims, and its use is now widely seen as depreciatory or offensive'.

References for this reading

Brutt-Griffler, J. (2002) *World English: A study of its development*. Clevedon: Multilingual Matters.

Bureau of Education (H. Sharp, ed.) (1920) *Selections from educational records, Part 1, 1781–1839*. Calcutta: Superintendent of Government Printing.

Education Commission Report (1883) Report of the Education Commission appointed by His Excellency Sir John Pope Hennessy, K.C.M.G. … to consider certain questions connected with Education in Hong Kong, 1882. Hong Kong: Hong Kong Government.

Howatt, A. P. R. (1984) *A history of English language teaching*. Oxford: Oxford University Press.

Loh Fook Seng, P. (1970) 'The nineteenth century British approach to Malay education'. *Journal Pendidekan*, *1*(1), 105–115.

Lugard, F. D. (1910) *Hong Kong University. Objects, history, present position and prospects*. Hong Kong: Noronha.

Macaulay, T. B. (1835/1972) Minute on Indian Education. In J. Clive & T. Pinney (eds), *Thomas Babington Macaulay. Selected writings*. Chicago: University of Chicago Press.

Pennycook, A. (1998) *English and the discourses of colonialism*. London: Routledge.

Pennycook, A. (2000) Language, ideology and hindsight: Lessons from colonial language policies. In T. Ricento (ed.), *Ideology, politics and language policies: Focus on English* (pp. 49–66). Amsterdam: John Benjamins.

Pennycook, A. (2002) Language policy and docile bodies: Hong Kong and governmentality. In J. Tollefson (ed.), *Language policies in education: Critical issues* (pp. 91–110). Mahwah, NJ: Lawrence Erlbaum.

Straits Settlements (1884) *Straits settlements annual departmental reports*. Singapore: Government Printing Office.

Straits Settlements (1894) *Straits settlements annual departmental reports*. Singapore: Government Printing Office.

Swettenham, F. (1894, July 6) In *Perak Government Gazette*. Perak.

Viswanathan, G. (1989) *Masks of conquest: Literary study and British rule in India*. London: Faber & Faber.

4　A global language

David Crystal

4.1　Introduction: the recency of World English

As early as 1780, John Adams, one of the founding fathers of the
United States of America and its second president, commented that
'English is destined to be in the next and succeeding centuries more
generally the language of the world than Latin was in the last or French
is in the present age' (Adams, 1852). Throughout the 1800s others
echoed his prediction. But it was not until the second half of the
twentieth century that his prediction became a literal reality.

A language achieves a truly global status only when it develops a special
role that is recognised in every country. The notion of 'special role' is
critical. It is obviously present when large numbers of the people in a
country speak English as a first language, as happens in the USA,
Canada, Britain, Ireland, Australia, New Zealand, South Africa and a
scattering of other territories. It is also present when it is made the
official language of a country, or is given joint-official or special-regional
status (the terms vary in different dispensations), and comes to be used
as the primary medium of communication in such domains as
government, the law courts, broadcasting, the press and the educational
system. English now has some kind of special administrative status in
over seventy countries, such as Ghana, Nigeria, Zimbabwe, India,
Singapore and Vanuatu. Then, in a different way, English achieves a
special role when it is made a priority in a country's foreign-language
teaching policy; it has no official status, but it is nonetheless the foreign
language which children are most likely to encounter when they arrive
in school, and the one most available to adults in further education.
Over 100 countries treat English as just a foreign language (chiefly in
Europe, Asia, North Africa and Latin America), and in most of these it
is now recognised as the chief foreign language being taught in schools,
or the one which a country would most like to introduce (if only more
trained staff and teaching resources were available).

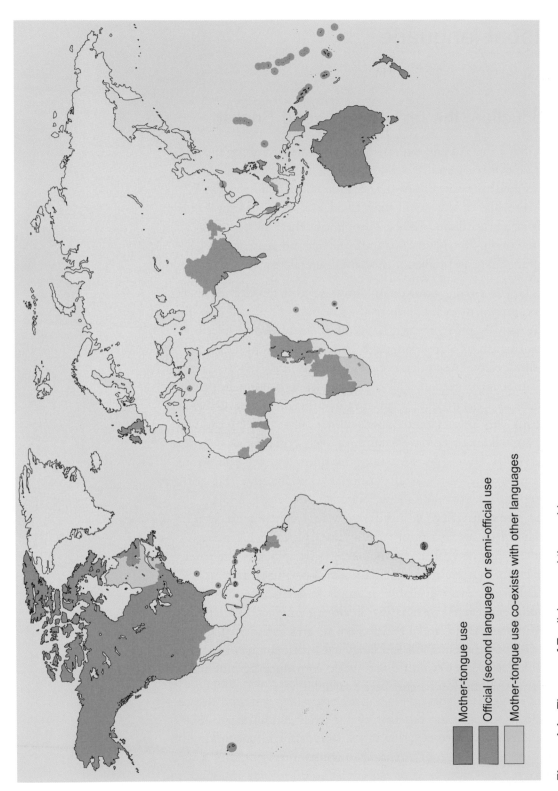

Mother-tongue use

Official (second language) or semi-official use

Mother-tongue use co-exists with other languages

Figure 4.1 The use of English around the world

The term 'global English' thus has a genuine application in the first decades of the twenty-first century. However, it could not have had such an application in the mid-twentieth century. Although the notion of a lingua franca is probably as old as language diversity itself, the prospect that a lingua franca might be needed as a practical tool for the whole world is something which has emerged strongly only since the 1950s (notwithstanding the efforts of the various artificial language movements during the first half of the century). Not only was there then a post-war demand for a mechanism enabling nations to talk and listen to each other on a regular basis, the actual number of nations in the world participating in that mechanism was soon to increase significantly. The United Nations had only fifty-one member states when it began in 1945, but this had risen to 192 members by the turn of the century. The consequence was an increasing reliance on the concept of a 'working language', as an alternative to expensive and often impracticable multi-way translation facilities, with English more likely to be the mutually accessible language than any other. Although the point has not received the historical study it should, relevant anecdotes abound. Alex Allen, High Commissioner for Australia in the late 1990s, recalls being present at the meetings which led to the formation of the European Bank for Reconstruction and Development: simultaneous translation took place routinely into various languages, but only until 10 o'clock, when the interpreters had to go off-duty – at which point discussion would often continue into the early hours, with everyone using English (Allen, 1999). Reports of this kind of thing happening at political gatherings are commonplace now, notwithstanding the pressure to safeguard and maintain other languages at an official level, and are reflected in the daily realities of interaction in the worlds of business and education.

Translating daily experience into reliable linguistic statistics is virtually impossible, given the absence of routine data-gathering procedures about language use in the population censuses of the world. When it comes to global statistics, we are in the business of informed guesswork. Still, international organisations, linguistic surveys and individual authors, using various criteria, have come up with some figures, usually separating native (first-language) and non-native use of English, and sometimes further distinguishing second-language use (where English has special, often official, status within a country) and foreign language use (where it does not). Each category has an in-built uncertainty, the nature of which needs to be appreciated before the totals can be used with any cogency.

The first-language totals cited at the turn of the century have been swinging between 400 and 500 million – a considerable range, probably because of differences of opinion as to what should be included under this heading. The chief factor must be the status of pidgins and creoles historically derived from English. If these are considered now to be 'varieties of English', then their speakers will be included, and we will move towards accepting the higher total; on the other hand, if they are thought to be separate languages, whether on grounds of mutual unintelligibility or sociopolitical identity or both, then their numbers will be excluded, and the lower total will be more acceptable.

The non-native totals are even more difficult to be sure about, for the obvious reason that fluency is a continuum, and, as was discussed in Chapter 1, commentators differ in their view about how much competence in English a person needs before being counted as a member of the community of world English users. A criterion of native-speaker-like fluency would clearly produce a relatively small figure; including every beginner would produce a relatively large one. A widely circulated British Council estimate – more informed than most, as it was based on reports of numbers attending courses and taking examinations, as well as on market intelligence provided by its 'English 2000' project – has referred to a billion (i.e. one thousand million) people engaged in learning English (British Council, 1997). That figure needs to be interpreted cautiously, because it includes all learners, from beginners to advanced. If we take, as a criterion, a medium level of conversational competence in handling domestic subject-matter, then we might expect between half and two-thirds of this total to be counted as 'non-native speakers of English'. However, there need be only small variations in percentage estimations in the more populous countries (chiefly, India and China) to produce a large effect on the figures. In India, for example, estimates of the numbers of English speakers have varied between 3 per cent and 33 per cent (Kachru, 2001) – which in real terms represent a range between 30 million and over 330 million. The 2001 census data report a figure roughly halfway between these two totals (Graddol, 2010). In China, estimates of around 220 million at the turn of the century are thought to have increased significantly in the period leading up to the 2008 Beijing Olympic Games (Feng, forthcoming).

Faced with such notable variations, in which people with particular political agendas can argue for English being stronger or weaker, a cautious temperament will use averages of the most recent estimates, which would mean a grand total of between 1500 and 2000 million speakers from all sources (for predictions of the larger total, see Graddol, 2006). This figure permits a convenient summary, given that world population passed the six billion mark during late 1999. It suggests that approximately one in three of the world's population are now capable of communicating to a useful level in English.

Table 4.1 Annual growth rate in population, 2002–7: selected countries

	%
Australia	1.2
Canada	1.0
New Zealand	1.2
UK	0.5
USA	1.0
Average	0.98
Ghana	2.4
India	1.7
Malaysia	1.8
Nigeria	2.3
Philippines	2.0
Average	2.04

(Graddol, 1999)

Two comments must immediately be made about this or any similar conclusion. First, if a third of the world's population are able to use English, then two-thirds are not. Nor do we have to travel far into the hinterland of a country – away from the tourist spots, airports, hotels, and restaurants – to encounter this reality. Populist claims about the universal spread of English thus need to be kept firmly in perspective. Second, there is evidently a major shift taking place in the centre of gravity of the language. From a time (in the 1960s) when the majority of speakers were thought to be first-language speakers, we now have a situation where the ratio of native to non-native speakers is around 1:4. Moreover, the population growth in areas where English is a second language is about twice that in areas where it is a first language (see Table 4.1), so that this differential is steadily increasing. David Graddol

(1999, p. 61) suggests that the proportion of the world's population who have English as a first language will decline from over 8 per cent in 1950 to less than 5 per cent in 2050. The situation is without precedent for an international language.

4.2 Explanations for the emergence of world English

Allow about
10 minutes

Activity 4.1

What factors do you think led to the emergence of English as the leading global language in today's world? Take a few minutes to write down some possible reasons. There is no separate comment for this activity but my thoughts can be found in the discussion that follows.

For a reminder of the terminology used in describing the different features that comprise a language, please see Appendix 2.

There are several explanations as to why English has emerged as the pre-eminent international language in the world today. Some are plausible; some are not. A good example of an implausible explanation is the argument that there are properties in the language (*intrinsic linguistic factors*) which make it especially attractive or easy to learn. The imagined simplicity of English is frequently cited, with its relative lack of inflectional endings, the absence of grammatical gender and lexical tone, and the non-use of honorifics sometimes cited as evidence. Ignored by this account are such matters as the language's syntactic, lexical and stylistic complexity, or the proportion of irregularity in its spelling system. Linguists, respecting the axiom that languages are equivalent in their structural complexity, have no difficulty rejecting intrinsic arguments of this kind. It need only be pointed out that languages which are strongly marked by inflection and grammatical gender, such as Latin and French, have been international languages in their day, to demonstrate that global stature has nothing to do with linguistic character.

A language becomes a world language for *extrinsic* reasons only – that is, reasons related to things other than the properties of the language itself – and these all relate to the power of the people who speak it. 'Power', in this connection, has a variety of applications in political (military), technological, economic and cultural contexts. Political power is seen in the form of the colonialism that brought English around the world from the sixteenth century (as was discussed in the previous chapter), so that by the nineteenth century, the language was one 'on which the sun does not set' (Quirk, 1985, p. 1). Technological power is present in the sense that the Industrial Revolution of the seventeenth and eighteenth centuries was very significantly an English-language event. The nineteenth century saw the growth in the economic power of the United States, rapidly overtaking Britain as its population grew, and adding greatly to the number of world English speakers. And in the twentieth century, cultural power manifested itself in virtually every walk of life through spheres of American influence. We can identify several domains within which English has become pre-eminent in this way: politics, economics, the press, advertising, broadcasting, motion pictures, popular music, international travel and safety, education and communications. Given this spread of functionality, it is not surprising that so many countries have found it useful to adopt English as a medium of communication, either for internal or external purposes.

Politics

As just suggested, pre-twentieth-century commentators would have had no difficulty giving a single, political answer to the question, 'Why world English?' They would simply have pointed to the growth of the British Empire, a legacy which carried over into the twentieth century. The League of Nations was the first of many modern international alliances to allocate a special place to English in its proceedings: English was one of the two official languages (along with French), and all documents were printed in both. English now plays an official or working role in the proceedings of most major international political gatherings, such as ASEAN (Association of South East Asian Nations).

Economics

By the beginning of the nineteenth century, Britain had become the world's leading industrial and trading nation (Parker, 1986, p. 391). Its population of five million in 1700 had more than doubled by 1800, and during that century no country could equal its economic growth, with a gross national product rising, on average, at 2 per cent per year. By 1800, the chief growth areas, in textiles and mining, were producing a range of manufactured goods for export which led to Britain being called the 'workshop of the world'. Over half of the leading scientists and technologists during the Industrial Revolution worked in English, and people who travelled to Britain (and later America) to learn about the new technologies had to do so through the medium of English. The early nineteenth century saw the rapid growth of the international banking system, especially in Germany, Britain and the USA, with London and New York becoming the investment capitals of the world. The resulting 'economic imperialism' brought a fresh dimension to the balance of linguistic power.

Figure 4.2 A copy of the *New York Daily Times* from 1851

The press

The English language has been an important medium of the press for nearly 400 years. The nineteenth century was the period of greatest progress, thanks to the introduction of new printing technology and new methods of mass production and transportation. It also saw the development of a truly independent press, chiefly fostered in the USA, where there were some 400 daily newspapers by 1850 (see Figure 4.2), and nearly 2000 by the turn of the century. Censorship and other restrictions continued in Continental Europe during the early decades, however, which meant that the provision of popular news in languages other than English developed much more slowly. Today, about a third of the world's newspapers are published in countries where English has special status (*Encyclopaedia Britannica*, 2008, p. 804ff.), and the majority of these will be in English. This high profile was reinforced by the way techniques of news gathering developed. The mid-nineteenth century saw the growth of the major news agencies, especially following the invention of the telegraph. Paul Julius Reuter started an office in Aachen, but soon moved to London, where in 1851 he launched the agency which now bears his name. By 1870, Reuters had acquired more territorial news monopolies than any of its continental competitors. With the emergence in 1856 of the New York Associated Press, the majority of the information being transmitted along the telegraph wires of the world was in English. Some degree of linguistic balance would later emerge, but not for a considerable time.

Advertising

Towards the end of the nineteenth century, a combination of social and economic factors led to a dramatic increase in the use of advertisements in publications, especially in the more industrialised countries. Mass production had increased the flow of goods and was fostering competition, consumer purchasing power was growing, and new printing techniques were providing fresh display possibilities. In the USA, publishers realised that income from advertising would allow them to lower the selling price of their magazines, and thus hugely increase circulation. Two-thirds of a modern newspaper, especially in the USA, may be devoted to advertising. During the nineteenth century the advertising slogan became a feature of the medium, as did the famous 'trade name'. The media capitalised on the brevity with which a product could be conveyed to an audience: posters, billboards, electric displays, shop signs and other techniques became part of the everyday scene. As international markets grew, the 'outdoor media' began to travel the world, and their prominence in virtually every town and city is now one of the most noticeable global manifestations of English language use. American English ruled: by 1972, only three of the world's top thirty advertising agencies were not US-owned.

Broadcasting

It took many decades of experimental research in physics before it was possible to send the first radio telecommunication signals through the air, without wires. Marconi's system, built in 1895, carried telegraph code signals over a distance of one mile. Six years later, his signals had crossed the Atlantic Ocean; by 1918, they had reached Australia. English was the first language to be transmitted by radio. Within twenty-five years of Marconi's first transmission, public broadcasting became a reality. The first commercial radio station, in Pittsburgh, Pennsylvania, broadcast its first programme in November 1920, and there were over 500 broadcasting stations licensed in the USA within two years. A similar dramatic expansion affected public television twenty years later. We can only speculate about how these media developments must have influenced the growth of world English. There are no statistics on the proportion of time devoted to English-language programmes the world over, or on how much time is spent listening to such programmes. But if we look at broadcasting aimed specifically at audiences in other countries (such as the BBC World Service or the Voice of America), we note significant levels of provision – over a thousand hours a week by the former, twice as much by the latter, at the turn of the millennium. Most other countries showed sharp increases in external broadcasting during the post-war years, and several launched English-language radio programmes, such as the Soviet Union, Italy, Japan, Luxembourg, The Netherlands, Sweden and Germany.

Figure 4.3   The Voice of America

Motion pictures

The new technologies which followed the discovery of electrical power fundamentally altered the nature of home and public entertainment, and provided fresh directions for the development of the English language. The technology of this industry has many roots in Europe and America during the nineteenth century, with England and France providing an initial impetus to the artistic and commercial development of the cinema from 1895. However, the years preceding and during the First World War stunted the growth of a European film industry, and dominance soon passed to America, which oversaw from 1915 the emergence of the feature film, the star system, the movie mogul and the grand studio, all based in Hollywood, California. As a result, when sound was added to the technology in the late 1920s, it was spoken English which suddenly came to dominate the movie world. And despite the growth of the film industry in other countries in later decades, English-language movies still dominate the medium, with Hollywood coming to rely increasingly on a small number of annual productions aimed at huge audiences. It is unusual to find a blockbuster movie produced in a language other than English, and about 80 per cent of all feature films given a theatrical release are in English (Dyja, 2005), although this figure needs to be set against the amount of dubbing into other languages, which is steadily increasing.

Popular music

The cinema was one of two new entertainment technologies which emerged at the end of the nineteenth century: the other was the recording industry. Here too the English language was early in evidence. When in 1877 Thomas A. Edison devised the phonograph, the first machine that could both record and reproduce sound, the first words to be recorded were 'What God hath wrought', followed by the words of the nursery-rhyme 'Mary had a little lamb'. Most of the subsequent technical developments took place in the USA. All the major recording companies in popular music had English-language origins, beginning with the US firm Columbia (from 1898). Radio sets around the world hourly testify to the dominance of English in the popular music scene today. By the turn of the century, Tin Pan Alley (the popular name for the Broadway-centred song-publishing industry) was a reality, and was soon known worldwide as the chief source of US popular music. Jazz, too, had its linguistic dimension, with the development of the blues and many other genres. And by the time modern popular music arrived, it was almost entirely an English scene. The pop groups of two chief English-speaking nations were soon to dominate the recording world: Bill Haley and the Comets and Elvis Presley in the USA; the Beatles and the Rolling Stones in the UK. Mass audiences for pop singers became a routine feature of the world scene from the 1960s. No other single source has spread the English language around the youth of the world so rapidly and so pervasively.

International travel and safety

For those whose international travel brings them into a world of package holidays, business meetings, academic conferences, international conventions, community rallies, sporting occasions, military occupations and other 'official' gatherings, the domains of transportation and accommodation are chiefly mediated through the use of English as an auxiliary language. Safety instructions on international flights and sailings, information about emergency procedures in hotels, and directions to major locations are now increasingly in English alongside local languages. A special aspect of safety is the way that the language has come to be used as a means of controlling international transport operations, especially on water and in the air. English has become the international language of the sea, in the form of Essential English for International Maritime Use – often referred to as **Seaspeak** (Weeks et al., 1984). **Airspeak**, the language of international aircraft control, emerged after the Second World War, when the International Civil Aviation Organisation was created, and it was agreed that English should be the international language of aviation when pilots and controllers speak different languages (a principle which is not always respected in practice, as air disasters sometimes bring to light).

Education

Issues to do with the role of English in global education are discussed in a later book in this series, Hewings and Tagg (eds) (2012) *The Politics of English: Conflict, Competition, Co-existence.*

English is the medium of a great deal of the world's knowledge, especially in such areas as science and technology, and access to knowledge is the business of education. When we investigate why so many nations have in recent years made English an official language or chosen it as their chief foreign language in schools, one of the most important reasons is always educational. Since the 1960s, English has become the normal medium of instruction in higher education for many countries – including several where the language has no official status. Advanced courses in The Netherlands, for example, are widely taught in English. No African country uses its indigenous language in higher education, English being used in the majority of cases. The English language teaching (ELT) business has become one of the major growth industries around the world in the past half century. However, its relevance to the growth of English as a world language goes back much further. In the final quarter of the eighteenth century, we find several examples of English grammars, such as Lindley Murray's, being translated into other languages (Tieken-Boon van Ostade, 1996).

Communications

If a language is a truly international medium, it is going to be most apparent in those services which deal directly with the task of communication – the postal and telephone systems and the electronic networks. Information about the use of English in these domains is not easy to come by, however. It is thought that three-quarters of the world's mail is in English, but as no one monitors the language in which we write our letters, such statistics are highly speculative. Only on the internet, where messages and data can be left for indefinite periods of time, is it possible to develop an idea of how much of the world's everyday communications (at least, between computer owners) is actually in English. The internet began as ARPANET, the Advanced Research Projects Agency network, in the late 1960s, in the USA. Its language was, accordingly, English, and when people in other countries began to form links with this network, it proved essential for them to use English. The dominance of this language was then reinforced when the service was opened up in the 1980s to private and commercial organisations, most of which were (for the reasons already given) already communicating chiefly in English. At the turn of the century, it was thought that some 70 per cent of usage – at least on the World Wide Web – was in English, although the proportion has been steadily reducing as more languages and non-English sites come online.

Table 4.2 is based on a sample of nearly 1.5 million internet users during the second quarter of 2010 (carried out by Internet World Stats). English still holds the leading position, but Chinese is rapidly catching up, with a percentage growth rate that is three times that of English over the previous eight years. By 2003, less than half the host servers in the world were in English-speaking countries. A similar predominance for English has also been observed in more recent developments, such as social networking forums and microblogging sites like Twitter. Internet usage will in due course probably reflect the balance of linguistic power in the outside world. On the other hand, the head start English has had means that there is more high-quality content on the internet in English than in other languages, so that even though the proportion of websites in English is falling, the number of hits on those sites (i.e. individuals calling up specific web addresses) will remain disproportionately high for some time.

Table 4.2 Most widely used languages on the internet in 2010

Top ten languages in the internet	Internet users by language	Growth in internet use (2000–2010)	% of total internet users	World population for this language (2010 estimate)
English	536,564,837	281.2%	27.3%	1,277,528,133
Chinese	444,948,013	1277.4%	22.6%	1,365,524,982
Spanish	153,309,074	743.2%	7.8%	420,469,703
Japanese	99,143,700	110.6%	5.0%	126,804,433
Portuguese	82,548,200	989.6%	4.2%	250,372,925
German	75,158,584	173.1%	3.8%	95,637,049
Arabic	65,365,400	2501.2%	3.3%	347,002,991
French	59,779,525	398.2%	3.0%	347,932,305
Russian	59,700,000	1825.8%	3.0%	139,390,205
Korean	39,440,000	107.1%	2.0%	71,393,343
Top 10 languages	1,615,957,333	421.2%	82.2%	4,442,056,069
Rest of the languages	350,557,483	588.5%	17.8%	2,403,553,891
World total	1,966,514,816	444.8%	100.0%	6,845,609,960

(Internet World Stats, 2010)

4.3   English and globalisation

All these factors that have contributed to the emergence of English as the pre-eminent world language are examples of social processes which can be grouped together under the term **globalisation**. This is a key concept for discussions of English in the world today, and so it is worth examining in some detail.

Activity 4.2

Before we turn to Reading A on the subject, take a few moments to think about what the term 'globalisation' means to you. In what contexts have you come across it before? Was it presented as primarily a positive or a negative phenomenon in these contexts? What effects was it portrayed as having for society?

Now turn to Reading A: *English and linguistic globalisation* by Philip Seargeant, which outlines the theoretical scope of the concept, and considers the nature of its relationship with language-related issues.

Part 1

To begin with, read the first section of the article only: 'Defining globalisation' (pages 178–183). While reading, pay particular attention to the different definitions of the phenomenon, and to what the reading suggests are the common threads that run throughout them. You may find it helpful to make notes on the key terms identified in the article (those which are italicised). These are important concepts for the second section of the article, which examines the relationship between language and globalisation.

Comment

While the discussion in this chapter so far has considered the range of historical factors that have contributed to English's current position in the world (factors ranging from the influence of political institutions such as the League of Nations to the impact of the movie industry and the invention of new communications technology), Reading A considers the issue in a more abstract and theoretical way, drawing out the key processes which constitute globalisation. It suggests that different commentators interpret the effects of globalisation in different ways. Some take a very positive view of the commercial opportunities it appears to offer, while others focus on the detrimental effects it is having on 'traditional' cultures and the way it is increasing inequality around the world. A further interpretation suggests that it is resulting in 'hybrid' cultures: where a mix of the contemporary and the traditional, the local and the imported, is creating new cultural and social practices.

In many ways all these perspectives are accurate appraisals of the way that increased interconnectivity is affecting the way things operate in the world, and one can readily find examples which back each of these up. The article goes on to argue that for this reason it is helpful to think in terms of the underlying *processes* which result in all these effects, because these processes can help explain the many different (and often contrasting) social effects that globalisation is producing. Key to the concept of globalisation is the way that new technologies – especially communication and transport technologies – are offering different ways for people to relate to one another. It is now significantly easier than it was a few decades ago to interact with someone on the opposite side of the globe, and to send information, money and goods long distances in a short space of time. Because of this, the world is 'shrinking' and becoming ever more interconnected. These changes in the way that people interact result in changes in social organisation. Society is no longer so 'local', but instead people are likely to move across or connect with different cultures and communities on a far more regular basis.

Part 2

Before reading the second half of the article, give some thought to the role that language might play in the processes of globalisation. What do you think the relationship between language and globalisation might be, and what influences are globalising forces having on the English language specifically?

Now turn to the second section of the article: 'Language and global society'. As you are reading it, consider what aspects of globalisation are of particular importance for the nature and status of English in the world today. Because the article deals primarily in theoretical (that is to say, abstract) concepts, you may find it helpful to try to relate these abstract ideas to the concrete historical processes that we discussed above in relation to the emergence of English as the pre-eminent international language.

Comment

The reading suggests that the relationship between language and globalisation is a two-way street. On the one hand, the increased mobility in society and the way that so many aspects of modern life operate on a global rather than a local scale lead to the need for a common means of communication which transcends national boundaries. If a business organisation is going to trade with partners on the other side of the world, for example, it is important to have a common working language. And English has emerged as the language which mostly readily fulfils this role.

But the obverse of this is that because English is used in ever more diverse contexts, it is also changing to adapt to the circumstances in which it is used. Language contact – which we discussed in the previous chapter – results in new varieties of English developing, which are influenced by the linguistic and communicative practices of the communities which adopt the language. So there are two different forces at work here – one which creates the need for a common language which can be used (and understood) across national and cultural boundaries, and another which results in continued and greater diversity in the language.

4.4   The future of English as a world language

Given the factors outlined in Section 4.2 and in Reading A that have led to the emergence of English as a global language, what is in store for the future of the language? Will it continue to gain in prominence and further cement its position as *the* global language? Are the factors we have looked at so far going to continue to privilege English, or are other languages likely to emerge as rival forces on the global linguistic stage? And if English does continue to spread, what will the consequences be for its form and shape?

Language is an immensely democratising institution. To have learnt a language is immediately to have rights in it. You may add to it, modify it, play with it, create in it, ignore bits of it, as you will. And it is just as likely that the course of the English language is going to be influenced by those who speak it as a non-native language as by those who speak it as a mother tongue. Fashions count, in language, as anywhere else, and fashions are a function of numbers. As we have seen, the total number of mother-tongue speakers in the world is steadily falling, as a proportion of world English users. It is perfectly possible for a linguistic fashion to be started by a group of non-native learners, or by those who speak a creole or pidgin variety, which then catches on among other speakers: the phenomenal spread of rapping is an example. As numbers grow and non-native speakers gain in national and international prestige, usages which were previously criticised as 'foreign' – such as a new concord rule ('three person' rather than 'three people'), variations in countability ('furnitures', 'kitchenwares'), or verb use ('he be running') – can become part of the standard educated speech of a locality, and may eventually appear in writing.

In the next chapter we will examine in detail the features of some of these different Englishes from around the world. For the moment, let us focus on the political, social and sociolinguistic issues which accompany this diversity in the language. We can start by asking what power and prestige is associated with these new varieties of English? It is all happening so quickly that it is difficult to generalise. But impressionistically, we can see several of these new linguistic features achieving an increasingly public profile in their respective countries. Words become used less self-consciously in the national press – no longer being put in inverted commas, for example, or given a gloss. They come to be adopted, often at first with some effort, then more naturally, by first-language speakers of English in the locality. Indeed, the canons of local political correctness, in the best sense of that phrase, may foster a local usage, giving it more prestige than it could ever have dreamed of – a good example is the contemporary popularity in New Zealand English of Maori words (and the occasional Maori grammatical feature, such as the dropping of the definite article before the people name 'Maori' itself). Above all, the local words begin to be used at the prestigious levels of society: by politicians, religious leaders, socialites, pop musicians and others. Using local words is then no longer to be seen as slovenly or ignorant, within a country; it is respectable; it may even be 'cool'.

The next step is the move from national to international levels. These people who are important in their own communities – whether politicians or pop stars – start travelling abroad. The rest of the world looks up to them, either because it wants what they have, or because it wants to sell them something. The result is the typical present-day scenario: an international gathering (political, educational, economic, artistic, etc.) during which senior visitors use, deliberately or unself-consciously, a word or phrase from their own country which would not be found in the traditional standards of British or American English. Once upon a time, the reaction would have been to condemn the usage as ignorance. Today, it is becoming increasingly difficult to say this, or even to think it, if the visitors have more degrees than the visited, or own a bigger company, or are social equals in every way. In such circumstances, one has to learn to live with the new usage, as a feature of increasing diversity in English. It can take a generation or two, but it does happen. It happened within fifty years between Britain and America: by 1842, Charles Dickens (in his *American Notes*, revised in 1868) made some observations about American linguistic usage – such as his amazement at the many ways that Americans use the verb 'fix' – all expressed in tones of delight, not dismay. But, whatever your attitude towards new usages – and there will always be people who sneer at diversity – there is no getting away from the fact that, these days, regional national varieties of English are increasingly being used with prestige on the international scene.

If these **New Englishes** are becoming standardised, as markers of educated regional identity, what is taking their place elsewhere within the social spectrum of these communities? Here, very little descriptive research has been done, but there are enough anecdotal reports to suggest the way things are going. When actual examples of language in use are analysed, in such multilingual settings as Malaysia and Singapore, we immediately encounter varieties which bring elements of different languages together (*code-mixing*) and make use of informal features that would not be used in standard British or American English. Conversations of this kind, between well-educated people, are now heard at grass-roots level in communities all over the English-speaking world (Mesthrie, 1992; Siegel, 1995). However, establishment attitudes towards these varieties are still generally negative. In 1999, for example, Prime Minister Goh Chok Tong of Singapore devoted several minutes of his National Day Rally speech to a plea for Singaporeans to cut down on their use of **Singlish** (a hybrid of English, Chinese and Malay) and to maintain the use of standard English, if the country's aims for a greater international role were to be realised. He illustrated this part of the speech with some Singlish expressions, then focused his anxiety on the influence of the media, and in particular the leading character from the country's highly popular television sitcom, Phua Chu Kang ('PCK'), known for his rapid, fluent Singlish. The prime minister then approached the Television Corporation of Singapore, and asked them to do something about it; they then agreed to enrol PCK in some basic English classes so that he could improve his standard English. The action was widely reported both within the country (e.g. *The Straits Times*, 23 August 1999) and abroad, and not without scepticism. As *The Independent* put it (17 October 1999), the chastising of PCK 'was something like the Queen rebuking Del Boy during the opening of parliament'.

Figure 4.4   The Speak Good English Movement in Singapore

That language should receive such a high profile in a 'state of the union' address is itself surprising, and that a head of government should go out of his way to influence a television sitcom is probably unprecedented in the history of language planning! But it illustrates well the direction in which matters are moving. Singlish must now be a significant presence in Singapore for it to attract this level of attention and condemnation. The nature of the reaction is also a good illustration of the nature of the problem which all New Englishes encounter in their early stages. It is the same problem that older varieties of English also encountered: the view that there can only be one kind of English, the standard kind, and that all others should be eliminated. From the days when this mindset first became dominant, in the eighteenth century, Britain and a few other countries have taken some 250 years to confront it and replace it with a more egalitarian perspective in educational curricula. The contemporary view, as represented in the National Curriculum for England, is to maintain the importance of standard English while at the same time maintaining the value of local accents and dialects. The intellectual basis for this policy is the recognition of the fact that language has many functions, and that the reason for the existence of standard English (to promote mutual intelligibility) is different from the reason for the existence of local dialects (to promote local identity). The same arguments apply, with even greater force, on a global scale. There is no intrinsic conflict between a standard variety of English and Singlish in Singapore, as the reasons for the existence of the former, to permit Singaporeans of different linguistic backgrounds to communicate with each other and with people abroad, are different from the reasons for the emergence of the latter, to provide a sense of local identity. Ironically, the prime minister himself recognised the importance of both these goals, in emphasising that the future of Singapore needed both an outward-looking set of economic and cultural goals as well as an inward-looking sense of the 'something special and precious' in the Singaporean way of life. A bidialectal (or bilingual) policy allows a people to look both ways at once, and would be the most efficient way of the country achieving its aims. Fostering a standard English is one plank of such a policy. Condemning Singlish is not.

We will encounter similar attitudes in all parts of the world where English is developing a strong non-native presence, and at all levels. Teachers of English as a Second or Foreign Language have to deal with the situation routinely, with students increasingly arriving in the classroom speaking a dialect which is markedly different from standard English. The question of just how much local phonology, grammar, vocabulary and pragmatics should be allowed in is difficult and contentious. But there seems no doubt that, gradually, there is a definite ameliorative trend around the English-speaking world, with expressions which were once heavily penalised as local and low-class now achieving a degree of status. How fast this trend develops depends on economic and social factors more than on anything else. If the people who use mixed varieties as markers of their identity become more influential, attitudes will change, and usages will become more acceptable. In fifty years time, we could find ourselves with an English language which contains within itself large areas of contact-influenced vocabulary, borrowed from such languages as Malay or Chinese, being actively used in Singapore, Malaysia and emigrant communities elsewhere. First-language speakers from those areas would instinctively select this vocabulary as their first choice in conversation. Everyone else would recognise their words as legitimate options, passively at least, with occasional forays into active use. It is a familiar story in the history of the English language, though operating now on a global scale.

Indeed, such a scenario would not be so different from that already found in English. There are over 350 living languages given as vocabulary sources in the files of the *Oxford English Dictionary*. For example, there are already over 250 words with Malay as part of their etymology in the *OED* so the foundation is already laid. The contact-language words of the future will of course include more alternative rather than supplementary expressions – localised words for everyday notions, such as tables and chairs, rather than for regionally restricted notions, such as fauna and flora – but the notion of a lexical mosaic as such is not new. It has always been part of the language.

4.5   An English family of languages?

The future of world English is likely to be one of increasing multidialectism, but could this become multilingualism? Is English going to fragment into mutually unintelligible varieties, just as Vulgar Latin did a millennium ago? The forces of the past fifty years, which have led to so many New Englishes, suggest this outcome. If such significant change can be noticed within a relatively short period of time, must not these varieties become even more differentiated over the next century, so that we end up, as Tom McArthur (1998) argues, with an English 'family of languages'?

Allow about
15 minutes

Activity 4.3

Take a few moments to think of reasons which might lead to English fragmenting into a family of discrete and mutually unintelligible languages. What aspects of modern global society might prevent this from happening?

Comment

The question of whether we will end up with an English 'family of languages' does not have a single answer. The history of language suggests that fragmentation has been a frequent phenomenon (as in the well-known case of Latin), but the history of language is no longer a guide. Today, we live in the proverbial global village, where we have immediate access to other languages and varieties of English in ways that have come to be available only recently, and this is having a strong centripetal or standardising effect. With a whole range of fresh auditory models becoming routinely available, chiefly through satellite television and on the internet, it is easy to see how any New English could move in different directions at the same time. The pull imposed by the need for identity, which has been making New Englishes increasingly dissimilar from British English, could be balanced by a pull imposed by the need for intelligibility, on a world scale, which will make them increasingly similar. At the former level, there may well be increasing mutual unintelligibility; but at the latter level, there might not.

None of this disallows the possible emergence of a family of English languages in a sociolinguistic sense; but mutual unintelligibility will not be the basis of such a notion in the case of New Englishes, any more than it has been in relation to intranational accents and dialects. Although there are several well-known instances of dialect unintelligibility among people from different regional backgrounds, especially when encountered at rapid conversational speed – in Britain, Cockney (London), Geordie (Newcastle), Scouse (Liverpool) and Glaswegian (Glasgow) are among the most commonly cited cases – the problems largely resolve when a speaker slows down, or they reduce to difficulties over isolated lexical items. This makes regional varieties of English no more problematic for linguistic theory than, say, occupational varieties such as legal or scientific. It is no more illuminating to call Cockney or Scouse 'different English languages' than it would be to call Legal or Scientific by such a name, and anyone who chooses to extend the application of the term 'language' in this way finds a slippery slope which eventually leads to the blurring of the potentially useful distinctions between 'language', 'variety' and 'dialect'.

The intelligibility criterion has traditionally provided little support for an English 'language family'. We have learnt from sociolinguistics in recent decades, however, that this criterion is by no means an adequate explanation for the language nomenclature of the world, as it leaves out of consideration linguistic attitudes, and in particular the criterion of identity. It is this which allows us to say that people from Norway, Sweden and Denmark speak different languages, notwithstanding the considerable amount of intelligibility which exists between them. It seems that if a community wishes its way of speaking to be considered a 'language', and if they have the political power to support their decision, there is nothing which can stop them doing so. The present-day ethos is to allow communities to deal with their own internal policies themselves, as long as these are not perceived as being a threat to others. However, to promote an autonomous language policy, two criteria need to be satisfied. The first is to have a community with a single mind about the matter, and the second is to have a community which has enough political-economic 'clout' to make its decision respected by outsiders with whom it is in regular contact. When these criteria are lacking, any such movement is doomed.

Autonomous language policy is discussed further in Chapter 6.

There are very few examples of English generating varieties which are given totally different names, and even fewer where these names are rated as 'languages' (as opposed to 'dialects'). There are some cases among the English-derived pidgins and creoles around the world (e.g. Tok Pisin, Gullah), but any proposal for language status is invariably surrounded with controversy. An instance from the mid-1990s is the case of **Ebonics** – a blend of Ebony and phonics – proposed for the variety of English spoken by African-Americans, and which had previously been called by such names as 'Black Vernacular English' or **African-American Vernacular English** (McArthur, 1998, p. 197ff.). Although the intentions behind the proposal were noble, and attracted some support, it was denounced by people from across the political and ethnic spectrum, including such prominent individuals as Education Secretary Richard W. Riley, the black civil rights leader Rev. Jesse Jackson and writer Maya Angelou. Quite evidently the two criteria above did not obtain: the US black community did not have a single mind about the matter, and the people who had the political-economic clout to make the decision respected also had mixed views about it.

By giving a distinct name, Ebonics, to what had previously been recognised as a variety of English, a hidden boundary in the collective unconscious seems to have been crossed. It is in fact very unusual to assign a novel name to a variety of English in this way, other than in the humorous literature, where such names as *Strine* (a spelling of an imagined casual Australian pronunciation of the word 'Australian') can be found. There are indeed many world English locations which have generated their regional humour book, in which the local accent or dialect is illustrated by comic 'translations' into standard English (Crystal, 1998). Exchanges of this kind, however, are part of the genre of language play, and recognised as such by author and reader. They are not serious attempts to upgrade the status of the dialect into a separate language. The notion of translation which they employ is purely figurative. Indeed, the humour depends on a tacit recognition of the fact that we are dealing with a variety which is 'non-standard', and that people can recognise what it is saying. There is no true intelligibility problem and no problem of identity status.

In all cases of emerging linguistic status – such as the Ebonics example – the number of speakers involved has been a minority within a much larger sociopolitical entity. We have yet to see whether the same situation will establish itself in countries where the New English speakers are in a majority and hold political power, or in locations where new, supranational political relationships are being formed. For example, although several languages are co-official in the European Union, pragmatic linguistic realities result in English being the most widely used language in these corridors. But what kind of common English emerges, when Germans, French, Greeks and others come into contact, each using English with its own pattern of influence or 'interference' from the mother tongue? There will be the usual sociolinguistic accommodation (Giles and Smith, 1979), and the result may be a novel variety, of Euro-English – a term which has been used for over a decade with reference to the distinctive vocabulary of the Union (with its 'Eurofighters', 'Eurodollars', 'Eurosceptics', and so on), but which must now be extended to include the various hybrid accents, grammatical constructions and discourse patterns encountered there. English-as-a-first-language politicians, diplomats and civil servants working in Brussels have been heard to comment on how they feel their own English is being pulled in the direction of these foreign-language patterns. A common feature, evidently, is to accommodate to an increasingly syllable-timed rhythm (i.e. a pattern where roughly equal time is given to each syllable, as is the case with French). Others include the use of simplified sentence constructions, the avoidance of idioms and colloquial vocabulary, a slower rate of speech, and the use of clearer patterns of articulation (avoiding some of the assimilations and elisions which would be natural in a first-language setting). It is important to stress that this is not the 'foreigner talk' reported in an earlier ELT era. These people are not 'talking down' to their colleagues, or consciously adopting simpler expressions, for the English of their interlocutors may be as fluent as their own. It is a natural process of accommodation, which in due course could lead to new standardised forms in Europe, and even beyond. Some scholars, such as Jennifer Jenkins (2007), now argue that common patterns of non-native usage will emerge around the English-speaking world, resulting in a new version of **English as a Lingua Franca (ELF)** – a phenomenon that is beginning to receive empirical study (the VOICE project of Seidlhofer, 2010).

Figure 4.5 The official languages of the European Parliament

Activity 4.4

Now turn to Reading B: *English in Finnish society* by Sirpa Leppänen and Tarja Nikula. This extract outlines the role played by English in modern Finland, a country with two official languages: Finnish and Swedish. It gives an example of the type of English used in one particular domain, that of the media. While reading, consider the following questions:

- How has the status of English changed in Finland in line with the language's growing global status?
- To what extent is the type of English illustrated in the talk show example a new or distinct variety of English (a type of 'Euro-English')?

The transcript conventions used for the extract from the talk show include a great amount of detail about how the utterances were spoken. It is not necessary to follow this detail for the purposes of this activity.

Comment

In the last fifty years, English has become increasingly important in Finland, according to Leppänen and Nikula. It now plays a role in almost all domains of social life, and has a significant role in the education system. Attitudes towards the language are mixed, with some voicing concern about the impact that its growing status has on the local languages and culture, while others see it as an important element for the internationalisation of the country.

With regard to the question of whether the English spoken in Finland represents a distinct variety of the language (i.e. whether it has features which mark it out as a specific lingua franca usage), Leppänen and Nikula are somewhat sceptical. In their analysis of the data from the talk show, they note that there *are* indeed features of the interaction which diverge from standard English, and that these could be considered a product of the lingua franca situation. On the other hand, many of these features are also to be found in most spoken interaction – be it in a standard or non-standard variety – which often exhibits 'flaws' or inconsistencies in areas such as syntax and word choice (they discuss the example of 'word searches', i.e. trying to find the right word for what one wants to express), but nevertheless operates smoothly and efficiently as an act of communication. For Leppänen and Nikula, therefore, the issue of whether a 'Euro-English' is in fact emerging remains an open question, and is one that requires further empirical research.

4.6   Conclusion

Global English remains an evident functional reality, but its linguistic character has become increasingly difficult to define. The emergence of hybrid trends and varieties raises all kinds of theoretical and pedagogical questions, several of which began to be addressed during the 1990s (e.g. by Schneider, 1997, and Foley, 1999). They blur the long-standing distinction between 'native' and 'non-native', and between 'first', 'second' and 'foreign' language. They make us reconsider the notion of 'standard', especially when we find such hybrids being used confidently and fluently by groups of people who have education and influence in their own regional setting. They present the traditionally clear-cut notion of 'translation' with all kinds of fresh problems, for, in a code-mixing situation where speakers are switching between English and other languages, at what point in a conversation should we say that a notion of translation is relevant, as we move from 'understanding' to 'understanding most of the utterance precisely' to 'understanding little of the utterance precisely ("getting the drift" or "gist")' to 'understanding none of the utterance, despite its containing several features of English'? And, to move into the sociolinguistic dimension, hybrids give us new challenges in relation to language attitudes: for example, at what point would our insistence on the need for translation cause an adverse reaction from the participants, who might maintain they are 'speaking English', even though we cannot understand them? There may have been analogous situations earlier in the history of English. William Caxton was the first to comment on it, in his Prologue to Virgil's *Booke of Eneydos* (see the account in Chapter 2). We are being faced again with *egges* and *eyren*, but on a global scale.

READING A: English and linguistic globalisation

Philip Seargeant

Specially commissioned for this book.

Defining globalisation

Globalisation and cultural homogeneity

Since the late twentieth century the concept of 'globalisation' has risen to such prominence in discussions about the nature of modern society that it could be said to define the era in which we live. The social, economic and political processes that are grouped together under the term 'globalisation' are such that they have a bearing on almost all aspects of modern life. The daily existence of people around the world is significantly affected in one way or another by 'globalising' forces, to the extent that an understanding of this single idea has become central to an understanding of life in early twenty-first century society.

Specifying what exactly is meant by 'globalisation', though, is far from straightforward. The meaning that finds its way most readily into dictionaries, and is most often found in the mainstream media, refers to the ways in which businesses are taking advantage of the expansion of world markets. The *Oxford English Dictionary*, for example, defines globalisation as 'the process by which businesses or other organisations develop international influence or start operating on an international scale, widely considered to be at the expense of national identity' (revised edition, 2009). From a neoliberal perspective, such expansionism is regarded as a natural stage in the history of capitalism and thus a positive development in the social organisation of the world. The ability to trade freely across the entire globe, to tap into new markets and take advantage of cheap foreign labour costs, enhances the money-making capabilities of companies. For those opposed to these developments, 'globalisation' is something that is having pernicious effects on societies around the world. A key complaint voiced by 'anti-globalisation' advocates is that it leads to cultural homogeneity: that the cultural prerogatives of politically and economically dominant countries (most noticeably the USA) are spreading at the expense of local or indigenous cultural identities, and that there is a 'flattening out' of the rich diversity of human cultures. Globalisation, according to this characterisation, is akin to a mixture of economic and cultural imperialism, with powerful corporations and countries exploiting resources and workforces across the globe, while simultaneously imposing a bland and standardised cultural impress on diverse local traditions. Such a view is characterised by the existence of such things as McDonald's outlets in cities across the globe, or of Coca-Cola advertisements in remote rural communities in Africa or South Asia. In terms of language-related issues, this view of globalisation highlights the way in which large, powerful languages (most noticeably English) are spreading across the globe at the expense of other smaller languages.

Figure 1   A McDonald's restaurant in Masqat, Oman and a Coca-Cola advertisement in Agra, India

'Glocalisation' and cultural hybridity

Yet this negative view of globalisation is not shared by everyone. For some, the spread of cultural practices or values does not necessarily lead to homogeneity, but to the emergence of new, hybrid cultural practices. Roland Robertson (1995) uses the term 'glocalisation' – a blend of globalisation and localisation – to describe the way in which practices that spread across the globe will be 'nativised' by local cultures. The phenomenon can be seen in the way that multinational corporations adapt their global marketing strategies to take account of local cultural practices or preferences (McDonald's using Asterix rather than Ronald McDonald in its advertising campaigns in France, for example[1]), and in the way that imported cultural trends get adopted in a modified form by local populations (resulting in phenomena such as Korean hip-hop or Japanese R&B). And whereas the above outlined concept of globalisation saw cultural influence as only flowing in one direction – from politically and economically 'centre' countries to less powerful 'periphery' countries – an approach which stresses hybridity sees influence as a two-way street. So, for example, while US comic-book culture had a strong influence on post-war Japanese culture, this was then transformed into an indigenous Japanese cultural art form, manga, which in turn has been exported back to the US where it is having a significant influence on the US comic market. Rather than homogeneity, globalisation in this guise leads to a continued diversity, albeit one which disrupts traditional local ways of doing things. The cultures of the powerful countries are not simply imposed on those of less powerful countries, yet they do influence them, and the result is often radical change to traditional cultural practices.

When this view of globalisation is applied to language-related issues, the stress is on the way that the spread of a language such as English results in the development of new 'indigenised' varieties, sometimes referred to as New Englishes (e.g. Australian English, Indian English, etc.), which are a result of contact with local languages and cultural practices (Kachru, 1986). And again, the process operates in two directions. So, for example, the English of 'Inner Circle' countries is also being influenced by the language practices of new immigrant communities (Harris, 2006).

Figure 2   Manga in a bookstore

Globalisation as process

What is apparent from this brief sketch is that these alternative views of globalisation lead to very different – and in many ways conflicting – interpretations of what is happening in the world. As such it is perhaps best to consider these as *effects* of globalisation, rather than integral aspects of the process in their own right. In other words, globalisation does not necessarily lead to one or the other of these scenarios, and so it can be misleading to view it solely in these terms. A more flexible approach for theorising the topic is to focus on the *processes* rather than the *products* of globalisation: to look at what it is about the dynamics of the present historical period which leads, under certain circumstances, to these particular effects.

If we consider globalisation in terms of processes rather than end products, a concise definition would be that it is the complex of processes by which the world is being transformed into a vast, interconnected global system. In the words of Robertson (1992, p. 8), it is 'the compression of the world and the intensification of consciousness of the world as a whole'. At the heart of this process is the collapsing of traditional ideas and constraints of *time* and *space*, and the subsequent opportunities for *mobility* to which this gives rise. That is to say, human beings are now no longer bound in the way they were even a generation ago by the rules of time and space in terms of the way they can communicate and interact. Due to rapid developments in technology (specifically in computers, telecommunications and transport), it is now far easier for people to communicate instantly over great distances, and for people, commodities, information and money to travel around the world in very short periods of time.

The result of all this is that fresh opportunities now exist for the way that a host of everyday social activities take place. Rather than operate on a predominantly local scale, in many contexts it is now as easy for people to conduct a range of affairs with participants scattered all across the globe. Video teleconferencing means one can have business meetings with colleagues on different continents without anyone having to go anywhere; online banking means one can send money to distant locations with a click of the mouse; mobile phone technology allows one to be in constant contact with home or work wherever one may physically be in the world. This movement of ideas, goods and people is a key catalyst for all the developments that are happening in the name of globalisation, and so the concept of *mobility* is central to an understanding of how it works as a process.

The result of all this opportunity for movement is a fundamental *change in traditional social structures*. Anthony Giddens (1999) gives the example of the way that for many people around the world, the face of Nelson Mandela is more recognisable than that of their own neighbour. He suggests that this illustrates that people interact with society in a noticeably different fashion from that of previous eras, and that in today's globalised world the local environment is no longer as important as it once was for the everyday necessities of life or for a sense of one's identity. Many people around the globe – especially those living in modern urban societies – are now as likely to identify with events happening on the other side of the world as with those on their own doorstep. In other words, the different opportunities for social activity that have been brought about by the dissolution of the constraints of time and space bring with them different ways of organising society, and the net result is that people are now as connected to a worldwide system of social interaction as they are to their local environment. Other examples of this global interconnectedness include everything from the year-round importing of seasonal fruit for sale in local supermarkets, to the use of international call-centres by local banks and businesses, to the impact that financial crises on one side of the world have for the economies of countries on other continents. In each case, systems of social organisation are operating on a *global* scale, and this has inevitable implications for the role and status of the *local* environment. We should add to this that not everyone has equal access to the technologies which propel globalisation, and so the experience of the changes in social organisation are felt in different ways by different people. For example, increased mobility might mean cheaper international tourism for some, while for others it will be experienced in terms of refugee migration.

The concept of community in a globalised world

A major consequence of this shift in social organisation is that it alters the nature of what is understood as a *community*. Traditional ideas of a community being a group of people living in a local environment are no longer necessarily valid. Nowadays, some communities exist more as networks of people who interact by means of a communication technology which allows them to be dispersed across the globe and never physically meet. For example, social networking sites such as Facebook, Bebo or Mixi allow one to keep in touch with groups of 'friends' whom one may rarely physically see, or indeed, may never have met in person at all. With the increased mobility brought about by globalisation, communities are also likely to be more fluid than in the past, with people migrating to and fro.

The implications of this shift in the nature of community is that cultural practices which are rooted in tradition (that are the habitual ways of doing things which evolve within a settled community) come under a great amount of pressure. The shift in the way people interact means that new cultural practices (i.e. ways of doing things) emerge along with new communities, and that different traditions rub up alongside each other. In other words, while diversity and change have been constants in the cultural history of humankind, they now happen with greater speed and scope than ever before. Globalisation, therefore, can be seen as a process whereby increased mobility brought about by rapid developments in technology is producing a globally interconnected system of social organisation, and this is having a profound effect on the way people relate and interact, as well as on the cultural practices which mediate this interaction.

Language and global society

Globalisation and international communication

What role does language play in all this? The short answer is that it plays a highly significant role. Broadly speaking, the relationship between globalisation and language is one of mutual influence: globalisation processes are affected greatly by language-related issues; and different languages can be significantly influenced by the processes of globalisation. In this section, I will look at this relationship from both perspectives, with a particular focus on the case of English (the 'global language'), and will suggest that the era of globalisation has brought with it a fundamental shift in the way we think about languages in the world today. For a full understanding of the role that language plays in the lives of modern societies it is therefore necessary to look at how the forces of globalisation are exerting pressure on the way we both use and think about the language we employ daily. And, as will be discussed below, it is the way that globalisation is refashioning concepts of community and having an impact on cultural practices that produces the most significant changes in global language practices (Blommaert, 2010).

A first point of note is that language facilitates globalisation. The social interaction that now takes place on a global scale invariably involves people across the world communicating with each other, and this means that language-related issues are an essential aspect of the process of globalisation. For people across the globe to be able to interact successfully, they need some system of communication through which to do so. It is in this context that the issue of an international or global language emerges: a single code to unite the peoples of the world linguistically. At this present moment in time, it is English that has emerged as the pre-eminent international language, and, as is often noted, more people today use the language as a *lingua franca* (i.e. as a means of communicating with people with whom they do not share a first language) than have it as their native language (Seidlhofer, 2001). In this respect, English already has a distinctly global profile, and while globalisation processes are facilitated by the spread of English around the world (people use it for communicating across national and linguistic boundaries), globalisation then further propels this spread (English is actively promoted as an international language in policy initiatives and education curriculums). As such, the spread of English can be seen as a key element in what we understand by globalisation.

English as a local language

The emergence of English as a code for international communication is not, however, the be all and end all of linguistic globalisation. With the spread of one language comes contact between that language and different contexts, cultures and communities. And this in turn results in different forms, functions and beliefs for the language. So, for example, rather than one standard form of English spreading inexorably across the globe, different varieties (or New Englishes) emerge as the language is shaped by the new communities which adopt it.[2] As was discussed above, one of the main consequences of globalisation has been the reconfiguration of communities and the development of new cultural practices by these communities. So although the spread of English is a result (and facilitator) of globalisation, the phenomenon that produces the spread (i.e. increased mobility in the world) also produces a continued diversity in the way that the language itself alters as it adapts to the emergent cultures of the diverse communities using it.

One notable consequence of this – which illustrates how the spread of English results in new forms of diversity – is that we can no longer assume things about the culture of the people we are talking to even when we are superficially speaking the same 'language'. Two and a half centuries ago, Dr Johnson wrote in his preface to his book *A Dictionary of the English Language* that 'it is incident to words [...] to change their manners when they change their country' (1755, p. v). He was referring to the way in which a word that is adopted into English from a different language may change its original meaning once it is established as part of the vocabulary of English. An example would be 'mutton', derived from the Old French *mouton* meaning 'ram' or 'sheep', but once integrated into the English language being used to refer only to the 'meat' from sheep.[3] This same process occurs in the everyday use of the language in globalised contexts, as English forms are now constantly changing context and country and, in the process, changing their 'manners'. The result is that an item of vocabulary might have one shade of meaning in British English, but a quite different shade in one of the New Englishes. For example, the word 'dresses' in British English refers to a particular type of clothing, but in Cameroon English it is used to mean clothes in general. A global language such as English thus becomes *multiplex* – it no longer has one centre (e.g. the UK) which influences its shape and usage, but instead has several different centres located in the communities which now use it.

Figure 3   Localised use of English in Jodhpur, India

In addition to having different meanings depending on the contexts in which they are used, linguistic forms are also likely to have different *values* (Hymes, 1966). For example, in the USA using English may simply be taken as commonplace (it is the dominant language in the country), but in Japan it might be seen as a symbol of an international outlook, while in Bangladesh it might be associated with economic prestige. Likewise, English spoken with a Nigerian accent in Lagos will have a different value from the use of the same accent in London; in the former context it will be the norm – most people will speak it with much that accent – while in the latter it is likely to be seen as an index of 'foreignness' by the mainstream community, and may well attract forms of discrimination.

As we can see, therefore, the consequence of this difference in meaning and value is that we can no longer speak of a single cohesive 'English speech community'. Due to the increased mobility in global society, assumptions about meanings and values become complicated as the language spreads from country to country and culture to culture. Even if people across the globe speak what is notionally the 'same' language, they are still likely to be faced with a variety of intercultural communication issues, which manifest themselves not only in terms of the way people are able to understand each other, but also in the way people perceive and evaluate each other's use of the language.

In conclusion, we can see that it is impossible simply to say that globalisation is leading to linguistic homogeneity (everyone speaking the same language), and that the spread of English around the world will result in a form of linguistic imperialism whereby the language practices of the politically and economically powerful Anglophone countries (especially the USA and UK) come to dominate other countries (Phillipson, 1992). While this dynamic is certainly a noticeable effect of linguistic globalisation in some contexts (e.g. in domains such as scientific research and academic writing where English is becoming ever more dominant), the actuality of day-to-day linguistic practices for many people around the world is far more complex in terms of the different influences and orientations they have (Pennycook, 2010).

Linguistic globalisation, then, is a result of the increased mobility in society which is a product of the advances in technology that are collapsing traditional constraints of time and space. With this increased mobility come changes in social organisation, and these in turn lead to different types of community. Ultimately, language practices are determined by the communities that use the language, and it is, therefore, the ways in which communities are changing due to the forces of globalisation that produces the new patterns of linguistic use and new forms of linguistic diversity which we experience in present-day society.

Notes

1 'Asterix Promoting McBurgers in France', 24 January 2002, *Toronto Globe & Mail.* Available at http://www.commondreams.org/headlines02/0124-03.htm (last accessed 30 March 2011).

2 Just as English is influenced by contact with other languages, so local languages will also alter, maybe adopting features or structures from the contact language, or, in some cases, gradually being replaced by it.

3 In New Zealand English, however, 'mutton' can still have the wider meaning of 'sheep'; while in Australian and South Asian Englishes it also refers to goat meat (*OED*, draft revision, 2009).

References for this reading

Blommaert, J. (2010) *The Sociolinguistics of Globalization*, Cambridge, Cambridge University Press.

Giddens, A. (1999) *Runaway World: How Globalization is Reshaping Our Lives*, London, Profile.

Harris, R. (2006) *New Ethnicities and Language Use*, Basingstoke, Palgrave Macmillan.

Hymes, D. (1966) 'Two types of linguistic relativity (with examples from Amerindian ethnography)' in Bright W. (ed.) *Sociolinguistics: Proceedings of the UCLA Sociolinguistics Conference, 1964*, The Hague, Mouton.

Johnson, S. (1755) *A Dictionary of the English Language*, London, J. and P. Knapton.

Kachru, B. B. (1986) *The Alchemy of English: The Spread, Functions, and Models of Non-native Englishes*, Oxford, Pergamon Press.

Pennycook, A. (2010) 'English and globalization' in Maybin, J. and Swann, J. (eds) *The Routledge Companion to English Language Studies*, Abingdon, Routledge.

Phillipson, R. (1992) *Linguistic Imperialism*, Oxford, Oxford University Press.

Robertson, R. (1992) *Globalization: Social Theory and Global Culture*, London, Sage.

Robertson, R. (1995) 'Glocalization: time-space and homogeneity-heterogeneity' in Featherstone, M., Lash, S. and Robertson, R. (eds) *Global Modernities*, London, Sage.

Seidlhofer, B. (2001) 'Closing a conceptual gap: the case for a description of English as a lingua franca', *International Journal of Applied Linguistics*, vol. 11, no. 2, pp. 133–58.

READING B: English in Finnish society

Sirpa Leppänen and Tarja Nikula

Source: adapted by the authors from: Leppänen, S. and Nikula, T. (2007) 'Diverse uses of English in Finnish society: discourse-pragmatic insights into media, educational and business contexts', *Multilingua*, vol. 26, no. 4, pp. 333–80.

English as the most important foreign language in modern Finland

Through a variety of historical, political, economic, social and cultural processes, English has acquired a unique role and status in Finland. Its spread received a distinct boost in the 1960s when Finland gradually began to associate itself more with the western, Anglo-American world – its politics, values, ways of life and its popular culture (e.g. Battarbee 2002). In so doing, it chose to distance itself from the culture and values of its former rulers, Sweden and Russia. In education, English quickly evolved from a relatively marginal foreign language (less important than German or French) into the first foreign language *par excellence*, the one studied by the majority of Finns born in and after the 1950s (Takala and Havola 1983; Takala 1998; Leppänen *et al.* forthcoming). Its current centrality in education is demonstrated by the fact that tuition is now offered, not only in the two official languages, Finnish and Swedish, but also in English, in the form of content-based language learning, IB gymnasiums and courses in higher education (Nikula and Marsh 1996; Phillipson 1992: 317–318; Phillipson 2004). In the media, English has had a strong presence since the 1960s. For example, from very early on, English films and TV series have been subtitled rather than dubbed (Vertanen 2003). In the print media – including youth magazines, advertisements, job announcements and trade names – and in the new media, English has established itself as an additional language, alongside Finnish and Swedish, (e.g. Sajavaara and Lehtonen 1981; Taavitsainen and Pahta 2003; Moore and Varantola 2005; Leppänen 2007; Leppänen *et al.* 2009; Leppänen and Piirainen-Marsh 2009). In professional life and business, English is quickly becoming a lingua franca or an intracultural means of communication (e.g. Louhiala-Salminen, Charles and Kankaanranta 2005, Virkkula and Nikula 2010).

In Finland, as in many other countries where the importance of English as [a second or foreign language] has increased, the spread of English has caused a great deal of debate, both among scholars and the general public. And just as elsewhere, the debates often recycle value judgements and arguments from more general discourses related to English. Comments range from lamentations on the role of English in what could be seen as an Anglo-American cultural and economic conspiracy to celebrations of English as an agent of progress, international understanding and co-operation (e.g. Crystal 1997); and further to utilitarian views of English as an effective tool for getting things done in, for example, multinational business life and international politics (Quirk 1985; Bhatt 2001; Brutt-Griffler 2002).

In Finland, the dystopian view of English is manifested in public concern for those sections of the Finnish population whose proficiency in English is non-existent or limited, and in arguments emphasising the spread of English into Finnish society as a factor creating a new kind of linguistic divide, one that will further marginalise part of the population and increase social and economic inequality (e.g. Nuolijärvi 1999). Strongly nationalistic pleas for the protection of the Finnish language/s are growing stronger in Finland, with some scholars worrying that Finns may now be in danger of losing their language/s either completely (e.g. Laurén 2001) or partially (e.g. Hiidenmaa 2003; Taavitsainen and Pahta 2003). Thus, in some recent work on the role of English in Finland (e.g. Taavitsainen and Pahta 2003; Hiidenmaa 2003) it is suggested that within particular domains and settings (e.g. higher education, youth culture, research and business) the native language/s are being lost to English. Still others argue that Finns are losing not just their native languages but also English: because of the trend in Finnish schools towards teaching content subjects through English, it is feared that students are, in fact, being forced to learn 'broken' or 'bad' English mediated by their Finnish teachers (Räikkälä and Reuter 1998). On the other hand, in business, politics and the media it is not uncommon for English to be equated with internationalisation – which is also seen as something that the Finnish society and economy should strive towards (Härkönen 2005). The debates concerning English clearly display conflicting opinions and attitudes, and overall, the issue of English in Finland is highly controversial […]

Despite the fact that English is officially a foreign language in Finland, in certain domains and settings it is often either officially or unofficially selected as the only language of communication […] They include two broad types of situations. First of all we have situations in which English is either a foreign language to all of the participants, or in which some of the participants are native speakers of English. In these situations, English is usually the only language shared by all the participants – a factor which explains why instances of code-switching rarely become an issue. But secondly, there are situations in which English is chosen as the primary means of communication, even when all or most of the participants are Finns. A remarkable characteristic of the situations in this category, no matter whether the participants are from different language backgrounds or Finns only, is that the choice of English is to a large extent an unquestioned phenomenon.

English in the Finnish media: the case of talk shows

As an illustration of a setting where English is selected as the language of communication, this section discusses an example from the domain of the media. From the early days of Finnish television, there have been regular broadcasts of programmes in English. In addition, there are nowadays domestic programmes – news and talk shows in particular – which either include sections in English within the Finnish or Swedish programme, or which are conducted completely in English. A typical example of these would consist of interviews with non-Finnish experts or guests. The programmes in English are usually subtitled in Finnish and Swedish, although in some cases, particularly if the English item is brief, the Finnish journalists may simply paraphrase the English comments in Finnish.

Our example […] (from Koskela 2005) is an illustration of a programme type which is entirely in English (but broadcast with Finnish subtitles): it is an episode from a talk show in which a Finnish journalist interviews foreign celebrities, native and non-native speakers, in English. In this type of interview English is the only language shared by the participants. Koskela (2005) approaches such interview data from a conversation analytic perspective, with special reference to how expertise is constructed in broadcast talk. One of her interests, looked at in more detail below, has to do with whether the lingua franca situation is somehow reflected in the language use. In [Table 1] the guest interviewed is a well known Bosnian film director, and the topic here is the theme of violence in his films:

[Transcription conventions are given at the end of the article. IE = Interviewee, IR = Interviewer]

[Table 1]   An extract from a Finnish talk show

1	IE	so violence is everywhere look at how the
2		°hh how they beh- behave on the:
3		°hh on the: in England in the football stadiums.
4		more °hh worse than any Balkanian uh: wild (.)
5		bunches they are even: **wor**se
6		so °hh uh- uh look at how they t:hrow the atomic b**o**mb.
7		what is that. that's the **ulti**mate expression
8		of this is uh s- still °hh folklore but when they

<pre>
                    o-----x------o   x = IE looks away from IR
</pre>

9		throw the atomic bomb, °hh it's the **ul**timate
10		u-u-uh power (.) that shows

<pre>
                  o—x—o   x = IE looks away from IR
</pre>

11		how the people are destructed.=
12	IR	=°hh but do we have to:
13		accept the violent nature of human:
14	IE	**n**[**o**:: .] we have to try to (.) correct it.
15	IR	[being]
16	IR	well **how**.
17	IC	[by the movies.]
18	IR	[°heh heh°]
		[...]
25	IE	in m**y** movies you are never disgusted
26		or neve:r (.) u:h neve:r uh (0.7)

<pre>
                      o-x-o   o---x---o   x = IE withdraws gaze from IR
</pre>

27		afraid of: of blood or I don't know
28		tho the images (.) you **feel** the-the-t- destroy-

<pre>
                           o----------x--------   x = IE withdraws gaze from IR
</pre>

29		uh uh °hh dis**tur**bed but not u:h (.)

<pre>
             ------------o
</pre>

30		**sho**cked I'm never doing this.=
31	IR	°hh what about betrayal. (.)
32		that's one of the themes in Underground.=
33	IE	=also constituent of the history he[re.]
34	IR	[mm]-h (0.8)
35	IE	lo[ook at me,] I'm betrayal
36	IR	[>in which way. <]
37	IE	I betrayed a **na**tion they say.
38		even I never felt °hh **be**ing part of this nation.
39		(.) so °hh i-it's like u- °hh it's like u:h for a psychi**a**trist
40		I think more it's a good to°hh it's like a projection:
41		you project to somebody::?
42		(.) what **you** feel. (.) and your feel- fee- uh

43		O----------X---	x = IE withdraws gaze from IR
		feeling of guilt is **so:** extended,	
44		-----------o	
45		°hh that's even (xx) or like uh with	
		°hh betrayal: traito:r and all- all this	
		O---------X--------------O	IR circular mvt forward with
46			right hand
47		(0.5)	IR nods slightly
48		sense of **g**uilt.	
		guilt °(guilt)° (.) g̲uilt of father,	
49		O---X--	x = IR lifts up index finger
	IR	**fa**ther's guilt it's a °hh >which is< **an**tique guilt	
50	IE	---------o	
51		that people feel here (.)	
52		and they just from generation to generation: uh (.)	
		they just proc**ee**d the guilt.	

[This] example […] has many features that previous research has found to be typical of lingua franca talk. Linguistically, lingua franca speech has been found to contain a number of lexico-grammatical features that deviate from the norms of standard English (see Seidlhofer, in Jenkins *et al.* 2001: 16). In this example, such features could include the occasional omissions of both indefinite and definite articles (ll. 13, 48, 49) and idiosyncratic lexical forms (l. 11 'destructed'). Other features that have been seen as typical of lingua franca speech include gaps in a speaker's vocabulary (Seidlhofer, in Jenkins *et al.* 2001: 16). In [Table 1], the interviewee's 'I'm betrayal' (l. 35) or 'proceed the guilt' (l. 52) could perhaps be seen as indicating lexical or collocational gaps in the interviewee's English […]

The extract would thus indeed show many characteristics of lingua franca talk, but Koskela (2005) argues that if the exchange is investigated from a perspective which does *not* take as its point of departure the fact that this is non-native talk, the very same phenomena may receive interpretations that do not highlight their problematic nature. For example, word searches may be seen as signs of insufficient target language mastery, and in line 45, the interviewee does indeed seem to search for a suitable word with his expression 'and all- all this'. However, word searches are also employed by native speakers, as pointed out by Goodwin and Goodwin (1986: 56), who found that in native-speaker talk, speakers often move their gaze away from the recipients during word searches. The withdrawal of the gaze is consequential for the recipient, as it shows that the speaker is engaged in a word search and that there is reason for the recipient to wait for the talk to continue. In a similar vein, the interviewee in [this] extract moves his gaze in lines 8, 10, 26, 28 and 42–43 to mark a word search and to indicate that no contributions are expected from the co-participant [...]

Furthermore, Koskela (2005) argues that in this television interview the participants orient themselves primarily to their institutional roles; the fact that the interview is conducted in English does not change the situation. Rather, both participants orient to the roles of interviewer and interviewee and jointly manage to construct an appropriate interview interaction in which the linguistic 'flaws' of their contributions do not seem to cause any significant problems. The need for participants to co-construct themselves and each other as competent and knowledgeable social actors is further accentuated by the specific nature of the situation: the interview is public and mediated to a large audience through the medium of TV, and the guest has been invited onto the programme specifically because he is a recognised expert in his field; thus his contributions are treated as valid and adequate.

The frequent use of English in Finnish TV programmes indicates that it now has the status of a self-evidently available language for communication in the Finnish media in the absence of other shared languages. As shown above, although such lingua franca interactions often display linguistic and interactional features that may seem 'problematic' at the outset, these are not necessarily treated as such by the interlocutors themselves who, rather than orienting themselves to language, focus more on the joint negotiation of the activity and the enactment of their institutional roles and expertise.

The example illustrates a typical contact situation in present-day Finland where English is used as a vehicular language by interlocutors who would not otherwise have a shared language. However, it is important to notice that in the changing sociolinguistic landscape of globalized Finland this situation represents only one particular case. Other typical contact situations include settings where English functions as an 'intracultural' means of communication between language users who may or may not share their native language. These can be, for example, workplace communities or groups sharing a common interest (e.g. a lifestyle; leisure time activity). Within this contact type, instances of code-switching may take on particular significance, in cases where the language users also have at their disposal shared codes apart from English [...] Yet another important contact situation is one in which English functions as an additional resource in bilingual communication – for example, on the internet, in the media, and in such everyday contexts as the playing of electronic games […] new media […], hobbies and lifestyles […] In this type of contact situation, speakers and writers draw on resources from both Finnish and English to varying degrees […].

Based on what we have observed, one of our main arguments is that if we are to provide nuanced and contextualised empirical evidence on which to base language and educational policies, research on global English (and the ways in which it is taken up and put to use in different domains, settings, situations and texts) will need to be multi-dimensional in nature. In our view, investigations of this kind should pay attention both to micro-level features and processes of language use and to language use as social practice, i.e. as shaping and shaped by the setting, the activity and the institutional context.

Table 2 Transcription conventions

emboldened talk	emphasis or stress
CAPITALS	increased volume
°high circles°	decreased volume
ta:::lk	prolongation or stretching of the preceding sound
tal-	cut-off word
°hhh	inbreath
hh	outbreath
(.)	a micropause of less than 0.4 seconds
(0.8)	a pause, timed in tenths of a second
ta[lk] [tal]king	overlapping utterances
talk= =talk	latching utterances
(talk)	uncertain transcription
(x)	unintelligible item, probably one word only
(xx)	unintelligible items, approximately of phrase length
(xxx)	unintelligible items, beyond phrase length
,	continuing intonation
.	falling intonation
?	rising intonation
↑	high pitch
>fast<	fast speech
<slow>	slow speech
£	altered tone of voice, e.g. when quoting somebody
ta(h)lk	breathiness, e.g. in laughter

References for this reading

Battarbee, Keith (2002). English in Europe: Finnish. In Görlach, Manfred (ed.), *English in Europe*. Oxford: Oxford University Press, 261–276.

Bhatt, Rakesh M. (2001). World Englishes. *Annual Review of Anthropology* 30, 527–550.

Brutt-Griffler, Janina (2002). *World English: A Study of its Development*. Clevedon: Multilingual Matters.

Crystal, David (1997). *English as a Global Language*. Cambridge: Cambridge University Press.

Goodwin, Marjorie H. and Charles Goodwin (1986). Gesture and coparticipation in the activity of searching for a word. *Semiotica* 62, 51–75.

Härkönen, Mari-Annukka (2005). The 'value' and 'meaning' of the English language in Finland as represented in newspapers in the early 2000's. Pro Gradu thesis. University of Jyväskylä: Department of Languages.

Hiidenmaa, Pirjo (2003). *Suomen kieli – who cares* ('The Finnish language – who cares'). Helsinki: Otava.

Jenkins, Jennifer, Marko Modiano and Barbara Seidlhofer (2001). Euro-English. *English Today* 17, 13–19.

Koskela, Heidi (2005). Invoking different types of knowledge in celebrity interviews. *SKY Journal of Linguistics* 18, 93–118.

Laurén, Christer (2001). Ovatko suomalaiset menettämässä kielensä? ('Are Finns losing their language?'). *Helsingin Sanomat*, 14.3.2001.

Leppänen, Sirpa (2007). Writing (trans)local gender in fan fiction. In Caldas-Coulthard, Carmen-Rosa and Rick Iedema (eds.), *Identity Trouble – Discursive Constructions*. London: Palgrave, 165–179.

Leppänen, Sirpa and Arja Piirainen-Marsh (2009). Language policy in the making: an analysis of bilingual gaming activities. *Language Policy* 8 (3), 261–284.

Leppänen Sirpa, Anne Pitkänen-Huhta, Arja Piirainen-Marsh, Tarja Nikula and Saija Peuronen (2009). Young people's translocal new media uses: A multiperspective analysis of language choice and heteroglossia. *Journal of Computer-Mediated Communication* 14 (4), 1080–1107.

Leppänen Sirpa, Anne Pitkänen-Huhta, Tarja Nikula, Samu Kytölä, Timo Törmäkangas, Kari Nissinen, Leila Kääntä, Tiina Virkkula, Mikko-Pekka Laitinen, Päivi Pahta, Heidi Koskela, Salla Lähdesmäki and Henna Jousmäki (Forthcoming). *Finns uses of and attitudes to English: Findings of a national survey*. *eVarieng*. http://www.helsinki.fi/varieng/journal/index.html.

Louhiala-Salminen Leena, Mirjaliisa Charles and Anne Kankaanranta (2005). English as a lingua franca in Nordic corporate mergers: Two case companies. *English for Specific Purposes* 24, 401–421.

Moore, Kate and Krista Varantola (2005). Anglo-Finnish contacts: Collisions and collusions. In Anderman, Gunilla and Margaret Rogers (eds.), *In and Out of English: For Better, for Worse?* Clevedon: Multilingual Matters, 133–152.

Nikula, Tarja and David Marsh (1996). *Kartoitus vieraskielisen opetuksen tarjonnasta peruskouluissa ja lukioissa.* ('A survey on the availability of foreign language instruction in lower and higher levels of the secondary school'). Helsinki: Opetushallitus.

Nuolijärvi, Pirkko (1999). Suomen kielitilanne 2000-luvulla ('The Finnish language situation in the 2000's'). http://www.tsv.fi/ttapaht/991/nuolijarvi.htm, accessed March 12, 2004.

Phillipson, Robert (1992). *Linguistic Imperialism.* Oxford: Oxford University Press.

Phillipson, Robert (2004). *English-Only Europe? Challenging Language Policy.* London: Routledge.

Quirk, Randolph (1985). The English language in a global context. In Quirk, Randolph and Henry Widdowson (eds.), *English in the World: Teaching and Learning the Language and Literatures.* Cambridge: Cambridge University Press, 1–6.

Räikkälä, Anneli and Mikael Reuter (1998). Kotimaisten kielten tutkimuskeskuksen kielipoliittinen ohjelma ('The language policy program of the research institute for the languages of Finland'). http://www.kotus.fi/kotus/kielipolitiikka.shtml, accessed February, 2004.

Sajavaara, Kari and Jaakko Lehtonen (1981). Anglismit nykysuomessa ('Anglicisms in modern Finnish'). *Virittäjä* 4.

Taavitsainen, Irma and Päivi Pahta (2003). English in Finland: Globalisation, language awareness and questions of identity. *English Today* 19, 3–15.

Takala, Sauli (1998). Language teaching policy effects – a case study of Finland. In Fisiak, Jaček (ed.), *Festschrift for Kari Sajavaara. Studia Anglica Posnaniensia: International Review of English Studies* XXXIII.

Takala, Sauli and Liisa Havola (1983). *English in the Socio-linguistic Context of Finland Englannin kieli Suomen yhteiskunnallisessa ja kielellisessä ympäristössä.* University of Jyväskylä: Institute for Educational Research.

Vertanen, Esko (2003). Personal communication on the history of subtitling English language TV programs on Finnish TV.

Virkkula, Tiina and Tarja Nikula (2010). Identity construction in ELF contexts: A case study of Finnish engineering students working in Germany. *International Journal of Applied Linguistics* 20 (2), 251–273.

5 English and Englishes

Jennifer Smith

5.1 Introduction

English has always been a highly mobile language, beginning with its arrival in the British Isles from Europe around the fifth century and its subsequent spread across the globe. As previous chapters have shown, this mobility has resulted in the emergence of diverse systems of language use, with the creation of unique varieties of English across time and throughout the world. The history of English demonstrates that one of the most important influences on the emergence of these varieties is the sociohistorical conditions in which they arose, including migration patterns, settlement history, geographical factors and contact with other languages. This chapter turns to the outcomes of such processes: to the linguistic characteristics of contemporary varieties of English.

As a basis for this description, the chapter broadly adopts Braj Kachru's (1992) idea of Circles of Englishes. While there are shortcomings with this idea, as discussed in Chapter 1, it nevertheless provides a good starting point for accounting for different varieties. I start with 'Inner Circle' Englishes spoken in the British Isles and Ireland – the 'Old World'. I then move on to how these highly diverse varieties became levelled and homogenised in their transplanted homes in the 'New World' during the colonial period: in North America, Australia and New Zealand. 'Outer Circle' Englishes, those which are used in parallel with indigenous languages, will include discussion of Indian English, and creolised varieties such as Bislama and Tok Pisin. While English has now spread widely across Kachru's 'Expanding Circle' (e.g. continental Europe, China, Japan), we cannot identify systematic varieties of English in these contexts in quite the same way as we can in the 'Inner' and 'Outer Circles' – I consider this point briefly towards the end of the chapter.

5.2 A sociolinguistic approach to studying varieties of English

The approach taken in this chapter largely adopts the model used in **sociolinguistics**, where the development of particular varieties of English is related to the historical, geographical and social contexts in which the language occurs. I touch on particular theories that have been proposed to account for variation in English, whether in terms of contact between English and other languages, contact between dialects of English, characteristics of speakers, or some other factor.

Sociolinguistics

Sociolinguistics is the study of language and society, or language and social life. A core area of interest for sociolinguists has been variation and change in English and other languages.

As you saw in the general introduction to this book, linguists draw on different linguistic levels in the description of English and other languages. In order to describe varieties of English, I refer mainly to the levels in the box below. This involves some technical description, particularly in relation to the sounds of language. If you are not familiar with linguistic description, Appendix 2 provides some brief guidance to the kinds of features we discuss.

Describing English

Levels of description adopted in this chapter include:

Lexis, or vocabulary: **lexical variation** refers to the use of words that are specific to particular varieties of English

Grammar: including particular word forms (*morphology*), or sentence structure (*syntax*)

Phonology: the sound systems of different varieties, including variation in the way particular sounds are pronounced, or 'phonetically realised'.

Activity 5.1

Allow about 5–10 minutes

Read through the following extract. Can you identify one or two examples of vocabulary (lexis) and pronunciation that seem to stand out in this variety? (You can't hear how the words are pronounced, but does the spelling give you any clues about possible pronunciations?) Don't worry about grammatical features for the moment – I'll come back to these later.

Speaker from the Shetland islands, off the north coast of Scotland

And we started driving oot and er I mind pulling up ootside this- we got into this, like, road, pulling up ootside this tiny peerie like hoose and there was all this like peerie kind of like corrugated iron shacks aroond it. And all this- just all this folk just wanderin' aboot and that, just dirt and mess everywhere and I just mind thinking 'Oh please God, let yon be his, let yon be his hoose'. And then he said 'This Lisa- this is w- where you're stayin'. And so I got oot of the car and then, the wife like kind of introduced me to this foak and I gied inside this tiny, tiny, peerie hoose, it was just two rooms. Probably the rooms put together was peerier as this room. And er gied in, they started speaking in yon !Xhosa, that's what the- like the kind of dialect they spoke.

(Smith and Durham, 2011)

Comment

In terms of vocabulary, you may have picked out the word *peerie*, which means 'little' in this variety. Other examples include *gie* (meaning 'go' – here in the past tense); and *yon*, meaning 'that' or 'those' (this is related to the word *yonder*).

A striking feature of pronunciation is the 'oo' vowel in *oot*, *ootside* and *hoose* ('out', 'outside' and 'house').

Descriptions of different language varieties tend to emphasise their distinctiveness, as I did in Activity 5.1, identifying and seeking to explain specific features. Varieties are compared to a perceived standard (often standard English in England). This perception of distinctiveness is also evident in the names given to varieties (e.g. 'Geordie' for a variety spoken in Newcastle upon Tyne, in the north-east of England; Indian English; American English; Scottish English; Scots, as opposed to English). However, as you will see in this chapter, the identification of varieties of English and related languages is not unproblematic, not least because while descriptions focus on their distinctive features, they also share many features in common. Peter Trudgill (1999, p. 6) points out that, for geographically neighbouring areas, there are usually no sharp dialect boundaries. Instead, dialects form a continuum of use and are best characterised as 'more or less' rather than 'either/or'.

So let us now turn to varieties of English worldwide and some of their defining linguistic features.

5.3   English in the 'Old World'

Chapter 2 provides an account of the development of English in England, and Chapter 3 begins with an account of its spread within the British Isles and Ireland.

One of the defining features of dialects in the 'Old World' – the United Kingdom and the Republic of Ireland – is just how many regional varieties of English there are: Cockney, Geordie, Doric and Hiberno-English, to name but a few. The diversity of the Old World Englishes has a number of explanations, including variation in the dialects spoken by different Anglo-Saxon tribes who first brought English to Britain. Other factors are the great **time-depth** of English in the region: the long history that has allowed further differences to develop; and, over this period, contact with other languages such as Celtic, Norse and French. Here I touch on a number of dialect areas in the British Isles and how their present-day use can be situated in their sociohistorical contexts.

English in England

Traditionally, there are said to be two major dialect groups in England: Southern and Northern. These may be the result of Anglo-Saxon settlement patterns from centuries ago, with physical barriers perpetuating this split. Trudgill (1999, p. 8) provides a striking example of this in one of the most important dialect boundaries which runs through the Fens in eastern England. The Fens, now mostly drained, was an isolated, swampy area which in the past was difficult to cross. Both north and south of this line people used to pronounce 'laugh' and 'butter' as *laff* (/laf/) and *bootter* (/bʊtə/). However, south of the line these pronunciations began to change, so 'laugh' became /lɑːf/ with a long /ɑ/ and 'butter', /bʌtə/, the modern, standard pronunciation. Because people couldn't make it across the swampy Fens, neither did the change, so they continue to say *laff* and *bootter* in more northern areas, even to this day, providing one of the most important **isoglosses** between north and south. Isoglosses are the geographical boundaries of particular linguistic features, represented by lines on dialect maps.

Figure 5.1   Dialect regions in England (Trudgill, 1999)

Note: Figure 5.1 shows a hierarchy of dialect areas in England. There is an initial broad division between 'north' and 'south'. 'North' is divided into 'northern' (further subdivided into 'northeast' and 'lower north'), and 'central' (further subdivided into 'west central' and 'east central'). 'South' is divided into 'southwest' and 'east'. Within these areas there may be smaller dialect regions. Trudgill's sixteen dialect regions occur at this local end of this hierarchy, including the 'northeast' (not further subdivided), 'central north', 'central Lancashire', etc.

Trudgill points out that change is a natural characteristic of human languages, but we cannot always explain why a particular change occurs where and when it does. Processes of change are discussed further in Chapter 7.

Most differences are much more fine-grained than a north/south split, however, due to different changes taking place across the country. Taking a number of pronunciation features into account, Trudgill identifies sixteen dialect regions of England, as in Figure 5.1, and points out a number of defining features of these areas such as the pronunciation of '*ng*' in Central Lancashire, Merseyside, Northwest Midlands and West Midlands so that *singer* rhymes with *finger;* and, in Newcastle, the use of the /a:/ vowel in certain words so that *all, ball* and *call* sound like *ahl, bahl* and *cahl*. Dialect divisions of the type shown in Figure 5.1 are continually changing, with changes stretching over hundreds of years. With increased social mobility and urbanisation, one of these changes is generally assumed to be dialect 'attrition' (the loss of traditional dialect forms) particularly in urban areas. However, the situation is not that simple, as will be shown in Reading A.

Activity 5.2

The complexities of the dialect situation in England are exemplified in Reading A by Esther Asprey who provides a description of Black Country English, an urban dialect which emerged as people migrated to the Midlands during the Industrial Revolution of the eighteenth and nineteenth centuries. Asprey's reading highlights the relationship between dialect and local **identity**: that is, how people feel about themselves, how they present themselves to others, and how this affects the way they speak. Asprey refers to the use of 'lexical sets' in her discussion of pronunciation – see the box below for an explanation.

As you read, consider the following questions:

- What aspects of language use are of interest to Asprey, and how does she investigate these?
- What kinds of features characterise the Black Country variety?
- What factors might encourage a Black Country speaker to use local dialect forms?

You may wish to compare this to your own situation: what kinds of features characterise the language variety, or varieties, in use in your area? To what extent is your own use of these features shaped by your sense of identity, or by the attitudes of others?

Comment

Esther Asprey was interested both in people's perceptions of the Black Country dialect – how they described the dialect and what they felt about it – and their own use of dialect forms. From the design of her research you can see how she tried to investigate this systematically. For instance, she made up a sample of informants who differed in certain ways, allowing her to make comparisons between groups of speakers (older and younger speakers, different social classes, as reported by the speakers themselves). Differences between older and younger speakers also allowed her to suggest that certain dialect features were changing.

Asprey analysed dialect features systematically across the levels of phonology, lexis and grammar.

Despite the stigma that its speakers often face, the Black Country dialect does not appear to be at risk of disappearing. There have been changes across generations, but the contemporary dialect is very much alive and kicking. Dialect forms include:

- **phonology**: how the vowels in several lexical sets are 'realised' or pronounced
- **lexis**: words for 'stream' and for 'playing truant'
- **grammar**: a particular system of negation, and the pronoun 'her' where in most other varieties we would find 'she'.

How to explain the persistence of such an old and stigmatised variety in a bustling urban area? Asprey cites a number of reasons. First, working class people, who are less likely to be mobile (either socially or geographically) and live in tight-knit communities, are more likely to use Black Country forms than others in the area. Second, social and demographic changes seem to alter the Black Country dialect (as with its increasingly atypical negation system, its pronunciation or even words like 'wag') rather than levelling out its features to reflect more standard ones. Finally, people seem proud of the variety and, as in other regions, their attitudes have a remarkably powerful effect on their use of local dialect forms. Perhaps because they are reluctant to use these in front of a researcher, people's responses to questions on their use don't always coincide with how they actually speak: one respondent claimed that the dialect had no words for playing truant, apparently unaware that she had used the phrase 'stop away'; while two speakers who said they never used 'her' for 'she' then went on to do so.

Lexical sets

Lexical sets are a means of comparing the pronunciation of vowels in different dialects. A lexical set is a group of words containing a vowel that has the same pronunciation in a given dialect. Each set is represented by a keyword. The BATH set, for instance, includes the keyword *bath* as well as other words such as *laugh, brass, ask* and *dance*. The vowel here is pronounced [ɑ:] in the south of England but [a] in the north.

English and Scots in Scotland

The English language in Scotland has considerable time-depth, and although written Scots was gradually supplanted by Scottish standard English from the seventeenth century onwards, spoken Scots features continue to be used to this day. This results in a linguistic continuum where the boundaries between Scots, Scottish standard English and even English English are fuzzy at best (e.g. Romaine, 1975).

Allow about 5–10 minutes

Activity 5.3

There is a plethora of characteristic features in Scots which differ from standard varieties of English, as illustrated below. Can you describe the highlighted feature in each example? (You met with some of these in the extract in Activity 5.1.)

So we a' **gied** down there.

I **selt** it a few year ago to the rowp man.

Doctor Paterson **telt** him right up, right **oot**.

Let **yon** be his, let **yon** be his hoose.

I **ken** you're right.

I **thocht** 'Och, I'm nae getting' intae that again'.

Can you not see her?

My hair needs **washed**.

There is no separate comment for this activity, but answers can be found in the discussion that follows.

It might be thought that these features arise from contact with Gaelic, the indigenous language in previous centuries. However, there are very few traces of the Gaelic language in Scots (Macafee, 2003). Instead, the unique nature of a number of features arises from two sources: innovations that have developed over time in Scotland, but not in other English-speaking contexts; and retentions from older forms of English. The first category includes grammatical features such as the regularisation of some irregular past tenses: *gied* for 'went' (from present tense *gie* meaning 'go'); also *selt* ('sold') and *telt* ('told'). An example from phonology is Scots 'l-vocalisation', where words like 'ball' and 'wall' are realised as *ba'* and *wa'* in most vernacular varieties (Macafee, 1983).

The second category, retentions from older forms of English, accounts for many present-day differences. The speaker's use of *oot* above is one example. Most speakers across the British Isles would have used this form in previous centuries but following a systematic change in the pronunciation of English vowels, known as the *Great Vowel Shift*, more southern varieties started using the sound /aʊ/ (often represented in writing by the letters <ou>). Northern varieties, however, maintained the earlier /uː/ sound. The word *yon* occurred throughout the British Isles a few centuries ago and can be found in Shakespeare's plays, but its use is now confined to more northern varieties. The same is true for the use of *ken* for 'know'. The sound, known technically as a 'velar fricative' /x/, is a very characteristic feature of Scots, so that 'night', 'fight' and 'thought' sound like *nicht*, *ficht* and *thocht*. This sound would have been heard in Old English but is rapidly dying out and is only heard in the more traditional, rural dialects in Scotland.

The Great Vowel Shift

The Great Vowel Shift was an ordered change in the sounds of the main vowels of English. It began in the fifteenth century and had its greatest effect in the south of Britain. This is why, for instance, 'house' is pronounced as *hoose* in more northern dialects: *hoose* is the original, unshifted pronunciation.

The use of non-prevocalic /r/ has been investigated in several dialects of English – we say more about this in Chapter 7.

Another of the most defining features of Scots is the use of **non-prevocalic /r/**, also know as **rhoticity** (where /r/ is pronounced at the end of words or before consonants, as in *car* and *card*). However, like the velar fricative, rhoticity may be in decline among younger speakers, especially in more urban areas (Scobbie and Stuart-Smith, 2008).

Most items in Activity 5.3 are features that people are overtly aware of and comment on. They tend to be used at the broad Scots end of the continuum. There are also 'covert' Scotticisms: forms which speakers don't even recognise as being Scots and are in fact surprised about when these are pointed out. These include the word order in the question *Can you not see her?* and the *need + -ed* construction in *My hair needs washed*, shown in Activity 5.3. These are used by all speakers regardless of class, and are also found in written contexts, as in the street sign below.

Figure 5.2   Street sign in Glasgow

A number of phonological forms also go unnoticed, including the pronunciation of *wh-* with initial aspiration (like 'hw') in words such as *where, when, whale* etc. This distinctive sound (represented by the symbol /ʍ/) occurs in some other varieties but is rare in standard English. Where the sound occurs, *whales* and *Wales* are different – they begin with two different sounds – leading Trudgill (1999, p. 39) to point out that the breakfast cereal *Weetabix* doesn't work very well in these varieties as *wheat* and *Weetabix* don't have the same initial sound.

The above features can be heard throughout Scotland. However, quite a number of features are distinctive to particular varieties of Scots. Today, there are several dialect areas and their unique histories are reflected in their grammar, lexis and phonology. Figure 5.3 indicates some broad areas, including Insular Scots (Orkney and Shetland), Northern Scots, Central Scots, Ulster Scots and Southern Scots.

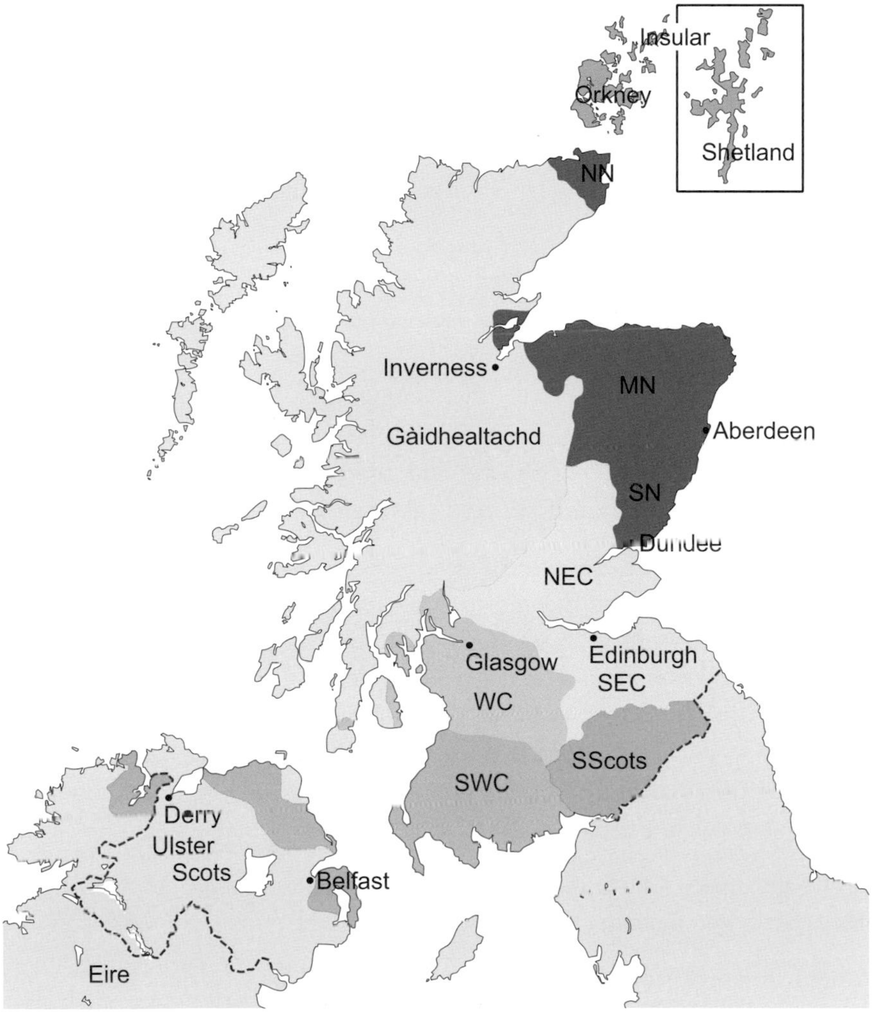

Figure 5.3 Main dialect divisions of Scots, www.scots-online.org, 2001. (Accessed 18 July 2011)

Notes: **Southern Scots** (SScots) along the Scots side of the border; **Central Scots**, subdivided into: South East Central (SEC), North East Central (NEC), West Central (WC), South West Central (SWC); **Northern Scots**, subdivided into: South Northern (SN), Mid Northern (MN), North Northern (NN); **Insular Scots** in the Orkney and Shetland Islands; **Urban Scots** refers to the dialects of Scots spoken in and around towns and cities, especially Edinburgh and Glasgow; **Ulster Scots** is found in the north of Ireland; **Gàidhealtachd**, the Gaelic for the Highlands and Islands to the west, refers to an area that, until fairly recently, was on the whole Gaelic speaking.

Varieties in the (rural) north-east – commonly referred to as Doric – are singled out as having a number of unique forms. This is no doubt due to their geographical isolation over the centuries, but also more sociocultural isolation which has allowed them to develop norms of their own, or internal innovations, little influenced by more mainstream developments. An example of this dialect is spoken in Buckie, a small fishing town on the north-east coast. In this dialect you can hear linguistic forms that seem very strange to an outsider, as in the examples below:

(a) **Far** you stayin' **fin** ye're here?

(b) **I na ken** far ye're gan.

(c) You dinna ken fit tae dee wi' **quines**.

As mentioned above, Scots has a separate sound /ʍ/ in words such as *where* and *when*. However, in Buckie and surrounding areas this sound becomes /f/ to give *far* and *fin* in (a) above.

The form in (b) is an example of *do* absence: instead of *I dinna ken* ('I don't know') the *do* is deleted in some contexts to give *Iø na ken* (the symbol ø is used here to mark deletion) (Smith, 2001). An important point about *do* absence is that it can only occur in certain environments: speakers in Buckie never delete *do* if the subject is *he, she, it* or a singular noun. So you would never hear something like *He na like it*, or *The girl na like it* in this dialect. This provides a very good example of how dialects have rules, just as standard English does.

One of the many lexical differences is in the use of *quines* and *loons* for 'girls' and 'boys' instead of the more widespread *lassies* and *laddies*.

It might be surprising that these forms are used by a variety in the British Isles, and even more surprising that the utterances come from a young speaker – a 26-year-old woman, Karen. However, the relative isolation and time-depth of English in the area explains the many differences found in this Scottish dialect, which has been allowed not only to retain features long since gone in more mainstream Scots dialects, but also to innovate features, free from standard norms. The survival of the variety is also attributed to the positive attitudes the speakers themselves have to the dialect and Buckie more generally, as Asprey discusses in Reading A in relation to Black Country English.

English in Wales

The time-depth of English in Wales is much shorter than in Scotland. Despite the fact that the Acts of Union in 1536 and 1542 saw the beginnings of English used in law, administration and education, until the start of the eighteenth century the vast majority of the population of Wales spoke the Celtic language Welsh. This changed with the Industrial Revolution, which brought a massive influx of English speakers, and also government policies which were concerned with 'the means afforded to the labouring classes of acquiring a knowledge of the English Language' (Education Report 1847, p. 1). By the twentieth century, the majority of speakers in Wales were monolingual English. However, this shift to English was highly geographically circumscribed to South Wales where immigration led to rapid expansion in Cardiff, Newport and communities along the South Wales Valleys. Elsewhere, particularly in rural west and north-west Wales, the population remained predominantly Welsh speaking, although by the start of the twentieth century contact with English had increased to the point that most speakers were bilingual.

This history has produced two broad dialect areas in present-day Welsh English. Dialects in the south are said to have strong affinities with dialects in the south-west of England and West Midlands, whereas the northern and western regions are said to be more influenced by the structure of Welsh, particularly in areas where English has the least time-depth.

A good example of the varying influences of Welsh and 'English' English is shown in the use of non-prevocalic /r/ in words such as *car*. In the densely Welsh-speaking and bilingual north of Wales the dialects are generally rhotic (as in Scots, discussed above), but in metropolitan or heavily anglicised areas such as Cardiff or Port Talbot, they are generally non-rhotic, in line with most southern English dialects.

Although the influence of the Welsh language on grammar is not so widespread, particular forms stand out. The highlighted examples below illustrate a striking verb feature:

(a)   **He goes** to the cinema every week.
(b)   **He do go** to the cinema every week.
(c)   **He's going** to the cinema every week.

(Thomas, 1985, p. 215)

Chapter 6 discusses other examples of 'language shift' in bi- or multilingual communities – where one language takes over the functions of another.

These examples are alternative ways of indicating 'habitual aspect' in verbs – where the verb refers to a habitual or repeated action. The standard (*he goes* ..., as in (a)) is in general use in Wales. A form using *do* (*he do go* ..., as in (b)) is found in areas of early anglicisation and is linked to Midlands dialects. A form using the auxiliary *be* + *-ing* (as in (c) *he's going* ...) is largely confined to late anglicisation areas and can be connected to the influence of Welsh.

Finally, the influence of the Welsh language is said to be particularly evident in **prosody** (a feature of pronunciation that includes stress, rhythm, intonation, etc.). John Wells (1982, p. 392) notes that '[p]opular English views about Welsh accents include the claim that they have a "sing-song" or lilting intonation' and this may have substance in linguistic analysis: the vowel in the final unstressed syllable for words such as *sofa* and *butter* is lengthened and has a fuller quality when compared to standard English in England, and this may be perceived as melodic. This is attributed to the Welsh language, where final unstressed syllables are not reduced, and is a feature generally shared throughout Wales.

The examples above provide a snapshot of the different influences on the development of English in Wales, and how these impact on present-day dialects of Welsh English.

English in Ireland

The use of English in Ireland dates back to 1250, but just as in Wales, widespread use did not come about until much later, around the seventeenth century, with the organised colonisation of Ireland by the British Crown.

Hickey (2007, p. 142) states that 'it is obvious that linguistically, as well as politically, Ireland is divided into two broad sections, the north and the south' and these are largely related to patterns of settlement. The broad dialect areas are shown in Figure 5.4.

The northern area can be further divided into three major dialect regions which developed during the period of colonisation: Ulster Scots, derived from the Lowland Scots settlers; Mid-Ulster English, derived from settlers coming largely from northern England; and a variety spoken in the west of Donegal arising from forms of Ulster English in contact with Irish. Added to these three main varieties is the capital of Belfast, where a number of different varieties converge.

Figure 5.4   Dialect areas in Ireland (Hickey, 2004)

The impact of settlers on the developing varieties is demonstrated by traditional Ulster Scots, which has much in common with traditional versions of Lowland Scots in Scotland. Phonological features include:

a low, unrounded back vowel so that *soft* sounds like *saft* (/sɑːft/)

the 'velar fricative' /x/ in words like *thought*

'l-vocalisation' in words like *ball* (to give *ba'*)

See above for examples of the velar fricative and l-vocalisation in Scots.

Many grammatical forms can also be traced to Scots, such as the following examples, from an 80-year-old speaker in Cullybackey, Co. Antrim:

(a) **Youngsters gets** far too much and **they've** no manners some of them at all.

(b) And I would've **haen** to have **haen** the floor scrubbed and everything cleaned for him coming.

In (a), the third-person verb ending -*s* (singular in standard English) occurs after a plural noun (*youngsters gets*). However, this form does not occur after pronouns (so the speaker says *they've*, i.e. 'have' rather than 'has'). This is known as the Northern Subject Rule, and dates back to the thirteenth century in Scotland. In (b) the form *haen* is used for the past participle of 'have' (standard 'had'). Despite attempts to establish official language status for Ulster Scots, many of these distinctly Scottish features are now in decline.

In the southern area, Irish slowly receded from east to west, resulting in two broad dialect areas for Southern Irish English, also known as Hiberno-English. The first is the variety spoken on the east coast from Waterford up to and beyond Dublin, an area first settled by the English from the late twelfth century. The second is in the south-west and west where the shift from Irish to English came later. The centre of the country is characterised as 'a diffuse and dialectally indeterminate' region (Hickey, 2004, p. 24). Put very simply, the Irish language has more influence on varieties spoken in the west and English has more influence on varieties spoken in the east. However, disentangling the origins and subsequent development of individual forms is no easy task.

Chapter 3 discussed the sentence *They are after doing the work*. It is generally agreed that this sentence structure arises from the influence of Irish. However, the origins of other grammatical constructions used in Hiberno-English may be more contentious, as exemplified by the following, which was recorded in Wicklow near Dublin (Filppula, 1991, p. 55):

It's looking for more land a lot of them are.
[A lot of them are looking for more land.]

This type of sentence structure is technically known as 'it-clefting'. Many commentators have claimed that it reflects a similar construction in Irish. Irish, however, has not been spoken in Wicklow for more than 200 years. There may be another explanation: many grammatical patterns in Hiberno-English may derive, not from Irish, but from varieties of seventeenth-century English which were taken to Ireland by colonists and have since become obsolete (or at least very scarce).

This demonstrates that there is a range of influences on how a variety develops, and disentangling from where particular features originate can be problematic. However, it seems clear that historical patterns of settlement from Scotland and England, and the influence of the Irish language, have had varying influences on the development of Irish English.

5.4   English in the 'New World'

'New World' Englishes such as American English, Australian English and New Zealand English all have their origins in British and Irish varieties of English, so why do they sound so unique today? If we could transport ourselves back to these areas during the colonial period, what we would hear is a collection of Northern Irish, Geordie, Scots, Cockney and any number of other dialects mixing and mingling in the burgeoning homesteads, villages and towns in the New World territories. But through time this sandpit of varieties changed: the settlers' children, and their children's children, began to sound less like their parents and more like each other. This **dialect levelling** resulted in new dialects – unique varieties but with vestiges of the original inputs still evident today to varying degrees. One of the first continents colonised by speakers of English, North America, provides a good example of this new dialect formation in the New World.

English in the USA

The history of English in the USA goes back to 1607 with the first English-speaking colony in Jamestown, Virginia followed by Plymouth, Massachusetts in 1620. The colonisers in this first wave of migration primarily came from southern England and their continuing political and cultural ties with Britain may be one of the reasons why the varieties spoken in New England and the South share linguistic features with southern British English. The aristocratic nature of the input is said to be best preserved in the 'Boston Brahmin', families in New England who claim direct descent from the original Protestant settlers who founded Boston. When you hear these speakers, they do indeed sound like upper-class British speakers, and are often parodied on film and television for their 'posh' accent.

In the following years, thirteen colonies were established along the eastern seaboard, but in contrast to the first wave of settlers, these colonisers were of very different stock: mostly indentured servants from northern England, Scotland and Ireland. The speech of these people is said to have constituted the basis of colonial mid-Atlantic American speech, which later became the basis for the mainstream, inland-northern and western type of American English (Schneider, 2004). As the colonisers moved west and intermingled, this gave rise to a further process of linguistic mixing and blending, with marked forms (i.e. those which are unusual) disappearing in favour of unmarked forms (i.e. those which are shared by a large number of dialects). This resulted in rather levelled, homogeneous varieties in the West, but with more divergent varieties remaining along the east coast.

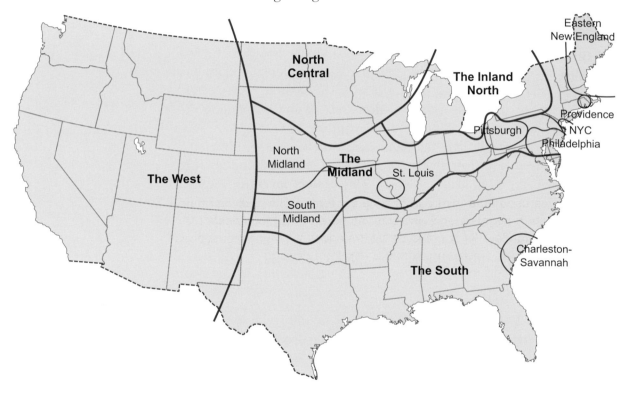

Figure 5.5 The urban dialect areas of the United States (adapted from Labov et al., 1997, Map 1)

Hans Kurath began work in the early twentieth century on the *Linguistic Atlas of the United States and Canada*, postulating three main dialect areas in the United States: northern, midland and southern, and this was further defined by Craig Carver (1987). Figure 5.5 is a more recent map of regional dialects in US English based on the work of William Labov, Sharon Ash and Charles Boberg. It identifies major urban dialect areas on the basis of their vowel systems.

Although there is more homogeneity in North America when compared to the British Isles and Ireland, a number of local varieties stand out. A good example is the Ocracoke dialect, spoken on an island in the Outer

Banks of North Carolina, first settled by British ship pilots in the 1700s. Because of its isolation over the last 300 years, the people in this small community have retained many features from the history of English in southern and western England, the birthplace of the original founder populations to the area. At the same time they have innovated and restructured, resulting in a unique variety which uses phonological and grammatical forms not found elsewhere.

Activity 5.4

Allow about 5–10 minutes

Grammatical forms characteristic of Ocracoke include the following. What seems distinctive about the highlighted forms?

(a) **She weren't** there

(b) She's **to the house**

(c) He kept **a-looking** for the rain

(d) He **might could** do it … he **useta could** do it

(e) It's **nasty-some** out there today.

Comment

In (a) *were* is used as a third person singular form of the verb *be* (this mainly occurs in negative environments, as here). In (b) *to* indicates location (the standard form would be '*at* the house'). The construction in (c) is referred to as a-prefixing, with the *-ing* form of verbs. The sentences in (d) include 'double modals' (i.e. a combination of two modal verbs, *might could*, and *used to could*). In (e) *some* is used as an 'intensifier', to strengthen the adjective *nasty*.

A number of pronunciation features also exist in Ocracoke. Particularly striking are forms such as *oncest* and *twicet* ('once' and 'twice'), where /t/ is added after a final /s/ sound; as well as *extry* ('extra') and *sody* ('soda') where the sound /i/ replaces a final /ə/. However, the 'Ocracoke Brogue', as it is known, is now said to be an endangered dialect, undergoing rapid attrition as tourism and depopulation dilute the original ancestral variety.

Activity 5.5

Reading B, *Extracts from 'New York Tawk'* by Michael Newman, considers a rather different variety of American English. This is a popular account of the New York dialect, intended in part to increase its readers' awareness of spoken diversity in the United States, and to challenge the negative way in which 'Brooklynese' is often portrayed. As you read, consider the following questions:

- How does Newman describe the English spoken in New York City?
- What similarities can you find between this and Asprey's account of Black Country English?

Comment

Newman identifies certain linguistic features of the New York dialect. He focuses particularly on pronunciation features, including the /r/ sound identified in this chapter as non-prevocalic /r/ – a feature I have discussed in relation to several other varieties. What stands out in this case is the absence of non-prevocalic /r/, compared to a US norm in which the sound is generally pronounced. By contrast, in England non-prevocalic /r/ has disappeared from the standard variety although it is retained in certain regional varieties. Newman also refers to a number of distinctive lexical items, including words introduced by successive waves of immigrants.

Newman points to the stigmatised nature of New York speech, relating this to the attributes of its speakers. A person's dislike of 'r-less' pronunciations, for instance, is a statement about the group of speakers who use these, rather than reflecting feelings towards the linguistic feature itself: Newman suggests that the association of this pronunciation with working-class speakers in New York may have affected people's perceptions. For those who speak the dialect, however, this is part of their identity as New Yorkers. This recalls Asprey's discussion of attitudes towards the Black Country dialect, which is disparaged by those who do not speak it, but a source of pride to those who do.

As well as this connection between dialect and identity and the often negative attitudes this involves, other similarities between Newman's and Asprey's readings are that they both describe living and adapting urban varieties whose younger speakers are also introducing innovations.

So far I have been considering American English as an 'Inner Circle' English – defined as a variety in direct descent from British English, brought to its region in the colonial period, and spoken as a first language. One variety of English in North America provides a controversial, and fascinating, challenge to this definition: African-American Vernacular English (henceforth AAVE). This variety fits

Kachru's description of an 'Inner Circle' variety: a variety of English spoken as a native language in a largely monolingual context. However, how it got to its current state is the subject of heated debate, especially given the backdrop of race relations in the USA. Some facts are clear: Africans in large numbers were enslaved and brought to North America. They came speaking a range of West African languages and learned English subsequently in North America, resulting in a shift from their ancestral languages to English. Today, AAVE is largely thought to be a variety of English, but the details of the mechanisms of change from one language to another are subject to much debate, both in the linguistics world and more widely.

Two major hypotheses are at the centre of this debate: the 'Anglicist Hypothesis' (e.g. Kurath, 1964) *vs.* the 'Creolist Hypothesis' (e.g. Dillard, 1972). The Anglicist Hypothesis, dating from the 1950s onwards, suggests that the origin of AAVE can be traced to the same sources as earlier European American dialects of English – the varieties of English spoken in the British Isles. In this case, the slaves learnt the regional varieties brought by the initial settlers to North America, and within a few generations nearly all traces of the ancestral languages were wiped out. The Creolist Hypothesis advocates of the 1960s and 1970s challenged these ideas. They proposed that the contact situation that existed for the slaves was very different from that of the European settlers. They had little contact with their enslavers: the contact was with other slaves who all spoke different African languages. It is hypothesised that this linguistic and social context led to the development of a creole, which was neither English nor an ancestral language, but a new language created from the **superstrate** (mainly English) and **substrate** (African language) mix. This creole provided the foundations for present day AAVE.

Substrate and superstrate languages

'Substrate' and 'superstrate' refer to the direction of influence of languages in a bilingual community. A substrate language is a less dominant language that influences a socially dominant language. A superstrate language is a dominant language that influences a less dominant language. Chapter 3 discussed the influence of substrate languages on English in India and West Africa. In pidgin and creole studies, substrates are believed to make important contributions to the grammars of new (pidgin and creole) varieties, whereas

> superstrates have a major influence on the vocabulary of the new variety.

Proponents of the Creolist Hypothesis call on a number of test case linguistic features as evidence of creole origins. These are reported to be widespread in English-based creoles but are said not to exist, or to be very infrequent, in the original settler dialects (e.g. Wolfram and Schilling-Estes, 2006, p. 214).

Grammatical examples include:

(a)   Sometimes my ears **be** itching (use of the verb form *be* for habitual or intermittent activity)

(b)   **She sick** (absence of a 'copula' or 'linking verb' – compare 'she is sick')

(c)   She **walk** down the street every day (absence of -*s* in third person singular verb forms)

(d)   **Jack** car (absence of the possessive -*s* form)

(e)   I saw two **dog** (absence of the plural -*s* form)

(f)   I **been** known him a long time (use of *been* to mark a state or action that happened a long time ago but is still relevant – sometimes termed 'remote been').

Phonological examples include:

(g)   **Lif'** up the box (the reduction of consonant clusters – here /ft/ – where the following word begins with a vowel)

(h)   She live on the **skr**eet (*skr* for *str* in initial consonant clusters)

(i)   I **aks** him for money (use of 'metathesis', where consonant order is switched).

It is argued by some that although these grammatical and phonological patterns may be shared with other varieties of English, and, in particular, dialects in the southern states of America, the details differ. For example, in other varieties consonant cluster reduction (in (g) above) tends to happen when the following word begins with a consonant (e.g. *bes' kind*); the absence of plural -*s* forms (in (e) above) is largely restricted to weights and measures (*five pound, four mile*), but in AAVE it is much more widespread. Proponents of the Creolist Hypothesis would argue that this is because AAVE has different roots from English. However, recent work on 'traditional' or 'relic' dialects in the British Isles (i.e. dialects that preserve earlier states of the language), have shown that many of these so-called creole features have their origins in the non-standard Englishes brought by the original settlers in the eighteenth century. For example, verbal -*s* forms (in (c) above) are used variably in original settler dialects from Lowland Scotland and Northern Ireland. This 'Neo-Anglicist' position (e.g. Poplack and Sankoff, 1987) argues that AAVE has diverged from these initial settler dialects over the years, so that it now sounds quite different from other white non-standard varieties in the United States. These differences are said to arise from identity-based motivations and include the increasing use of examples such as *had* + verb for simple past and *ain't* for 'didn't':

> Yesterday she **had fixed** the bike and **had rode** it to school.

> He **ain't** go there yesterday.

Thus, according to this argument, the differences are not due to different origins, but arise from the evolving nature of African-American speech during the twentieth century.

This debate remains unresolved and will probably continue for many decades to come. Whatever the underlying reasons for the linguistic patterns of use, the divergence of AAVE from more mainstream American norms continues today, where a trans-regional (i.e. a common set of features across different regions) urban AAVE is emerging and intensifying, with even higher rates of distinctive AAVE features than in the past. In the process, AAVE has become more ethnically distinct than it was a century ago, perhaps due to the persistent segregation in American society and a growing sense of ethnic identity.

English in Australia and New Zealand

English came to Australia and New Zealand relatively late – in the late eighteenth century. The majority of the first Australian settlers were convicts, who arrived in 1788. By the mid-nineteenth century, there were around 130,000 prisoners, mostly from the south-east of England. Until 1947, most of the emigrants were white British, and still today, despite substantial immigration from Asia and the South Pacific, this number stands at just under 75 per cent, with other Europeans (20 per cent), Asians (6 per cent) and Aborigines (1 per cent) making up the rest of the population.

Settlement to New Zealand began in the late 1800s, after the signing of the Treaty of Waitangi between the British Crown and various Maori chiefs in 1840, bringing New Zealand into the British Empire. Settlers came from Germany, Scandinavia and other parts of Europe, as well as from China and India, but again British and Irish settlers made up the vast majority, and did so for the next 150 years.

Peter Trudgill has worked extensively on the spread of English to Australia and New Zealand. He states that the 'most important ingredients in the mixture that was to lead to the development of these new forms of English were the dialects and accents of the language brought with them by native speakers of English' (Trudgill, 2004, p. 13). His basic premise is that if we know where the people came from, and in what proportions, and if we can discover what dialects they spoke, then we can actually predict what a dialect will look like in future years. Following migration and contact between speakers there is a levelling out of the variation in individual linguistic features in a number of stages. The selection of particular features to form a stable, focused new dialect is normally achieved by the second native-born generation.

Not all researchers accept Trudgill's argument. Some opposing views are discussed in Chapter 7.

Trudgill suggests that the origins of Australian English lie in the language of settlers from London and areas to the north-east of London, such as Norfolk, around the beginning of the nineteenth century, with fully fledged new dialect formation occurring with children around the 1850s. Subsequent migrations between 1850 and 1900 due to the Gold Rush may have diluted the influence of settler dialects, but vestiges of this initial input can still be heard across a number of features. For New Zealand, Trudgill estimates that 50 per cent of British settlers were from England, 27 per cent from Scotland and 23 per cent from Ireland and he suggests that a distinct variety developed around 1840, with a fully fledged variety spoken by the first years of the twentieth century. The national standards, Australian English and New Zealand English, were recognised towards the end of the twentieth century.

Australia and New Zealand share many linguistic features. In their grammar, they are virtually indistinguishable from each other, or from standard English in England, and this may result from the levelling that Trudgill proposes in the first generations of speakers. In terms of pronunciation, similarities include 'linking r' (so that 'law and order' becomes *lawr and order*); 'l-vocalisation'; and the pronunciation of the /t/ sound between vowels so that 'writer' and 'rider' would sound the same. They also share an intonation feature known as a 'high rising terminal' (HRT) where a declarative clause (or statement) has rising intonation at the end, making it sound like a question. This is sometimes referred to as Australian Questioning Intonation, although it is now also found in several other varieties of English.

However, there are some differences between Australian and New Zealand English, most noticeably with the vowel in 'bit'. In Australia this is raised and fronted (pronounced higher and towards the front of the mouth) so 'fish and chips' sounds more like *feesh and cheeps*. In New Zealand, it has gone in the opposite direction, resulting in a pronunciation something like *fush and chups*.

Of course, Australian and New Zealand English are not monolithic: not surprisingly, geographical and social differences exist. A good example within New Zealand English is the Southland dialect, which is rhotic, in comparison to the rest of New Zealand which does not pronounce non-prevocalic /r/. This is said to be due to settlement patterns: the influence of Scottish immigrants who settled in the southern part of the South Island.

A number of other 'ethnic' varieties exist in Australia and New Zealand, including New Zealand Maori English (e.g. Meyerhoff, 1994) and Aboriginal Australian English (e.g. Leitner, 2004). In addition, New Australian English or 'Ethnic Broad' (Horvath, 1985) is a variety spoken by immigrants who have arrived since the 1960s – from Greece, Italy and Lebanon among other regions – which is to some extent shaped by their first language.

5.5   'New Englishes' in Africa and Asia

The previous section has provided some insight into the development of English in the New World, where British and Irish people made up the majority of the settler population. I turn now to Kachru's 'Outer Circle', beginning in this section with the development of what are sometimes termed 'New Englishes' in Africa and Asia. The number of second language/'Outer Circle' speakers of English far exceeds that of 'Inner Circle'/first language speakers. In these contexts, the indigenous languages were not submerged by the colonising language, but instead existed side by side with it in a situation largely characterised by bi- or multilingualism. This very different environment from 'Inner Circle' Englishes affected the types of English that arose in these situations, giving rise to different forms over time.

The colonial expansion of Britain was vast and continued over a number of centuries across the Caribbean, Africa and Asia, as detailed

Chapter 3 discussed Schneider's model of a five-stage process whereby English could develop from a colonial language to an established local variety.

in Chapter 3. English was mainly restricted to the colonial administration, leading to the survival of indigenous languages and the development of bi- or multilingualism. However, over time the foreign language, English, sometimes shed off its foreignness through processes described in Chapter 3. This involved the establishment of the separate linguistic and sociolinguistic identity of, in particular, postcolonial African and Asian varieties of English.

The colonisation of India and subsequent spread of English there provides a good example of the linguistic processes that may operate in these 'New Englishes'. The British first arrived in India in the early 1600s and soon established trading posts in a number of cities under the control of The East India Company. By 1765 the Company's influence had grown to such an extent that the British were effectively controlling most parts of the country. This date is often taken as the start of what is referred to as *The Raj* – a period of British rule in India that lasted until Independence in 1947. Initially, English was only taught to the local population through the work of Christian missionaries, but by the 1700s, English had established itself as the language of administration, and by the nineteenth century it was increasingly accepted as the language of government, of the social elite and of the national press.

Chapter 4 cites estimates of English speakers in India ranging from 30 to 330 million.

Estimates on what percentage of the population have some competence in English differ enormously, but for the vast majority of these speakers it remains a second language. A number of phonological and grammatical forms now characterise the range of varieties that fall under the umbrella of Indian English. For instance, Indian English is generally rhotic. A noticeable feature is that /t/ and /d/ have 'retroflex' pronunciations, where the tongue tip is curled backwards. The sounds /v/ and /w/ are not distinguished.

In terms of grammar, speakers often use 'progressive' verb forms where these would not occur in other varieties. For example:

I **am believing** you

She **is liking** music

(Compare 'I believe', 'she likes'.)

Interrogative constructions often do not invert subject and verb:

Where **you are** going?

What **you would** like to buy?

(Compare 'Where are you going?' 'What would you like to buy?')

Isn't it is found as a generalized (invariant) question tag:

They are coming tomorrow, **isn't it**?

(Compare '… aren't they?')

(McArthur, 2002)

The complex multilingual situation in India makes it quite difficult to establish the influence of particular Indian languages on these forms in many cases: the forms may be the result of transfer from, for example, Hindi, Punjabi, Gujarati or indeed a combination of languages.

Another outcome of these multilingual settings is frequent switching between English and other languages, and sometimes the development of mixed varieties such as Hinglish, a mixture of Hindi and English. This is discussed further in Chapter 6.

Chapter 6 focuses on how English is used alongside other languages in multilingual contexts.

5.6   English-related varieties: pidgins and creoles

As you saw in Chapter 3, although pidgins and creoles developed in many 'Outer Circle' contexts, they are rather different from the varieties discussed in Section 5.5 above. As pointed out in Chapter 3, there is some debate as to whether they count as varieties of English or entirely separate languages. For this reason I have referred to them in the title of this section as 'English-related varieties'. The distinction between varieties known as 'pidgins' and 'creoles' is also not clear-cut (again, as discussed in Chapter 3).

The box below provides an example of a variety known as Bislama. The speaker was recorded by Miriam Meyerhoff as part of her research on this variety.

Bislama text

long lanis ya. mi mi bin kambak long wok. mi kakae finis ale mi wantem gobak long wok mi singaotem hem. blong toktok long hem. se mi gobak long wok. mi singaot. mi singaot. mi singaot. no gat. Togo i haed nomo. i stap antap. mi mi talem mifala evriwan. mi wetem haosgel blong mifala. mitufala i traem. blong lukaot raon

---

long haos. no gat. go insaed. go afsaed. mifala i raonem haos. no gat. mifala i no faenem Togo.

Translation:

long lanis ya	it was lunchtime
mi mi bin kambak long wok	I'd come back from work
mi kakae finis	and I'd eaten
ale mi wantem gobak long wok	and so I wanted to go back to work
mi singaotem hem	I called out to him
blong toktok long hem	to talk to him
se mi gobak long wok	to say I was going back to work
mi singaot	I called
mi singaot	and I called
mi singaot	and I called
no gat	couldn't find him
Togo i haed nomo	T was just hiding
i stap antap	he was up the tree
mi mi talem mifala evriwan	I said, all of us
mi wetem haosgel blong mifala	me and our housegirl
mitufala i traem	the two of us tried
blong lukaot raon long haos	to find him round the house
no gat	but he wasn't there
go insaed	we went inside
go afsaed	we went outside
mifala i raonem haos	we went all round the house
no gat	no sign of him
mifala i no faenem Togo	we couldn't find T

(Original transcript and translation kindly provided by Miriam Meyerhoff)

Bislama is spoken in Vanuatu, an archipelago in the South Pacific Ocean, east of Australia. Its date of origin is placed at around 1840 where contact between English traders and the indigenous peoples of Vanuatu gave rise to this new variety. The emergence of new language varieties normally proceeds at glacial pace: what is unusual about Bislama and others like it is that in the space of just fifty years it became a fully fledged variety, widely spoken in the coastal communities around Vanuatu.

It was not until the 1960s that linguists began to investigate pidgins and creoles in any serious way. They had previously been thought of as forms of 'broken English', corruptions of much 'better' European languages. Leonard Bloomfield writing in the 1930s (1933, p. 471), for example, describes them as 'aberrant'. However, although pidgins and creoles may contain features that have been reduced or simplified, serious analysis found that this process does not occur on an ad hoc basis, but has fixed structural norms. In other words, these varieties have rules, just as any other variety does. The only difference between pidgins and creoles and 'ordinary' language development is the speed at which these developments take place. Thus, over the last few decades, pidgins and creoles have proved to be a goldmine for linguistic research: changes in grammar, phonology and lexis can be tracked in a 'telescoped' period of time, allowing unparalleled access to the processes involved in contact and change.

Chapter 3 discussed the often controversial ideas about the origins and historical development of pidgins and creoles and also whether there exist clear cut distinctions between the two. I focus here on some of their linguistic characteristics. It has been claimed that pidgins and creoles have the same structural design (e.g. Bickerton, 1984) – that is, they all look very similar linguistically – but this is disputed (e.g. Mufwene, 1986). For this reason, the examples below are indicative only.

In the extract above, some of the words may look familiar to you: *gobak* ('go back'), *wok* ('work'). This is because the 'lexifier' of Bislama – the language from which the basic initial vocabulary is taken – is English. In pidgins and creoles, the majority of the lexis comes from the superstrate language – that is, the language of power – but some also comes from the substrate: an example here is *kaikai* meaning 'food' or 'eat' in Polynesian languages. A third category is made up of internal innovations as detailed below.

A defining feature of many pidgins and creoles is a relatively small vocabulary. Due to the limited nature of the vocabulary, there is maximum use of a minimum lexicon; in other words, much 'polysemy', where words have multiple meanings. For example, *banis* ('bandage') has a wider semantic range than in English: it has come to mean a ribbon, fence or any type of enclosure. The word *gras* ('grass') can come to mean anything which grows. Vocabulary can also become more semantically specific through 'circumlocution': the use of many words to describe one thing. So, for example:

> *gras bilong het* means something that grows out of the head ('hair')

> *gras bilong fes* means something that grows out of the face ('beard')

> *gras bilong salwara* means something that grows in the sea ('seaweed')

These circumlocutions may in time be shortened: thus *ma bilong mi* ('man belong me', or 'my husband') becomes *mamblomi*. 'Compounding' – putting two or more words together to form a new word – is also characteristic, so that *kot bilong ren* ('coat belong rain' or 'raincoat') becomes *kotren*.

Pidgins and creoles may have fewer sounds when compared to the input languages. For example, in standard English in England there are said to be around twenty-six vowels (a very high number compared to most languages in the world), but in pidgins and creoles this can be limited to five or seven plus a number of nasal vowels. Sounds which are unusual in the world's languages, or are acquired later by children, are avoided. For example, in the extract of Bislama you can see the use of *finis* rather than 'finish' and *lanis* rather than 'lunch'.

Another feature said to be common to a number of pidgins and creoles is a syllable structure referred to as 'CV': each syllable is made up of a consonant and a vowel. This may result from the deletion of vowels at the beginning of words (e.g. *American* becomes *Merican*, 'afraid' becomes *frede*) or from 'epenthesis' – the insertion of a vowel between consonants, so that 'six' becomes *sikis*, 'straight' becomes *sitirit*. In line with this is the avoidance of consonant clusters – two or more consonants side by side – 'bandage' becomes *banis*, without the /nd/ consonant cluster.

In terms of grammar, features such as verb tenses tend to be expressed by additional words rather than by changes to the verb itself. The following forms come from West African Pidgin:

i bin kam (where *bin* marks the simple past, 'he came')

i don kam (where *don* marks the perfect tense, 'he has come')

i go kam (where *go* marks the future tense, 'he will come')

With negation, the negative particle tends to appear before the verb with no other marking:

i no sabi ('I don't know')

Prepositions are usually multifunctional with again an example from Bislama: *long* can mean 'in', 'on', 'at', 'from' or 'with' as in:

*mi mi bin kambak **long** wok ... ale mi wantem gobak **long** wok* ('I'd come back **from** work ... and so I wanted to go back **to** work')

While a pidgin may be characterised by simplification and reduction, an expanded pidgin – one which begins to be used in more domains, for instance government and schooling – is characterised by elaboration and expansion. One result of this is greater syntactic complexity. For example, in Tok Pisin, spoken in Papua New Guinea, the form *-im* is used to indicate that a verb is used transitively (i.e. with a direct object):

Em i rit ('He is reading')

*Em i rit**im** book* ('He is reading a book')

The term *olsem* is used as a 'complementiser' to link two sentences (like 'that' in standard English) as shown in the example below:

Mi no save. Ol i wokim dispela haus

becomes

*Mi no save **olsem** ol i wokim dispela haus* ('I didn't know that they built this house')

As with other Englishes worldwide, there is a susbstantial amount of variation in the use of pidgins and creoles. Figure 5.6 shows an example from Jamaica where there is a range of forms running from the broadest creole (termed the 'basilect') through to a Jamaican standard (termed the 'acrolect'). This also occurs in other varieties and is sometimes referred to as a 'Creole continuum'.

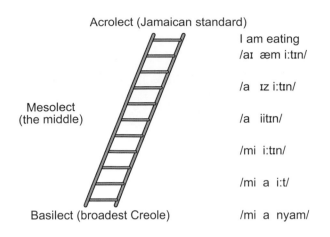

Acrolect (Jamaican standard)

I am eating
/aɪ æm iːtɪn/

/a ɪz iːtɪn/

Mesolect
(the middle)

/a iitɪn/

/mi iːtɪn/

/mi a iːt/

Basilect (broadest Creole)

/mi a nyam/

Figure 5.6 Visual representation of the 'Creole continuum' in Jamaican Creole (Sebba, 1997, p. 211)

5.7 The expanding circle of Englishes?

These ideas are
discussed in Chapter 1.

Within 'Expanding Circle' contexts, English has been seen as having a different status from that in the 'Inner' and 'Outer' circles: learnt primarily as a foreign language; and 'norm-dependent' (i.e. looking towards the Inner Circle for its linguistic models). It is in the Expanding Circle, however (China, Indonesia, Saudi Arabia, Japan, throughout continental Europe and Scandinavia), that the use of English is increasing dramatically, contributing to the contemporary position of English as a global language. In such countries, English may be restricted to certain domains (education, the media, commerce), but in many cases its role is changing: for instance, Philip Seargeant claims (Chapter 1) that in Scandinavian countries English has become 'an integral part of everyday life', and is 'moving towards a situation where it almost has the status (in practice if not in name) of a second language'.

English is also used widely as a lingua franca between speakers of different languages, and David Crystal notes (Chapter 4) that the use of ELF (English as a Lingua Franca) is now the object of much academic study. Sirpa Leppänen and Tarja Nikula (Chapter 4, Reading B) identify some features of what could be viewed as 'lingua franca' talk in a television interview in Finland that was conducted in English. However, despite the prevalence of English in Finland, the fact that it is used when most of those present are Finns, and the fact that it includes some 'non-native' forms, Leppänen and Nikula make no claims about its status as a distinct variety: they are discussing 'English in Finland' rather than 'Finnish English'.

Crystal himself (Chapter 4) seems slightly more hopeful about the potential of a more general variety: 'Euro-English'. He identifies several characteristics (use of a syllable-timed rhythm, simplified sentence construction, avoidance of idioms and colloquial vocabulary, slower rate of speech, clearer patterns of articulation), arguing that these go beyond being 'foreigner talk', and may indeed lead to new standardised forms. This view, however, remains controversial. Jenkins et al. (2001) and Jenkins (2003) have discussed the potential of Euro-English as a new variety appropriate to the European experience, and one which is on the way to developing its own norms. However, Sandra Mollin (2007) argues that it is not consistently used across a wide range of domains within European countries; linguistic features said to characterise 'Euro-English' are not, for the most part, in systematic use; and speakers still claim to be orienting to native speaker or 'international' norms. Whether we can talk about such varieties as 'Englishes', in the same way as Indian English, is, then, at least open to question.

Another area of interest in 'Expanding Circle' contexts is the influence of English on local languages, and in turn the influence of local languages on English, evident through the use of loanwords and codeswitching between languages. In Japan, for instance, estimates suggest that around 10 per cent of all vocabulary in Japanese consists of English loanwords (e.g. Stanlaw, 1992; Yano, forthcoming), despite the fact that English loans are a relatively recent phenomenon.

Switching between English and Japanese in conversation is also common. So, while a 'Japanese English' variety (on the model of Indian English) is unlikely to emerge, influences from English are nevertheless embedded in the everyday language practices of Japan.

'Codeswitching' between English and other languages is discussed in Chapter 6.

5.8   Conclusion

In this chapter I have discussed some linguistic characteristics of contemporary varieties of English. I have suggested that, to understand these, we need to be aware of their history. The features of contemporary varieties show a range of influences, including earlier settlement patterns: the mix of varieties of English brought to different parts of the world by colonists or settlers, and subsequent contact between these varieties; contact with other local languages; and the 'time-depth' that allows particular linguistic features to change over time. The balance of these influences varies in different contexts.

I have also illustrated how varieties may be described systematically according to particular linguistic levels (my focus in this chapter has been on phonology, lexis and grammar).

Local Englishes are often described in terms of their distinctive features – usually those features that distinguish them from a standard variety of English. I pointed out, however, that boundaries between varieties are not clear-cut. Varieties tend to form a continuum of use across particular geographical areas. There may be a great deal in common even between geographically distant varieties.

Varieties of English have important social meanings for their speakers and others who encounter them. Readings A and B pointed to the negative associations of Black Country and New York English, but also noted their powerful association with local identities, which may help explain their continuing vibrancy. A further point touched on in these readings was social variation and change within varieties – for instance, the association of Black Country English with working-class speakers, and the fact that younger speakers are introducing changes into the dialect. We return to these social aspects of language in Chapter 7.

Towards the end of the chapter, I considered the potential of 'Expanding Circle Englishes', pointing out that whether these count as varieties of English remains controversial.

Contact between English and other languages has been an important theme in this chapter, in relation to how this has influenced the development of certain varieties of English. Chapter 6 continues this theme, focusing on the contemporary status of English, and how this is used in multilingual contexts in different parts of the world.

READING A: Black Country English and Black Country identity – a case study

Esther Asprey

Specially commissioned for this book.

Introduction to the region and language variety

Black Country English is spoken in the West Midlands (England) in an area known as the Black Country, roughly fifteen miles across and immediately neighbouring Birmingham. It is a typical Midlands variety, lying on the isoglosses for several features which distinguish northern versus southern varieties.

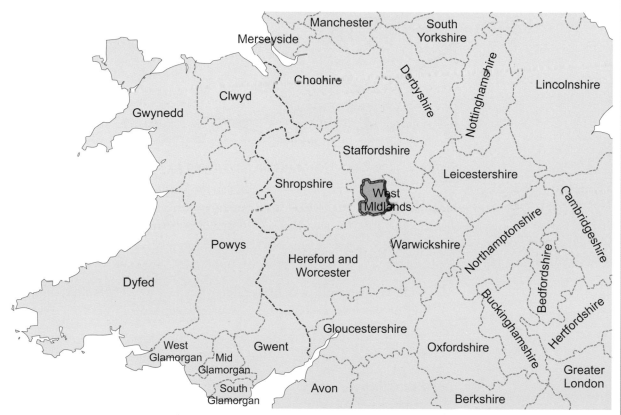

Figure 1   Approximate location of the Black Country (shown in pink) in relation to surrounding English and Welsh counties

Black Country is an interesting regional variety because it thrives even among younger speakers, despite being heavily stigmatised across the UK. It regularly tops polls as the most undesirable accent to have, and it is often equated with stupidity. Coupland and Bishop (2007, p. 79)

analysed data from a BBC accent ratings poll and found that of the thirty-four accents under investigation, only Asian and Birmingham accents ranked lower than Black Country for both 'social attractiveness' and 'prestige'.

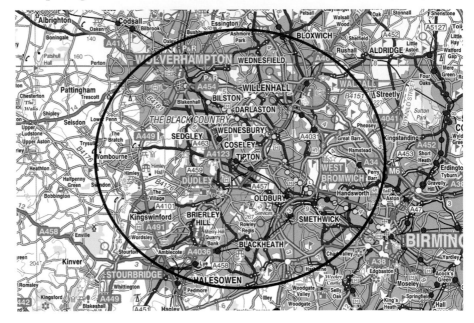

Figure 2   The Black Country (map reproduced by kind permission of the Ordnance Survey)

Many speakers in the Black Country, however, are proud of their dialect. The BBC Voices Black Country chat board (2005) shows posts like these:

> Ours is a very old way of speaking this is why people take the 'p' out of the way we talk. (Lucy, Wolverhampton)

> The Black Country language is one of the oldest still surviving in England we should be proud of it! (Kat, London)

> I can't believe that the black country accent has been voted the worst it is proper old English. (Michael, Stourbridge)

This conflict – between the low social status accorded the variety and the community pride in it – formed the basis of my investigation into the relationship between attitudes and language use in the Black Country.

Introduction to the study

My research was carried out between 2002 and 2007 (Asprey, 2007). In this time, I collected data from twenty men and nineteen women of white British or Irish ethnicity aged between seventeen and eighty-one. These speakers were split into age groups based on what Eckert (1997, p. 159) terms 'life stages': childhood, adolescence, early adulthood, middle age and old age. These divisions take into account socialising patterns and employment patterns, as well as societal positions. Retired people, for example, may face less pressure to 'speak correctly' if they no longer interact with the public at work.

I used my own social networks to contact 'friends of friends', as in the work of Milroy (1987), and augmented the sample with an appeal in a local newspaper. Data was collected using the *Survey of Regional English* method (Kerswill et al., 1999) which was later used in the *BBC Voices* online survey (www.bbc.co.uk/voices). The method uses Sense Relation Networks (SRNs), illustrated in Figure 3. Informants completed SRNs with 'their own' and 'local' words for concepts such as 'the time between summer and winter', and brought the sheets to the interview. As Llamas (2000, p. 98) explains, the idea is to empower informants during the interaction and, through discussion of their chosen words, phonological, lexical and (to a lesser extent) grammatical data is produced.

This method enabled me to identify several features of Black Country English, as well as some interesting examples of change in the dialect. I discuss these below.

Phonology

Black Country phonology is partly a combination of northern and southern forms, but it also contains phonological features typical only of the West Midlands. Table 1 shows the pronunciation of certain vowels, described using Wells' idea of *lexical sets* (1982, p. 120).

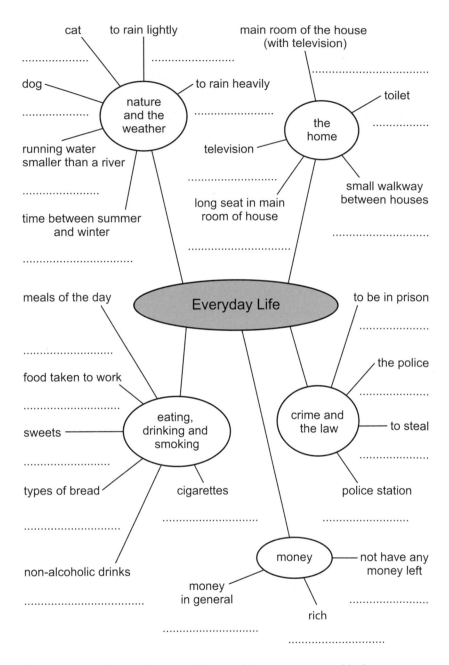

cat   to rain lightly

main room of the house
(with television)

....

....

dog

to rain heavily

toilet

nature
and the
weather

the
home

....

....

running water
smaller than a river

television

small walkway
between houses

....

....

long seat in main
room of house

time between summer
and winter

....

....

meals of the day

Everyday Life

to be in prison

....

....

the police

food taken to work

....

eating,
drinking and
smoking

crime and
the law

....

sweets

to steal

....

....

types of bread

cigarettes

police station

....

....

....

non-alcoholic drinks

money

not have any
money left

....

money
in general

....

rich

....

....

Figure 3   A 'Sense Relation Network' (reproduced by kind permission of the University of Leeds)

Table 1   Some major features of the Black Country phonological system

BATH	Like northern speakers, Black Country speakers use [a] for this lexical set where southern varieties use [ɑː].
TRAP	In Black Country as in southern dialects, the vowel in TRAP is realised as [a].
FOOT	The FOOT set comprises words which appear in southern varieties with the vowel sound [ʊ] – these are often, though not always, spelt with <oo>, so for example, *good, stood, look* but also *wolf, pudding, bullet*. This also occurs in the Black Country.
STRUT	As a Midlands variety, Black Country English uses several pronunciations here; from the more southern [ʌ] through a middle variant [ɤ] to a more northern [ʊ], where STRUT would rhyme with FOOT.
PRICE	Older speakers' Black Country English resembles northern varieties in that words like <price> are pronounced with a long vowel [ɑː]. Younger speakers are more likely to use vowel sounds like [ɑɪ], [ɒɪ], or even [ɔɪ] (the same vowel as in the word *foil*). This reflects the increasing influence of Birmingham on the Black Country variety, since these variants are historically from Warwickshire and the South-West.
FACE	The older pronunciation for this set is [æː]: older speakers say [fæːs] while younger speakers use a more standard diphthong [feis]. Further north in the Potteries, [æː] is still present.

Over time, the Black Country accent has moved away from northern norms. However, it is not moving to a great extent towards *standard* norms. Its Midlands realisation of the FOOT and STRUT sets is different both from the north (where there is no difference in the vowels of the two sets) and from the south, where the STRUT set is more obviously different from the FOOT set. The Black Country preserves a northern variant [a] in the BATH set where its neighbour Birmingham sometimes has the southern [ɑː], but the PRICE set *is* undergoing change to become more like its larger urban neighbour variety, Brummie [Birmingham] English.

Lexical variation in the Black Country

Peter Trudgill (1999, p. 20) suggests that while variation between accents may be maintained, or even growing, vocabulary is becoming more uniform: people know fewer traditional dialect words, and the words themselves are confined to narrower functions and to smaller geographical areas. Nonetheless, the existence of several 'Black Country Dictionaries' suggests that many words typical of the Black Country are still in use. I selected a list of words described by interviewees as typical 'Black Country words' and investigated how people talked about their use of these words. Lexis can tell us many interesting things about change and difference between older and younger speakers.

Running water – smaller than a river?

This example is also discussed in Chapter 2.

Change in the use of *brook* (variants across the UK include *stream*, *burn*, *beck* and *rill*) illustrates the loss (or attrition) of traditional dialect words well. The conditions set by some speakers in order for something to be a *brook* include size: 'a brook's smaller than a stream and a stream is smaller than a river.' This is interesting because older speakers quizzed about size being a possible qualifying condition report that a brook can be as large as a river: the Wom Brook near Wolverhampton, for example, is far too large to step over safely. Younger speakers often associated *brook* only with such waterways which carried the name:

> Erm, there's a place called the brook by my house which is just a stream. Everyone calls it the brook but I don't think I'd say it apart from to talk about that place.

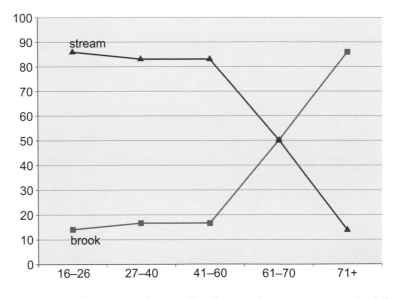

Figure 4 *Running water smaller than a river* – responses by informants of different ages

Note: the horizontal axis of the chart gives the age ranges of informants. The vertical axis shows the percentage of speakers who said they used *brook* (squares) or *stream* (triangles). To see patterns of change you need to read the chart from right to left (i.e. from older to younger speakers).

These narrowing conditions contribute to the widely used UK form *stream* gaining ground. Figure 4 shows that there is a change in reported usage across the age range, with older speakers mainly saying they used *brook*, and speakers in the 41–60 age range and below mainly saying they used *stream*.

Play truant

Social change can also bring new words. As older machinery, handtools and foodstuffs cease to be used, the words which describe them fall from use, but in the same way, new social norms and customs generate new terms. The term *play truant*, for example, did not elicit many terms from speakers over fifty. People had their own reasons for this, one informant reporting that 'everybody used to be frightened to death of stopping away' – in the process in fact using the Black Country dialect term *stop away* to refer to playing truant. However, the general perception was that parental control used to be tighter. Informants reported that the 'school mon' or 'school board man' would visit the houses of children reported absent from school to check that their absence was genuine. In contrast, younger speakers in the Black Country give *wag* as their term for 'play truant', a term also in use in other dialect areas. This lexical item is so productive that it has undergone semantic extension and now appears in the noun *waggy man*, who in turn drives a *waggy van*.

Grammar

Negation in Black Country

Black Country grammar shows how difference can persist despite, or even because of, social mobility and change. The dialect has an unusual method of forming the negative of auxiliary verbs. Rather than adding *not*, or *n't* (to give forms such as *do not*, or *is not*), Black Country marks negation by changing the vowel in the stem of the verb, so that *do not* becomes *doh*, and *did not* becomes *day*. Some examples are given in Table 2, together with what I call 'intermediate' forms which co-exist with the more Black Country forms.

Table 2 Auxiliary verb negation in Black Country English

Standard form	Black Country form	'Intermediate' form
has not/have not	ay	ain't
is not/are not	ay/bay (bay is older)	ain't, baint
do not	doh	doht, doh
cannot	cor	cort
did not	day	dain't, dait
shall not	share	shairt

Informants in my research regularly used forms such as *I day see nothing*, *I cor go* and *It doh matter* at interview. However, in discussion the same speakers would report their dislike of some of these terms:

Interviewer: so 'ay'(.) you wouldn't use 'ay'(.) does that grate on *you* [EMPHATIC] as well?

Informant 5: it doesn't really grate on me (.) but a lot of people use it

Informant 2: 'ay' doesn't (.) 'day' does [LAUGHS] (.) 'day' is the worst

Informant 5: yeah I don't like 'day'(.) I don't mind 'ay' (.) but

Informant 2: a lot of people say 'ay'

Although the verb forms look unusual they are likely to be derived from non-standard forms used more widely across England. Migration into the area was high during the Industrial Revolution, especially from Shropshire, and it led to an influx of many different linguistic forms. It is clear from sources such as Ellis (1889) that speakers have been using more widespread non-standard forms (what I referred to earlier as 'intermediate forms' like *ain't* and *dain't*) since the nineteenth century. Academic evidence from across time suggests that a form with [nt] was the original dominant form in the Black Country, and that the [n] element and then the [t] element were lost. Rather than being an old preserved feature, the Black Country's distinctive negation is in fact a result of language contact and change.

Third person singular feminine object pronoun

Another peculiarly Black Country variant which persists is the use of *er* or *her* for the third person female subject pronoun (as in 'He can't drive, but *her* can', where *she* would be used in standard English). The *her* form used to be used as far north as Derbyshire and Lancashire, and as far east as Oxfordshire, and it remains in widespread use in the

Black Country despite there being considerable stigma attached to it within the region. I looked at speakers' self-reports of their use of this form versus their actual use of it. The variant is clearly well-known among the speech community. Of thirty-nine informants, thirty-four had heard the construction in their local area, although only seven of these reported using it themselves. Nine informants actually used the *her* form in interview, generally alongside the standard form. The greater use of the standard form in interviews may simply reflect the fact that informants consider this more appropriate for an interview with a university researcher. More telling were the reports given by two speakers who said they never used the *her* form but then went on to do so.

Those using high levels of the local *her* variant all described themselves as of working-class origin. It seemed that those who declared themselves to be middle class distanced themselves from using local forms, while those reporting a label of working class to define themselves used more local features.

Conclusions

Black Country is an urban linguistic variety in an area which has long experienced inmigration on a large scale, yet it retains non-standard features at high levels of use even among younger speakers. This contradicts theories suggesting that older and more unusual forms fall out of favour as standard or unmarked (less noticeably different) forms are preferred. Black Country is not a variety untouched by change. It has been subject, for example, to exposure to a wider non-standard form of negation, which it has now made peculiarly its own. This does not indicate levelling, where dialect differences are smoothed out; if anything it proves that regional dialects have their own norms, which may change over time but then restabilise.

It was the working-class speakers in my sample whose varieties were the 'most regional' and whose speech differed most from the standard. This suggests that speakers less likely to be in contact with standard language speakers – those working and living in the same village or town, interacting with a small number of friends and an extended family who all live in the same place – are the section of any community likely to retain regional forms in their everyday usage.

Finally, speakers in my sample were aware that the variety was stigmatised and could report instances where they felt using it was inappropriate; the continued use of it by some even at interview may suggest a link between feeling 'Black Country' and speaking 'Black Country'.

References for this reading

Asprey, E. (2007) *Black Country English and Black Country Identity*, unpublished doctoral thesis, University of Leeds.

BBC Voices Black Country (2005) *Have Your Say*, available at: http://www.bbc.co.uk/blackcountry/have_your_say/accents/accents.shtml (Accessed 14 September 2009).

Coupland, N. and Bishop, H. (2007) 'Ideologised values for British accents', *Journal of Sociolinguistics*, vol. 11, no. 1, pp. 74–93.

Eckert, P. (1997) 'Age as a sociolinguistic variable' in Coulmas, F. (ed.) *The Handbook of Sociolinguistics*, Oxford, Blackwell.

Ellis, A. (1889) *On Early English Pronunciation, with Especial Reference to Shakspere and Chaucer*, Part V, London, Trübner and Co.

Kerswill, P., Llamas, C. and Upton, C. (1999) 'The first SuRE moves: early steps towards a large dialect project', *Leeds Studies in English*, vol. 30, pp. 257–69.

Llamas, C. (2000) 'A new methodology: data elicitation for social and regional language variation studies', *Leeds Working Papers in Linguistics*, vol. 8, pp. 95–118.

Milroy, L. (1987) *Observing and Analysing Natural Language – A Critical Account of Sociolinguistic Method*, Oxford, Blackwell.

Trudgill, P. (1999) *The Dialects of England* (2nd edn), Oxford, Blackwell.

Wells, J. (1982) *Accents of English Volume 1: An Introduction*, Cambridge, Cambridge University Press.

READING B: Extracts from 'New York Tawk'

Michael Newman

Source: Newman, M. (2006) 'New York Tawk (New York City, NY)' in Wolfram, W. and Ward, B. (eds) *American Voices: How Dialects Differ from Coast to Coast*, Oxford, Blackwell, pp. 82–7.

Back in the early 1970s, all the students in my Manhattan high school were given speech diagnostic exams. I passed, but the boy next to me was told he needed speech class. I was surprised and asked him why, since he sounded perfectly normal to me. 'My New York accent' he explained unhappily. Actually, this reason made me less thrilled with my exemption, as if my Detroit-born parents had deprived me of being a complete New Yorker.

As my classmate's predicament shows, my longing for New Yawk sounds was a distinctly minority taste. My school was hardly alone; there was a time when many New York colleges, including my present employer, Queens College, had required voice and diction courses, and their curriculum targeted certain local dialect peculiarities. Furthermore, a person with too many of these features was not allowed to teach in the New York City public schools.

Although these efforts were abandoned decades ago, many New Yorkers still talk of their speech as a problem to be overcome. When I was researching this article, a number of my former schoolmates claimed that their accents weren't 'that bad' or boasted that they had overcome 'the worst features'. As a New York accent fan, I would be more depressed by these claims if they were not actually based almost entirely on denial. Take the case of the *r*, which New York dialect speakers tend to leave out whenever it comes after a vowel sound. Many New Yorkers believe that dropping *r*'s is a serious flaw, but they usually imagine that it is someone else's. An employment agency owner once proclaimed to me that anyone who did not pronounce their *r*'s could not possibly qualify for a professional job – all the while calling them *ahs*.

Perhaps because this man was middle-class, he believed he had to be pronouncing his *r*'s. In fact, he was not altogether wrong; he sometimes put an *r* in where none belonged, a feature called intrusive *r*. It may seem bizarre to pronounce *r*'s that aren't there while skipping over those that are, but in fact, intrusive and missing *r*'s are two sides of the same coin. For *r*-droppers words like *law* and *lore* and *soar* and *saw* are homophones. However, they do not usually drop *r*'s all the time. They sometimes maintain them, particularly when a final *r* sound comes right before another word that begins with a vowel sound. Just as the *r* is sometimes pronounced in *lore and legend,* so it can appear in *law-r-and order.* When they are speaking carefully New Yorkers even occasionally maintain *r*'s when there is no following vowel. You get the idear? […]

My colleague Chuck Cairns developed a diagnostic list of 12 [New York] features […]. A particularly important one involves the vowel sound sometimes written as *aw,* as in *all, coffee, caught, talked,* or *saw* and the New York *r*-less *shore.* In New York dialect, this vowel becomes closer to the vowel *u* in *pull* or *put* followed by a slight *uh.* Strong New York dialect speakers say *u-uhl,* for *all* and *cu-uhfee,* for *coffee,* and they don't distinguish between *shore* and *sure.* A similar process applies to the short *a* in *cab, pass,* and *avenue.* In this case, the vowel can come to sound like an *i* or even *ee,* again followed by *uh.* Many New Yorkers try to catch *ki-uhbs* that *pi-uhss* by on Fifth *i-uhvenue,* although not all of us are so extreme.

In our pronunciation of these vowels, we New Yorkers are not unique; related pronunciations can be found from Baltimore to Milwaukee. However, none reproduce exactly the same pattern. Specifically, in New York all the *aw*s are affected, but many short *a* words are not – a differentiation called the 'short *a* split'. So in New York, *pass, cab,* and *avenue* have different vowels from *pat, cap,* and *average.* In most cities between Syracuse and Milwaukee, by contrast, *aw* is nothing like it is in New York, while all the short *a*'s are pronounced like *i-uh.* They not only say *pi-uhss* for *pass* – as in New York – but also *pi-uht* for *pat,* which no New Yorker would ever do. Detective Andy Sipowicz on *NYPD Blue* may seem like the archetypal New York City cop, but his *aw*'s and short *a*'s are obvious clues that Dennis Franz, the actor who plays him, is really from Chicago.

To be fair, it might be hard for Franz to sound like an authentic New Yorker. While there are rules that determine which short *a* words are shifted and which are not in New York, they are quite complicated. For instance, *can* is *key-uhn* in *can of soup* but not in *yes, I can.* The system is so complex that most unfortunate New Yorkers whose parents speak another variety of English never really learn them. We are condemned to not be full New York dialect speakers.

Although these vowel changes are an inherent part of the mix that receives condemnation, New Yorkers seem less concerned about them than they are about *r*'s. Only the most extreme pronunciations receive condemnation. In fact, there is an aspect of their speech that many New Yorkers appear to be actually proud of – the distinctive vocabulary. There are childhood games like *Ring-a-levio,* a kind of street hide-and-seek, *stickball,* baseball played with a broomstick, and *salugi,* the snatching of a kid's bag or hat, which is then thrown from friend to friend, just out of the victim's reach. More widely known are the Yiddishisms, such as *schlep* – to travel or carry something an annoying distance – to pick one out of many. Such terms are used by Jews of Eastern European origin the world over, but in New York they have extended to other communities. A teenage Nuyorican (New Yorker of Puerto Rican heritage) rap artist I know rhymed, *I'm gonna spin you like a dradel,* a reference to a top used in Chanukah celebrations. His schoolmate, also Latino, often says, *What the schmuck!* as an expression of surprise, misusing, or perhaps just appropriating, the vulgar Yiddish term for 'penis'. Some of these terms may be in decline – I don't hear many young Latinos using *schlep* – but there are recent replacements from other immigrant languages. Besides Nuyorican itself, there is the offensive *guido,* an ignorant Italian American tough guy. More positively, we have *papichulo,* a suave, well-dressed Latino ladies' man.

The appeal of these words lies in their evocation of immigrant roots, and New York dialect, like the city itself, serves as a kind of counterpoint to mainstream Anglo America. The dialect is often called Brooklynese, more because of Brooklyn's status as an icon of urban ethnic life than any real linguistic priority of that borough over other parts of the metropolitan area. The key to understanding the disparagement of New York pronunciations is similarly that they symbolize lack of integration into the American mainstream, and so being stuck in the working class. […]

Those, like my high school speech teacher, who wished to cure us of such features as intrusive *r*'s did so because they thought it would be a social and professional handicap. They were mistaken. Many middle- and upper-middle-class New Yorkers of all ethnicities use the dialect, to say nothing of billionaires like Donald Trump. One dialect speaker, former Governor Mario Cuomo, even became nationally famous for his eloquence. Instead, as New York dialect speakers have moved up socially, their speech has lost much of its outsider status. Older speakers may think they speak badly, but they do so almost out of inertia. In fact, many professional Latinos, Asian Americans, Caribbean Americans, and African Americans have adopted their distinctive dialect features, in whole or in good part.

In assuming what has become a common New York middle-class dialect, these speakers either leave behind or alternate with the speech commonly associated with their ethnic communities. Today, this working-class minority speech has taken on the outsider status the classic Brooklynese has left behind. Among young New Yorkers, *r*-lessness is replaced by *aks* for *ask* and *toof* for *tooth* as examples of how one shouldn't speak. Some expressions, such as using *mines* instead of *mine,* in the sentence *That's mines,* occupy a kind of middle ground for these minorities (actually together the majority of the city) of marking roots while still being understood as 'incorrect.' Again, minority youths often seem proud of their special vocabulary, which expresses their roots in urban life. The speech of minorities is less unified than that of the previous generations of children of European immigrants. But, despite the variation, there is a tendency for some characteristics to be shared widely. Also these forms often extend to other immigrants, particularly Middle Easterners, and even to many European Americans and Asian Americans who associate with rap and hip-hop culture generally. […]

A former Nuyorican student of mine remarked after he got out of the Army, 'No matter where I went, people could tell I was from the city.' He was obviously pleased by that fact, just as I am when out-of-towners identify me as having a New York accent despite my over-abundant r's and lack of a proper short *a* split. The ultimate resilience and uniqueness of New York dialects lies in our intense local pride, and this is as true for the minority versions as it is for the so-called Brooklynese.

Further reading

William Labov's mammoth study, *The Social Stratification of English in New York City* (Washington, D.C. Center for Applied Linguistics, 1966), is still considered to be the authoritative work on English in New York City.

6 English and other languages

Kay McCormick

6.1 Introduction

As you know from earlier chapters, English has co-existed throughout its history with other languages across nations, institutions and communities.

Earlier chapters have discussed how contact with other languages has affected the development of English – from the influence of Scandinavian languages and Norman French on Old and Middle English (Chapter 2) to the distinctive features of New Englishes in several parts of the world (Chapters 3 and 5). This chapter continues the discussion of **language contact**, focusing on the status and use of English alongside other languages in contemporary multilingual contexts. This is of interest not only to linguists but also to non-linguists who speak more than one language. If you use more than one language in your daily life, while you are reading this chapter you may frequently find yourself prompted to think about your own patterns of language choice and what shaped them.

See also the historical timeline (Appendix 1) which indicates the main influences of other languages on English throughout its history.

Bilingual individuals and communities commonly deploy their languages in complementary ways, using one language for some functions and others for other functions. The selections are often made unconsciously, being based in habitual patterns. The patterns, in turn, are shaped by the circumstances under which English came into the community, by practical considerations, and by qualities associated with each language: progress or conservatism; cultural rootedness or neutrality; a particular religion, ethnic group or social class. It is often the case that languages accrue several associations, some of which are in tension with one another. As a result, people may be very ambivalent about a language. For example, they may value it because they see it as giving access to certain economic benefits and upward social mobility, but also dislike it because it is the mother tongue of people who oppress(ed) them. English has been and still is the subject of this kind of ambivalence, particularly in former British colonies. Thus, as we will see in this chapter, the spread of English among speakers of other languages receives both support and opposition.

In the following section we look at how, in various multilingual contexts, speakers of other languages may come into contact with English. Because of its perceived benefits and dangers, English has often been the subject of regulation as governments attempt to promote or limit its use in relation to other languages, and we turn to this topic in Section 6.3. In Section 6.4 we explore how English is used in bilingual communities and families, and the effects this may have, over time, on other languages. Finally, in Section 6.5 we look at how people may 'speak bilingually', focusing on the detail of what happens in conversations which combine English and other languages in various ways and to different effects.

A note on terminology:

- Most of the phenomena discussed here occur in both **bilingual** and **multilingual** communities. I sometimes use the terms 'bilingual' and 'bilingualism' as general terms to avoid awkward repetition of 'bilingual and multilingual', or 'bilingualism and multilingualism'.

- By **home language(s)**, I mean the language(s) habitually used in a home and acquired by its children. The scope of the term is similar to 'first language', but it allows for the fact that in some homes it isn't clear that one language is 'first' in the sense of being acquired first or in the sense of ranking.

- At times I refer to people who *use* English, rather than to people who *speak* English, for two reasons. First, the term reminds us that in the contemporary world, there are many people who frequently read English (on the internet) but seldom speak it. Second, it is an appropriate way of referring to people who use some of the resources of the English language for limited purposes, but don't have sufficient proficiency in it to be seen by themselves or by others as 'English speakers'.

6.2   Encounters with English

As an illustration of English language teaching in China, look back to Kingsley Bolton's discussion in Chapter 1, Reading B.

In countries where it is a foreign language, such as those in Kachru's 'Expanding Circle' (Kachru, 1992), the school classroom is the main site where speakers of other languages meet up with, learn and use English. Where opportunities for face-to-face teaching and learning in English are very limited, people might still be able to gain some ability to read and write the language through a combination of self-instruction manuals, CDs and DVDs. Their main use of it may be for accessing the English language radio and television programmes, available through satellite technology. These programmes – particularly dramas – can expand the range of English varieties that people become acquainted with and learn to understand, aided by visual and aural context. Formal teaching and learning favours standard Englishes, whereas radio, television and the internet are more hospitable to other varieties of English. This expanded competence is not automatically used in speech or writing, of course, but this may happen, as we see in a study carried out by Alastair Pennycook. He describes the ways in which a Japanese rap group, Rip Slyme, attempts to incorporate the English of American rap subculture in their lyrics. Pennycook (2003, p. 527) argues that this is used 'more symbolically than mimetically'. In other words, the use of English symbolises an affinity with American rap subculture, but does not actually sound much like the English of the rap artists it imitates.

As you saw in Chapter 4, English is the language most widely used on the internet. People do not need to have an excellent command of the language as a whole in order to navigate and participate in the virtual worlds of the internet. Starting with basic vocabulary and grammar, they can pick up the style appropriate to the domains they enter. Reading and writing in internet communication may be all that many people will use English for – they may never need to speak it. The rest of their lives can be carried on in their other languages.

Unfettered access to English language programmes and internet content sometimes gets a mixed reception. On the one hand, the language may be welcomed by some people as a carrier of a rich range of new ideas and possibilities. On the other hand, that very quality may make other people fear or reject it, seeing it as a bearer of ideas that could erode traditional knowledge, practices and values. Both responses were evident in Taleban-controlled sectors of Afghanistan in the late 1990s: according to a BBC report on 12 January 2009, '[e]ven during the Taleban era, there were some English-language centres where pragmatic and ambitious Taleban members were learning the language. However, the extremists among them shunned it as the language of "infidels"'.

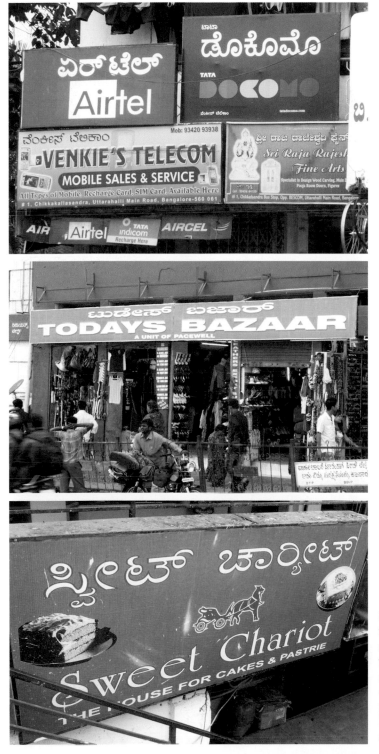

Figures 6.1–6.6   People may elect to use English, but in multilingual communities there are also many fortuitous encounters. These street signs, in which English sits alongside other languages, come from Singapore (English, Chinese, Tamil and Malay) and Bangalore in India (English and Kannada).

Although informal access to English is becoming easier, pressure to have access to classes where English is taught systematically and intensively to adults is on the increase throughout the world. The British Council and hundreds of TESOL (Teaching English to Speakers of Other Languages) and TEFL (Teaching English as a Foreign Language) language schools provide resources and classes which cater for the needs of adults who want to interact with business, professional or academic colleagues internationally. As has been discussed in earlier chapters, English is very widely used as a lingua franca for communication between people who do not speak one another's home languages.

The contemporary teaching of English, and translation between English and other languages, are discussed in another book in this series: Hewings and Tagg (eds) (2012).

Because it is difficult for adult learners to become proficient in a new language in a short space of time, what is gained from adult language classes often needs to be complemented and supported by the provision of translation and interpreting services in international contact situations.

Having looked at some of the ways in which speakers of other languages come into contact with English, we turn now to see why and how governments may attempt to promote or limit the use of English in their countries.

6.3   Regulating English: policy and planning

Obviously, English could not be the viable lingua franca that it is in international communication if it were not already a prominent language in a large number of countries. As you saw in earlier chapters, in Kachru's 'Inner Circle' countries English has a high profile because it is now the mother tongue of the numerical majority, who are also the most powerful group politically and economically.

In countries where English is not a majority home language, its high status relative to other languages has usually been achieved through legislation to implement government policy decisions.

Language policies and language planning that affect English are also addressed in Hewings and Tagg (eds) (2012).

National language policy and planning in multilingual countries

Language policy is the set of broad goals – political, social, economic, linguistic – that policy developers hope to achieve by focusing on aspects of the use of languages in particular countries or institutions. **Language planning** identifies the processes of policy implementation.

The development of a new language policy at national/governmental level usually takes place only at times of major political change; for example, after a war, or at the time of declaring independence. A country's language policy is usually determined by politicians, based on their vision of what the country needs internally, and how they want it to be positioned in its region and in the world. Thereafter, plans to implement the policy have to be devised. At that stage, it sometimes becomes clear that politicians who devised the policy have not fully considered all the conditions in the country (or institution) and therefore come up with a policy that is impossible to implement.

Typically, legislation regulates which languages are to be used for official purposes in government at all levels (national, regional and local), in the civil service, educational institutions, the legal domain, and in relations with other countries. As **official languages**, these are given high status. They may have official language status throughout the country or only in certain regions. Some countries also identify an indigenous language as a **national language**. Its main value is symbolic. At a language policy conference in South Africa in 1991, sociolinguist Ralph Fasold answered a question about the difference in meaning between the terms 'national language' and 'official language'. He said that a national language is rather like the flag: it is valued as a symbol of national identity and people feel strongly about it. An official language is more like the post office: it is valued as an institution through which things get done, communication happens, but people don't feel strongly about it. (Not all countries have both a national and an official language.)

The process of planning how to give effect to these decisions is called **status planning**. It is usually accompanied by what is known as **acquisition planning**, which is planning for how people will learn the official languages and other languages which the government regards as necessary for economic or other reasons. Both status and acquisition planning are involved in implementing what is always a crucial decision – the choice of language(s) for use as a medium of instruction in schools and tertiary education institutions. Much of the detailed work in acquisition planning is done by people involved in education: teacher trainers, curriculum specialists and developers of educational materials.

Major political changes sometimes bring to power groups of people who were formerly marginalised. Such groups sometimes insist that their languages be given the status and functions of official languages, partly as a sign of respect for the speakers, but partly to make it easier for them to gain access to state services, by using their own language. All languages develop in order to do whatever their speakers need them to do, but that kind of spontaneous development is usually rather piecemeal. Something more systematic needs to be done to equip a language to handle the range of new functions that come with being an official language. Its linguistic 'body' or *corpus* has to be developed: vocabulary has to be greatly expanded (e.g. to teach mathematics); new discourse forms need to be developed (e.g. to use in the formulation of laws). Working out how that can best be done, and doing it, is the domain of **corpus planning**, which involves linguists and educators. It is a time-consuming process.

Language policy identifies goals, but in practice, goals are not always met. Recognition of discrepancies between policy and practice does not immediately lead to reformulation of policy, however. Because thorough implementation is slow and expensive, language policies usually stay in place until there is very strong political or economic pressure for them to be scrapped or amended.

English has a long history of serving as an official language or a language of education in many countries. As a result, its corpus is highly developed for those functions. This has put it in a position of advantage over many other languages in situations where new language policies are being considered. However – and this is very important – it has not automatically ensured that English is accorded high official status in multilingual countries, nor even that it is retained as an official language in countries where it once had an established presence. As we will see in the examples below, pragmatic considerations are not the only ones that shape language policy: perceptions of historical legacy and desired national identity are also taken into account.

After they gained independence, many former British colonies initially retained English in key domains. In some countries there was little or no organised resistance to the retention of English, but in others there was. Two former colonies where the status of English was contested are Pakistan and Tanzania.

Pakistan was part of a large area in south Asia which had been under British control for about ninety years, from the mid-nineteenth century. In 1947, Britain relinquished control of this area, having forged agreements with political leaders that, on independence, the territory would be divided into two self-governing dominions, Pakistan and India. Pakistan consisted of two territories, West Pakistan (now Pakistan) and East Pakistan (now Bangladesh), which split into independent countries at the end of 1971.

During the period of British control, English was the main language of administration and it became fairly widely known through formal education. Also during that period, several other languages of the region were used as identity symbols for various ethno-nationalist and religious movements. Because English had not been associated with any of these movements it could be seen as neutral in relation to them. This was ideologically useful to the post-independence government of Pakistan, which was trying to unify a newly established political entity while at the same time carrying on the day-to-day tasks of education and administration, many of which had previously been carried out in English. These factors favoured keeping English as an official language. However, its retention was strongly opposed by religious parties 'who felt that maintaining the status of English symbolized a new form of colonization' (Mahboob and Ahmar, 2008, p. 245). They wanted an Islamic state which used a local language spoken by Muslim communities. Of the possible contenders, Urdu received the strongest support. In response, successive governments in the first thirty years of the postcolonial period passed recommendations to develop and elevate the status of other languages, Urdu in particular, but did little to implement them before 1977. In that year a military coup led by General Zia-ul-Haq paved the way for more comprehensive Islamisation and an attempt at Urduisation in all domains. For example, in 1978 all schools were instructed to move towards Urdu as sole medium of instruction, starting with the first grade in the following year. Schools for the elite continued to teach in English and the demand for English medium education grew, even – covertly – among government supporters. By 1987 it was clear that political will in regard to Urduisation in education and administration was losing strength. Thus, realising that they had embarked on this policy too hastily and without adequate planning, the government withdrew it. Language policy in subsequent governments has promoted English because of its value in linking the country's development into global political and economic spheres.

According to Rahman:

> The ruling elite as a whole supports the continued use of English in formal official domains because it ensures its social distinction from the non-elite; facilitates the entry of members of its own class, including the younger generation, into the elitist positions and increases the possibility of opening up the international job market.
>
> (Rahman, 1997, p. 179)

Urdu is currently (in 2012) the national language, while English and Urdu have official language status.

The East African country, Tanzania, gained its independence from Britain in 1961. Although it had been under British colonial rule for far less time than Pakistan – only forty years – English was already firmly established as the language of colonial government. The post-independence government wanted to turn away from Western capitalist models and build a classless society based on Ujamaa, an African form of socialism and self-reliance. The unifying linguistic vehicle for this was to be an African language, Swahili, rather than English. Although Swahili was the dominant home language in only one area of the country, it was widely used as a lingua franca locally and had the added advantage of also being used in some neighbouring countries. (The new government paid very little attention to other indigenous languages.) The period from 1967 to 1974 was one of strong antagonism towards Britain and other capitalist countries, and during those years Swahili was strongly promoted to replace English. To that end, enormous efforts were put into corpus and acquisition planning. However, despite this, and despite strong political commitment to it, full Swahilisation did not come about. This was because political events and economic pressures nationally and internationally changed Tanzanians' perceptions of their country's ability to remain isolated from the West. Recognising the need for more political and economic interaction with Britain and other countries of the West, the government put measures in place to facilitate this. In 1974, as part of the process of political and economic liberalisation, President Nyerere advocated equalising the status of English and Swahili. Since then 'English has regained its pre-1967 prestige, while Swahili has attained an unprecedented level of spread and importance in use' (Blommaert, 1999, p. 98). This is not surprising since both languages had been and still are used in modernisation. Within the country today, both languages are used in political discourse, and in education albeit at different levels. Swahili is used more than English in primary and adult basic education, while English predominates in secondary and tertiary education. In these domains the standard varieties of the two languages are promoted but as research conducted by Blommaert (2005) shows, in their everyday lives, Tanzanians make creative use of elements of other varieties of these languages which have local value. For instance, they may blend sounds and words from non-standard Swahili and non-standard English to create written texts such as shop signs. A similar mixed variety is also found as a spoken form – an urban vernacular used by young people who are diverse in ethnic and class backgrounds but who are united in their 'awareness of being in the margins of the world' (Blommaert, 2005, p. 405). (I discuss such mixed varieties further below.)

Former British colonies are not the only multilingual countries where English has been elevated to the status of official language. This has been done in Rwanda, Madagascar and Namibia, none of which had ever been part of the British Empire. The first activity gives you the opportunity to apply what you know about the complexity of the spread of English, in an analysis of aspects of Namibia's language policy. Keep in mind the factors involved in language policy decisions made and rescinded in Tanzania and Pakistan.

Activity 6.1

Allow about 15 minutes

Read the following thumbnail sketch of Namibia's pre-independence background, and the brief account of its language policy history. Think about what policy makers would have been weighing up when they made their decisions to have English as the only official language, and to designate it as the only medium of instruction in state schools after the third grade. What would they have seen as the advantages of prioritising English? What do you think the problems would have been with implementing the policy in parliament, the civil service and schools? Can you think of any solutions to those problems?

Language policy in Namibia

Namibia is located in the south-western region of Africa, bordered by Angola, Botswana and South Africa. Most of the area that is now Namibia was a German colony from 1894 to 1915, and German was the language of administration. During the First World War, neighbouring South Africa occupied the territory, and in the post-war deliberations, South Africa was appointed by the League of Nations to administer it. After the Second World War, the United Nations (which had superseded the League of Nations) wished to withdraw South Africa's mandate, but South Africa refused to surrender its control over the country. It continued to run it on lines similar to those operating in South Africa, including the institutionalising of racial discrimination, emphasising ethnic differences among the indigenous population, repressing black political organisations, and denying the franchise to black people. South Africa resorted to military force to maintain its presence and to counter the growing liberation movement.

Although both English and Afrikaans were official languages during the period of South African control (1915–1989), in fact the much-resented military and administrative control was exercised largely through Afrikaans, the South African official language most strongly associated with that country's white nationalist government. This led to negative associations with Afrikaans among oppressed indigenous people. But in spite of that, they were willing to learn it because it was the main language of schooling from the fourth grade on, and therefore the main language of access to employment. As a result, Afrikaans became known widely enough to function as a lingua franca in most of the country. None of the indigenous languages could compete with it in that regard. Nor could English, which was rarely used except in a few urban areas and was the home language of less than 2 per cent of the population.

However, English became the lingua franca of Namibian political exiles and it was the language through which most of them furthered their education while in exile. The liberation movement was led by the South West African People's Organization (SWAPO), founded in 1960. Its public meetings were banned from 1963. Thereafter many of its members went into exile because of severe repression. While in exile, they developed a language policy as part of their vision for a new democratic order within the country, and active participation in the globalising world (published by the United Nations Institute for Namibia (UNIN) in 1981). This policy formed the basis for the one adopted at independence in 1990.

The new constitution declared English the sole official language but, according to Ndjoze-Ojo (2004), it was deliberately not explicit about the status and roles of other languages. The wording gave the impression that permission could be given for their use in administration, education and judicial functions where appropriate.

The language policy for education allowed for the continuation of mother tongue instruction up to the end of Grade 3, and stipulated that in all state schools English was to be rapidly phased in to replace Afrikaans as the sole medium of instruction in senior primary and secondary schooling. The new policy demanded that rote learning be replaced by interactive teaching and learning in languages and other subjects.

At independence in 1990, Namibia had an estimated population of 1.3 million. Except for a few urban areas, population density was low. Distances between settlements were vast, and road and communication infrastructures were not strong. There were approximately thirty indigenous languages, half of which did not have a written form. According to a Ministry of Education and Culture report at the time, '60% of the teachers are unqualified with a further 30% underqualified' (MEC, 1990, p. 23, quoted in O'Sullivan, 2002, p. 225).

(adapted from O'Sullivan, 2002; Ndjoze-Ojo, 2004; Pütz, 2006; Tätemeyer, 2009)

Comment

Language policy makers would have had to weigh the advantages and disadvantages of the status quo in regard to official languages: Afrikaans was a reasonably effective lingua franca; English was rarely used and not widely known. Retaining Afrikaans as an official language and as the medium of instruction beyond Grade 3 would have had the advantages of continuity, the ability to use existing human and material resources, and the language's established status as a lingua franca. But Afrikaans had strong negative associations among oppressed people because of the repressive uses to which it had been put in Namibia and South Africa. In contrast, English was associated with the liberation movement. Its retention could also be seen as tapping into the advantages of a global language; for example, its facilitation of trade and the exchange of ideas. Moreover, retaining English would not privilege a particular ethnic group. It could be regarded as the most ethnically neutral language in the country and could thus be seen to be a unifying factor. However, it was not neutral with respect to class – the few who did know English well constituted an elite, whether members of the former ruling class, or the well-educated political leadership who had been in exile.

Elevating an indigenous language to the status of co-official language, or national language, or medium of instruction beyond the lower primary level would have been problematic for political and practical reasons. It would have favoured one ethnic group above the others; and on the practical front, extensive corpus planning would have been required, since no indigenous language had previously served the functions of an official language or medium of instruction beyond the third grade. Making English the main medium of instruction in higher primary and secondary schools could be seen as a way of fast-tracking increased proficiency in English. A vast array of educational and other information resources had already been developed in other countries and could be made available in Namibia.

In practice, serious challenges emerged with the implementation of the language policy. I list just three:

1   Many delegates elected to the first parliament were unable to participate in its discussions or study its documents because they did not have the necessary proficiency in English. Although theoretically other languages could be used in parliamentary debates, in fact there was not adequate provision for interpreting and translating to and from English.

2   Very few higher primary and secondary school teachers were sufficiently proficient in English to be able to teach their subjects in English, or even to understand the specialist discourse of the syllabi.

3   It was very difficult for learners to start using English for all their academic work when they had only studied it as a subject at school and had little or no opportunity to use it outside school.

In spite of the challenges, the prioritising of English in the language policy for education has not been rejected by teachers. Attempts are being made to provide support for its implementation. For example, teachers' views and the paucity of resources were taken into account in the 1997 rewriting of the English syllabi. Teacher advisers have been appointed. The 2003 revised policy allows for the use of mother tongue 'in a supportive role' in higher primary classes (Ministry of Basic Education, Sport and Culture, 2003, p. 4). Whether the scale and reach of the support is going to be sufficient remains to be seen.

In these accounts of the changing status of English in Pakistan, Tanzania and Namibia, some general points about the positioning of English in a multilingual country can be derived. For instance, we noted that there may be tensions between ideological and pragmatic forces which can cause mismatches – if not contradictions – between policy and practice, and may even prompt a series of policy decisions and reversals. We also saw that, in the contemporary world, national language policies in multilingual countries should take account of both the country's internal situation and the wider regional and global contexts within which it is located.

6.4   English and other languages in communities and families

Language policies may influence but they certainly do not determine how people will use languages and the resources that come with them. Communities and families are key sites where relationships between languages are established and challenged. Thus, we turn now to an exploration of the ways in which English may be incorporated into the linguistic repertoires of communities and families which also use one or more other languages. The box below provides a schematic account of what may happen after a new language – referred to as N – is introduced into communities or families already using one or more other languages – referred to as O.

Patterns of bilingualism

When changes of language policy or changes in circumstances (such as alterations to national borders, new trade opportunities, or migration) bring a new language (N) within reach of a community or family, members of the community or family will learn and use it only if they perceive that they will benefit from doing so. If they do learn it, they may continue using their other languages (O) for most functions, while using N exclusively for interactions emanating from the change in circumstances. That configuration may be stable over a long period of time. Or it may change over time. N may come to be used increasingly alongside O in established domains such as schools, and later also in homes, until it is eventually accepted as an additional home language. In such cases it may be used for the same functions as O, but it is more likely to be used for some kinds of topics and interactions, while O continues to be used for others. If this co-existence persists over a long period, we describe it as stable bilingualism.

Stable bilingual communities or families are usually characterised by a strong sense of the importance of their heritage and of O, the language originally associated with it. Their beliefs and daily practices promote what is called **language maintenance** in regard

---

to O. However, if a community or family begins to associate N exclusively with identities or a way of life that they prefer to their own, it may gradually come to use only N for functions that O used to perform, until over three or more generations, O is abandoned entirely in favour of N. This process, known as **language shift**, is seldom smooth and uncontested. Individuals or groups may seek to halt or reverse the process by maintaining their own use of O, and by teaching it, and aspects of the heritage it carries, to children. If they are unsuccessful, and if no other communities speak or read this language, **language death** may be said to have occurred. Of course, if there are written texts, the language does not necessarily pass into total oblivion.

Stable bilingual or multilingual communities which use English but do not neglect their own languages are to be found not only in predominantly English-speaking countries and former British colonies such as India, but also in countries which have no history of control by Britain. Scandinavian countries and the Netherlands are examples of the latter. Members of such communities learn and use English for some purposes (such as access to ideas disseminated primarily in English) but not for others. They move comfortably within the English-speaking world without wanting to identify with it at the expense of their own. In some stable bilingual communities English has become part of the linguistic repertoire of the home, along with other languages, but it does not displace the original home languages. The movement of English into the home domain is often facilitated by children. It is more likely to occur when they don't just study it as a subject, but have all of their schooling in English. In such cases, children often speak English to their siblings and friends in the playground, and out of habit, they continue to use English with their siblings at home when talking about things associated with life outside the home. If their parents can also speak English, it is possible for 'home topics' to be spoken of in English. In this way English becomes a home language. This process is occurring in Singapore, South Africa and many other parts of the world, particularly among urban middle-class families. Writing about India, Rakesh Bhatt refers to 'local ownership of global English – as "one of our own"', and he argues that 'We have to abandon the use of the label "non-native speaker" for multilingual subjects from postcolonial contexts. In the case of communities which have appropriated English and localized its usage, the members should be treated as "native speakers"' (Bhatt, 2005, pp. 35, 48).

Where communities' own languages seem to have little currency in the wider world, younger people may not want to continue using them. In a community, language shift may take several generations to run its course. This seems to be the case with the shift from a Gaelic language to English in Britain and Ireland. Extensive contact with English goes back several centuries in some Gaelic-speaking areas, but not in all. In more geographically isolated areas, such as the Uist and Aran islands, contact with English was sporadic before twentieth-century developments in transport and communication technology decreased their isolation. Gaelic speakers have had to gain proficiency in English in order to access education and most kinds of economic opportunities. There are hardly any local employment opportunities that do not involve some use of English. In some communities, there are organised attempts at language maintenance. In the west of Ireland, for example, Irish-medium preschools have been established to serve families who use only Irish at home, and also bilingual families who want to maintain the language (Hickey, 2009).

In Wales, efforts to halt the shift to English and to revitalise the use of Welsh have met with noticeable success during the past three decades. Cooperation between strong civil society organisations and the Welsh Assembly Government has been a key element in this success. The process of revitalisation is complex and is affected by political and economic factors, and by differing perceptions of the connection between the Welsh language and Welsh identity (Coupland and Aldridge, 2009; Williams, 2009). Some people regard the revitalisation of the Welsh language primarily as part of a long process of resisting political and economic domination by English speakers. Others do not see English as an outsider language since many people whose families have lived in Wales for generations are English-speaking and speak very little Welsh, while regarding themselves as Welsh. Williams's interviewees express a range of views on the centrality of the Welsh language to a sense of Welsh identity.

In the United States, the shift from indigenous languages to English seems to be ongoing in communities whose language of origin has not already died out. However, some Native American communities are trying to prevent their languages from dying out. The Linguistics Department at the University of New Mexico offers assistance to such communities by working with community members to develop descriptions of the languages and dictionaries. These interventions alone, however, are not enough to halt or reverse language shift – that would require wider and more intensive community involvement and extensive state support – but they can provide resources for those who want to learn the languages.

Migration is discussed further in another volume in this series – see Hewings and Tagg (eds) (2012).

Families isolated through migration often undergo language shift in as little as three generations. This is the time frame seen in many immigrant families who settle in English-speaking countries and live in neighbourhoods where their home language is not known. A typical pattern in such cases is that, if they do not already know English, the adult immigrants speak their language of origin at home and try to learn as much English as they need for their daily lives outside the home. Children born in the new country speak the language(s) of their parents, but also have to learn and use English for educational and social purposes. When they in turn have children they may choose to use English in interactions with them at home, so that they will settle easily at school and integrate with local English-speaking children. It is in the second generation that decisions are taken which lead to language maintenance or language shift in a family.

If adults of the second generation feel that their ancestral language stigmatises them and minimises their life-chances, they may encourage children to use only English. One example is that of a poor Jewish community of Yiddish-speaking immigrants in early twentieth-century Cape Town. The editorial of *The South African Jewish Chronicle* of 5 June 1903 puts it bluntly: 'anything which cultivates the art or practice of Yiddish speaking in a European colony is actually detrimental to the Jewish people and their cause'. Within about three generations that community became English-speaking, like the city's longer established middle-class Jewish community. Li Wei discusses a more recent and complex example from a British/Chinese community on Tyneside, where patterns of shift varied between different sections of the community (see box below).

Although across the globe there is evidence that English is in high demand, it is not seen only as the bringer of advantages. There are also concerns about its effects on other languages and the cultures with which they are associated. In recent decades the promotion and rapid spread of English throughout the world has lead to a fear that it will inevitably result in the eventual death of the languages with which it comes into contact.

Language shift on Tyneside

Li Wei (1998) carried out a study of a British/Chinese community on Tyneside, in the north-east of England. Some of the community came originally from Ap Chau, a small island near Hong Kong; others came from various parts of Hong Kong and from Guang Dong Province in mainland China. Li Wei found evidence of a language shift: from the oldest generation, and also some women in the middle generation, who spoke Chinese (mainly Cantonese) monolingually through to the youngest (British-born) generation who were bilingual in English and Chinese, with English as their dominant language. However, patterns of language choice among the British-born speakers varied depending on the family's region of origin. Those whose families had come from Ap Chau seemed to have maintained their use of Chinese more than those from other regions. This may be because families from Ap Chau had a relatively high level of contact with others from the island. A major focus for such contact was the local evangelical church which provided opportunities for several social and cultural activities, including Chinese language lessons for British-born children.

This fear has been strongly expressed in metaphors of war such as the 'invasion' by English into the territories of other languages; English has been labelled a 'killer language', and its effect on other languages has been seen as a form of 'linguicide' (Skutnabb-Kangas and Phillipson, 2001). It is important to note that while the contemporary spread of English is threatening the survival of other languages in some places, it does not always have this effect. Even where English is accorded high status nationally, it may not precipitate language shift towards English, as we see in Tanzania, for example.

The perceived threats posed by English to other languages are discussed further in another book in this series: Hewings and Tagg (eds) (2012).

6.5   Speaking bilingually: switching between English and other languages

In previous sections, we have looked at what may motivate bilingual speakers to choose English or another language for interactions in multilingual contexts. But bilinguals do not always have to choose only one language for a conversation – they may switch between their languages within one conversation. The moment-by-moment alternation between languages is termed **codeswitching**, where 'code' may refer to a distinct language or language variety: for example, a dialect, or accent. Here I focus on switching between English and other languages; switching between different varieties of English is considered in Chapter 7.

A speaker may switch from one code to another for just one phrase, or for much longer. Switches may occur within sentences as well as between them. Codeswitching may be planned or unplanned, conscious or unconscious. There is evidence to indicate that bilinguals are not always aware of which language they are speaking, or of when they are switching.

In the rest of this section we explore different forms and functions of switching between English and other languages. We start with switches that involve only brief inserts of words or phrases from a different language, move to those in which there is frequent movement from one language to another, and conclude with examples where two languages are so tightly intertwined in vernacular speech that we could regard them as constituting a bilingual or hybrid code. The functions of switches are practical (e.g. making the best use of available vocabulary), social (e.g. signalling aspects of identity) and stylistic (e.g. heightening contrast).

The briefest excursion into another language would be for a **loanword**, or **borrowing**. As you know from earlier chapters, English has absorbed many borrowed words, and has been the source of loans to other languages. Contemporary examples of borrowing between English and French would include (French into English): *haute couture, de rigueur*; and (English into French): *un scoop, un squat, un lifting* [a face lift]. Filling vocabulary gaps is one function of loanwords. For recent borrowings that still retain signs of their origins, there may also be a social function: signalling something about oneself or one's perception of one's interlocutor. Marie-Noëlle Lamy has commented on the situation in France: 'English may be seen as fashionable, particularly by young French people who wish to identify with the prestigious dynamic Anglo-American culture conveyed to them through TV, the Web, pop music and films' (Lamy, 2007, p. 36).

Even a brief excursion into another language can signal particular 'belonging'. The primary function of a process that is sometimes termed **emblematic switching** is symbolic. It is often used to indicate ancestry in cases where the speaker is no longer thoroughly familiar with his or her ancestral language. For example, monolingual English-speaking descendants of Yiddish-speaking immigrants from Eastern Europe sometimes use Yiddish words and idioms when talking to others who share or are familiar with that background. The Yiddish phrases are passed down in families across generations, even when the rest of the language is no longer used. Emblematic switching to Yiddish accesses concepts which the speaker feels could not be adequately rendered in English, for example 'I can't bear the *kvetching*.' [persistent complaining] or 'He's such a *schmuck*!' [stupid person, oaf]. It also signals the solidarity of shared heritage with other participants in the conversation.

A superficially similar kind of switching occurs among people who pick up and use words or phrases from a language which is *not* part of their heritage. Such switching is known as **language crossing**, defined as the use of a language, or language variety, that isn't generally felt to 'belong' to the speaker. This is similar to emblematic switching in that the person who engages in it does not have established proficiency in the language or dialect to which he or she makes brief excursions, but is able to use a few of its words, phrases or accent features. The main difference is that the crosser has no insider status in the group whose language she or he is drawing on. For instance, in Ben Rampton's study of young people in a British multi-ethnic urban community, a school student of Pakistani descent uses creole expressions to add emphasis to an unfavourable comment about a teacher (Rampton, 2005). Such behaviour tends to stand out, going against expectations about speakers and language use. It may indicate some degree of identification with the other language and its speakers. Equally, however, it may involve negative stereotyping, as when a speaker 'takes off' another language, which is why instances of it may be regarded with suspicion.

Switching between languages may be deeply involved in the enactment of identity. Consciously or unconsciously through the way we speak in various interactions, we signal something about ourselves, or about how we would like to be seen: as learned/cool/exotic/working class, etc. Sometimes people switch to a particular language as part of an attempt to present themselves favourably. For example, Sabrina Billings (2009) reports that contestants in national beauty pageants in Tanzania go to great lengths to present themselves on stage as fluent speakers of English, even when they are not. (Some prepare for their on-stage interviews by learning likely dialogue sequences by rote.) Contestants know that physical appearance is not enough; they also have to appear to be well educated, and in the eyes of judges and audience fluency in

The use of Yiddish expressions as a feature of New York English is also referred to in Chapter 5 Reading B.

English – unmixed with Swahili – is taken as evidence of elite education.

The range of things we signal about ourselves through our linguistic choices is enormous, since none of us has a single identity. Social scientists talk of people 'enacting identities', rather than 'having an identity'. We construct identities in interaction. We all have several 'reference points' or 'reference groups' in relation to which we construct our identities. Jan Blommaert puts it this way:

> the social environment of almost any individual would by definition be *polycentric*, with a wide range of overlapping and criss-crossing centres to which orientations need to be made, and evidently with multiple 'belongings' for individuals (often understood as 'mixed' or 'hybrid' identities).
>
> (Blommaert, 2005, p. 394)

As an example, Rosaura Sánchez describes the way Spanish-English bilinguals in the south-western United States 'place' themselves through their speech which is characterised by frequent switches – she calls them 'shifts' – between Spanish and English: 'These shifts ... are often considered to be the mode of expression that best captures the bilingual, bicultural situation of the Mexican-origin population residing as a minority within an English-dominant society' (Sánchez, 1982, p. 41).

In some communities it may be generally regarded as appropriate to speak different languages in different places, such as English at the sports club and Swahili at the market. For some subject matters, bilinguals have the necessary vocabulary only in one language and would thus always switch to it for talking about that subject. Examples would be the use of an ancestral language such as Xhosa for talking about a coming-of-age ritual, and English for talking about technology. However, even when they do have relevant vocabulary in both languages, established habits may perpetuate the use of only one for a particular topic or situation. Thus, in a wide-ranging conversation, a topic shift to 'the economy' might be marked by switching to English. Similarly, after informal chat in a local language, a switch to English could mark the start of the formal business of a meeting.

Switching into or out of English isn't simply a matter of habitual association, though. There are forms of codeswitching which occur without being triggered by 'big' factors such as shifts in topic or situation. They are much more fluid, and serve subtle interpersonal, stylistic or rhetorical functions.

Switching from one language to another can be a way of momentarily evoking a different role or aspect of one's own identity, or that of an interlocutor. As an illustration, Carol Myers-Scotton discusses the following conversation in which a young man comes into the office of a manager in a Nairobi company to ask about a job. The languages at play here are English (in plain text) and Swahili (in italics). An English translation of Swahili utterances is given in the right hand column of the transcript.

Young man (English)	Mr Muchuki has sent me to you about the job you put in the paper.	
Manager (Swahili)	*Ulituma barua ya* application	Did you send a letter of application?
Young man (English)	Yes, I did. But he asked me to come and see you today.	
Manager (Swahili)	*Ikiwa ulituma barua, nenda ungojee majibu. Tutakuita ufike kwa* interview *siku itukupofiku.*	If you've written a letter, then go and wait for a response. We will call you for an interview when the letter arrives.
	Leo sina la suma kuliko hayo.	Today I haven't anything else to say.
Young man (Swahili)	*Asante. Nitangoja majibu.*	Thank you. I'll wait for the response.

(Myers-Scotton, 1989, pp. 333–46)

Activity 6.2

Allow about 5 minutes

What do you think may be going on in the extract above? Conversations need to be interpreted with some understanding of the context in which they occur, so you won't be able to give a full interpretation here. But can you think of some reasons why the young man might begin speaking in English then switch to Swahili?

Comment

Myers-Scotton notes that one function of codeswitching in her data was the negotiation of identities between people. In offering an interpretation of the extract she notes that, while both English and Swahili are possible choices for these speakers, the young man's use of English may be an attempt to negotiate the higher status associated with the language. The manager's insistence on Swahili denies the young man this opportunity and he switches to Swahili following the manager's lead.

Even when there are very strong associations in a community between its languages and non-linguistic factors (such as solidarity, economic privilege, religion), switches from one language to another during a conversation are not always linked with these associations. We should be careful not to import knowledge mechanistically of what a language *can* signify in a speech community into our interpretation of how it is *actually* functioning in a particular bilingual conversation.

Switches might be doing nothing more than achieving stylistic effects. A range of such effects can be seen in the following examples of Afrikaans/English switching (McCormick, 2002, p. 177).

A switch from one language to another can highlight a sense of balance in a two-part construction, as in the following 'if–then' sequence where the *if* clause is in Afrikaans and the *then* clause in English:

> *as it gevat is* then we leave it [if it is taken …]

A commonly reported stylistic function of language switching is rather like that of opening inverted commas – to signal that what follows is a quotation, as in:

> when I get home I tell them *bring nou julle twee randjies* [bring your two rand]

(Such switches are not necessarily a faithful representation of which language the speaker actually used at the time.)

Another common stylistic practice is to switch languages when repeating something for emphasis. In the following example, the English clause repeats exactly what is in the Afrikaans one:

kyk ek raak nie aan die kerk nie look I don't touch the church

The following extract of Spanish/English codeswitching in a school staffroom shows switches from one language to the other for set phrases ('day and age', 'head of year'), but there are other switches where triggers are less readily apparent.

T: *No tienen educación, ¿eh? Las niñas ...*
     [They don't have any manners, hmm? The girls ...]
A: *¿Qué no tienen?*
     [They don't have what?]
T: *Ha salido un lote de niñas* including fifth years, and sixth years.
     [There is a group of girls who have turned out ...]
     Both fifth years. Have stood ... I'm holding the door. I'm
     holding the door.
A: For them, *claro.*
                    [of course]
T: For them. And then two sixth years and a fifth year stood back
     and said come in. I was waiting for that.
E: *Pero tú te esperas que en este, en este, en este* day and age
     [But do you expect that in this, in this, in this ...]
     que se cojan las niñas y te dejan a ti de pasar, porque te llamas /?/
     [that the girls are going to stop and let you pass because just
     because you are called (or your name is)?]
A: Heh, heh.
E: *Vamos, porque sea el* head of year *de aquí.*
     [come on, because you're the]   [here]
T: *No /?/. Además yo no soy* head of year.
     [No. Besides I'm not ...]
E: Sorry.

(adapted from Moyer, 1998, pp. 229–30)

In these extracts from McCormick's and Moyer's data, many of the switches to and from English occur in the middle of sentences. One slightly longer switch into English marks a brief narrative – holding the door for students, then some students standing back and saying come in – and this may therefore have a stylistic function, as discussed above.

However, switches don't seem to be triggered by shifts in topic or mood. In the Spanish/English conversation, both speakers use both languages. Melissa Moyer gives this extract as an example of typical conversation among friends in a Gibraltar school staffroom, where switching between Spanish and English is the normal way to talk.

Prolonged language contact can result in a weaving of languages which is even tighter than that seen in the examples given above. In Gardner-Chloros (1995), Agnihotri (1998), Meeuwis and Blommaert (1998), among others, we find the argument that at some level two languages can become sufficiently integrated in the minds of speakers for them to be able to draw on both without always attending to their (also) being different systems. Gardner-Chloros (1995, p. 71) speaks of bilinguals being able to 'let down the mental barriers between two languages'. This happens in some bilingual communities with a long-established history of prolific linguistic borrowing and codeswitching. The local varieties of the two languages may converge sufficiently in phonology and syntax to facilitate combination into one code – a **hybrid** or **mixed code**. Such codes are common in many parts of the world, particularly in 'Outer Circle' communities where they are associated with young, urban, educated speakers. In earlier chapters you have encountered 'Manglish' (Malaysia, Chapter 1), 'Singlish' (Singapore, Chapter 4) and 'Camfranglais' (Cameroon, Chapter 3, Reading A). You may also have heard of 'Hinglish' in India. The example below comes from an area of Cape Town known as District Six.

Kombuistaal in District Six, Cape Town

Sharing most of the features of Afrikaans syntax, but drawing heavily on English for vocabulary, is the local mixed variety known as Kombuistaal ('kitchen language'). A speaker comments on this variety:

Ek dink nie dis stupid *nie. Kyk hier: ons* coloureds *het opgegroei am te praat kombuistaal, ne?* Which is *Afrikaans en Engels ge*mix.

[I don't think it's stupid. Look here: we coloureds grew up speaking Kombuistaal, right? Which is Afrikaans and English mixed.]

Characteristic of the mixed code are: the speaker's incorporation of English words into Afrikaans phrases; the retention, in nouns, of

---

English plural forms (as in 'coloureds') but with verbs taking on the Afrikaans tense form (as in '*ge*mix'); the word order (in '*ons coloureds … kombuistaal*' where the object does not precede the infinitive as it would in standard Afrikaans but follows it as it does in English and in some non-standard Afrikaans dialects. 'Afrikaans' itself is 'bivalent', belonging both to Afrikaans and English, so that in this clause it is not possible to say exactly where the English string stops and Afrikaans begins.

(adapted from McCormick, 2002, pp. 93–4)

Such hybrid codes are often denigrated and regarded as inappropriate in a public domain, but they may also be publicly accepted, as they have recently become in South Africa where, for example, they often occur in popular local soap operas on state television channels (McCormick, 2010).

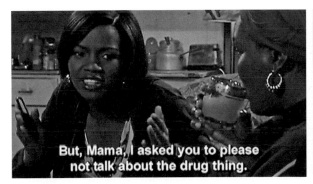

Transcription: **Maar** *Mama wa itsi ke le kopile, ke le kopile*, please don't talk about the drug thing

Transcription: Yeah **maar** *Mama* mistake *ya Papa eyan-* costa **nou**

Figures 6.7 and 6.8 These images come from the South African soap opera *Rhythm City*, in which characters routinely codeswitch between different languages. The young woman, a medical student, is talking to her mother. She expresses concern that her father told her boyfriend that she had had drugs counselling when younger. She switches between the family language, Tswana (*italic*), English (in plain text) and Afrikaans (in **bold**).

In this section I have discussed different ways in which speakers may switch between English and other languages in everyday conversation: from the use of loanwords, through 'emblematic switching' and 'language crossing', to more routine and habitual conversational 'codeswitching'. I have suggested that the choice of one language over another may be associated with particular settings, or conversational topics, but that codeswitching may serve more subtle interactional functions, enabling speakers to negotiate particular identities, or to achieve certain stylistic effects (e.g. to emphasise a point, or highlight a contrast). Sometimes the practice becomes so habitual, with closely interwoven switches, that the result is better seen as a 'hybrid' or 'mixed' code.

Activity 6.3

In order to review your work in this section, turn now to Readings A and B. In Reading A, *Code alternation studies: a trajectory*, Suresh Canagarajah discusses codeswitching (he refers to this as 'code alternation') in three bilingual contexts: in the Tamil community in Jaffna, Sri Lanka, where many speakers alternate between Tamil and English, and language choice has also been affected by language policy decisions; in a Tamil community in the USA, where there is a language shift, across generations, from Tamil to English; and in his teaching of bilingual students in US higher education. In Reading B, *Extracts from 'Metrolingualism: fixity, fluidity and language influx'*, Emi Otsuji and Alastair Pennycook focus on a single context: a workplace in Sydney, Australia, where Japanese and English are used for business and social purposes. In both readings the authors argue that we need to develop new ways of thinking about people's linguistic resources in order to account for how these are actually used. As you read, identify the main points made by the authors, and how these relate to earlier discussion in this section.

Comment

In Reading A, Canagarajah adopts a historical perspective. He argues that earlier research often focused on relatively straightforward relationships between the associations of particular languages and their use by speakers. So, for instance, in Jaffna in Sri Lanka, Tamil would signal 'in-group solidarity' and English 'out-group relations or formality'. Canagarajah's own work, however, has focused on more complex processes in which English and Tamil are drawn on strategically in particular contexts, to 'shuttle between different communities' and 'signal shifting identities': for instance, to mark a shift in roles and relations in an English lesson, to secure attention in a market, to signal conformity to a local language policy, and, in a US family, to mark a connection with a grandparent. This is consistent with discussion in this section, where I have tried to show that speakers switch between English and other languages to a range of effects in particular contexts of use. Canagarajah adds that we need a more complex understanding of 'multilingual competence' to account for these practices. Rather than thinking of a speaker's knowledge of, or competence in, English and Tamil, for instance, multilingual language use suggests a more 'integrated repertoire' where languages are complementary. Canagarajah offers the term 'code-meshing' to indicate that one can 'mesh diverse codes into a textual tapestry'. In a student essay, for instance, the writer 'meshes' Arabic and English. Arabic occurs in Arabic script, in translation and transliteration, and also influences grammar and idiom in the 'English' part of the text.

In Reading B, Otsuji and Pennycook argue that staff in the company they studied drew on a set of 'multilingual resources'. This is consistent with Canagarajah's idea that speakers have an integrated multilingual repertoire. They also argue, like Canagarajah, that speakers draw on these resources to negotiate identities in complex ways. Of interest here is that, while speakers make use of both English and Japanese, their linguistic choices do not seem to be related to their own or their interlocutor's dominant language, and in fact they often seem unaware of which language(s) they have used. Otsuji and Pennycook use the term 'metrolingualism' to refer to what is often seen as a contemporary urban phenomenon in which people's language use, and associated identities, are 'hybrid' and 'fluid', as demonstrated in the conversational extracts they cite. Alongside this apparently ubiquitous fluidity, however, they suggest that people do have fixed conceptions of language and identity – for example, saying that they are 'bastardising English and Japanese', or that their language is 'chaotic', suggests they do also have a sense of orderly language use. For Otsuji and Pennycook these metrolingual practices combine 'fixity' and 'fluidity'. Both are 'mobilised' (compare here Canagarajah's reference to the 'strategic' use of language) in the negotiation of contemporary mobile identities.

6.6   Conclusion

In the early twenty-first century most speakers of English in the world have another language as their first language: language contact phenomena are, then, common rather than exceptional in the lives of people who speak English today. In the many multilingual countries where English is an official language, it is usually also the main language of post-primary education and is thus perceived as the language of access to higher education, to well-paid employment and to the wider world. While there are fears that such positive associations will lead to neglect or loss of a community's other languages, this is not necessarily the case. For instance, local languages may be regarded as the only appropriate languages for important cultural domains.

In contact situations, speakers may also frequently, even routinely, draw on English alongside other languages, switching between these in everyday conversation to a range of stylistic and interpersonal effects. Readings A and B illustrate the complexity and creativity of such everyday bilingual conversations.

READING A: Code alternation studies: a trajectory

Suresh Canagarajah

Specially commissioned for this book.

When I began studying the communicative practices of my native Sri Lankan Tamil community, the dominant orientation in codeswitching research was correlationist (see Blom and Gumperz, 1972, for an example). Languages were seen as associated with particular social meanings, and speakers could call up these meanings by selecting one language or the other. From this perspective, Tamil will be associated with in-group solidarity and English with out-group relations or formality. In my study of interactions in local secondary school ESL classrooms, I found that things were rather more complex: teachers and students used these associations strategically to negotiate relationships (see Canagarajah, 1995a). For example, when a teacher asks students to take out their homework for grading, a student replies in Tamil that he hasn't brought the assignment to class. Thus, the student brings into play a more personal voice to step out of institutional relationships, evoke in-group solidarity, and claim special treatment from the teacher. By the same token, a teacher might switch to English to evoke her institutional authority – as in the following example:

> T: *piLLayaL, katirakaLai vaTTamaai pooTunkoo. cattam pooTaamal. ketiyaa pooTunkoo.* [Children, arrange your chairs into a circle. Without making a noise. Arrange quickly.]
>
> **Turn to page forty for today's lesson.**

(Note: Tamil is in italics and English in bold text.)

Although the teacher starts the class in Tamil, establishing rapport and conversational informality, the switch to English marks that the routinised teacher/student roles have now begun. In a context where 'English Only' is the policy for classroom interactions, I found it interesting that teachers and students unwittingly violated the policy and gained practice in a discourse strategy that was widespread outside the classroom.

In studies in other contexts, I found that speakers might strategically violate the conventional values attached to a code to suit their purposes. The code alternation can help to renegotiate the context subtly, enabling

The term 'correlationist' suggests that earlier research focused on establishing the relationship between a language and particular speakers, contexts of use or social meanings.

speakers to move into and out of identities and relationships. In a typical Jaffna rural market, the less educated fish vendors will be expected to use Tamil and the middle-class buyers (often English-educated) will be expected to use English among themselves, although they will use Tamil to talk to the vendors. However, I found that some fish vendors will use the few English words they know to complicate this social stratification (Canagarajah, 1995b). Consider the following interaction in a crowded fish market when a vendor notices a trouser-clad buyer turning away from another vendor after finding the latter's fish too expensive:

> V: *ayyaa Raal irukku vaankoo. ancu ruupaa Raal.* [Sir, come, I have prawns. Prawns for five rupees]

> (Buyer does not respond; goes toward other vendors)

> V: **fay rupi.** [Five rupees]

> (Buyer turns round, and comes toward V)

When the vendor utters the price in English, he attempts to establish an in-group identity with the buyer, which situates him favourably for winning the bargain in the heavily competitive market. Buyers I interviewed said that they felt flattered by being addressed in English. The English uttered by the vendor enables him to achieve a special bond with the buyer, in a way that non-English speaking vendors cannot do. Through the code alteration, then, the vendor reconstructs the social context and relationship, at least temporarily, in his favour. Monolinguals can thus strategically employ even the few tokens at their disposal to great symbolic and material advantage.

The values and relationships that are negotiated by speakers through code alternation cannot be treated as neutral. There are ideological implications behind code choice. During the 1990s, Tamil militant youth who were waging a separatist struggle against the Sinhala government controlled the region and proclaimed a Tamil Only policy. Signs and billboards using English words were immediately altered to Tamil. In rallies and speeches, officials of the military regime reinforced this linguistic policy by warning people that the use of English could damage traditional Tamil culture and hinder the nationalist struggle. The regime also used the civil institutions and political infrastructure under its control to promote the use of Tamil and to enforce its sole usage.

Officials were able to enforce their policy by turning back petitions or applications tendered in other languages or in mixed Tamil to the police department, pass office (for movement outside the liberated zone), law courts and village councils. The censorship was more direct in face-to-face verbal interactions like the following where a woman applies for a permit to leave the region and travel to the capital city:

1   Officer: *appa koLumpukku een pooriinkaL?* [So why are you travelling to Colombo?]

2   Woman: *makaLinTai* **wedding**-*ikku pooren.* [I am going for my daughter's 'wedding']

3   Officer: *enna? unkaLukku tamiL teriyaataa?* **England**-*ilaiiruntaa vantaniinkal?* [What? Don't you know Tamil? Have you come here from 'England'?] *enkai pooriinkaL?* [Where are you going?]

4   Woman: *cari, cari, kaLiyaaNa viiTTukku pooren, makan.* [Okay, okay, I am going to a wedding, son]

The petitioner's single use of the English word *wedding* doesn't pass unnoticed. Although it takes some time for her to realise her blunder, she corrects herself as her petition can easily be turned down for such violations. However, note how the officer who chastises the petitioner for using an English word himself uses one (in turn 3). Though the Tamilised form of 'England' is *inkilaantu,* he chooses the former. He is probably indicating to the petitioner that his insistence on the use of the vernacular should not mean that he is himself rustic, ignorant, or uneducated. By using English, he is implying to the addressee that he feels comfortable with more urbane values. The strategy might be aimed at levelling the inequalities of status in the relationship (see Heller, 1992, p. 134). Although the monolingual official has more power in political terms, he may desire to level off the symbolic inequalities with those proficient in English. Thus, despite the Tamil Only policy at the macro-level, I found that in face-to-face interactions at the micro-level people used English, sometimes surreptitiously, to display their symbolic capital and claim urbane, cosmopolitan, or educated identities. Even traditionally monolingual speakers from less educated backgrounds can deploy certain English words to claim an urbane ethos or educated group status when they need it, subtly resisting the language ideology of the military regime.

We can treat the English used by Tamil monolinguals to negotiate roles and relationships with bilinguals in their own community and adopt new identities as a form of *styling* (Rampton, 1999). I find creative forms of styling in the more recent formation of diaspora Tamil communities in the West (Canagarajah, 2008). Since the youth in the community are not proficient in the heritage language (Tamil), many of them use the few Tamil words at their disposal to style a Tamil identity and establish in-group relationships. Rather than adopting the language of an out-group (as in *language crossing*), they are switching to the in-group language to achieve solidarity. We may call this an act of *self-styling,* as their limited Tamil proficiency compels them to 'perform' their own in-group identity. Consider the following example. Visiting a house in Lancaster, California, one of the newest settlements of Sri Lankan Tamils in the post-1983 exodus from war-torn Sri Lanka, I find that only 'grandma' is available for an interview. Our conversation turns quickly to the topics everyone in the community is discussing these days; that is, that the Tamil language is dying in the diaspora as children are increasingly adopting English for everyday communication; and that in the next fifty years there won't be a Sri Lankan Tamil community in migrant locations, as ethnic identity will die with the heritage language. Grandma is disappointed that most Tamil children, including her grandchildren, are becoming monolingual in English while people of her age group remain monolingual in Tamil, preventing both groups from establishing strong bonds. As we talk, her teenage grandson Raju comes out of his room. A late riser, ready to have a quick lunch and leave the house, he addresses the grandmother in part-greeting, part-request:

1   Raju: Hi, *caniyan.* Where's my *cooRu* [rice]?
2   Grandma: *ankai meeseelai irukku, pooi paaRum.* [It's over there on the table. Go and see.]

Raju could have easily said 'rice' for *cooRu,* a word that has become a well-used borrowing for most Tamils, which even his grandmother would be expected to understand. However, Raju is clearly choosing a Tamil word that would establish a better connection with his grandmother. His nickname for the grandmother, *caniyan,* is more difficult to translate. Deriving from the planet Saturn (*cani* in Tamil) which portends misfortune in Hindu astrology, it is a term of insult referring to those who are unlucky or evil. However, the grandmother doesn't treat this form of address as an insult. She suspends the usual negative meanings of the word as she is aware of the grandson's status as lacking full proficiency in Tamil. The coupling of the name with the more casual youth greeting 'Hi!' also makes it clear to her that he is only half serious, and probably using it for a special rhetorical purpose. Though she could have easily rejected the grandson's attempts at bonding, she signals uptake by giving him the information he is seeking. Perhaps she is mildly amused, and even appreciative, that her grandson is using Tamil words to establish rapport with her.

Raju's receptive proficiency in Tamil, which helps him go to the dining table and get his plate of rice, is also interesting. This puts into question Grandma's views on the demise of Tamil language and the decline of inter-generational communication. I have found other cases in diaspora contexts where youth use their passive competence in Tamil to participate in in-group interactions. Though the Tamil youth respond in English, their interlocutors use Tamil. Such interactions are called *polyglot dialogue* (Posner, 1991). This is a widespread communicative practice in many multilingual communities (see Khubchandani, 1997, for South Asia).

The implications of such code alternation for identity construction are far reaching. In traditional approaches to codeswitching, speakers were assumed to orchestrate identities that were predefined and preconstructed. Codeswitching was assumed simply to reflect the available identities and relationships in a context. However, in more recent work, identities are seen as linguistically constructed in interpersonal relationships through skilful language choice. Scholars prefer to use the term 'identification' for such practices. The new term conveys the fact that identities don't pre-exist or exist free of language; they are actively constructed and brought into being through language in situated social relationships. Code-alternation practices such as styling and polyglot dialogue offer important language strategies for migrant groups in late modernity to shuttle between different communities and signal shifting identities.

A more complex understanding of multilingual competence has recently produced a radical turn in code-alternation studies, inspiring scholars to consider the languages as part of an integrated repertoire, accessed along a continuum according to one's needs and interests. Furthermore, the languages do not involve separate competencies, but constitute an integrated competence, perhaps a multi-competence (Cook, 1999) that is qualitatively different from that of monolingual speakers. In some circles, this activity is known as *translanguaging*. García provides the following definition for this activity:

Rather than focusing on the language itself and how one or the other might relate to the way in which a monolingual standard is used and has been described, the concept of translanguaging makes obvious that there are no clear cut borders between the languages of bilinguals. What we have is a languaging continuum that is accessed.

(García, 2009, p. 47)

Such an integrated orientation to the languages in one's repertoire has radical implications for code-alternation studies. Since languages are an integrated repertoire, multilinguals may not have full competence in all the languages. The languages are complementary. Therefore, the languages do not replicate the same functions. Multilinguals develop the proficiencies that are adequate for the different purposes the respective languages perform. Moreover, languages may influence each other in translanguaging. What may have been perceived as interference errors in traditional studies will be perceived as creative influences in translanguaging.

I have recently adopted the term *code meshing* to reflect the new insights into code alternation and to apply them to areas that have not featured prominently in codeswitching studies. I have been especially interested in studying how multilingual scholars and students bring diverse codes into English writing for purposes of voice and identity. Code meshing conveys the possibility that one can mesh diverse codes into a textual tapestry to make meaning. Though formal literacy in contemporary 'western' communities has been associated with the use of one language or code at a time, this has not always been the case in multilingual communities. In a precolonial practice known as *manipralava* writing (literally, 'stringed beads') in South Asia, Tamil people combined their regional language with Sanskrit, which was considered the elite language for religious and learned discourse. This way, they appropriated the dominant language for their purposes, infusing it with their values. We have similar evidence from other multilingual communities (e.g. de Souza, 2002). For subjects for whom diverse languages form an integrated competence, literacy does not involve keeping the codes separate. Codes are meshed together in texts.

Consider how a Saudi Arabian student opens her essay in one of my courses in the US:

يعش ابد الدّهر بين الحفر~~~ ومن يتهيّب صعود الجبال

'I doon't want to!' was my response to my parents request of
enrolling me in a nearby preschool. I did not like school. I feared
it. I feared the aspect of departing my comfort zone, my home, to
an unknown and unpredictable zone. My parents desired to enroll
me in a private preschool. Due to my fear, I refused. My parent's
face discolored and the sense of disapproval appeared in their tone
of speech. To encourage me, they recited a poetic line that I did
not comprehend as a child but live by it as an adult. They said
'Who fears climbing the mountains ~~ Lives forever between the
holes.' … My experience learning English has interesting twists. In
many different stages of my life, I had a different motivation. At
the end of the road, however, knowledge became the key for
freedom, *ma sha Allah*.

The essay moves fluidly between Arabic and English. Note that the
Arabic epigraph is translated later in the paragraph. Note also the
transliteration of *ma sha Allah*. Other grammatical and idiomatic
peculiarities will also be attributed to translanguaging influences, and not
treated as errors by multilingual scholars. Similarly, I have studied how
Tamil scholars in Sri Lanka code mesh English and Tamil in local
publications (see Canagarajah, 2006). Popular magazines in the
community also show writers shuttling between both languages. Not
only are proper names or nouns printed in English in a Tamil text,
there is a range of other lexical items and phrases that occur in English
without translation. The reader has to do a bilingual reading to interpret
these stories and poems. Such examples show that this form of code
meshing in texts is widespread in the community and constitutes
everyday communication.

As we continue to conduct studies along the new theoretical
perspectives on multilingual communication, we are moving away from
face-to-face conversational interactions to study many new domains of
communication. In chat forums on the internet, youth from diverse
communities are code meshing effectively (Williams, 2009). New art
forms such as hip hop feature fascinating forms of code meshing
(Pennycook, 2007). Linguistic landscape research also shows that codes
are meshed in creative ways in street signage and commercial displays
(Gorter, 2006). As we develop more knowledge on the strategies
undertaken for both production and reception in these sites, we are also
able to develop pedagogies for teaching code meshing. As many

scholars have noted, we haven't progressed far in developing teachable strategies of code alternation (Lin and Martin, 2005; Creese and Blackledge, 2010). We are gradually moving away from the position that language mixing is a mongrel form of communication that violates the purity of languages and should be kept out of schools. We now see mixing as a very normal multilingual communicative practice with significant symbolic and material implications, which needs fostering in education.

References for this reading

Blom, J. P. and Gumperz, J. (1972) 'Social meaning in linguistic structures: code-switching in Norway' in Gumperz, J. and Hymes, D. (eds) *Directions in Sociolinguistics: The Ethnography of Communication*, Oxford, Basil Blackwell.

Canagarajah, A. S. (1995a) 'Functions of code switching in the ESL classroom: socialising bilingualism in Jaffna', *Journal of Multilingual and Multicultural Development*, vol. 16, pp. 173–96.

Canagarajah, A. S. (1995b) 'Use of English borrowings by Tamil fish vendors: manipulating the context', *Multilingua*, vol. 14, pp. 5–24.

Canagarajah, A. S. (2006) 'Toward a writing pedagogy of shuttling between languages: learning from multilingual writers', *College English*, vol. 68, pp. 589–604.

Canagarajah, A. S. (2008) 'Language shift and the family: questions from the Sri Lankan Tamil diaspora', *Journal of Sociolinguistics*, vol. 12, pp. 1–34.

Cook, V. (1999) 'Going beyond the native speaker in language teaching', *TESOL Quarterly*, vol. 33, no. 2, pp. 185–209.

Creese, A. and Blackledge, A. (2010) 'Translanguaging in the bilingual classroom: a pedagogy for learning and teaching?', *Modern Language Journal*, vol. 94, no. 1, pp. 103–15.

De Souza, L. M. (2002) 'A case among cases, a world among worlds: the ecology of writing among the Kashinawa in Brazil', *Journal of Language, Identity, and Education*, vol. 1, pp. 261–78.

García, O. (2009) *Bilingual Education in the 21st Century: A Global Perspective*, Oxford, Wiley-Blackwell.

Gorter, D. (2006) *Linguistic Landscape: A New Approach to Multilingualism*, Clevedon, Multilingual Matters.

Heller, M. (1992) 'The politics of codeswitching and language choice' in Eastman, C. (ed.) *Codeswitching*, Clevedon, Multilingual Matters.

Khubchandani, L. M. (1997) *Revisualizing Boundaries: A Plurilingual Ethos*, New Delhi, Sage.

Lin, A. and Martin, P. (eds) (2005) *Decolonisation, Globalisation: Language-in-Education Policy and Practice*, Clevedon, Multilingual Matters.

Pennycook, A. (2007) *Global Englishes and Transcultural Flows*, London, Routledge.

Posner, R. (1991) 'Der polyglotte Dialog', *Der Sprachreport*, vol. 3, pp. 6–10.

Rampton, B. (1999) 'Styling the other: introduction', *Journal of Sociolinguistics*, vol. 3, pp. 421–7.

Williams, B. T. (2009) 'Multilingual literacy strategies in online worlds', *JAC*, vol. 29, pp. 255–8.

READING B: Extracts from 'Metrolingualism: fixity, fluidity and language in flux'

Emi Otsuji and Alastair Pennycook

Source: Otsuji, E. and Pennycook, A. (2010) 'Metrolingualism: fixity, fluidity and language in flux', *International Journal of Multilingualism*, vol. 7, no. 3, pp. 240–54.

(1) J ふふ~ ワインを１６本。(*Ha ha...16 bottles of wine*)
(2) H Yeah
(3) Ad なんで、どこからもらったの？(*Why? Where did you get them from?*)
(4) J Ah, I bought them off the internet. There is like a sale, special cellar masters at the moment
(5) H う~ん。(*Ri::ght*)
(6) J Offering a 16 bottle dozen,
(7) H Uuu
(8) J For a hundred twenty nine dollars. From all over the country
(9) H Oh, wow
(10) J Some Margaret river stuff, Coonawarra
(11) H Oh, 言ってよ。(*You should have told me!*)
(12) J まだあるよ。(*They still have some*)

At first glance, there is nothing very remarkable about this conversational fragment between J (James), Ad (Adam) and H (Heather). Code-switching, we know, is common and widely attested in contexts where two languages are used in daily interaction (Myers-Scotton, 2006; Wei, 2005). In this workplace in Sydney, in a company [named Japaria] where Japanese and English are frequently used for both business and social purposes, it is common to find dialogues such as this where participants switch and mix between English and Japanese. What might give us pause, however, is that none of the participants in the conversation, J, Ad and H is 'Japanese' (though as we shall see, all such identity categorisations will need careful consideration). At the very least, then, we can note that such instances of English/Japanese mixed code use derive not so much from the use of different first and second languages but rather as the result of a mixed Japanese/English code becoming the lingua franca of the workplace. […]

The following two excerpts from the same workplace show the staff using their *multilingual* resources. In Excerpts [1] and [2], Heather is jokingly reporting the same telephone conversation with a Japanese client to different participants, first with James in Excerpt [1], and then with Asami, her Japanese colleague, in Excerpt [2].

Excerpt [1] (H: Heather, J: James)

(1) H   James, Chiba san said to me もしもし、9日にシドニーに行って、そのままニュージーランドに行ったほうがいいですか? 私に聞くなよ。　[laugh] 何考えているのよ。「あ、それは千葉さんのご都合で」[laugh]
("*Hello, Is it better to go to Sydney on the 9th and go straight to NZ?*" *Don't ask me.*[laugh] *What is he thinking?* "*Well, It's up to your schedule, Mr. Chiba*" [laugh])

(2) J   ニュージーランドに9日だったら。(*If NZ is on the 9th.*)

(3) H   then he said「で1日ゴルフで1日ニュージーランドって無理でしょうかね」。("*Is it possible to play golf one day and go to NZ for one day?*")

(4) J   だって9日だったらもう僕らいないんだよ。もどってきているんだよ。(*If it's 9th, we are not there anymore. We are already back here*)

(5) H   なに言ってるの？ばかだな:: (*What is he saying? He is ma::d*)

Here again, though both James and Heather are non-Japanese (in the usual sense) and the conversation was held exclusively between the two, Japanese and English were mixed not only to quote the actual dialogue in the conversation (which might, of course, be an obvious trigger for Japanese use) but also in James' comments about the conversation in lines 2 and 4. Ten minutes later, Heather reports the same telephone call to Asami.

Excerpt [2] (H: Heather, J: James, As: Asami)

(1) H   What is he thinking?

(2) J   吸いすぎじゃないの？(*Maybe he is smoking too much?*)

(3) As   [laugh] what did he say?

(4) H   He asked me should he go to New Zealand instead of playing golf? Should he go to N.Z to the ロケ地？(*location?*) どうして私の判断を。。。 (*Why my decision…*)

(5) J   ゴルフね。(*Golf, huh?*)

(6) As   He is not coming till Monday. What did you say?

(7) J   She said

(8) H   I said it is up to you 千葉さんのご都合で。(*Its up to Chiba-san*)

In this excerpt, Heather is reporting to Asami the same conversation about the Japanese crew asking her to decide their schedule. This time, as opposed to Excerpt [1] where she quoted the actual conversation in Japanese (line 1, Excerpt [1]), she rephrases the quote in English (line 4, Excerpt [2]). It is interesting to note that while in Excerpt [1], Heather reported to an 'English' dominant speaker in 'Japanese', she uses 'English' with Asami, a 'Japanese' dominant speaker. [...]

The above staff, moreover, reported little awareness of using one language or the other: *In Japaria I don't consciously speak in English or in Japanese. I choose the one I feel comfortable with at the time.* Another reported that *I don't have any awareness that I am choosing language* or *when I recall a particular conversation, it is often the case that I can't remember in which language it was spoken.* While they thus reported little conscious language choice, they were nevertheless aware of the mixture they used as a result: *what we are doing here is bastardising English and Japanese* or *in a casual conversation, language is chaotic.* In this light, we will look at how language is invented, disinvented and re-constituted by examining everyday conversation and what it means to people as a local practice.

From multilingualism to metrolingualism

Rather than describing such language phenomena in terms of monolingualism, bilingualism, code-mixing or code-switching, we shall look at this in terms of what we have called *metrolingualism*. [This tries to bring together contemporary ideas of hybridity and fluidity across languages and cultural identities with an awareness that more fixed notions of language/cultural identity may still be salient for speakers. Indeed, one of the driving forces to be different and multiple and dynamic is the interaction between fixed and fluid cultural identities.]

The underlying assumption of the previous interview statements *what we are doing here is bastardising English and Japanese* as well as *in a casual conversation, language is chaotic* is that even though they do not have a sense of treating languages separately in their use, they have a set of ideal and orderly linguistic practices that are reflected in such terms as *bastardising* and *chaotic.* Our argument is that we need to account for this within our understanding of *metrolingualism,* especially if [...] it is incumbent on us to include the local perspectives of language users who appear to incorporate within their own hybrid practices both fluidity and fixity. [...]

Metrolingualism describes the ways in which people of different and mixed backgrounds use, play with and negotiate identities through language; it does not assume connections between language, culture, ethnicity, nationality or geography, but rather seeks to explore how such relations are produced, resisted, defied or rearranged. […]

The *metro* as we understand it, […] is the productive space provided by, though not limited to, the contemporary city to produce new language identities. Such an interpretation is intended to […] accommodate the complex ways in which fluid and fixed, as well as global and local, practices reconstitute language and identities. […]

Metrolingualism, fixity and cultural change

At the same time that metrolingualism presents possibilities of borderless language crossing and flexible identifications, it nevertheless always rubs up against the fixed identity markers of modernity. For the participants in these metrolingual conversations, these may mean that while they are conducting fluid conversations in a mixture of English and Japanese, they may also mobilise ascriptions of identity along static lines. One of the workers at Japaria, Atsuko, for example, said in an interview *In Japan, people are different depending on the person. I stop thinking it is different because s/he is Japanese and I don't consciously think that I am a Japanese. I stop being aware of noticing people as Japanese or Australian.* And yet, in other conversations, she nevertheless showed herself to be capable of ascribing quite monolithic characteristics to French speakers.

Excerpt [3] (A: Atsuko, Ad: Adam)

(1) A   フランス語？フランス語しゃべる人ってかわいしし 格好良いと思う。
       (*French? I think people who speak French are cute and cool*)
(2) Ad [laugh]   みんな？国全体がかわいくて格好良いと思う？   (*Everyone?   You think everyone in the country is cute and cool?*)
(3) A   おとこ おとこの人がフランス語話すとセクシーだし 女の子が話すとかわいい と思う フランス人はみんな。(*Men. If men speak French, they are sexy and if girls speak French, they are cute. All French people*)

Such generalisations, however, are immediately challenged by Adam, and though she continues to assert her desire to generalise here, she soon sides with Robert in critiquing the essentialist direction the conversation takes when other participants started to provide extreme comments about French people.

Excerpt [4] (A: Atsuko, R: Robert)

(1) A   みんなすごい。 (*All of you are extreme*)
(2) R   すごい差別だよ。(*Extreme prejudice*) [everyone laughs]

Likewise, Asami, another participant in the essentialising moves in this conversation, commented negatively during the interview about over-generalised views about Japan: *there are many people who think 'Japanese people are like this', or 'Japanese people always eat fish' and I do not like that.* In a later discussion, she told us *After I started to live in Dubbo* [a rural town in Australia], *I noticed that a small town is a closed society. It is not a bad thing. It can't be helped. It must be the same in the countryside in Japan.* Here she struggles between a generalising move about small town mentalities and a relativising move across locations. This is the push and pull between fixity and fluidity, the capacity to both mobilise and critique essentialised identity ascriptions. [...]

None of these staff members, moreover, are easily categorised along common lines of ascribed identity. Atsuko moved to Australia from Japan with her family at the age of 11 due to her father's business assignment, and has been living in Australia since then. She is an Australian citizen, having given up her Japanese nationality. Adam was born in the northern part of Japan to New Zealander missionary parents, and lived in Japan until the age of 13. In the interviews, they challenged, attested, compromised and sometimes ignored the issues of linguistic and cultural borders. Under these circumstances, what it means to be 'Japanese' or to speak 'Japanese' shifted back and forth from fixed to fluid understandings, which leads us to ask how we can reconcile a certain level of borderlessness with a certain level of fixed cultural views and language use.

Another of our research participants presents us with a slightly different way of approaching these questions. Osman, who works for a working holiday maker's advisory office in Australia, was in his late 20s, an Australian national born in Australia to a mother of Turkish descent and a father of Anglo-Saxon background. He speaks English and Japanese and can understand Turkish but not speak it. During the interview, Osman demonstrated a distance from both Australian and Turkish communities, reflected in remarks such as *I could not fit into either Turkish or Australian culture and I was always unconsciously searching for a place where I belonged, I always thought that I was not a typical Aussie and I like the Japanese way of thinking and I have a feeling that I could live in Japan for the rest of my life.* While expressing an intriguing fluidity on the one hand in his rejection of Turkish/Australian identities and his adoption of Japanese, he also operates at another level with quite fixed interpretations of these cultural and linguistic entities. [...] In contrast to the conversation amongst the staff at Japaria where a mixed code was common, Osman was determined to speak exclusively in Japanese in every context at work.

Excerpt [5] (O: Osman, R: Rie)

(1) O　どう りえちゃん この曲 ?(*What do you think, Rie chan?*)
(2) R　ん？あんた きのうも 聞かなかった？(*Huh? Didn't you ask that yesterday as well?*)
(3) え ?(*What?*)
(4) R　昨日も聞いたでしょ? (*You asked that also yesterday, didn't you?*)
(5) 昨日ちがう曲じゃん。(*Yesterday was different music*)
(6) R　うそ。(*liar*)
(7) ん 記憶良くないね 君 。(*Huh, you do not have a good memory, you*) [silence]
(8) りえちゃんは 君って呼んだらすごくおこるからさ。(*I know that Rie chan gets very angry when I call you KIMI*)

By using Japanese, his endeavour can also be interpreted as an attempt to break the connection between one language and attached ethnicity and cultural background in order to create a new tie between another ethnic/cultural background and language. It is interesting, however, to note that his creative attempt to break borders is, in fact, supported by his understanding of a fixed relationship between language and culture/ethnicity. Osman's example is a good case in point where someone operates on one level with a fairly borderless identity – a Turkish-Australian immersing himself in Japanese language and culture as a preferred identity – and yet at another, by insisting on Japanese and trying to claim Japaneseness, he also operates simultaneously at a level of linguistic and cultural fixity.

Excerpt [5] is intriguing in another sense. The conversation was held between Rie and Osman during office hours. Notwithstanding the fact that Rie is his manager, Osman's language directed to Rie is very informal and indicates the close relationship between the two. First of all, Osman addressed Rie, his manager, as *Rie chan* (*chan* is used to show an intimate relationship). Superiors are normally addressed by their family names and positional terms, such as *Suzuki Bucho* (Suzuki manager), when addressed by subordinates. Although it is also true that the use of language is in a state of flux, and a more creative use of Japanese language by younger generations has been studied by various researchers (Inoue, 2006; Kubozono, 2006), it is still not common for a superior or person in a high position to be addressed by their first name with *chan* by subordinates in a Japanese work context. He also used plain form (informal verb form) with colloquial language じゃん [Jan] in line 5 which is informal slang from the Tokyo and Nagoya areas, normally used by young people.

Moreover, in lines 7–9, Osman is challenging Rie with an address term 君 [Kimi] which is normally used by a superior to a subordinate (Kunihiro, 1991). He did so knowing that Rie would not like the choice of term, suggesting that aside from the particular relation between the two, he was also interested in pushing the boundaries of acceptable behaviour in Japanese. He was also, one might argue, taking advantage of the *outsider* privilege to play with Japanese norms. Here, then, we see a complex mixture of fixed and fluid practices. On the one hand, Osman had a strong desire to associate himself with 'Japanese' culture and language, to leave his own ascribed identities behind in search of alternatives, but on the other, he was also able to mobilise his outsider identity to challenge standard practices by his deliberate language choices within less hierarchical relationships.

Fixity and fluidity in metrolingual language use

Assumptions about multilingualism are so deeply embedded in predominant paradigms of language studies that they are rarely questioned. […] As Makoni and Pennycook (2007) argue, current approaches to diversity and multilingualism frequently start with the enumerative strategy of counting languages and romanticising a plurality based on these putative language counts, a presupposition that 'clear borders exist between languages, that they can be counted, catalogued with certainty and that, above all, their vitality can be promoted and their disappearance prevented' (Duchêne, 2008, p. 8). By rendering diversity a quantitative question of language enumeration, such approaches overlook the qualitative question of where diversity lies while continuing to support those very language ideologies that we need to supersede (Canagarajah, 2007a, 2007b; Heller and Duchêne, 2007). […]

The idea of metrolingualism sheds light on processes of social change and the kinds of linguistic, cultural and social issues that are involved in creating different kinds of language and identities. Both data from Japaria and the case of Osman indicate the complexity and flux of cultural and linguistic understanding, as people move between fixed and fluid views. They attest to the point that hybridity and fluidity […] cannot on their own disassemble relations between language, culture and nation. Similarly, they show how fixity, within a metrolingual frame, becomes meaningful only through the interaction with fluidity. Metrolingualism, therefore, can be conceived as the paradoxical practice and space where fixity, discreteness, fluidity, hybridity, locality and globality coexist and co-constitute each other. This is different from multilingualism, which is either based on a pluralisation of fixed linguistic categories, or hybridisation, which cannot accord any legitimacy to the mobilisation of fixity. Metrolingualism, by contrast, can assign an alternative meaning to essentialism as part of a process of social change. What therefore sets metrolingualism apart is its productive power to overcome common ways of framing language, its capacity to deal with contemporary language practices, and its ability to accommodate both fixity and fluidity in its approach to mobile language use.

Note

Data in this paper are drawn from a large study of casual conversation in bilingual workplaces, based on over 120 hours of recorded data, as well as 19 interviews at five different worksites in Sydney. Names of people and companies and places are pseudonyms.

References for this reading

Canagarajah, S. (2007a) 'After disinvention: Possibilities for communication, community and competence', in Makoni, S. and Pennycook, A. (eds) *Disinventing and Reconstituting Languages*, Clevedon, Multilingual Matters, pp. 233–239.

Canagarajah, S. (2007b) 'The ecology of global English', *International Multilingual Research Journal*, vol. 1, no. 2, pp. 89–100.

Duchêne, A. (2008) *Ideologies Across Nations: The construction of linguistic minorities at the United Nations*, Berlin, Mouton de Gruyter.

Heller, M. and Duchêne, A. (2007) 'Discourses of endangerment: Sociolinguistics, globalization and social order', in Duchêne, A. and Heller, M. (eds) *Discourses of Endangerment: Ideology and interest in the defence of languages*, London, Continuum, pp. 1–13.

Inoue, I. (2006) 'Net shakai no wakamono kotoba', *Gekkan Gengo*, vol. 35, no. 3, pp. 60–67.

Kubozono, H. (2006) 'Wakamonokotoba no gengo koozoo', *Gekkan Gengo*, vol. 35, no. 3, pp. 52–59.

Kunihiro, T. (1991) 'Koshoo no shomondai', *Gekkan Gengo*, vol. 20, no. 7, pp. 4–7.

Makoni, S. and Pennycook, A. (2007) 'Disinventing and reconstituting languages', in Makoni, S. and Pennycook, A. (eds) *Disinventing and Reconstituting Languages*, Clevedon, Multilingual Matters, pp. 1–41.

Myers-Scotton, C. (2006) *Multiple Voices*, Malden, MA, Blackwell.

Wei, L. (2005) '"How can we tell?" Towards a common sense explanation of conversational code-switching', *Journal of Pragmatics*, vol. 37, pp. 375–389.

7 Variation and change in English

Miriam Meyerhoff and Anna Strycharz

7.1 Introduction

Speakers of English sound rather different from one another. Variation between speakers may be caused by physical differences. Some people tense their vocal cords more when they speak and this gives them a hoarse, creaky voice quality. Some people talk very rapidly, and so forth. These differences are idiosyncratic and hard to predict. But there is also more systematic variation between speakers related to the social groups they belong to, their lifestyles and patterns of interaction with others and, on any one occasion, how they position themselves in relation to those they are talking to, the topic under discussion, etc. These are the topics we discuss in this chapter: we look at how tiny variations in the way we speak serve to position us in relation to others around us.

Very subtle forms of contemporary variation also relate to the processes of language change over time. We look at some of the 'mechanics' of how English changes, gradually giving rise to distinct varieties of English associated with people born in small islands off the coast of the United States and colonies many thousands of miles from the British Isles.

Contemporary changes in English can help us understand longer term historical change: the subject of earlier chapters in this book. The study of language variation and change assumes that whoever we are, at any given moment in time, we are unexceptional and the ways we use language are quite ordinary and typical. This means that, if we can understand what patterns and principles are associated with the inception and the subsequent transmission of variation among speakers today, we will have a better idea of how similar patterns and principles might have operated on changes in the past. Contemporary variation and change can then provide a window on the kinds of social and linguistic factors that have shaped the development of English.

Like other chapters in this book, we draw on research from sociolinguistics (the study of language and society, or language and social life). The particular branch of sociolinguistics which focuses on language variation and change is sometimes referred to as **variationist sociolinguistics**. This chapter is more methodological than earlier chapters. We try to make clear how sociolinguists carry out their work, so you will gain some insights into the types of evidence that researchers have drawn on to piece together their accounts of varieties of English.

7.2   Studying variation over time

Allow about
15 minutes

Activity 7.1

Have you observed differences in your own language use and that of:

- older family members or friends?
- younger family members or friends?

Think about different words you might use to describe the same thing or different ways of pronouncing the same word. Make a list of a few of them and see if you can generalise about where the major differences lie. Why do you think there are these differences?

Comment

Readings A and B in Chapter 5 discuss some differences between older and younger speakers in, respectively, the Black Country and New York.

You were probably able to think of one or two words associated with older or younger speakers. For example, younger New Zealanders are more likely to talk about goods being transported in *trucks* and older New Zealanders are more likely to talk about *lorries*. And while Scottish mothers used to tell their children *straighten yer face* or pack them a *play piece* in their school lunch, now they usually say *cheer up* or pack them a morning *snack*. Some words cycle in and out of fashion quickly: in New Zealand English, hand-held personal telephones were called *cellphones* in the early 2000s, but by 2010 the most usual term used was *mobile phone*.

While pronunciation is not always so noticeable, you may have identified some differences between older and younger speakers. In the Scottish English spoken in Edinburgh, for instance, most people over the age of forty clearly pronounce a non-prevocalic /r/ sound at the end of words like *here* and *hair,* but speakers under twenty are much less likely to have an /r/ sound in this position. In many varieties of English today, the traditional British pronunciation of *news* is giving way to something more like the American English pronunciation, so people in Canada and New Zealand and many middle-class speakers of British English are more likely to say *nooz* than *nyooz*.

In sociolinguistic terms, the examples in the actvity above (*cell-* vs *mobile phone*, *hair* with or without the /r/, the /u/ sound in *news* with or without the initial 'glide') can be considered a **variable**. That is the technical term for something that varies in people's use of English. The alternative forms of a variable are termed **variants**, so *hair* with an /r/ sound and *hair* without an /r/ sound are variants of the (r) variable. These concepts provide a means of describing variation and change in English. We can look at which variants of a particular variable (pronunciations, words, etc.) are used by different kinds of speakers and in different situations. It is different pronunciations that have been particularly well studied in research on contemporary variation and change, and these make up most of the examples in this chapter.

Sociolinguists can analyse how this variation is used among groups of speakers of very different sizes, from the speech community to smaller social networks and communities of practice. There are many different definitions of **speech community**, but for our purposes here we can think of it as a group of people who share norms and expectations with regard to language use. Examples of studies of particular speech communities would be William Labov's research on Martha's Vineyard and New York City, discussed below. On the other hand, our **social networks** are made up of people we are in contact with. There can be many different types of social networks, and most people are involved in more than one network. For example, you can think of your social networks in terms of people you work or study with, but you are also part of social networks that can include your neighbours, or people you chat with online. **Communities of practice** tend to be smaller kinds of networks in which members *do* things together for a purpose, such as workplaces or the close friendship groups that form in school.

A foundational study: Martha's Vineyard

A significant study within variationist sociolinguistics was William Labov's research on variation on Martha's Vineyard (Labov, 1972). Martha's Vineyard is a small island lying three miles off the coast of Massachusetts. In 1961, when Labov visited the island, it had a permanent population of about 6000, but during the summer the number was nearly seven times greater. The increase was due to the summer residents, who most of the year lived on the mainland and came to Martha's Vineyard only for vacations. The social distance between the groups is summed up by the island saying 'Summer People, some are not'.

Curved brackets, e.g. (r), are used to represent linguistic variables. For this discussion and elsewhere in the chapter, please also refer to Appendix 2 on the notation used to represent sounds in the study of English.

When Labov came to the island in 1961, most of the permanent inhabitants lived in the eastern part of the island, 'Down-Island', in the bigger townships, but this was also the area favoured by the summer-only people. The 'Up-Island' region, centred on the fishing village of Chilmark, was more rural, with fewer residents. The permanent population of the island consisted of people of English ('early settlers') descent, of Portuguese descent and Native Americans (Wampanoag) (see Figure 7.1).

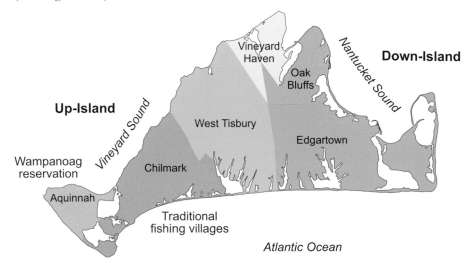

Figure 7.1 Map of Martha's Vineyard

Labov chose to investigate the pronunciation of two sounds in the speech of the permanent residents on the island: the diphthongs (ay), as in *price* or *side*, and (aw), as in *mound* or *mouth*. These sounds function as linguistic variables because their pronunciation varies in the community. In this case, they were sometimes pronounced [aɪ] and [aʊ], as on the nearby mainland. But they were also pronounced with a more raised, centralised 'onset' (i.e. where the beginning of the diphthong is pronounced higher, and towards the centre of the mouth – phonetically [əɪ] and [əʊ]). These alternatives are variants; that is, different ways of pronouncing the linguistic variable.

Labov discovered that speakers' pronunciations were affected by linguistic factors, in this case the following consonant. The centralised [əɪ] and [əʊ] occurred more frequently in words such as *white*, *twice*, *wife* and *out*, *shout* or *house* (i.e. when they came before a voiceless plosive such as [t], or a fricative such as [s] or [f]). On the other hand, [aɪ] and [aʊ] were favoured in words such as *time*, *file* and *found* or *owl* (before nasals such as [m] and [n] and the lateral approximant).

See Appendix 2 for an explanation of these terms.

Activity 7.2

Try saying the words listed above. Can you hear any subtle differences in how you pronounce the words in these two different groups?

Comment

The pronunciation of sounds is generally affected by their linguistic environment – the sounds that precede or come after them. For instance, in the case of the diphthongs investigated by Labov, all speakers of English have a slightly more raised and centralised onset before voiceless consonants like /t/ than they do before voiced ones like /d/ (try saying two similar words such as *write* and *ride*). It's simply something voiceless consonants do to the preceding vowel. In Martha's Vineyard, this phonetic fact has taken on a life of its own, and has been co-opted for social meaning, as we will see below.

Labov also found some relationships between the choice of variant and a number of social factors, such as speakers' age, ethnicity, place of residence on the island and occupation. The age patterns identified by Labov were quite complex. A comparison with earlier records showed that the centralised forms, which had been the norm in the area, had been in decline historically, but this decline was reversing. The use of centralised forms had been increasing, peaking in the 31–45 age group, but it then declined again for younger speakers. This general pattern obtained across ethnic groups: 'early settlers' (of English descent), those of Portuguese descent and Native Americans. Labov discovered that people in the 'Up-Island', more rural areas (especially those around Chilmark), were more likely to use the centralised variants than people living 'Down-Island'. As far as occupation is concerned, people who were working in the traditional fishing industry were most likely to use the centralised variants.

Having talked to a number of people on the island Labov identified another factor, which had not been obvious from the beginning of his study; people he had recorded differed in their attitudes towards living on the island. Most of the people were very positive about living there, and felt connected with the traditional ways of life; some had gone away and come back to settle on Martha's Vineyard. But there were also those who felt unsure, or even those with negative feelings about the island and who hoped to leave. Labov divided people into three categories: those with positive, neutral and negative feelings towards

Martha's Vineyard, and found striking differences between them. People with positive attitudes were most likely to use the centralised variants of the two diphthongs, those with neutral attitudes followed, and the ones with negative feelings towards the Vineyard were the least likely to use these centralised variants. Taken all together, the distribution of the centralised variants suggests that centralisation 'indexed', or pointed towards, a local, 'island' identity, someone with traditional ties to Martha's Vineyard, unlike the summer visitors. The age patterns suggest an increase in identification with the island. Speakers in the 31–45 age group had often made a choice to remain on the island, or in some cases had returned to the island after living on the mainland, which could explain their high levels of centralisation. On the other hand, Labov suggested that many of the younger speakers, who used less centralisation, did not intend to remain on the island.

This study of the sociolinguistics of variation, therefore, shows that very subtle linguistic features may be intertwined with larger and more obvious social facts such as occupation and attitudes. Labov also discovered that the study provided a possible window on to ongoing change in pronunciation. By using 'apparent time' (comparing younger and older speakers), as well as comparing current speech against older dialect records, Labov suggested that this could be a way of tracing change as it is taking place.

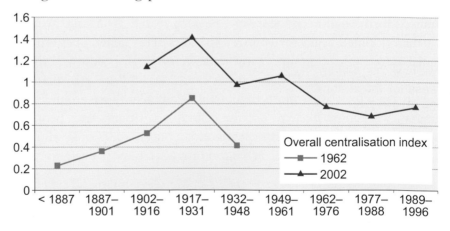

Figure 7.2 Labov's 1962 data compared with data from Pope's 2002 study (Pope et al., 2007, p. 622)

Forty years later Jennifer Pope (Pope et al., 2007) decided to re-study Martha's Vineyard, to see whether Labov's inferences of change based on apparent time could be verified in real time. She looked at the same variables on Martha's Vineyard – the pronunciation of (ay) and (aw) – and replicated Labov's methods to make the results of the two studies directly comparable.

This real-time study showed strong support for Labov's original results (Figure 7.2), suggesting that we can indeed draw reliable inferences about ongoing language change from an apparent-time study that compared the language use of older and younger speakers.

Activity 7.3

Allow about 10 minutes

Figure 7.2 shows to what extent speakers in different age groups used centralised pronunciations of (ay) and (aw). Don't worry about the detail of the 'centralisation index' shown in the figure. The main point is that the higher the centralisation index, the more raised and centralised the pronunciation of these variables. Speakers are grouped according to when they were born – oldest on the left, youngest on the right. The brown line, with squares, shows the results of Labov's study carried out in 1962. The red line, with triangles, shows the results of Pope's repeat study, carried out in 2002.

Can you explain the most striking *similarity* between the lines charting centralisation in 1962 and 2002 on Martha's Vineyard?

Can you explain the most striking *difference* between these lines?

Comment

In both cases the chart illustrates the increase in the use of centralised variants mentioned above, peaking in speakers born between 1917 and 1931, then declining for younger speakers. The 2002 study shows how this pattern has continued more recently, with a slight increase for those born between 1949 and 1961, then a levelling off. The 1902–16, 1917–31 and 1932–48 figures allow a direct comparison between speakers in both studies; that is, they show similar groups of speakers, forty years apart. The 2002 data replicates the general pattern of the 1962 data exactly.

Figure 7.2 also shows a difference between the lines in the chart: the figures for Pope's study are always higher than those for Labov's, indicating that all speakers are using more centralised variants in 2002 than they were in 1962. Apparent-time data cannot tell us about the rate of a linguistic change. A change can speed up as it spreads throughout a community, something we can see clearly in Figure 7.2.

These studies all serve to show that there is an intimate link between variation in how people talk *right now* and how changes unfold over time. English has changed greatly over the millennia and we can assume with hindsight that those changes were preceded by variation in the language use of different speakers in the speech communities of the time. We may not have records of the details of that variation, but sociolinguists believe that no change is possible without some preceding variation and that what we see as change (with hindsight), is one of several competing forms winning out and becoming the new norm.

New dialect formation in the southern hemisphere

Another interesting case study, where the combination of real- and apparent-time data has produced thought-provoking results in recent years, is in the description of the southern-hemisphere Englishes. These include South African, Australian, New Zealand, Tristan da Cunha, St Helenian and Falkland Islands English. To many outsiders, South African English (SAE), Australian English (AusE) and New Zealand English (NZE) sound quite similar, and they do share many similarities which cannot all be attributed to continued contact among the speakers. So we would like to know why this might be.

Peter Trudgill (2004) presents the most thorough exploration of this question, and the underlying linguistic and sociohistorical facts uniting and differentiating these varieties of English. Chapter 5 discussed Trudgill's study of AusE and NZE, but he argues more broadly that similarities between the southern-hemisphere Englishes can be explained by linguistic factors: that most of the features of SAE, AusE and NZE were present in the initial pool of emigrants, and they were present in the proportions necessary for subsequent propagation and stabilisation.

Trudgill rejects any significant role for non-linguistic factors such as prestige or identity in the earliest stages of new dialect formation; that is, among the first generation of English-speaking children born in the colonies. He argues that this first generation 'level out' the different pronunciations of their parents' generation strictly according to linguistic constraints, including the overall frequency of particular variants. The processes of dialect levelling seem to be central to much language change in the southern-hemisphere Englishes, and we will discuss these processes in more detail below. By this argument, southern-hemisphere Englishes are mainly non-rhotic (they do not pronounce non-prevocalic /r/ in words such as *car* and *card*) because the bulk of the English colonists who moved there were already speakers of varieties of English that had lost an /r/ in this position (by contrast, North American Englishes do use non-prevocalic /r/ because they were settled earlier, before the /r/ started to disappear in south-eastern British dialects).

Janet Holmes and Paul Kerswill (2008) take strong issue with Trudgill's claim that identity issues don't matter. They argue that identity formation is implicated at all stages of new dialect formation, and point out that settlers in new urban areas might have been particularly sensitive to which dialects from the 'old country' were markers of prestige. New settlers might have seen moving to Australia or New Zealand as a chance to start again, and been willing to try to do so linguistically as well as socially and economically. Gareth Baxter et al. (2009) use computer modelling to ask whether it is reasonable to suppose that NZE might have developed into what it looks like today simply on the basis of linguistic factors. This involves taking data about what the colonists and early settlers sounded like, what the current speakers of NZE sound like, and trying to get a computer to fill in the gaps to see how one might have changed into the other. They conclude that some kind of 'accelerating' force – for example, speakers' attitudes about prestige variants or a desire for distinctiveness – may have been needed to get NZE sounding the way it does today in only 150 years or so. Elizabeth Gordon et al. (2004) also argue that the English speech communities in the southern hemisphere were attuned to what was prestigious and what was not, from the very early stages of new dialect formation.

These studies of new dialects in the southern hemisphere show how important it is to understand their history. How the original speakers of English talked when they colonised these parts of the world partly shapes the way people speak today. However, these new varieties of English don't exist in a social vacuum, and now that they have taken root, they also show how contemporary, ongoing variation and change can become a marker of social factors that are important within the speech community. An example is Rajend Mesthrie's study of pronunciation change in South African English.

Activity 7.4

In Reading A, *Social change and changing accents in South Africa*, Mesthrie discusses one example of a sound change: the pronunciation of /uː/ (the vowel in words such as *goose, school, true*, etc.). He refers to this as the 'GOOSE vowel', where *goose* is used as the keyword for the 'lexical set' of words that share this vowel. The pronunciation of the vowel is becoming 'fronted' (pronounced further forward in the mouth) in

Esther Asprey, in Chapter 5 Reading A, also drew on the idea of 'lexical sets' in her account of Black Country English.

southern-hemisphere English, and Mesthrie gives an example of how this is related to race and class in South Africa.

Mesthrie's work provides a good example of how sociolinguists need to design a study that allows them to look systematically at an aspect of variation and change. As you read, consider how Mesthrie sets out on this kind of systematic investigation.

Comment

Mesthrie gives the context for his study: widespread social change following the end of apartheid, which finds a reflex in the way people use language. While several aspects of language are likely to be affected, Mesthrie focuses here on the pronunciation of a single vowel.

Mesthrie consults historical records which provide evidence of an earlier ethnic difference, where the fronting of /u:/ was perceived as a 'peculiarly White' phenomenon. In comparing the speech of White and Black speakers in his own contemporary study, Mesthrie pays attention to several factors, including:

- *Selection of speakers*: Mesthrie selects the same number of White and Black speakers who are similar in several other respects (all students, in the same age-range, from middle-class backgrounds, who have been to similar schools).
- *Samples of speech*: all speakers take part in a similar interview, and read out a word list. This combination of interview and word list comes from the work of William Labov, which we discuss further in Section 7.3.
- Mesthrie also pays attention to the *linguistic environment* of the /u:/ vowel (other surrounding sounds that may affect its pronunciation).

This method of holding other social factors, the contexts in which people are speaking, and the linguistic environment reasonably constant allows Mesthrie to focus on the point that interests him – a comparison between the pronunciations of White and Black speakers. While it is possible to hear differences in pronunciation, Mesthrie also uses computer analysis to provide an objective measure of these. He is able to demonstrate that these young Black speakers have adopted a pronunciation formerly associated with White South African English. He argues therefore that the vowel has been 'deracialised' and is now 'a marker of youth and middle-class status'. This is, as he notes, only one aspect of sociolinguistic change and 'other processes are at work in other social groups'.

Other aspects of dialect contact

The processes governing new dialect formation in the southern hemisphere differ from the formation of new dialects elsewhere in one crucial respect: there was no 'native' dialect of English in the southern hemisphere when English speakers arrived. Work by Paul Kerswill on new dialect formation in the British new town of Milton Keynes shows that children whose families moved to Milton Keynes from other parts of Britain create a new dialect that has vestiges of the old local dialect, but which usually discards linguistically marked forms in favour of new forms found in abundance in the speech of their parents' generation.

As in the changes that occurred in NZE discussed above, this is a process of *dialect levelling*: the differences between the dialects that have come in contact with one another decrease and there is a levelling of the linguistic playing fields, so to speak. When this happens in a speech community like a new town or when it happens across regional dialect boundaries, dialects become less diverse and more similar to each other. In Milton Keynes, for example, the settlers in the new town brought many different pronunciations of the vowel in *mouth* and *loud* with them and the traditional dialect in Milton Keynes had a very distinctive, fronted pronunciation. But none of the children interviewed by Kerswill and Ann Williams (2000) who grew up in the new town had the traditional distinctive pronunciation. A few still used pronunciations that they might have picked up from their parents, but the majority of the time, they pronounced words like *mouth* with what seems to be a new marker of localness.

Milton Keynes is one of a number of new towns set up in Britain. Founded in 1967, it attracted significant in-migration from London and the south-east of England, but also from elsewhere in Britain.

Recent work looking at the spread of variation through contact between dialects suggests that, as a general rule, it is uncommon for different varieties of English to use a variable that is being passed on from one variety to another in exactly the same way. Miriam Meyerhoff and Nancy Niedzielski (2003) discuss how global innovations and trends in language can be given a local flavour, sometimes referred to as **glocalisation**.

A good example is the use of the form *be like* as a way of introducing reported discourse, as in:

See Chapter 4 for more on English and globalisation, as well as glocalisation.

> We drove past the cop … *I'm like* 'What? Oh my God, oh my God.'

This form is said to have originated in US English but is now found in several other varieties. Isabelle Buchstaller and Alexandra D'Arcy (2009) studied its contemporary use by speakers of US English, British English and NZE. While there are many similarities in the use of this form, Buchstaller and D'Arcy argue that it also seemed to have been given a local spin, in rather the same way as global products such as McDonald's and Coca-Cola are. For instance, NZE favoured the use of the expression in the historic present (where the present tense is used to narrate events in the past, as in the example cited above). While this also occurs in US English, it is a more striking feature of NZE, but not of British English. Buchstaller and D'Arcy suggest that global linguistic resources need to be integrated into local norms and practices – they come to occupy 'a slightly different niche in different varieties' (Buchstaller and D'Arcy, 2009, p. 318).

In this section we have looked at how English is continually changing and how this may be studied systematically: either by comparing contemporary speech with historical records or by comparing the speech of different age groups. We have suggested that such changes do not take place in a social vacuum: in Martha's Vineyard change was associated with the expression of a particular 'island' identity; identity was also said to be at stake in the development of southern-hemisphere Englishes; and a pronunciation shift in South Africa was associated with the redrawing of 'race' and 'class' boundaries. Change is, then, bound up with patterns of contemporary variation in English. We look at some of these patterns in greater detail in the following section.

7.3   Social and stylistic variation in English

One of the key features of variation in English (and other languages) is that language is used variably by speakers from different social groups or communities. Even though we know that no two individuals talk alike (i.e. there is variation in the way particular people speak even in one small community), it is possible to observe certain patterns across individuals.

There are a number of social factors which typically influence how speakers use a linguistic variable. We look below at social class and gender, and the social networks people belong to. We also consider how individuals vary the way they speak, according to different speaking styles.

Social class

Reading B in Chapter 5 discussed a number of pronunciations that characterise the speech of New York City, including the absence of non-prevocalic /r/ among many speakers. In Labov's early work in New York City (1972) he identified a social pattern in the way (r) was pronounced: those from higher social classes did use non-prevocalic /r/, at least more than speakers from lower social classes, with quite clear 'stratification' (i.e. division) of other classes in between. Non-prevocalic /r/ is the norm for General American English and is recognised as more 'standard' even by New Yorkers who do not use it very often in casual speech. Given that this variant has connotations of standardness or prestige, it is unsurprising to find that speakers of higher social classes in New York City tend to use it more: just as members of the highest social class are likely to display their markers of economic prestige and success (occupation, car, private school), they are also likely to display linguistic markers of prestige and success. In other words, part of being 'posh' or 'successful' is *talking* posh or sounding like what we expect someone who is successful to sound like.

But social class distinctions can be found in variables that are below the level of conscious awareness too. In Philadelphia, for instance, there is a sound change in progress where (aw) and (ey) (the vowels in *mouth* and *face*) are being raised (pronounced higher in the mouth). Labov (2001) has noted a class distinction in the raising of these vowels. These changes are taking place below the level of awareness, and, as is common in such cases, the new variants tend to be favoured by lower middle-class or upper working-class speakers, not the highest social classes who are following behind.

Change from above and below

We talk about a **change from above** when the change is conscious (above the level of social awareness). As such, it may be the subject of overt comments. It is usually first found in careful speech, and often introduced by the dominant social class. An example is the increasing use of non-prevocalic /r/ in New York City. **Change from below**, on the other hand, is unconscious, and is usually first found in the vernacular. As it is below the level of awareness it is not commented on by the speakers. Most non-lexical language change is below conscious awareness. An example here, as mentioned above, is the raising of the vowels in *mouth* and *face* in Philadelphia.

Speaking style

Allow about
10 minutes

Activity 7.5

Make a list of some of the different ways you can say someone had too much to drink. Which ones would you use when describing the situation to:

- a close friend
- an elderly neighbour
- the emergency services.

Would you be likely to use different words if you were making the story into a joke for your friend, or if it was a serious story about danger?

Comment

The kinds of choices you made about whether to say *drunk*, *inebriated*, *smashed*, *pissed*, *three sheets to the wind*, etc. are the kinds of choices that reflect 'style-shifting'. You might be more likely to use *pissed* in everyday conversation with a friend, or *three sheets to the wind* if you are turning it into a mocking story. You might use *inebriated* to emergency services, and *drunk* as a default term. You will no doubt have identified several other terms that could be used. This kind of variation is triggered by changes in who you are talking to, what you are talking about, and what the tone of the conversation is. Such variation in vocabulary reflects shifts in style, and is often accompanied by similar changes in pronunciation and grammar.

Style and style-shifting

We use the term **style-shifting** to talk about alternations between the different speech **styles** of any individual speaker. This might mean speaking differently according to the person addressed, the topic under discussion, the particular setting, etc.

Labov's New York City study looked at different modes of speech among people in the Lower East Side of Manhattan. Labov identified several speaking styles, associated with the different speech activities speakers are engaged in. He saw these as running along a continuum ranging from casual (speech to family members or friends), through to careful (speech to an interviewer), to reading passages, word lists and, finally, minimal pairs (pairs of words that differ with respect to a single sound, such as the initial sounds in **th**in and **t**in). Labov argued that people pay more attention to their speech when talking to an interviewer (careful) than when chatting with a friend or a family member (casual), and that they pay even more attention when reading aloud.

One of the linguistic variables in Labov's study was (th) – the first consonant in **th**in or **th**ought. This can be pronounced as a 'dental fricative' [θ], an 'affricate' [tθ] or a 'plosive' [t]. The fricative is the standard/prestige form, while the plosive has less prestige in this case and is seen as non-standard. When we look at the patterning of this variable according to Labov's style continuum, we find that on average all the speakers used most fricatives (so the more standard, or prestigious, variant) in read speech, fewer in careful interview speech, and the fewest in casual speech. This kind of stylistic pattern emerged in all variables examined in the New York City study.

Significantly, this variation between different styles paralleled the variation associated with different social groups: the variants typical of all speakers' reading speech tended to be the ones favoured by the higher social class. This parallel between careful styles and higher social class strengthens the association between class and prestige mentioned in the last section.

Since Labov's work, there has been considerable interest in style among linguists. Labov's notion of style as having to do with attention paid to speech has generated criticism and a number of questions. Allan Bell (1984) and others have argued that attempting to quantify 'attention to speech' is problematic. In an alternative approach known as **audience design**, Bell (1984) suggests that people change the way they speak not as a result of the attention they pay to their own speech, but rather as a response to differences in their audience; that is, who they are talking to. For the researcher, it is easier to identify changes reliably in someone's audience than it is to identify changes in how much attention they are paying to the way they talk.

You may remember that, in Reading A, Rajend Mesthrie used a combination of interviews and word lists to collect samples of speech.

John Rickford and Faye McNair-Knox (1994) tested this proposal with a series of interviews with an African-American teenager, 'Foxy'. Foxy was interviewed by both African-American and White interviewers over the course of some years. The frequency of African-American Vernacular English features in her speech was significantly higher in the interviews with the African-American fieldworker than with the White fieldworker. This, they argued, shows the importance of audience or interlocutor on a person's speech.

This approach is built on seeing shifts in style as a *response* to the audience, but it also foreshadows more recent developments in how sociolinguists analyse style. These see style-shifting as a more active process, enabling speakers to construct relationships with others in certain ways. Natalie Schilling-Estes (2004) analyses the style shifts in a conversation between two young male friends, in this case shifts towards and away from the norms of different regional and ethnic varieties of US English. For example, both friends use pronunciations typical of Southern American English when they are talking about topics to do with the South. Schilling-Estes argues that, in adapting their pronunciation in this way, the speakers are not simply responding to the topic under discussion. They are also conveying particular stances, motivated by their desire to position themselves in relation to the topic and their addressee. In using similar pronunciations, for instance, speakers may be aligning themselves with each other, whereas the use of different pronunciations may serve to highlight their distinctiveness. This trend towards seeing speakers' style-shifting as a relatively active process is discussed further below.

Gender

Like social class, gender has frequently been studied as a social grouping that might affect how people use language. Summarising the results of several years of sociolinguistic research in this area, Labov (1990) proposed the following principles:

1   With stable variables, women use the standard variant more than men from the same class and age group.
1a   In change from above, women favour the incoming prestige variant more than men.
2   In change from below, women are most often innovators.

Note that principle 1 talks about stable variables which are not changing, while 1a and 2 describe a change in progress.

In trying to explain (and explore) these general patterns a number of researchers have argued that it is not enough simply to look at gender independently: explanations are said to lie in understanding its relationship with other social factors, as well as the social and cultural roles of women and men in a given community.

Sylvie Dubois and Barbara Horvath (2000) looked at the English spoken in a Cajun community in Louisiana to gain a better understanding of the roles of men and women in language variation and possible language change. Their study involved three generations of speakers (over a 100-year span), and analysed a number of traditional Cajun variables. They found that there was some effect of gender in the use of all the variables, but:

- different variables were affected by gender in different ways, and
- other social factors played a large role in the patterning of some variables.

One of the variables Dubois and Horvath examined was the set of voiceless plosives (p, t, k). These are traditionally pronounced without aspiration in Cajun English, whereas in standard US English they are aspirated when they occur at the beginning of a syllable. (To understand this, hold your hand in front of your mouth, and say the words *pan*, *pen*, *pun*. Can you feel a sharp burst of air on your hand? If so, you are pronouncing the /p/ sound with aspiration.)

Dubois and Horvath found that, for all these variables, there is an interaction between gender and age in the Cajun speech community: older men and women use the Cajun unaspirated variants at least half the time, but middle-aged and younger men and women use aspirated variants more than half the time. The difference between older women and men is minimal, but between the middle-aged and younger women and men, there are very significant differences. Women have almost entirely given up the traditional Cajun variant, but men still use it about 40 per cent of the time. If we say that women are leading this change towards standard English (i.e. non-Cajun) pronunciation of /p, t, k/, then we might conclude that it is an example of linguistic behaviour covered by principle 1a. However, note that 1a refers to changes 'from above' the level of conscious awareness, and this change is below the level of awareness – Dubois and Horvath note that there is absolutely no awareness in the Cajun community of the alternation between unaspirated and aspirated plosives and it was not targeted for correction in formal schooling. Because this change has some of the properties of a change from above and some of a change from below and because there is such a huge difference between what women and men are doing, it is not entirely clear that Labov's principles help understand or explain all the data observed.

Dubois and Horvath found a different pattern when they looked at another variable: whether people used 'nasalised' pronunciations of vowels. Nasalised pronunciations had been traditional in the community but were thought to be disappearing. Dubois and Horvath found that, although the patterns were different, once again age and gender seemed to be related:

- As might be expected with a pronunciation that is disappearing, middle-aged speakers used far less nasalisation than older speakers.
- This pattern held for both male and female speakers – that is, there was no significant difference between men and women in these older and middle generations.
- In the younger generation, however, men used traditional nasalised pronunciations almost 98 per cent of the time, while women used almost none of these pronunciations.

The social history of nasalisation is more complex than for many variables, and tests the limits of Labov's generalisations in its complexity. The loss of nasalisation was a change in progress, showing no clear gender differences for two generations. But by the time the third (young) generation came along, nasalisation had become strongly stereotyped as sounding really 'Cajun'. Young men involved in the tourism and entertainment industries had therefore re-adopted it as a signal of their identification as authentic Cajuns. Because women were largely closed out of the tourism and entertainment work, they did not need to project 'Cajunness' through nasalisation, and for them the change continued unchecked towards loss of nasalisation.

Because the younger men nasalised even more than the older speakers and are reversing a shift away from nasalisation, Dubois and Horvath call this 'recycling'. Recycling describes the resurgence of a variant that had been disappearing in the speech community. It seems to be an option that occurs with variables above the level of conscious awareness more than with those below – that is, a variable that is strongly stereotyped as sounding really 'Cajun', like nasalisation was, may be available for recycling in ways that variables below conscious awareness are not. Recycling seems to be tied to speakers' ideologies and beliefs about language.

While there are indeed differences in the ways men and women use traditional variants in the Cajun community, it is also important to remember that gender (along with other social variables) does not influence the way we speak in ways that are completely independent of other considerations. The examples above show that we need to know *which women* (how old they are) and *which variables* (ones the speakers are aware of or not).

Social networks

The notion of social networks was brought into the study of language from sociology and social anthropology. An individual's social network is described as an 'aggregate of relationships contracted with others', and is a way of capturing 'the dynamics underlying speakers' interactional behaviours' (Milroy, 2002, p. 549). Social networks group people from the point of view of the individual: they take into consideration factors such as who you spend most time with, who you consider to be your best friends, who you talk with on a daily basis, who you work or go to school with. This is different from grouping people according to categories such as social class or gender which, on their own, don't take any account of people's actual social behaviour. Social networks have a big influence on how information and innovation spread throughout society. It is therefore an attractive notion for sociolinguists, who are interested in (among other things) how language change occurs. If social networks play a role in the diffusion of changes in, for example, fashion, do they also play a role in how language change spreads? The answer seems to be 'yes'.

Carmen Fought (1999) examined the use of negative concord (as in 'I *did*n't tell **no***body* about it') among Latino teenagers in Los Angeles, looking at a number of linguistic and social factors. The most important one turned out to be the speaker's social network – the more involvement speakers had with gangs and gang culture, the more likely they were to use negative concord. Another smaller social network of teenagers who go out tagging – spraying artistic graffiti in public spaces – had the highest use of negative concord of all. For this study, it was the degree of engagement and involvement in a particular network that was really important.

Networks also proved significant in Dubois and Horvath's study of traditional Cajun variants discussed in the section above. In this case Dubois and Horvath looked at the variables (th) and (dh) – the initial sounds in **th**in*k* and **th***is*. In the Cajun community these sounds may be pronounced as plosives, to give /tɪŋk/ or /dɪs/). Dubois and Horvath found an important correlation between people who used the traditional plosive variants and what kind of social network they had.

Dubois and Horvath distinguished between *open* and *closed* networks. People with closed networks are those who have more ties within their local community, and spend most of their time with other members of their community; those with open networks have ties outside it and their circles are not limited to their local community. For Cajun women, there was a strong correlation between the choice of the variant and network type – women with closed networks used the typically Cajun [t] and [d] much more than those with open networks (this was true especially for women in the older and younger generation). This relationship is not as evident for men, and Dubois and Horvath make it clear that other factors are at play here. Engagement in open or closed networks for men is mostly about whether or not they work in the town. For women, on the other hand, it defines most of their lifestyle – women with open networks work outside the house, interact with outsiders, have ties with the non-Cajun population, maybe even get married outside the Cajun community, while those with closed networks lead a more traditional life, looking after the house and children. This shows that it is important to interpret social network effects on variation and change in the context of a particular community. Labov's principles say nothing about networks, and work like Dubois and Horvath's is important for pushing our understanding of the complex relationship between language change and gender further.

The study of social networks foreshadows variationists' use of even smaller networks known as communities of practice (Eckert and McConnell-Ginet, 1999) as the basis for analysing how variation acquires social meaning, is transmitted and results in change. Communities of practice are networks defined by members' participation in shared practices, goals and enterprises. The taggers in Fought's study would be a good example of this because as well as socialising together at school, they are engaged in an enterprise of getting their tags (graffiti) in as many places as possible. However, ways of talking are among the kinds of practices people can share.

Style, attitudes and social positioning

We referred above to research by Natalie Schilling-Estes which saw speakers' adoption of particular speaking styles as a relatively active process that enables them to construct relationships in certain ways.

This is less deterministic than seeing style simply as a response to a particular situation. It is part of a broader trend within sociolinguistics that also questions ideas about social categories such as social class and gender, evident in earlier research. We can document a development in ideas from seeing gender (for instance) as a fixed category that affects how people speak (so that you speak as you do because you are a woman or a man – something evident in Labov's earlier work); to taking into account the interaction between gender and other factors (gender and age in Dubois and Horvath's Cajun study); looking at patterns of interaction (social networks) that affect how people speak (e.g. women's and men's social networks in the Cajun community); and looking more closely at the detail of particular instances of language use – at how speakers may adopt a speaking style or shift between speaking styles as a way of emphasising or playing down certain aspects of their identity. These more recent ideas highlight the importance of speaker 'agency', where more weight is placed on the speaker's active use and creation of different styles, rather than stylistic choices being a reaction to external categories.

As an example, Rusty Barrett (1998) looked at the language of African-American drag queens. Barrett found that, in their performances, these speakers switched between standard American English and African-American Vernacular English to actively construct different identities and relationships, on different occasions highlighting their identities as drag queens, African Americans and gay men. Standard American English, for instance, was often associated with an ostentatious 'drag queen' performance.

Activity 7.6

In Reading B, *Variation and agency*, Robert Podesva reviews these newer approaches to language study that place a greater emphasis on speakers' agency and social meaning. As you work through the reading, consider what these add to our understanding of variation and change in English.

Comment

Ideas of speaker agency, for Podesva, highlight the capacity of speakers not simply to reflect, but also to redefine particular interactional contexts, sets of relationships, etc. (e.g. his example of a doctor making a medical consultation more informal). Podesva argues that, whenever speakers select one way of using language over another (adopting certain pronunciations, or pitch ranges, for instance), they are 'subtly altering the social world'. He does concede that there are some constraints – key here are his comments that not all speakers are equal in terms of power, and that whatever we do needs to make sense to others.

These ideas are based on the idea that linguistic features are socially meaningful: they 'index' particular stances, personal characteristics and identities. However, social meanings are 'indeterminate' – not fixed, and not clear-cut. For Podesva, this allows speakers creatively to 'rework' meanings: they can 'exploit the elastic mapping between linguistic form [a particular linguistic feature] and meaning'.

Meanings also change over time, though Podesva argues that traces of prior meanings may remain (his example of the word *queer*). This will contribute to their indeterminacy at any one time. Podesva's argument extends to the historical development of varieties of English, discussed in earlier chapters. We need to consider, he suggests, how particular varieties (dialects, speaking styles) come to be recognised as meaningful and distinct (the establishment of a 'Geordie' accent, for instance).

As we pointed out above, this combination of ideas extends 'traditional' research on language variation and change. Podesva notes, however, that it also raises questions – if we regard linguistic meaning as, at least in part, fluid, indeterminate, emerging in particular contexts, how can researchers be sure of their interpretations of speakers' utterances?

Podesva, like other work discussed in this chapter, focuses on variation *in English*. However, in these recent approaches to style and style-shifting, speakers' choice of particular styles in English begins to look very similar to the way speakers switch between English and other languages in multilingual contexts, as discussed in Chapter 6.

7.4   Perceiving and learning variation

In this final section, we consider a fundamental puzzle about variation: how does variation spread between individuals and over time? To address this, we will consider children's acquisition of variation, a process involving a connection between perception (what children hear) and production (how they speak). Children need to perceive structured variation as more than just random differences between individual speakers, and it seems that they do this by evaluating what they are hearing in relation to their own emerging understanding of the fact that social and personal information is organised systematically in their speech community.

There are still only a few studies that systematically investigate how children acquire variation. Some generalisations that have emerged from these so far are:

- Children master simple linguistic constraints, or linguistic factors that affect variation, by age 3–4 years (Roberts, 1994; Roberts and Labov, 1995).

- Children require much longer to acquire some grammatical constraints (Guy and Boyd, 1990).

- Preschoolers of both sexes first acquire changes that are led by women (Roberts, 1994; Foulkes et al., 2005). Roberts suggests this may be because most of the children in her sample were cared for by mothers or other women, so that both boys and girls had more opportunity to pick up variants that women favour.

- However, caregivers also seem to tailor how they talk to children according to their own expectations and knowledge of the speech community. Foulkes et al. (2005) observed that caregivers use variants preferred by women more with girls and variants preferred by men with boys.

Research by Jennifer Smith, carried out in Buckie, north-east Scotland, provides the most extensive study of the acquisition of variation to date, looking at a large number of children and also looking at variables from different levels of linguistic structure – phonetics, grammar and vocabulary.

The Buckie study compared the variation in both mothers' speech when talking to children and the children's own speech against the norms of the wider community (Smith, 2000; Smith et al., 2007). Two important and closely related findings emerged. There was a clear difference in how children acquired the variation associated with variables above and below the level of conscious awareness in the community as a whole. Children learnt how to use the different variants differently, depending on whether the variable was above or below conscious awareness. For variables above the level of conscious awareness, such as (au) – that is, the alternation between a pronunciation close to the standard English [aʊ] and the local Buckie [u] in words like *trousers* and *now* – children acquired a distinction between different social styles or stances as quickly as they acquired linguistic constraints on the variable. For variables below the level of conscious awareness, such as the alternation between third person plural -*s* on verbs (*the children shows their toys* versus *the children show their toys*), the children produced patterns that replicated the linguistic constraints on the variable in adult speech, but they did not distinguish different styles. This shows that 'awareness' of a variable is something we can assess at the societal level (e.g. what people make jokes about and express stereotypes about) and also something that influences how individual speakers relate to and learn the variation around them: both society and the individual are intimately involved in reproducing sociolinguistic facts.

The complex relationship between social and linguistic constraints is also a problem for older learners. In a study of Polish teenagers who moved to the UK, Erik Schleef and his associates (Schleef et al., 2011) looked at their use of the (ing) variable. This variable has often been studied in sociolinguistic research. It refers to the pronunciation of -*ing* in words such as ru*nn***ing** and *go***ing**: whether this is pronounced [ɪŋ] or [ɪn] (the latter is sometimes represented in writing as *runnin'*). Schleef et al. found that the migrant teenagers were rather good at attuning to the relative frequency of [ɪŋ] and [ɪn] in the London and Edinburgh communities they had moved into, and they also showed sensitivity to some of the local linguistic constraints on (ing). But in general, they seemed to be doing a lot of work to *create* systematicity in (ing) even where it was not present in their locally born teenage peers' speech. For example, for the London-born teenagers there was no difference between boys' and girls' use of the different variants of (ing), but among the Polish teenagers, boys were more likely to use one variant and girls the other. This echoes the evidence that H. D. Adamson and Vera Regan (1991) found for learner creativity when they looked at (ing) in the speech of adult Asian migrants to the USA.

Finally, there is growing evidence to suggest that the variation we learn as children can only minimally be 'unlearnt'. Miriam Meyerhoff and James Walker (2007) looked at variation in the speech of 'urban sojourners' on Bequia (an island in St Vincent and the Grenadines). Urban sojourners are people who worked overseas for a number of years and later returned to Bequia. Meyerhoff and Walker looked at presence/absence of the verb *be* in sentences like *She (is) the boss* and *The boss (is) showing her the door*. In sentences like these, urban sojourners used *is* more often than their stay-at-home peers did, but the sojourners still favoured and disfavoured presence of *be* in the same linguistic contexts that their stay-at-home peers did. This suggests that they had retained their original grammar of variation.

These case studies indicate not only how much there is to learn when you are acquiring variation, but also how important it is to consider what kind of variable it is. Not all variables are learnt the same way, and this has larger implications for the extent to which they can be the target of correction or amendment by formal education. This in turn feeds into the way the next generation will respond to a variable – as we noted earlier, few of the factors that influence variation in language operate independently of all the other factors.

7.5 Conclusion

English, as we have seen, varies in a number of different ways and on a number of levels: it varies across different localities, across different groups of speakers in one community, and, finally, variation can be found in the speech of every single individual. This variation is present in our lives all the time, and more often than not we just take it for granted. What is important (and interesting for sociolinguists) is how language variation can be translated into social reality. As we have seen, tiny linguistic differences (often those that speakers themselves are unaware of) can be socially very significant. Not only can they add to our understanding of social structures of communities or societies, but they can also be used by the speakers themselves to manipulate who they are perceived as (a very powerful notion indeed).

Apart from seeing language variation as embedded in everyday social reality, studying it can also lead to a deeper understanding of the history of English and to developments that have taken place in the past. It is clear from earlier chapters that the shape of English today is radically different from the way it used to be. Understanding the mechanisms behind language variation now (as we have seen in the many examples in this chapter) may help us understand and explain some of the processes that have led to the current shape of English, even though we have no recordings of it from the past.

READING A: Social change and changing accents in South Africa

Rajend Mesthrie

Specially commissioned for this book.

Introduction

This reading examines the degree of sociolinguistic change in the English of young middle-class South Africans of different ethnic backgrounds in relation to new post-apartheid opportunities and friendships. Once tightly controlled under the policy of apartheid, social networks of young people of middle-class background have been deracialising since the 1990s. Under apartheid, a system of rigid social control between 1948 and 1994, there was little social mixing between the country's four major social groups: Whites, Blacks, Coloureds and Indians. (Coloured is a South African term for people of multiple ancestries, one of which may be that of the indigenous Khoesan population different from the Bantu-speaking Black population.) Given that people from the population groups (as they were termed) could not reside in the same areas, go to school together, socialise in restaurants, hotels, bars, etc., or intermarry, it is not surprising that their language practices tended to differ. In particular there were at least four easily identifiable social dialects of English corresponding to these groups. These were either home languages or second languages learnt via schooling or work, which differed not just in terms of accent but in terms of grammatical features too.

The original paper on which this shortened version is based examined whether young people of the major ethnic groups are simply adopting prestige White middle-class English norms, adapting them or resisting change. It did this in relation to one particular vowel, the high, back rounded vowel traditionally transcribed as /uː/ and also referred to as the GOOSE vowel – *goose* being one of hundreds of English words having this vowel (also *fool, who, true, crude*, etc.) This shortened version will focus on the Black subgroup. The significance of this research extends beyond the analysis of a particular vowel. My interest lies in the full range of linguistic norms: the set of vowels and consonants, intonation and rhythm, grammatical properties, vocabulary and slang, etc. Since the study of these phenomena at a scholarly level would take many years, sociolinguists have to make do with studying individual elements like the GOOSE vowel to begin with.

Since the 1990s, perhaps for the first time in the country's history, English itself was beginning to deracialise. In particular young children of all backgrounds whose parents could afford it started to attend high-quality private schools once reserved for Whites alone. There were also formerly White schools (designated Model C) that were not private but afforded a high-quality education. Initially White children predominated in both types of school. They still do in the private schools but much less so in the Model C schools. Social networks and friendship groups developed which favoured the English of this group. Black, Coloured and Indian children who were in a minority accommodated to these prestige norms. In the 1990s it became noticeable that one could no longer identify the race (or ethnic group) of some young speakers purely by their accent (say from a telephone conversation or overhearing a conversation without seeing the speakers). This 'crossing over' of accents had many interesting social ramifications. First, it broke down stereotypes about the English of Black people: here were young people confidently using the prestige accent and social dialect of the most educated people. It also marked off a new middle-class social group, in which race was no longer a barrier to friendship and social relationships. But there were other less positive ramifications of the new socialisation. One was the potential generation gap between children and their elders. Going to English-dominant schools and shifting to the dominant variety of English made many Black children lose full proficiency in their home language, especially if their parents had moved to the 'suburbs' or high-quality housing in former White areas. This increased the gap between these children and their grandparental generation (who might not always have a command of English).

Equally, moving into the middle classes (or new elite) opened up class divisions between Black children who had been to private and formerly White schools and those whose activities still revolved around life and education in the townships. The extreme solidarity among Black people facing hardships and injustices under apartheid gave way to a sense of differentiation over being 'authentically' Black or not. In the 1980s, a sense of division emerged at university when Black pupils of such disparate backgrounds studied together. The difference eventually became encapsulated in the term 'coconut': a jesting or mocking term for those who are allegedly 'dark on the outside, White on the inside'. The linguistic crossing over of the middle-class Black students is part of a broader change in lifestyle, values and symbolism. Linguists also caution that the pre-eminence of this group could lead to the eventual decline of the indigenous languages like isiZulu, isiXhosa and Sesotho.

Clearly very large issues are at stake when it comes to changing accents and lifestyles. It is therefore important to analyse these linguistic changes objectively. Are young Black middle-class children simply adopting what used to be the norms of middle-class Whites? Do they bring something along to the party; that is, are they introducing some features of accent into this variety, making it truly multi-racial?

Descriptions of GOOSE in older South African Englishes

The first scholarly study of South African English (SAE) was that of Hopwood (1928), a British-trained phonetician who gives us the earliest description of the GOOSE vowel in South Africa. His description indicates that this vowel was beginning to be 'fronted' (i.e. articulated further forward in the mouth) in the White communities as early as the 1920s, within a century of the first English settlements in the country. This makes fronting likely to be a transported feature from the United Kingdom, rather than one that began anew. Fifty years after Hopwood's work, Lanham (1978, pp. 153–4) maintained that the fronted variant was widespread in South African English, in both middle-class and broader varieties; for the latter, especially among younger speakers. Crucially for this paper, fronting was once uncommon in the varieties of SAE spoken by Blacks, Coloureds and Indians. Lass (1995) forcefully contrasts this state of affairs with the White speakers as follows:

> The central-to-front quality is an ethnic as well as a social marker; it is (on anecdotal evidence at least) perceived by Black [= all speakers who are not White – RM] speakers as peculiarly 'White'. Vernacular Indian and Coloured varieties have a back vowel, often even backer than Conservative [= pronunciation oriented towards the British accent Received Pronunciation – RM]; and there is a strong tendency for Indian and Coloured speakers to avoid the fronter values even in very standard registers (the only exceptions being media personalities).

> (Lass, 1995, p. 99)

Where Whites were concerned, one can paraphrase Lass (1995, p. 98) slightly as follows: the higher up the class scale and the younger the speaker, the fronter the vowel.

The sample and methods

This paper reports on twenty-four young, middle-class students from the White and Black groups (twelve from each group). All had been to Model C or private schools which were multi-racial to varying degrees. They were between the ages of seventeen and twenty-four, with one exception of a 29-year-old mature student returning to university. The majority either lived in a university residence or at home with family; only a few lived in 'digs' (i.e. a rented house shared by students). However, all had been brought up in segregated suburbs, given that they were born before 1990. The families of about half of the Black students have since moved into suburbs that are predominantly White.

The project employs the technique of the 'Labovian' interview, long familiar in sociolinguistics. Topics under discussion included childhood games, primary and high school memories, righteous indignation over wrongful blame, relations with students of different backgrounds, and favourite pastimes. In lieu of the 'danger of death' question often asked in such interviews, interviewees were asked whether they had witnessed, heard of, or been the victim of any robbery – as every South African has a crime story to tell. At the end interviewees read out a word list.

It is increasingly common in the study of contemporary sound change to use computer-generated analyses of vowels, rather than relying on ear-training alone. The free software PRAAT (Boersma and Weenink, 2008) measures vowels in terms of frequencies in the sound wave, which linguists have been able to analyse to identify aspects of pronunciation – in this case the degree of fronting of the /uː/ vowel. In this paper (and generally) a measure of 0.4 denotes a back vowel value and 2.0 a front vowel value. A fully central value is 1.0. For ease of description I describe vowels between 0.6 and 0.8 as backish and 1.2 to 1.4 as frontish.

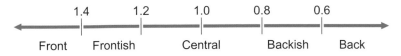

| 1.4 | 1.2 | 1.0 | 0.8 | 0.6 |
| Front | Frontish | Central | Backish | Back |

Figure 1 A fronting scale for the GOOSE vowel, based on acoustic analysis

It is usual in the sociolinguistic study of pronunciation to focus on specific environments which influence the variable under study. In this reading I will present the results for the most important of such environments, viz. when the GOOSE vowel is preceded by a sound that is sometimes termed a 'glide' or 'semi-vowel'. Examples of words where there is a glide before the /uː/ vowel are *few, new, cute* and *tune*.

Some pronunciations were discarded; for example, occasions when the vowel was unstressed so not fully pronounced as /uː/, and unclear data caused by simultaneous speech or background noise.

The data and its analysis

All parts of the interview were considered fair game for analysis: it was not possible to divide the transcripts into formal and casual style, as this would involve somewhat arbitrary divisions.

The White speakers

For GOOSE, there was a high degree of internal consistency within the White speakers, irrespective of whether the speakers were from different cities (Cape Town and Durban). Table 1 provides a bird's eye view of the norms of this group, showing the distribution of speakers into the relevant categories of fronting.

Table 1 Number of White speakers in each category of fronting after a glide

Front	Frontish	Central	Backish	Back
9	3	–	–	–

Table 1 shows that the GOOSE vowel of White speakers after a glide always falls into the front or frontish category.

Young, middle-class Black speakers

Particular interest lies in the sociophonetics of Black speakers, who have faced the most far-reaching changes of all South Africans in a relatively short space of time. The new middle-classes have moved from being among the more oppressed to among the more significant beneficiaries of legal and social change. The true advantage is felt by their children, who reap the benefits of good quality education in a relatively open society. Not surprisingly these children have made the greatest sociolinguistic transitions as well. I coin the term 'older Black South African English' for the variety in place during the apartheid era. Phonetically, this variety indexed the rift between Black and White cultures in the old South Africa. Even educated speakers and venerated politicians (with very few exceptions) drew on a system in English that was derived from that of Southern Bantu languages (such as isiXhosa and isiZulu) in terms of phonetics. In particular the vowel systems of Black and White English could not have been any more different.

Broader White varieties tended to raise short front vowels, centralise /ɪ/ and to pronounce the diphthongs of the PRICE and MOUTH sets as monophthongs. Very few of these were evident in older Black English. The most salient feature of older Black South African English (BSAE) is the absence of a distinction between long and short vowels (Lanham, 1978). GOOSE in older BSAE is accordingly a back vowel that has a tendency to merge with FOOT (see Van Rooy, 2004). The middle-class speakers studied here give no indication of any of the hallmarks of this older variety. A casual inspection of the database shows that for them GOOSE is always long, in contrast to FOOT. More significantly GOOSE is fronted to varying degrees, as Table 2 shows, which compares the distribution of the White and Black speakers in the fronting categories.

Table 2 Number of White and Black speakers in each category of fronting after a glide

	Front	Frontish	Central	Backish	Back
White	9	3	–	–	–
Black	8	3	1	–	–

Table 2 shows the following trends:

- There is a slightly greater spread of Black speakers compared to the White group. Statistical tests carried out in the longer version of this paper showed that this difference is not significant.

- Only one Black speaker has a central value, and none have a backish or back value. Most speakers have front or frontish values, with eight speakers being fully front.

- The group of Black speakers thus falls in quite closely with the trends shown by the White group, showing none of the vowel neutralisations and fully-back vowel typical of their immediately older generation. In effect they speak a different variety, more akin to what was historically White South African English.

Conclusion

This study demonstrates that middle-class South African students with English as their first language are fronting the GOOSE vowel. Fronted realisations were once firmly associated with 'Whiteness', but in the intervening twelve years since Lass's observations, this vowel has been adopted to varying extents by middle-class speakers from other groups.

In doing so they have turned it into a marker of youth and middle-class status, thereby deracialising the vowel to a large extent.

However, elsewhere, young Black speakers of less privileged school backgrounds than those of this study are embarking on creating an intermediate dialect, one with older Black English as a base, but with some new variants (see Da Silva, 2007), possibly carving out a difference between lower and upper middle class in the process. That is to say, this study focuses on the crossing over of the most elite Black varieties, but other processes are at work in other social groups.

References for this reading

Boersma, P. and Weenink, D. (2008) 'Praat: doing phonetics by computer' (Version 5.0.08) [Computer program], retrieved 11 February 2008, from http://www.praat.org/

Da Silva, A. (2007) 'South African English: a sociolinguistic analysis of an emerging variety', PhD thesis, University of the Witwatersrand.

Hopwood, D. (1928) *South African English Pronunciation*, Cape Town, Juta.

Lanham, L. (1978) 'South African English' in Lanham, L. W. and Prinsloo, K. P. (eds) *Language and Communication Studies in Southern Africa*, Cape Town, Oxford University Press.

Lass, R. (1995) 'South African English' in Mesthrie, R. (ed.) *Language and Social History: Studies in South African Sociolinguistics*, Cape Town, David Philip.

Van Rooy, B. (2004) 'Black South African English' in Schneider, E., Burridge, K., Kortmann, B., Mesthrie, R. and Upton, C. (eds) *A Handbook of Varieties of English*, vol. 1, *Phonology*, Berlin, Mouton de Gruyter.

READING B: Variation and agency

Robert J. Podesva

Specially commissioned for this book.

Introduction

Regan is a gay Asian-American man in his early thirties who grew up and lives in California. Like everyone, the way he talks varies considerably from one situation to the next. Sometimes he has a strong Californian accent, which comes through mainly in his vowels, while other times his regional accent is barely detectable. Sometimes he uses a wide pitch range, speaking high and low in the same sentence, while other times his pitch is more monotonic. The way Regan combines these two features is not predictable from the situation. In one rather informal setting, in which he is talking with friends about drinking and partying in gay clubs, he uses his most Californian vowels and widest pitch ranges. Yet in another situation that is equally informal and also highlights his gay identity – when talking about dating with a close friend, also gay – Regan's vowels are significantly less Californian and his pitch ranges are not as wide. Although many factors – the speaker, his social characteristics, the formality of the situation, and the foregrounding of gay identity – are constant across the situations, Regan's linguistic behaviour is rather different. In the former situation, Regan is highlighting a fun, party-going aspect of his identity.

Traditional approaches to variation have shown that many patterns of language use can be described in terms of the formality of the setting and the general social categories (like gender, class, age, and ethnicity) to which speakers belong. It might be tempting to conclude that variation patterns simply reflect social category membership and formality, but such a view fails to recognise that speakers – like Regan above – design their speech, moment by moment, to change subtly but constantly the social world. Minor shifts in linguistic behaviour can enable speakers to communicate a variety of messages, including alignments ('I agree with you'), stances ('I am passionate about this topic'), and displays of identity ('Even though it wasn't relevant a moment ago, I am emphasising that I identify as a gay man right now'). This reading sketches some of the ways that thinking about linguistic variation as a particular communicative strategy employed by speakers advances our understanding of variation and change in English.

Agency

A sociolinguistic variable is, very generally, more than one way of saying the same thing. Many variationists have come to believe that at some level (though not necessarily a conscious one), using one variant over another is a choice. The choice is strongly governed by both linguistic and social factors. For example, the sound /t/ at the end of the word *best* is sometimes pronounced strongly, but often not – for instance, saying *bes'* rather than *best*. To name just two of the many factors influencing deletion, /t/ is more likely to be omitted if the following word begins with a consonant (a linguistic constraint) and if the speaker is talking with peers as opposed to a superior (a social constraint). While linguistic and social constraints account for many of the patterns observed, they do not tell the whole story. The missing part of the story is speaker agency, or 'the socioculturally mediated capacity to act' (Ahearn, 2001, p. 112). Even though speakers might be encouraged by external forces to use one linguistic form (*best*) over another (*bes'*), they may have reasons for using the disfavoured variant. For example, even though talking with a patient might generally lead a doctor to pronounce /t/ rather frequently, the doctor could elect at some point to omit /t/, perhaps in an attempt to make the interaction more casual for the uneasy patient. In this case, the doctor's linguistic variation is not merely dictated by external factors; instead it transforms the situation into a more casual interaction.

Although I have used rather active language to characterise what speakers do with language, referring to the linguistic variants that they *choose* and the ways that they *transform* the situation, it is important to recognise that agency is constrained. As Ahearn's (2001) definition above implies, the capacity to act is neither a given nor constant. In the hypothetical doctor–patient interaction above, the patient could not have reframed the situation as casual as easily as the doctor could have simply by omitting /t/. Few interactions, if any, present speakers with an even playing field; approaches to variation that seek to account for speaker agency remind us to keep power in sight when analysing variation patterns. Issues of power aside, agency is further constrained by cultural intelligibility. The doctor's move to make the situation more casual can be successful only if speakers share the knowledge that '/t/-less' speech styles are typically less formal. Such shared knowledge renders the doctor's stylistic switch interpretable, or intelligible. Had the doctor altered her speech in some other way, perhaps by using very low pitch levels, the situation could not have been read as casual, since low pitch is not conventionally associated with more relaxed interactional styles.

Recognising agency does not mean that speakers always make conscious or deliberate linguistic choices. To be sure, sociolinguistic variables are often used in highly conscious, purposeful ways to construct various kinds of identity. Schilling-Estes (1998), for example, discusses how Rex O'Neal, an inhabitant of the Outer Banks, North Carolina, employs vernacular features of the Ocracoke Brogue when theatrically performing the local dialect. At the same time, linguistic features are also drawn on in subtler ways. Consider the relationship between pitch and gender. Though there are meaningful exceptions, men typically speak with lower pitch levels than women, due to a number of physiological and cultural factors. This gender pattern is learnt in early childhood before sex-based physiological differences arise (Graddol and Swann, 1989). By the time many men reach adulthood, using the lower reaches of their pitch ranges may have more to do with habit than a desire to project masculinity. Even though the use of low pitch contrasts in many respects with Rex O'Neal's theatrical Ocracoke Brogue performance, it is still said to be *performative* of identity. All men use high pitch on occasion (e.g. to emphasise words), revealing that even everyday, seemingly automatic linguistic practices like using low pitch require that speakers, on some level, exercise choices. Whenever speakers have the option of how to utter a sound, word, or phrase, they are subtly altering the social world by selecting one of the options over the other(s). Even if they end up using the most unmarked or expected form given the circumstances (e.g. a man's use of low pitch levels), they are reaffirming a previously assumed (e.g. masculine) identity.

Social meaning

That speakers can do things in the world with linguistic variation presupposes that linguistic features are socially meaningful. *Social meaning* refers to the stances, personal characteristics, and identities indexed through the deployment of linguistic forms in interaction. By way of example, a strongly articulated vowel can mean many things: it could mean that its speaker is speaking emphatically (stance), that the speaker is articulate (personal characteristic), or that the speaker is affiliated with a particular social group, such as geeks or nerds, that in the USA have been found to orient to clear, precise ways of speaking (identity).

The importance of social meaning has been recognised since the birth of modern sociolinguistics, when Labov (1972) found that patterns of phonological change in Martha's Vineyard depended on where Vineyarders stood with respect to an ideological divide between a local economy and an encroaching tourist economy relying heavily on mainland visitors. Yet, as Eckert (2005) points out, it is only recently that researchers have shown renewed interest in the topic. The social meaning approach extends the focus of research on language variation and change toward what variation, at any one time, means to speakers and hearers. As noted above, a given feature can index a number of different meanings, and one or other of these meanings will become salient in a particular context (Silverstein, 2003). Recognising this multiplicity of meanings that any given linguistic feature can index, Eckert (2008, p. 453) suggests that we think of meanings as an indexical field, or a 'constellation of ideologically related meanings, any one of which can be activated in the situated use of the variable'.

Given the variety of social moves linguistic features can be used to make, we can conclude that the social meaning of any particular feature is largely indeterminate – it cannot be determined in advance, and may not be clear-cut when actually uttered, an issue explored in greater depth by Jaffe (2009). The indeterminacy of social meaning is a crucial concept, as it is precisely the fact that indexical meanings are not predetermined that allows for meanings to be creatively reworked. In a study of a gay medical school student, Heath, I argue that Heath uses strongly released stops (on the other extreme from the omission of /t/ in words like *best*, discussed above) to index a 'prissy' stance when talking with his friends (Podesva, 2006). This stance derives from more conventional readings of /t/ releases as 'clear' and 'precise.' It would be misleading to label Heath's speech clear or precise, since his speech in this particular setting is characterised by a number of reductions that include the deletion of sounds, syllables and entire words. It is Heath's unique packaging of a hyper-precise feature (strongly released stops) in what is an otherwise informal style that facilitates the 'prissy' (or 'precise to an extreme') interpretation. Approaches to variation that focus on the importance of speaker choice in particular contexts of use highlight the fact that speakers can exploit the elastic mapping between linguistic form and meaning.

Language change

Studies of language change have traditionally been concerned first and foremost with changes in linguistic form, under the assumption that meaning is held constant during this process. Recently, variationists have begun attending to the ways in which meanings change as linguistic forms are held constant. Importantly, as the meanings of linguistic variants change, traces of former meanings are left behind. Consider the word *queer*. Once used primarily in a derogatory manner, the term was reclaimed by the queer movement as an emblem of pride. While *queer* generally refers to sexual minorities, it crucially has strongly subversive connotations. The term's subversiveness would not be recoverable if its earlier use as an epithet were not in some sense still part of its meaning. As McConnell-Ginet (2002) argues in her discussion of this and other terms, *queer* should not be viewed as an exceptional case, for all words 'figure in discursive history, a history that is never fully determinate and that looks back to sometimes conflicting assumptions and forward to a range of alternative possibilities'.

Viewing social meaning through a historical lens also encourages us to consider how speech varieties are recognised as such, through a process Agha (2003, p. 231) calls *enregisterment*, the process by which dialects or speaking styles come to be recognised and labelled as meaningful ways of speaking. Rather than taking the existence of speech varieties as descriptive facts, or focusing on the linguistic features that characterise them, we might instead examine the social processes that imbue dialects and styles with meaning. Beal (2009) investigates historical evidence dating back to the nineteenth century to uncover the emergence of the speech varieties spoken in Newcastle upon Tyne and Sheffield, in the north of England. She finds that popular descriptions of both varieties refer to linguistic features that are not unique to either variety. Beal argues that linguistic constructs like the 'Geordie' accent are not objective truths and that they must be sustained through a fair amount of ideological work. Treating a speech variety as a process, emerging through history, rather than a static object, enriches the study of language change because it enables us to examine not just how linguistic features take on new meanings, but how they come to be viewed as components of a speech variety in the first place.

Methodological considerations

Thinking of variation in terms of speaker agency encourages us to collect and analyse data from a wider range of social contexts than are typically considered. If speakers are doing things with variation, we should expect to see that their patterns of language use shift as the things they are doing change. Sociolinguistic variation studies have, from the beginning, emphasised the importance of eliciting a variety of styles, often thought of in terms of levels of formality. Labov (1972), for example, illustrated that the use of vernacular features increases as the level of formality decreases, a pattern that has been replicated many times over. Yet there is reason to believe that even interviews are limited in their ability to capture the extremes of linguistic behaviour. In their study on the retention of Asian English features among second generation British Asians, Sharma and Sankaran (2010) report that some speakers who consistently use standard, non-Asian features during sociolinguistic interviews may use Asian features far more extensively in more familiar contexts, like at home.

When we narrow our focus down to single individuals and specific moments of interaction, it is advantageous to examine how multiple linguistic features work together. Looking at combinations of features that serve similar interactive functions may highlight stretches of discourse when speakers' performances are particularly strong. In my study of Heath discussed above – in which I examined strongly released stops, high pitch levels and large drops in pitch on declarative statements, and falsetto voice quality – I found that the three features tended to cluster at points in the interaction when Heath was performing what I termed a gay 'diva' persona, when Heath portrays himself as socially superior and beautiful. The point here is that speakers do not merely use a feature here or there to construct their identities; they artfully recruit features across the levels of language to present coherent stylistic packages.

Conclusion

This reading has examined recent thinking on language variation that sees this as agentive, interactive and socially meaningful. I have considered a number of contributions this makes to our understanding of variation and change in English. Although taking such an approach improves our understanding of the phenomenon of linguistic variation, so too does it open up a number of questions. To what extent should the social meaning of a linguistic feature be thought of as pre-existing and to what extent should it be viewed as 'emerging' in unfolding discourse? How do we give reliable interpretations of these emergent social meanings? We also need to consider the relationship between production (what people say) and perception (how this is understood by others): how does this bear on social meaning? Johnstone and Kiesling (2008), for example, have shown that the pronunciation of (aw) as a monophthong in Pittsburgh (as in *dahntahn* – 'downtown') is associated with a Pittsburgher identity, but only by those listeners who do not produce the monophthongal variant in their own speech. These are some of the many issues that researchers will continue to address as they refine this relatively new approach to variation as an agentive practice that shifts social relations and alters identity, however subtly, from one moment to the next.

References for this reading

Agha, A. (2003) 'The social life of cultural value', *Language and Communication*, vol. 23, pp. 231–73.

Ahearn, L. M. (2001) 'Language and agency', *Annual Review of Anthropology*, vol. 30, pp. 109–37.

Beal, J. C. (2009) 'Enregisterment, commodification, and historical context: "Geordie" versus "Sheffieldish"', *American Speech*, vol. 84, pp. 138–56.

Eckert, P. (2005) 'Variation, convention, and social meaning. Plenary presented at the Annual Meeting of the Linguistic Society of America', Oakland, CA.

Eckert, P. (2008) 'Variation and the indexical field', *Journal of Sociolinguistics*, vol. 12, pp. 453–76.

Graddol, D. and Swann, J. (1989) *Gender Voices*, Cambridge, MA, Wiley-Blackwell.

Jaffe, A. M. (2009) 'Indeterminacy and regularization: a process-based approach to the study of sociolinguistic variation and language ideologies', *Sociolinguistic Studies*, vol. 3, pp. 229–51.

Johnstone, B. and Kiesling, S. (2008) 'Indexicality and experience: exploring the meanings of /aw/-monophthongization in Pittsburgh', *Journal of Sociolinguistics*, vol. 12, pp. 5–33.

Labov, W. (1972) *Sociolinguistic Patterns*, Philadelphia, PA, University of Pennsylvania Press.

McConnell-Ginet, S. (2002) '"Queering" semantics: definitional struggles' in Campbell-Kibler, K., Podesva, R., Roberts, S. and Wong, A. (eds) *Language and Sexuality: Contesting Meaning in Theory and Practice*, Stanford, CA, CSLI.

Podesva, R. J. (2006) 'Phonetic detail in sociolinguistic variation: its linguistic significance and role in the construction of social meaning', PhD dissertation, Stanford University.

Schilling-Estes, N. (1998) 'Investigating "self-conscious" speech: the performance register in Ocracoke English', *Language in Society*, vol. 27, pp. 53–83.

Sharma, D. and Sankaran, L. (2010) 'Beyond the sociolinguistic interview: style repertoire and social change in a minority community', Paper presented at Sociolinguistics Symposium, Southampton.

Silverstein, M. (2003) 'Indexical order and the dialectics of sociolinguistic life', *Language and Communication*, vol. 23, pp. 193–229.

Appendices

Appendix 1

History of English timeline

Date	Event	Description
55 BC	First Roman invasions of Britain	Julius Caesar invades Britain in 55 and 54 BC.
AD 43	Roman conquest of Britain	The Emperor Claudius invades Britain, leading to 400 years of Roman control of much of the island. Latin becomes the dominant language of culture and government.
410	Romans leave Britain	The end of Roman rule in Britain, leading to a period of gradual Roman withdrawal.
449	Anglo-Saxon invasions	Germanic tribes from the north of Europe settle in Britain, bringing with them their indigenous dialects.
c.450	Start of the 'Old English' period	What is known as the 'Early Old English' period runs from c.450–c.850.
597	Augustine arrives in Kent	The Roman missionary Augustine arrives in Britain, beginning the conversion of the Anglo-Saxons to Christianity.
658–680	Caedmon's *Hymn*	Caedmon, often described as the first English poet, composes his *Hymn*, a short, alliterative poem in Old English.
c.700	Ruthwell Cross	Construction of the stone cross in the parish church of Ruthwell (in present-day Scotland), which includes inscriptions in Latin and Northumbrian.
c.700	*Lindisfarne Gospels*	Illuminated Latin manuscripts of the four gospels of the New Testament are produced on Lindisfarne in Northumbria.

731	Bede's *Ecclesiastical History*	Bede writes his account of the Anglo-Saxon invasions of Britain in the 400s (*Historia Ecclesiastica Gentis Anglorum* or *Ecclesiastical History of the English People*).
*c.*750	*Beowulf* composed	Composition of the anonymous Old English epic poem *Beowulf*.
793	Viking invasions	According to the *Anglo-Saxon Chronicle*, the Vikings first come to Britain in 783, but the date most often cited for the first Viking raid is 793, when a group lands on Lindisfarne.
*c.*850	Start of the 'Later Old English' period	The 'Later Old English' period runs from *c.*850–*c.*1100.
871	Alfred becomes King of Wessex	Alfred the Great (born 849) is King of Wessex from 871–899. He instigates the translation of many Latin works into English.
878	Alfred defeats Danes at Ethandun	Following the Battle of Ethandun, a treaty is signed acknowledging the rule of the Danish king Guthrum in the north and east of Britain.
886	Danelaw established	The area governed by the Danes in the north and east of Britain, known as the Danelaw, is established.
*c.*892	*Anglo-Saxon Chronicles*	The collection of Old English writings chronicling the history of the Anglo-Saxons is first composed. It is originally compiled on Alfred's orders.
*c.*950–970	Old English glosses added to *Lindisfarne Gospels*	Glosses in Old English are added to the *Lindisfarne Gospels* by Aldred the Scribe. These are the oldest surviving English version of the gospels.
1066	Norman Conquest	William of Normandy defeats Harold Godwin at Hastings. Norman French is introduced as the language of the nobility in Britain.
*c.*1100	Start of the 'Middle English' period	The 'Middle English' period runs from *c.*1100–*c.*1450.

1171	Invasion of Ireland	Henry II (r. 1154–1189) invades Ireland and creates the 'Lordship of Ireland'. English and Norman French are introduced into the island.
1204	King John loses Duchy of Normandy	King John loses his lands in Normandy to France.
1284	Wales annexed	Edward I (r. 1272–1307) passes the Statute of Rhuddlan, establishing English law in Wales. Legal use of the Welsh language is retained, however.
1314	Robert the Bruce defeats English at Bannockburn	Robert the Bruce defeats Edward II, thus reasserting Scottish independence following wars between the Kingdoms of Scotland and England from the late thirteenth century onwards
1337	Start of Hundred Years' War	The Hundred Years' War between England and France lasts from 1337–1453. It ends with the loss of all England's French territories with the exception of the Channel Islands.
1362	English first used in Parliament	In addition to being used in Parliament for the first time, English becomes the official language of the courts of law, replacing French.
1382–1395	Wycliffe's translation of the Bible	John Wycliffe translates the Vulgate (Latin) version of the Bible into English.
1385	Trevisa's *Polychronicon*	John Trevisa's English translation of Ranulf Higden's *Polychronicon*, a chronicle originally written in Latin. Trevisa notes that children are abandoning the learning of French in schools, and shifting to English.

1399	Accession of Henry IV	Henry IV (r. 1399–1413) becomes the first king in England since the Norman invasion to speak English as a first language.
1430s	Growth of Chancery Standard	Government documents begin to be written in English rather than French. The dialect chosen for them is that used by clerks in the Chancery at Westminster.
c.1450	The start of the 'Early Modern English' period	The 'Early Modern English' period runs from c.1450–c.1750.
1473	Caxton prints first English book	William Caxton produces the first English printed book, *History of Troy*, while living in Bruges. He later returns to England where his first publication is Geoffrey Chaucer's *The Canterbury Tales* in 1478.
1490	Caxton's *Eneydos*	Caxton publishes an English translation of Virgil's *Aeneid*, titled *Eneydos*.
1526	Tyndale's translation of Bible	The first publication of William Tyndale's English translation of the New Testament.
1534	English Reformation	Henry VIII breaks with the Roman Catholic Church.
1536	First Act of Union between England and Wales	The Act of Union of 1536 creates a single state by annexing Wales to England. It makes English the only language of administration and the legal system in Wales.
1542	Henry VIII declares himself King of Ireland	The Crown of Ireland Act of 1542 establishes that the king of England is also 'King of Ireland'. This title replaces the 'Lordship of Ireland'.
1549	*Book of Common Prayer*	Publication of the first prayer book with the forms of service written in English. This comes to be viewed as one of the major works of English literature.

1560s	The plantation of Ireland	From 1560–1650, English, and later Scottish, settlers begin colonising Ireland. English is established throughout the island.
1562	Hawkins starts British slave trade	Sir John Hawkins takes slaves from the coast of West Africa to the Caribbean, marking the beginnings of the British slave trade.
1564	Shakespeare born	William Shakespeare (1554–1616), who in later centuries becomes canonised as the greatest writer in the English language, is born in Stratford-upon-Avon.
1586	Bullokar's *Grammar*	William Bullokar writes the first English grammar book, *Pamphlet for Grammar*.
1589	Puttenham's *Arte of English Poesie*	George Puttenham publishes his style guide, *The Arte of English Poesie*.
1600	East India Company chartered	The East India Company is granted a Royal Charter by Elizabeth I on 31 December 1600.
1603	Union of the English and Scottish crowns	King James I of England (James VI of Scotland) unites the crowns of England and Scotland.
1604	Cawdrey's *Table Alphabeticall*	Robert Cawdrey publishes his *A Table Alphabeticall*, the first monolingual dictionary in the English language.
1607	English settlement at Jamestown	Establishment of the Jamestown colony in Virginia. This is the first permanent English settlement in the New World.
1611	Publication of the *Authorised Version*	James I authorises the use of this bible translation in both his kingdoms. Known as the *Authorised Version* or the *King James Version*, for centuries this remains the standard English-language bible throughout the world.

1620	Pilgrim Fathers found Plymouth Colony	Plymouth Colony is founded in Massachusetts by the Pilgrim Fathers, who arrived in the New World in *The Mayflower*.
1623	Shakespeare's first folio	The first folio of Shakespeare's plays is published.
1627	Colonisation of Barbados	Having been claimed in the name of James I in 1625, a party of settlers arrives to occupy the island in February 1627.
1635	Académie française established	Cardinal Richelieu establishes the Académie française to act as the official authority on the French language.
1647	Ligon's account of Barbados	Richard Ligon's *A True and Exact History of the Island of Barbados* is published.
1653	Wallis's *Grammar*	Wallis publishes his *Grammatica linguae Anglicanae*. It is the last English grammar to be written in Latin.
1660	Royal Society established	The Royal Society of London for Improving Natural Knowledge is founded in November 1660, five months after the Restoration of the monarchy.
1665	*Philosophical Transactions*	The Royal Society's *Philosophical Transactions* is founded, the first and longest-running scientific journal in the world. It is published in English.
1687	Newton's *Principia Mathematica*	Isaac Newton publishes his *Philosophiæ Naturalis Principia Mathematica* in Latin.
1704	Newton's *Opticks*	Newton publishes his *Opticks* in English.
1707	Act of Union	The Act of Union unites the Parliaments of England and Scotland, creating the United Kingdom of Great Britain.

1712	Swift's *Proposal*	Jonathan Swift, Anglo-Irish writer and satirist, writes *A Proposal for Correcting, Improving and Ascertaining the English Tongue*, in which he argues for the standardisation and 'fixing' of the English language.
*c.*1750	Start of the 'Modern English' period	The 'Modern English' period runs from *c.*1750–*c.*1950.
1755	Johnson's *Dictionary*	Samuel Johnson publishes his *Dictionary of the English Language*, which becomes the model for English language lexicography for the next century and a half.
1762	Lowth's *Grammar*	Robert Lowth, Lord Bishop of London, writes his *Short Introduction to English Grammar*, one of the most influential of eighteenth-century English grammars and still in use in early twentieth-century Britain.
1770s	Concept of 'national literature'	Starting in Germany and quickly spreading throughout Europe, the idea of linking the nation state, the national literature and the national language becomes an influential political and cultural concept.
1775–1783	American War of Independence	The war begins as a conflict over tax between the British Parliament and the colonists in North America. In July 1776, thirteen British colonies declare their independence and create a new nation, the United States of America. This is the first country beyond the British Isles to have English as its primary language.

1788	Penal colonies established in Australia	The 'First Fleet' arrives in New South Wales with one and a half thousand emigrants, approximately 800 of whom are convicts. The first European colony in Australia is established.
1795	Murray's *English Grammar*	Grammarian Lindley Murray writes *English Grammar*, one of the most influential of eighteenth-century grammars, particularly in the United States.
1800	Acts of Union unite Britain and Ireland	Acts incorporating Ireland into Britain, and creating the United Kingdom of Great Britain and Ireland, are passed.
1803	The Louisiana Purchase	The United States buys France's North American territories, thus vastly increasing its size.
1807	British slave trade ends	The British Parliament passes the Act for the Abolition of the Slave Trade. While this ends the British slave trade, slavery itself remains legal in the British Empire until the Slavery Abolition Act of 1833.
1828	Webster's *American Dictionary*	Most of the differences between British and American spelling can be attributed to Noah Webster, whose most influential work is his *American Dictionary of the English Language*.
1836	Anglicism in British colonies	Charles Trevelyan outlines why English literature is better than vernacular literatures by way of providing a rationale for education via the medium of English in British colonies.
1840	Treaty of Waitangi	Treaty in which the Maoris cede the rights of government in New Zealand to the British.

1858	Proposal for *New English Dictionary*	The Philological Society in London draws up a proposal for a new dictionary of English based on historical principles. This project develops into the *Oxford English Dictionary.*
1867	Canada given self-government	The Dominion of Canada is created.
1901	Australia given self-government	The Commonwealth of Australia is established.
1922	Irish Free State established	The Irish Free State – a self-governing Dominion of the British Empire – is established in December 1922 as a result of the Anglo-Irish Treaty of 1921.
1922	BBC founded	The British Broadcasting Corporation (originally the British Broadcasting Company) is founded, becoming the first national broadcasting organisation in the world.
1928	Publication of the first edition of the *Oxford English Dictionary*	The production of the ten-volume *Oxford English Dictionary* takes over half a century, and involves contributions from hundreds of scholars and editors, led by James Murray (1837–1915). The first edition is finally completed in 1928.
1931	British Commonwealth created	The Commonwealth of Nations is formally created by the Statute of Westminster.
1947	Independence from British colonial rule for India	Following successive waves of resistance to British rule, India finally gains independence from Britain.
*c.*1950	Start of the 'Late Modern English' period	The 'Late Modern English' period begins *c.*1950.

1957	Independence from British colonial rule for Malay states	The states of the Malay peninsula gain independence in 1957. In 1963 they are joined by Sabah, Sarawak and Singapore to create the country of Malaysia. Singapore leaves to become an independent state in 1965.
1963	Independence from British colonial rule for Kenya	After at least a decade of often violent opposition to British rule, Kenya gains independence in 1963.
1963	First edition of ASCII	The American Standard Code for Information Interchange (ASCII) is devised to enable texts created on one computer to be read on others. It places users of non-English languages at a disadvantage because initially it makes no provision for non-English writing systems.
1969	Foundation of the ARPANET	The founding of the ARPANET (Advanced Research Project Agency Network), a computer network funded by the US Department of Defense. It has developed into today's internet.
1970s	Political migration	The 1970s witness large-scale migration of political exiles fleeing oppressive regimes in countries including Chile, South Africa and parts of Eastern Europe, to settle in Western Europe, the USA and Canada.
1981	*Macquarie Dictionary* published	The first edition of the *Macquarie Dictionary*, which is 'the first comprehensive dictionary of Australian English', is published.
1986	*Decolonising the Mind*	The Kenyan writer Ngũgĩ wa Thiong'o writes *Decolonising the Mind*, in which he rejects an English language literature canon for Kenya.

1987	Publication of the first COBUILD dictionary	The Collins COBUILD dictionary is the first to be based on statistical analysis of contemporary English speech and text. The work is carried out by researchers at the University of Birmingham under the direction of John Sinclair.
1988	Proposal of UNICODE	Proposed by Joseph Becker, a computer scientist working for Xerox, UNICODE is a single code based on ASCII but potentially capable of representing every symbol in every human writing system. It has helped to erode the initial dominance of English on the internet.
1990	Creation of the first computer search engine	Archie, the first search engine, is created by Alan Emtage, a postgraduate student at McGill University. It is essentially an automatically updated index of all files available via the internet.
1991	Launch of the World Wide Web	The World Wide Web is launched by Tim Berners-Lee, a scientist working for the European Organisation for Nuclear Research.
1991	Launch of BBC World News	In the wake of the First Gulf War, the BBC World Service launches a television news channel to compete with CNN (the US cable news channel).
1994	End of apartheid in South Africa	Although South Africa gained independence from Britain in 1910, it is not until the first free elections of 1994 (four years after Nelson Mandela's release from jail) that apartheid is ended and all people of the country can be said to be 'free'.

1996	Founding of Al-Jazeera	Based in Doha, Al-Jazeera is the first major global news provider to have its headquarters outside the English-speaking world. Its English-language sister channel, Al Jazeera English, is launched in 2006.
1997	First social network site	SixDegrees is the first dedicated social networking site on the World Wide Web. It proves a commercial failure, but pioneers many of the features of later social network sites such as Facebook (launched 2004), Mixi (2004), Bebo (2005) and Twitter (2006).
1998	Launch of Google	Google – the company behind what becomes the world's most popular web search engine – is founded by Larry Page and Sergei Brin, two former Stanford University PhD students. In 2004, it begins its project for a searchable database of all printed books.
2000s	Citizenship tests	Citizenship tests, which have been used in the USA and Canada for many years, come into being in Britain and several European countries, as well as New Zealand and Australia.
2001	Launch of Wikipedia	Launched by the entrepreneur, Jimmy Wales, and the philosopher, Larry Sanger, Wikipedia is the world's first open content encyclopaedia.

2003	English-medium education policy introduced in Malaysia	English is reintroduced into Malaysian schools as a medium of instruction for science and mathematics, following its wholesale replacement by the national language over the previous thirty years. In 2010 this policy is reversed, with English once again becoming a subject rather than a medium of instruction.
2008	English-medium education policy introduced in Rwanda	The Rwandan government decides to remove French as one of the country's official languages, and introduce a policy of English-medium education to replace its existing French-medium system.

Appendix 2

A note on describing English

Joan Swann

In writing about English, we need a systematic way of describing the language. We refer to features of English throughout the book, but particularly in Chapters 5 and 7 where we discuss the characteristics of contemporary varieties and how linguists have studied continuing variation and change. Because the book is aimed at readers who may have little or no experience of linguistic study, we have tried to keep description fairly simple, but we do adopt certain principles and concepts that underpin linguistic description. The most important of these is that English, and other languages, tend to be described according to different linguistic levels, as outlined in the box below.

Levels of description

Lexis, or vocabulary: **lexical variation** refers to variation in vocabulary; for instance, the words used in different geographical varieties of English. For example, a stream is known as a *burn* in Scotland and parts of Northumberland and a *beck* in other parts of northern England, but neither term is used in the south.

Grammar: this includes word structure, or **morphology**. For instance, standard English has two present tense verb forms ('I, you, we or they *walk*'; but 'he/she/it *walks*') whereas different patterns ('I *walks*', 'she *walk*') are found in some other varieties. Grammar also covers sentence structure, or **syntax**. You will see in Chapter 5 that Irish English has the structure 'It's looking for more land a lot of them are' (compare the standard 'A lot of them are looking for more land').

Semantics, or meaning: Chapter 1 refers to historical changes in the meaning of the word *wife*, for instance.

Orthography, or writing system: Chapter 1 refers to changes in spelling conventions between Old English and contemporary varieties.

Phonology, or the sound system of a variety: for instance, whether you pronounce the 'r' sound in words such as *card* and *car*.

Within these levels we sometimes use further technical terms (e.g. for an aspect of grammar), but we always illustrate any points we want to make with examples, so that the meaning should be clear.

Describing sounds

Many studies of both longer term historical change and contemporary variation and change in English have looked at the sounds of language. Because conventional spelling is not always a good guide to pronunciation, we have used symbols provided by the International Phonetic Alphabet (IPA) to represent sounds more accurately and systematically. You can find similar symbols used in dictionaries to represent the pronunciation of words. We do not have space for a complete account of the sounds of English, but the main symbols used in this book are listed below. To illustrate these we use a guide word. Unless indicated otherwise the model of pronunciation is that of a high-status speaker from the south of England (you could also think of a newsreader on the BBC World Service).

Main vowel symbols used in this book

a	as in *pat* (northern English)
ʊ	as in *put*
ɒ	as in *pot*
ʌ	as in *putty*
ɛ	as in *pet*
ə	as in *about* (initial unstressed syllable)
i:	as in *key*
ɑ:	as in *car*
ɔ:	as in *port*
u:	as in *coo*
eɪ	as in *bay*
aɪ	as in *buy*
aʊ	as in *cow*
ɔɪ	as in *foil*

Describing vowels

Linguists describe sounds in relation to the way they are articulated. Vowels are described according to the highest point of the tongue during their articulation – whether this is relatively **high** or **low**; and towards the **front**, a **central** position or the **back** of the mouth. Two further dimensions are the duration of the vowel – whether it is **long** or **short** (the : symbol, rather like a colon, indicates a long vowel; we have shown this above for common long vowels in English, but the symbol may be added to any vowel to show lengthening); and whether it is produced with or without the lips **rounded**. In the list above, i: is a high front vowel; it is also a long vowel; and it is unrounded – pronounced without lip-rounding; by contrast u: is a high back vowel, long, and rounded. If you say these vowels you should be able to feel a difference. These dimensions are useful in describing variation and change. For instance, Chapter 7 refers to changes in varieties of English that involve certain vowels being 'fronted', 'raised' or 'centralised' – they are pronounced further forward, or higher in the mouth or in a more central position.

The last four vowels in the list above are **diphthongs**, where the tongue glides from one position to another. These are often represented, as above, by two symbols, indicating their starting and end point.

Main consonant symbols used in this book

Plosives:

p	as in *pea*		b	as in *bee*	[bilabial]
t	as in *toe*		d	as in *doe*	[alveolar]
k	as in *cap*		g	as in *gap*	[velar]

Fricatives:

f	as in *fat*		v	as in *vat*	[labio-dental]
θ	as in *thin*		ð	as in *this*	[dental]
s	as in *sip*		z	as in *zip*	[alveolar]
ʃ	as in *ship*				
ʍ	as in *why* (older pronunciation – like 'hw')				[labio-velar]
x	as in *loch* (Scots)				[velar]

Affricate:

tθ   a combination of t and θ: occurs in *thin* in some New York speech

Nasals:

m	as in *map*	[bilabial]
n	as in *nap*	[alveolar]
ŋ	as in *bang*	[velar]

Approximant:

r   as in *red*

Lateral approximant:

l   as in *led*

Describing consonants

Consonants are usually described according to three dimensions.

Their manner of articulation – this refers to how consonants are articulated, and is a dimension often used in describing variation and change. The list above identifies the following characteristics:

- Plosive: an obstruction is formed in the mouth which completely blocks the airstream. The air builds up behind the obstruction, and is then suddenly released in a little 'explosion'.
- Nasal: as with plosives, there is a complete obstruction in the mouth, but the air flows out through the nose instead.
- Fricative: the mouth is obstructed enough to cause friction, but not enough to block the airstream completely.
- Affricate: an affricate begins like a plosive, but the obstruction is released only slightly. Instead of a little 'explosion', the sound ends with friction. An affricate is a combination of a plosive with a fricative.
- Approximant: the vocal tract is narrowed, but not quite enough to cause friction.
- Lateral (approximant): in the pronunciation of lateral sounds, the tongue is held against the roof of the mouth, but it is lowered at the side to allow the air to escape around the edges.

Their place of articulation – for instance, the set of plosives, fricatives and nasals above are distinguished according to where in the mouth they are articulated:

- bilabial: produced with both lips together
- dental: produced with the tongue against the teeth
- labio-dental: produced with the teeth against the lower lip

- alveolar: produced with the tongue against the alveolar ridge (the ridge just behind the teeth)
- velar: produced with the back of the tongue against the velum (or soft palate)
- labio-velar: produced with the lips rounded and the back of the tongue against or near the velum (soft palate).

Whether or not they are voiced – 'voiced' sounds are produced with vibration of the vocal cords in the larynx, or voice box; 'voiceless' sounds are produced without vocal cord vibration. In the list of plosives and fricatives above, the sounds on the left are voiceless and those on the right are voiced (e.g. if you say 'p' and then 'b' you should hear a difference). The nasals and approximants are all voiced.

Phonological and phonetic transcription

As mentioned above, phonology refers to the sound *system* of a language. Each distinctive sound in a word (e.g. p, a, t in the word *pat*) is a **phoneme**. When they are transcribed, phonemes are conventionally represented between slashes – for example, /p/.

Another level of transcription is **phonetic** transcription, which seeks to give an accurate indication of pronunciation. In this case symbols are represented between square brackets – for example, [p]. Additional symbols may be added to make transcription more accurate – for example, the superscript ^{h} in [p^h] means that the sound is pronounced with aspiration.

This phonemic/phonetic distinction is evident in the description of varieties of English and other languages. For instance, Chapters 5 and 7 discuss differences in the distribution of the /r/ sound in different varieties of English (i.e. when the sound occurs and when not – in some cases /r/ occurs in words such as *car*, in others not). But linguists may also be concerned with differences in how sounds are actually pronounced: for instance, Chapter 7 discusses William Labov's study of speech in New York city where the initial consonant in words such as ***thin*** may be pronounced as a 'dental fricative' [θ], an 'affricate' [tθ] or a 'plosive' [t].

References

Adams, J. (1852) Letter to the President of Congress (5 September 1780) in Adams, C. F., *The Works of John Adams*, Boston, Little Brown.

Adamson, H. D. and Regan, V. M. (1991) 'The acquisition of community speech norms by Asian immigrants learning English as a second language', *Studies in Second Language Acquisition*, vol. 13, pp. 1–22.

Agnihotri, R. K. (1998) 'Mixed codes and their acceptability' in Agnihotri, R. K., Khanna, A. L. and Sachdev, I. (eds) *Social Perspectives on Second Language Learning*, New Delhi, Thousand Oaks, London, Sage.

Allen, A. (1999) Communication at the English Speaking Union world members' conference, Sydney.

Bailey, R. W. (1996) *Nineteenth-Century English*, Ann Arbor, MN, University of Michigan Press.

Bailey, R. W. (2006) 'English among the languages' in Mugglestone, L. (ed.) *The Oxford History of English*, Oxford, Oxford University Press.

Baker, P. and Eversley, J. (eds) (2000) *Multilingual Capital*, London, Battlebridge.

Barber, C., Beal, J. C. and Shaw, P. A. (2009) *The English Language: A Historical Introduction* (2nd edn), Cambridge, Cambridge University Press.

Barrett, R. (1998) 'Markedness and styleswitching in performances by African American drag queens' in Myers-Scotton, C. (ed.) *Codes and Consequences: Choosing Linguistic Varieties*, New York, Oxford University Press.

Bartlett, R. (1993) *The Making of Europe: Conquest, Colonization and Cultural Change, 950–1350*, London, Allen Lane.

Baxter, G., Blythe, R., Croft, W. and McKane, A. (2009) 'Modeling language change: an evaluation of Trudgill's theory of the emergence of New Zealand English', *Language Variation and Change*, vol. 21, pp. 257–96.

BBC (2009) *English Takes Hold in Afghanistan* [online], http://news.bbc.co.uk/2/hi/south_asia/7493285.stm (Accessed 5 May 2011).

Bell, A. (1984) 'Language style as audience design', *Language in Society*, vol. 13, pp. 145–204.

Bhatt, R. (2005) 'Expert discourses, local practices, and hybridity: the case of Indian Englishes' in Canagarajah, A. S. (ed.) *Reclaiming the Local in Language Policy and Practice*, New York and London, Routledge.

Bickerton, D. (1984) 'The language bioprogram hypothesis', *The Behavioral and Brain Sciences*, vol. 7, pp. 173–221.

Billings, S. (2009) 'Speaking beauties: linguistic posturing, language inequality, and the construction of a Tanzanian beauty queen', *Language in Society*, vol. 38, pp. 581–606.

Blommaert, J. (1999) *State Ideology and Language in Tanzania*, Köln, Rudiger Koppe Verlag.

Blommaert, J. (2005) 'Situating language rights: English and Swahili in Tanzania revisited', *Journal of Sociolinguistics*, vol. 9, no. 3, pp. 390–417.

Bloomfield, L. (1933) *Language*, New York, Holt.

British Council (1997) *English Language Teaching*, London, The British Council.

Bruthiaux, P. (2003) 'Squaring the circles: issues in modeling English worldwide', *International Journal of Applied Linguistics*, vol. 13, no. 2, pp. 159–78.

Buchanan, J. (1757) *Linguae Britannicae Vera Pronunciatio*, London.

Buchstaller, I. and D'Arcy, A. (2009) 'Localized globalization: a multi-local, multivariate investigation of "be like"', *Journal of Sociolinguistics*, vol. 13, pp. 291–331.

Carver, C. M. (1987) *American Regional Dialects: A Word Geography*, Ann Arbor, MI, University of Michigan Press.

Chambers, J. K. (1999) 'Canadian English: 250 years in the making' in Barber, K. (ed.) *The Canadian Oxford Dictionary*, Toronto, Oxford University Press.

Christian Science Monitor (2003) 'English Sans French' [online], *Christian Science Monitor*, 14 March, http://www.csmonitor.com/2003/0314/p10s02-comv.html (Accessed 10 February 2010).

CJGTC [Prime Minister's Commission on Japan's Goals in the Twenty-First Century] (2000) *The Frontier Within: Individual Empowerment and Better Governance in the New Millennium*, Chapter 1 Overview.

Cooper, C. (1687) *The English Teacher*, London.

Coupland, N. and Aldridge, M. (2009) 'Introduction: a critical approach to the revitalisation of Welsh', *International Journal of the Sociology of Language*, vol. 195, pp. 5–13.

Crystal, D. (1988) *The English Language*, Harmondsworth, Penguin.

Crystal, D. (1998) *Language Play*, London, Penguin.

Crystal, D. (2003) *The Cambridge Encyclopedia of The English Language* (2nd edn), Cambridge, Cambridge University Press.

Crystal, D. (2005) *The Stories of English*, London, Penguin.

Dillard, J. L. (1972) *Black English: Its History and Usage in the United States*, New York, Random House.

Dubois, S. and Horvath, B. (2000) 'When the music changes you change too: gender and language change in Cajun English', *Language Variation and Change*, vol. 11, pp. 287–313.

Dyja, E. (ed.) (2005) *BFI Film Handbook*, London, British Film Institute.

Eckert, P. and McConnell-Ginet, S. (1999) 'New generalizations and explanations in language and gender research', *Language in Society*, vol. 28, pp. 185–201.

Encyclopaedia Britannica (2008) *Britannica Book of the Year*, Chicago, IL, Encyclopaedia Britannica.

Feng, A. (ed.) (forthcoming) *English Language in Education and Societies across Greater China*, Bristol, Multilingual Matters.

Filppula, M. (1991) 'Urban and rural varieties of Hiberno-English' in Cheshire, J. (ed.) *English around the World: Sociolinguistic Perspectives*, Cambridge, Cambridge University Press.

Finegan, E. (2006) 'English in North America' in Hogg, R. and Denison, D. (eds) *A History of the English Language*, Cambridge, Cambridge University Press.

Foley, J. A. (ed.) (1999) *English in New Cultural Contexts*, New York, Oxford University Press.

Fought, C. (1999) 'I'm not from nowhere: negative concord in Chicano English', Paper presented at NWAVE 28, University of Toronto.

Fought, C. (2003) *Chicano English in Context*, Basingstoke, Palgrave Macmillan.

Foulkes, P., Docherty, G. and Watt, D. (2005) 'Phonological variation in child-directed speech', *Language*, vol. 81, pp. 177–206.

Freeborn, D. (1992) *From Old English to Standard English*, Basingstoke, Macmillan.

Freeborn, D. (2006) *From Old English to Standard English*, Basingstoke, Palgrave Macmillan.

Gardner-Chloros, P. (1995) 'Code-switching in community, regional and national repertoires: the myth of the discreteness of linguistic systems' in Milroy, L. and Muysken, P. (eds) *One Speaker, Two Languages: Cross-Disciplinary Perspectives on Code-Switching*, Cambridge, Cambridge University Press.

Giles, H. and Smith, P. (1979) 'Accommodation theory: optimal levels of convergence' in Giles, H. and St Clair, R. (eds) *Language and Social Psychology*, Oxford, Blackwell.

Gordon, E., Campbell, L., Hay, J., Maclagan, M., Sudbury, A. and Trudgill, P. (2004) *New Zealand English: Its Origins and Evolution*, Cambridge, Cambridge University Press.

Government of Ireland (2006) *Statement on the Irish Language* [online], http://www.pobail.ie/en/IrishLanguage/StatementontheIrishLanguage2006 (Accessed 13 May 2010).

Graddol, D. (1999) 'The decline of the native speaker' in Graddol, D. and Meinhof, U. H. (eds) *English in a Changing World*, AILA Review 13, pp. 57–68.

Graddol, D. (2006) *English Next*, London, The British Council.

Graddol, D. (2010) *English Next: India*, London, The British Council.

Guy, G. R. and Boyd, S. (1990) 'The development of morphological class', *Language Variation and Change*, vol. 2, pp. 1–18.

Harris, J. (1991) 'Ireland' in Cheshire, J. (ed.) *English around the World: Sociolinguistic Perspectives*, Cambridge, Cambridge University Press.

Haugen, E. (1966) 'Dialect, language, nation', *American Anthropologist*, vol. 68, no. 4, pp. 922–35.

Hewings, A. and Tagg, C. (2012) *The Politics of English: Conflict, Competition, Co-Existence* Abingdon, Routledge/Milton Keynes, The Open University.

Hickey, R. (2004) *A Sound Atlas of Irish English,* Berlin and New York, Mouton de Gruyter.

Hickey, R. (2007) *Irish English: History and Present-Day Forms*, Cambridge, Cambridge University Press.

Hickey, R. (2007) 'Southern Irish English' in Britain, D. (ed.) *Language in the British Isles* (2nd edn), Cambridge, Cambridge University Press.

Hickey, T. (2009) 'Code-switching and borrowing in Irish', *Journal of Sociolinguistics*, vol. 13, no. 5, pp. 670–88.

Holm, J. (1982) *Dictionary of Bahamian English*, New York, Lexik House.

Holm, J. (2000) *An Introduction to Pidgins and Creoles*, Cambridge, Cambridge University Press.

Holmes, J. and Kerswill, P. (2008) 'Contact is not enough: a response to Trudgill', *Language in Society*, vol. 37, pp. 273–7.

Horne, D. (1997) Foreword in Delbridge, A. (ed.) *The Macquarie Dictionary* (3rd edn), Sydney, Macquarie Library.

Horvath, B. M. (1985) *Variation in Australian English: The Sociolects of Sydney*, Cambridge, Cambridge University Press.

Internet World Stats (2010) *Internet World Users by Language: Top 10 Languages* [online], http://www.internetworldstats.com/stats7.htm (Accessed 30 May 2011).

Jenkins, J. (2003) 'Intelligibility in lingua franca discourse' in Burton, J. and Clennell, C. (eds) *Developing Interactive Skills in Spoken Discourse*, Alexandria, TESOL Publications.

Jenkins, J. (2007) *English as a Lingua Franca: Attitude and Identity*, Oxford, Oxford University Press.

Jenkins, J., Modiano, M. and Seidlhofer, B. (2001) 'Euro-English', *English Today* 68, vol. 7, no. 4, pp. 13–19.

Johnson, S. (1755) *A Dictionary of the English Language*, London, J. and P. Knapton.

Kachru, B. (1992) 'Teaching world Englishes' in Kachru, B. (ed.) *The Other Tongue: English across Cultures* (2nd edn), Chicago, IL, University of Illinois Press.

Kachru, B. (2001) 'World Englishes and culture wars' in Kiong, T. C., Pakir, A., Choon, B. K., and Goh, R. B. H. (eds) *Ariels: Departures and Returns: Essays for Edwin Thumboo*, Singapore, Oxford University Press.

Kerswill, P. and Williams, A. (2000) 'Creating a new town koine: children and language change in Milton Keynes', *Language in Society*, vol. 29, pp. 65–115.

Kurath, H. (1964) 'British sources of selected features of American pronunciation: problems and methods' in Abercrombie, D., Fry, D. B., MacCarthy, P. A. D., Scott, N. C. and Trim, J. L. M. (eds) *In Honour of Daniel Jones: Papers Contributed on the Occasion of His Eightieth Birthday 12 September 1961*, London, Longman.

Labov, W. (1972) *Sociolinguistic Patterns*, Philadelphia, PA, University of Pennsylvania Press.

Labov, W. (1990) 'The intersection of sex and social class in the course of linguistic change', *Language Variation and Change*, vol. 2, pp. 205–54.

Labov, W. (2001) *Principles of Linguistic Change: Social Factors*, Oxford, Wiley- Blackwell.

Labov, W., Ash, S. and Boberg, C. (1997) *A National Map of the Regional Dialects of American English* [online], http://www.ling.upenn.edu/phono_atlas/ NationalMap/NationalMap.html (Accessed 18 May 2011).

Lamy, M.-N. (2007) 'Franglais' in Graddol, D., Leith, D., Swann, J., Rhys, M. and Gillen, J. (eds) *Changing English*, Abingdon, Routledge/Milton Keynes, The Open University.

Leitner, G. (2004) *Australia's Many Voices: Ethnic Englishes, Indigenous and Migrant Languages, Policy and Education*, Berlin, Mouton de Gruyter.

Le Page, R. B. and Tabouret-Keller, A. (1985) *Acts of Identity: Creole-based Approaches to Language and Ethnicity*, Cambridge, Cambridge University Press.

Ligon (1647) *A True and Exact History of the Island of Barbados*, London, Moseley.

Li Wei (1998) 'Banana split? Variations in language choice and code-switching patterns of two groups of British-born Chinese in Tyneside' in Jacobson, R. (ed.) *Codeswitching Worldwide*, Trends in Linguistics: Studies and Monographs 106, Berlin, Mouton de Gruyter.

Macafee, C. (1983) *Varieties of English Around the World: Glasgow*, Amsterdam, Benjamins.

Macafee C. (2003) 'Studying Scots vocabulary' in Corbett, J., McClure, D. and Stuart-Smith, J. (eds) *The Edinburgh Companion to Scots*, Edinburgh, Edinburgh University Press.

Mahboob, A. and Ahmar, N. H. (2008) 'Pakistani English: phonology' in Mesthrie, R. (ed.) *Varieties of English 4: Africa, South and Southeast Asia*, Berlin, Mouton de Gruyter.

Mazrui, A. (1973) 'The English language and the origins of African nationalism' in Bailey, R. W. and Robinson, J. L. (eds) *Varieties of Present-Day English*, London, Macmillan.

McArthur, T. (1998) *The English Languages*, Cambridge, Cambridge University Press.

McArthur, T. (2002) *Oxford Guide to World English*, Oxford, Oxford University Press.

McCormick, K. (2002) *Language in Cape Town's District Six*, Oxford, Oxford University Press.

McCormick, K. (2010) 'From margin to mainstream: the growing domain of language switching and mixing in contemporary South African television drama' in Hoosnain, I. and Chauhudry, S. (eds) *Problematising Language Studies: Cultural, Theoretical and Applied Perspectives*, New Delhi, Aakar Publishers.

McCrum, R., Cran, W. and MacNeil, R. (1992) *The Story of English* (2nd edn), London, Faber & Faber/BBC Books.

Meeuwis, M. and Blommaert, J. (1998) 'A mono-lectal view of code-switching: layered code-switching among Zaireans in Belgium' in Auer, P. (ed.) *Code-Switching in Conversation: Language, Interaction and Identity*, London and New York, Routledge.

Mesthrie, R. (1992) *English in Language Shift*, Cambridge, Cambridge University Press.

Meyerhoff, M. (1994) 'Sounds pretty ethnic, eh?: a pragmatic particle in New Zealand English', *Language in Society*, vol. 23, no. 3, pp. 367–88.

Meyerhoff, M. and Niedzielski, N. (2003) 'The globalisation of vernacular variation', *Journal of Sociolinguistics*, vol. 7, pp. 534–55.

Meyerhoff, M. and Walker, J. A. (2007) 'The persistence of variation in individual grammars: copula absence in 'urban sojourners' and their stay-at-home peers, Bequia (St Vincent and the Grenadines)', *Journal of Sociolinguistics*, vol. 11, pp. 346–66.

Milroy, J. and Milroy, L. (1985) *Authority in Language*, London, Routledge and Kegan Paul.

Milroy, L. (2002) 'Social networks' in Chambers, J. K., Trudgill, P. and Schilling-Estes, N. (eds) *The Handbook of Language Variation and Change*, Oxford, Blackwell.

Ministry of Basic Education, Sport and Culture (2003) *The Language Policy for Schools in Namibia: Discussion Document*, Windhoek, Namibia, Ministry of Basic Education, Sport and Culture.

Mollin, S. (2007) 'New variety or learner English? Criteria for variety status and the case of Euro-English', *English World-Wide*, vol. 28, no. 2, pp. 167–85.

Moyer, M. G. (1998) 'Bilingual conversation strategies in Gibraltar' in Auer, P. (ed.) *Code-Switching in Conversation: Language, Interaction and Identity*, London and New York, Routledge.

Mufwene, S. (1986) 'The universalist and substrate hypotheses complement one another' in Muysken, P. and Smith, N. (eds) *Substrata Versus Universals in Creole Gensis*, Amsterdam, Benjamins.

Mufwene, S. (2006) 'Pidgins and creoles' in Kachru, B., Kachru, Y. and Nelson, C. (eds) *The Handbook of World Englishes*, Oxford, Blackwell.

Myers-Scotton, C. (1989) 'Codeswitching with English: types of switching, types of communities', *World Englishes*, vol. 8, no. 3, pp. 333–46.

Ndjoze-Ojo, B. R. K. (2004) 'Governance, institutional reform and policy outcomes in Africa: the case of the Namibian language policy in education' in Olowu, D. and Mukwena, R. (eds) *Governance in Southern Africa and Beyond: Experiences of Institutional and Public Policy Reform in Developing Countries*, Windhoek, Gamsberg Macmillan Publishers.

Orton, H. and Wright, N. (1974) *A Word Geography of England*, London, Seminar Press.

O'Sullivan, M. (2002) 'Reform implementation and the realities within which teachers work: a Namibian case study', *Compare: A Journal of Comparative and International Education*, vol. 32, no. 2, pp. 219–37.

Parker, G. (ed.) (1986) *The World: An Illustrated History*, London, Time Books.

Pennycook, A. (2003) 'Global Englishes, Rip Slyme, and performativity', *Journal of Sociolinguistics*, vol. 7, no. 4, pp. 513–33.

Pennycook, A. (2007) *Global Englishes and Transcultural Flows*, Abingdon, Routledge.

Pope, J., Meyerhoff, M. and Ladd, R. D. (2007) 'Forty years of language change on Martha's Vineyard', *Language*, vol. 83, pp. 615–27.

Poplack, S. and Sankoff, D. (1987) 'The Philadelphia story in the Spanish Caribbean', *American Speech*, vol. 62, no. 4, pp. 291–314.

Pütz, M. (2006) 'The dynamics of language policy in Namibia: a view from cognitive sociolinguistics' in van der Walt, C. (ed.) *Living through Languages: An African Tribute to René Dirven*, Stellenbosch, Sun Press.

Quirk, R. (1985) 'The English language in a global context' in Quirk, R. and Widdowson, H. G. (eds) *English in the World*, Cambridge, Cambridge University Press.

Quirk, R. (1990) 'Language varieties and standard language', *English Today*, vol. 6, no. 1, pp. 3–10.

Rahman, T. (1997) 'The Urdu–English controversy in Pakistan', *Modern Asian Studies*, vol. 31, no. 1, pp. 177–207.

Rampton, B. (2005) *Crossing: Language and Ethnicity among Adolescents* (2nd edn), Manchester, St Jerome Press (1st edn 1995, London, Longman).

Ramson, W. S. (ed.) (1988) *The Australian National Dictionary: A Dictionary of Australianisms on Historical Principles*, Melbourne, Oxford University Press.

Rickford, J. and McNair-Knox, F. (1994) 'Addressee- and topic-influenced style shift: a quantitative sociolinguistic study' in Biber, D. and Finegan, E. (eds) *Sociolinguistic Perspectives on Register*, New York, Oxford University Press.

Roberts, J. (1994) 'Acquisition of variable rules: (-t, d) deletion and (ing) production in preschool children', unpublished PhD dissertation, Philadelphia, PA, University of Pennsylvania.

Roberts, J. and Labov, W. (1995) 'Learning to talk Philadelphian: acquisition of short *a* by preschool children', *Language Variation and Change*, vol. 7, pp. 101–12.

Romaine, S. (1975) *Linguistic Variability in the Speech of Some Edinburgh Schoolchildren*, MLitt Thesis, University of Edinburgh.

Sánchez, R. (1982) 'Our linguistic and social context' in Amastae, J. and Elias-Olivares, L. (eds) *Spanish in the United States: Sociolinguistic Aspects*, Cambridge, Cambridge University Press.

Schilling-Estes, N. (2004) 'Constructing ethnicity in interaction', *Journal of Sociolinguistics,* vol. 8, pp. 163–95.

Schleef, E., Meyerhoff, M. and Clark, L. (2011) 'Teenagers' acquisition of variation: a comparison of locally-born and migrant teens' realisation of English (ing) in Edinburgh and London', *English World-Wide*, vol. 32, no. 2, pp. 206–36.

Schneider, E. (ed) (1997) *Englishes around the World*, Amsterdam, Benjamins.

Schneider, E. (2004) 'The English dialect heritage of the southern United States' in Hickey, R. (ed.) *Transported Dialects: The Legacy of Non-Standard Colonial English*, Cambridge, Cambridge University Press.

Schneider, E. (2007) *Postcolonial Englishes: Varieties around the World*, Cambridge, Cambridge University Press.

Scobbie, J. M. and Stuart-Smith, J. (2008) 'Quasi-phonemic contrast and the fuzzy inventory: examples from Scottish English' in Avery, P., Dresher, E. B. and Rice, K. (eds) *Contrast: Perception and Acquisition. Selected Papers from the Second International Conference on Contrast in Phonology*, Berlin, Mouton de Gruyter.

Sebba, M. (1997) *Contact Languages: Pidgins and Creoles*, London, Macmillan.

Sebba, M. (2009) 'Pidgins and creole Englishes' in Culpeper, J., Katamba, F., Kerswill, P., Wodak, R. and McEnery, T. (eds) *English Language: Description, Variation and Context*, Hounslow, Palgrave Macmillan.

Seidlhofer, B. (2010) 'Giving VOICE to English as a lingua franca' in Facchinetti, R., Crystal, D. and Seidlhofer, B. (eds) *From International to Local English – and Back Again*, Frankfurt, Peter Lang.

Sheridan, T. (1762) *A Course of Lectures on Elocution*, London, W. Strahan.

Siegel, J. (1995) 'How to get a laugh in Fijian: code-switching and humour', *Language in Society*, vol. 24, pp. 95–110.

Singh, I. (2005) *The History of English*, London, Hodder Arnold.

Skutnabb-Kangas, T. and Phillipson, R. (2001) 'Linguicide' in Mesthrie, R. (ed.) *Concise Encyclopedia of Sociolinguistics*, Oxford, Elsevier Science.

Smith, J. (2000) *Synchrony and Diachrony in the Evolution of English: Evidence from Scotland*, unpublished PhD dissertation, York, University of York.

Smith, J. (2001) '"*Ye o na hear that kind o' things*": negative *do* in Buckie', *English World Wide*, vol. 21, no. 2, pp. 231–59.

Smith, J. and Durham, M. (2011) 'A tipping point in dialect obsolescence? Change across the generations in Lerwick, Shetland', *Journal of Sociolinguistics*, vol. 15, no. 2, pp. 197–225.

Smith, J., Durham, M. and Fortune, L. (2007) 'Mam, my trousers is fa'in doon!' Community, caregiver and child in the acquisition of variation in a Scottish dialect, *Language Variation and Change*, vol. 19, pp. 63–99.

South African Jewish Chronicle (1903, 5 June).

Stallybrass, P. (1988) 'An inclosure of the best people in the world: nationalism and imperialism in late sixteenth century England' in Samuel, R. (ed.) *Patriotism: The Making and Unmaking of British National Identities*, London, Routledge.

Stanlaw, J. (1992) 'English in Japanese communicative strategies' in Kachru, B. (ed.) *The Other Tongue: English across Cultures* (2nd edn), Chicago, IL, University of Illinois Press.

Taiwo, O. (1976) *Culture and the Nigerian Novel*, New York, St Martin's Press.

Tätemeyer, A.-J. (2009) *Namibia's Language Policy and its Effect on Education* [online], http://www.newera.com.na/article.php?articleid=7944 (Accessed 5 May 2011).

The Star (2006) 'Gag order on using *bahasa rojak*', 2 April; available online at http://thestar.com.my/news/story.asp?file=/2006/4/2/nation/13849132&sec=nation (Accessed 29 January 2010).

Thomas, A. (1985) 'Welsh English: a grammatical conspectus' in Viereck, W. (ed.) *Focus on England and Wales*, Amsterdam, Benjamins.

Tieken-Boon van Ostade, I. (ed.) (1996) *Two Hundred Years of Lindley Murray*, Münster, Nodus Publikationen.

Toolan, M. (1997) 'Recentering English: New English and global', *English Today*, vol. 13, no. 4, pp. 3–10.

Trudgill, P. (1999) *Dialects of England* (2nd edn), Oxford, Blackwell..

Trudgill, P. (2004) *New-Dialect Formation: The Inevitability of Colonial Englishes*, Edinburgh, Edinburgh University Press.

Wales, K. (2006) *Northern English: A Social and Cultural History*, Cambridge, Cambridge University Press.

Walker, J. (1791) *Critical Pronouncing Dictionary*, London.

Walvin, J. (1993) *Black Ivory: A History of British Slavery*, London, Fontana.

Webster, N. (1828) *An American Dictionary of the English language*, New York, S. Converse.

Webster, N. (1991 [1789]) 'An essay on the necessity, advantages and practicability of reforming the mode of spelling, and of rendering the orthography of words correspondent to the pronunciation' in Crowley, T. (ed.) *Proper English?: Readings in Language, History, and Cultural Identity*, London, Routledge.

Weeks, F., Glover, A., Strevens, P. and Johnson, E. (1984) *Seaspeak Reference Manual*, Oxford, Pergamon.

Wells, J. C. (1982) *Accents of English*, Cambridge, Cambridge University Press.

Williams, E. (2009) 'Language attitudes and identity in a North Wales town: "something different about Caernarfon"?', *International Journal of the Sociology of Language*, vol. 195, pp. 63–91.

Wolfram, W. and Schilling-Estes, N. (2006) *American English* (2nd edn), Malden, MA and Oxford, Blackwell.

Yano, Y. (forthcoming) 'English as an international language and "Japanese English"' in Seargeant, P. (ed.) *English in Japan in the Era of Globalisation*, Hounslow, Palgrave Macmillan.

Acknowledgements

Grateful acknowledgement is made to the following sources:

Text

Page 9: Gardner, Gail I. (1917) 'The Sierry Petes', Orejana Bull, Sharlot Hall Museum Press. Copyright © 1917 Gail I. Gardner/Gardner Family Trust. With kind permission from Gail Steiger; page 10: 'Varg' by permission of the author, Robert Alan Jamieson; page 10: 'Kantoi', lyrics by Izyan Alirahman, P&P Songs; page 18: adapted from *The Christian Science Moninitor* (2003) 'English sans French', www. csmonitor.com, March 14. © The Christian Science Monitor; page 36: Thiong'o, W. N. (2004) 'Recovering the original' in Lesser, W. (ed) *The Genius of Language: Fifteen Writers Reflect on Their Mother Tongues*, Pantheon Books. Copyright © 2004 Ngugi wa Thiong'o; page 38: Bolton, K. (2003) *Chinese Englishes: A Sociolinguistic History*, Cambridge University Press. Copyright © Kingsley Bolton 2003. Published by Cambridge University Press, reproduced by permission; page 57: Copyright © Ian Lancashire (Department of English) and the University of Toronto; page 76: (2010) 'Greece bans smoking in enclosed public spaces', Guardian.co.uk, 1 September. Copyright © 2010 The Association Press; page 92: Mitchell, C. (2005) 'Johnson among the early modern grammarians', *International Journal of Lexicography*, vol. 18. Copyright © 2005 Oxford University Press, page 136: Schneider, W. E. (2007) 'Cameroon', *Postcolonial English: Varieties around the World*, Cambridge University Press. Copyright © 2007 Edgar W. Schneider, published by Cambridge University Press, reproduced with permission; page 143: Pennycook, A. (2007) 'ELT an colonialism', in Cummins, J. and Davison, C. (eds), *International Handbook of English-language Teaching*. Copyright © Springer. With kind permission from Springer Science +Business Media B.V.; page 188: Leppänen, S. and Nikula, T. (2007) 'Diverse uses of English in Finnish society: Discourse-pragmatic insights into media, educational and business contexts', *Multilingua*, 26:4, pp. 333–380. Copyright © Walter de Gruyter. Reprinted by permission of Walter de Gruyter GmbH & Co. KG; page 241: Newman, M. (2006) 'New York Tawk' in Wolfman, W. and Ward, B. (eds) *American Voices: How Dialects Differ from Coast to Coast*, Blackwell Publishing Ltd. Copyright © 2006 Blackwell Publishing Ltd. Reproduced with permission of Blackwell Publishing Ltd; page 283: Otsuji, E. and Pennycook, A. (2010) 'Metrolingualism: fixity, fluidity and language in flux', *International Journal of Multilingualism*, vol. 7, no. 3, August 2010, pp. 240–254. Copyright © 2010 Taylor and Francis Ltd. http://informaworld.com, reprinted by permission of the publisher.

Figures

Illustrations

Index